MAD AT THE WORLD

ALSO BY WILLIAM SOUDER

On a Farther Shore
Under a Wild Sky
A Plague of Frogs

John Steinbeck in 1954. *(Yousuf Karsh)*

MAD AT THE WORLD

A LIFE OF

JOHN STEINBECK

William Souder

W. W. NORTON & COMPANY
Independent Publishers Since 1923

Printed in the United States of America
First Edition

For information about permission to reproduce selections from this book, write to Permissions, W. W. Norton & Company, Inc., 500 Fifth Avenue, New York, NY 10110

For information about special discounts for bulk purchases, please contact W. W. Norton Special Sales at specialsales@wwnorton.com or 800-233-4830

Manufacturing by LSC Communications, Harrisonburg
Book design by Brooke Koven
Production manager: Anna Oler

Library of Congress Cataloging-in-Publication Data

Names: Souder, William, 1949– author.
Title: Mad at the world : a life of John Steinbeck / William Souder.
Description: First edition. | New York, NY : W. W. Norton & Company, [2020] | Includes bibliographical references and index.
Identifiers: LCCN 2020017019 | ISBN 9780393292268 (hardcover) | ISBN 9780393292275 (epub)
Subjects: LCSH: Steinbeck, John, 1902–1968. | Novelists, American—20th century—Biography.
Classification: LCC PS3537.T3234 Z86676 2020 | DDC 813/.52—dc23
LC record available at https://lccn.loc.gov/2020017019

W. W. Norton & Company, Inc., 500 Fifth Avenue, New York, N.Y. 10110
www.wwnorton.com

W. W. Norton & Company Ltd., 15 Carlisle Street, London W1D 3BS

1 2 3 4 5 6 7 8 9 0

For my wife, Susan Sperl

*Humanity is the mould to break away from, the crust to
break through, the coal to break into fire,
The atom to be split.*

CONTENTS

— **PART THREE** — *Travels*

LIST OF ILLUSTRATIONS

BETWEEN THE MOUNTAINS AND BY THE SEA

THE BOY NO ONE KNEW

I N THE CALIFORNIA winter, after the sun is down and the land
has gone dark, the cool air slips down the mountainsides that
flank the great Central Valley, settling over the fields and tules
below. When conditions are right, the night air forms a fog so dense
that you cannot see your own feet on the ground. These fogs can last
for days, and sometimes fill all 450 miles of the valley.

To the west of the Gabilan Mountains, in Monterey County near
the ocean, lies another, smaller valley. Once it was an arm of the sea.
Ninety miles long and shaped like a sword, it follows the course of
the Salinas River, which runs north to Monterey Bay. The valley is
flat between the Gabilans and the Santa Lucia mountains that separate it from the Pacific. Here, a different fog comes in summer, when
inland heating draws in a marine layer of cooler, moist air from the
ocean. This sea-born fog does not lie still on the land, but seeps over
the folded hillsides, rising and falling along the river bottom. When
the fog comes and the mountains are hidden, the world is an abstraction and you are alone with your thoughts. But the gray veil lifts. The
light returns, the scene changes, and the fog retreats. Day by day the
mountains turn from blue-black at dawn to pale gold under the sun
and the towering sky, and the earth of the valley floor is lined with
rows of lettuce, some a mile long.

In the winter of 1902, in the midst of a drought, the skies over the
Salinas Valley opened. On February 27, the *Salinas Daily Index* reported

that the Salinas River—which in the dry season ran underground in places—was out of its channel. Trees along the banks had water six feet up their trunks. A tangle of deadfall and debris had swept through the valley overnight in the flood, and those who had been praying for rain began praying for it to stop. That same day, in a large, Queen Anne–style house in a well-to-do neighborhood of the town of Salinas, Olive Steinbeck gave birth to her third child and only boy. They named him John—like his father, like his father's father.

One world was ending; another, beginning. The promise of the new century was that nothing would remain the same for long, including America's place in the world. With the Victorian Age barely over, the Steinbecks' baby boy hurtled into a future he would help to write. Before his second birthday, Wilbur and Orville Wright would fly. And within months of his death, Neil Armstrong would walk on the moon. In between, John Steinbeck tried to tell the story every writer hopes to get right, which is only how it was during one small chapter of history. It is not much to ask, but the hardest thing on earth to do.

Thousands of years before John Steinbeck opened his eyes, bands of nomadic Indians—most recently the Ohlone—ranged through the Salinas Valley. They lived on game, fish, and shellfish, plus plants and seeds gathered in the woods and on grasslands sustained by controlled burnings that kept down the brush. The Ohlone also raised tobacco and managed a fraught coexistence with rattlers, mountain lions, and the now-extinct California grizzly bear.

In 1602, a Spanish explorer, Sebastián Vizcaíno, sailed up the California coast as far as the estuary of the Salinas River. Captivated by the harbor near the river's mouth, and by the panorama of mountains and rocky headlands that curled into the Pacific around the northern and southern ends of a great bay, he named the place Monterey. In 1769, a Spanish expedition coming overland from Baja reached the southern tip of the Salinas Valley and found it an unpromising place. "The hills," their report read, "gradually became lower, and, spreading out at the same time, made the canyon wider; at this place, in sight of two low points formed by the hills, it extends for more than three leagues." The soil, the report continued, was poor and offered "treacherous footing," as it was "full of fissures that crossed it in all directions, whitish in color, and scant of pasture."

It would take more than two centuries for Spain to enforce its claim to Monterey Bay and throughout the rest of Alta California, as this region north of Baja was known. The Spanish established religious missions, built *presidios*, or forts, and connected the settlements with a 600-mile north-south road, El Camino Real. They brought livestock to the Salinas Valley—lean, compact cattle good for hides and tallow—and tried irrigation schemes at several of the missions, damming rivers, excavating canals and reservoirs, and building aqueducts. As poor as the land appeared, water transformed it into a garden of astonishing abundance. Almost anything would grow on it. The Spanish carved out *ranchos* for grazing, and introduced a novel form of bullfighting in which bulls were made to fight bears.

After Mexico gained its independence from Spain in 1821, Alta California was loosely administered as a Mexican territory. In 1846, the United States declared war against Mexico. It was the same year that a group of American settlers led by James Reed and George Donner became snowbound in the mountain passes near Truckee, in the Sierra Nevadas of northern California. Nearly half of the Donner Party, as it came to be known, perished. The others survived by eating their dead family members and friends. The tragedy demonstrated the arduousness of the journey at the heart of America's so-called Manifest Destiny, a call to occupy the country from sea to sea that was encouraged by President James K. Polk's administration. Immigrants from Europe, having crossed an ocean, now undertook the longer voyage across a continent, wresting the land from native peoples on whom they visited new diseases, the destruction of the bison herds, and a ceaseless war of conquest. The extent of the United States reached violently and inexorably westward. In February of 1848, the war with Mexico ended, and in the Treaty of Guadalupe Hidalgo the United States purchased a vast area between Texas and the Pacific Ocean, including Alta California, for a little more than $18 million. One month earlier, gold had been discovered at Sutter's Mill just east of Sacramento. As prospectors poured into California, it raced toward statehood, which was ratified on September 9, 1850, at Colton Hall in Monterey.

As the population swelled, ranching and farming in the Salinas Valley boomed. Heavier-bodied beef cattle arrived from the east. Two rich aquifers were discovered beneath the valley floor—one at a depth of 180 feet, the other down at 400 feet. Below that is more water, though no one knows how much. By the late 1800s, farmers were experimenting with deep wells and then with pumps powered by gasoline engines. At the turn of the century, 7,000 acres were irrigated. Grains, hay, alfalfa, beans, potatoes, and mustard seed—staples of so-called dry farming—made room for an explosion of new crops including strawberries and lettuce and sugar beets as irrigation spread across the valley. Beef, milk, and produce moved out of the valley to San Francisco on the Southern Pacific Railroad, which reached Salinas in 1872.

Salinas sat in the midst of five large *ranchos*, residue of the early Spanish licenses and later the many more Mexican land grants that by Steinbeck's time had been mostly broken up. A provision in the Treaty of Guadalupe Hidalgo promised to keep the *ranchos* intact and their owners in place. But three years later, the California Land Act of 1851 effectively erased many of those longstanding claims. Then, in the 1860s, periods of flooding alternating with drought devastated cattle herds, and over time the *rancho* owners fell into a downward spiral of debt and rising costs that made their huge holdings—some of the *ranchos* were nearly 9,000 acres—unsustainable. The *ranchos* failed, but their boundaries, which wandered along recognizable natural features such as rivers and mountain ranges, kept their identities alive informally. If you said you were from Llano de Buena Vista, anyone would understand that your people lived in the country south of Salinas. Crumbling adobes still stood in places, organic extensions of the earth from which the Spanish and Mexicans had raised them. Most people in Salinas could remember when and how their families had come to the valley. And although Salinas was dominated by its founding families, no one apart from descendants of the native Ohlone could claim to have been there first.

The *ranchos* were framed by the mountains, and Salinas was framed by the *ranchos*, so that the town felt like an island. Salinas had sprung up to the southwest of an imposing, pyramid-shaped mountain called Fremont Peak. The town occupied an eighty-acre tract nearly encircled by a sharp bend in a tule-choked waterway called the Alisal Slough, which passed through fields of mustard plants as tall as a man. In the early days, the slough serpentined through the town, though it was interrupted by so many footbridges and streets that it had become a scattering of sloughs without names. Salinas began as a stopping-off place for a stagecoach line, with a hotel and a saloon where patrons could wager on what time the next coach would arrive. The line's most celebrated and heavily bet-on driver was Charley Parkhurst. After Charley died in 1879, it came as a shock to everyone when they learned that he was a woman named Charlotte Parkhurst.

As a boy, John Ernst Steinbeck Jr. was not lonely, but he was mostly alone. Though he grew up with a handful of schoolmates who liked spending time with him, none felt they knew him well. As one childhood acquaintance put it, John "didn't have a lot of friends—but he could be friendly if he liked you." Remote and seemingly preoccupied by ideas he never shared, John was big-boned and rangy, with a blunt face and a thick mop of hair parted on the side. People said he looked like "an unmade bed," though his sapphire-blue eyes were striking and he had a piercing gaze that set him apart even more. Until high school, John wore knee pants. Nobody else did. In one important way, though, he was not alone. His older sisters, Esther and Beth, adored John and spoiled him when they were around. But it was his sister Mary from whom he was nearly inseparable. A bold little girl three years younger, she was pretty and had blonde, ringleted hair. Mary went where John went. And yet John remained a boy apart in a place unto itself, a small town disconnected from the larger world. From an early age, he bridled at the bland striving in this narrow universe and, later on, at the town's conventional propriety, which he came to see as a veneer concealing the darker human impulses that exist everywhere.

John's father, John Ernst, had been born in Florida during the Civil War, one of six sons of Johann Adolph Großsteinbeck, a German-born immigrant who shortened his name to Steinbeck on arriving in the United States. Johann Adolph brought his family to California, where they farmed a small acreage near the town of Hollister, north of Salinas. John Ernst studied accounting. Like so many polite and proper men, he was by nature unhappy and spent much of his life wishing he had done something else, without any firm idea of what that would have been—though he was a passionate gardener and at one low point said he wished he'd become a farmer. Instead he went to work for the Southern Pacific Milling Company in King City, at the southern end of the Salinas Valley, and later at Paso Robles, fifty miles to the south in San Luis Obispo County. In King City, he met and married Olive Hamilton, one of Samuel Hamilton's nine children.

Sam Hamilton had lived in Salinas, and signed the city charter in 1872 before homesteading a ranch near King City, in a ravine warped into the "dry, hard-looking hills," as one friend put it. Hamilton was as charming and wise as his land was poor. His formidable daughter, Olive, taught school but had higher ambitions, and these seemed to be realized when John Ernst became manager of the Sperry Flour Mill in Salinas, by then a growing town of 2,500. Salinas was the county seat of Monterey County, a vast region that touched Monterey Bay, followed the coast down around Carmel and along Big Sur, and included the Salinas Valley and the surrounding mountain ranges—a county larger by half than the state of Delaware.

The Steinbecks settled into Salinas's middle class. They bought a big house on Central Avenue, and they built a vacation cottage on a hillside overlooking Monterey Bay in nearby Pacific Grove. But the Sperry mill closed in 1911, following a period of decline during which John Ernst's salary had been cut in half. Now, with the plant shuttered, he was out of a job. He told Olive he didn't know what to do next. He complained of feeling "dippy" and became forgetful. He was, he confided to their daughter Esther, "a lost sheep." Olive, who kept up a brave front—she said John Ernst had been fortunate to escape a business that probably should have closed a year earlier—admitted in a letter to Esther that John Ernst was tormented and often woke in the middle of the night and remained up until dawn, a spectral figure pacing the silent house. One worry among many was how to keep Esther, who had enrolled at the University of California, Berkeley, in college. Olive reassured Esther that her father's unemployment would not interrupt her schooling, at least for the current term. Esther, meanwhile, contemplated transferring to Stanford. As the family teetered, John and his little sister, Mary, could not grasp what the trouble was. They had been under the impression that their father *owned* the mill.

John Ernst opened a feed store on Main Street, but after a few years, as horses gave way to automobiles, it, too, failed. Then he landed work as a bookkeeper at the Spreckels Sugar plant near Salinas, and the family regained its footing. Claus Spreckels was a German-born sugar and railroad magnate who, beginning in the 1870s, had acquired large tracts of former *ranchos* in northern California. Spreckels paid tenant farmers to grow sugar beets, eventually concentrating his efforts in the Salinas Valley. At first he shipped the beets by train to processing plants to the north, but in 1898 he put up a new facility—at the time the largest sugar-processing plant in the world—just four miles south of Salinas. Spreckels built a community of small houses for workers near the plant, and this became the factory town of Spreckels. Much of the Salinas Valley, including the town of Salinas, orbited Spreckels. And now, so did the Steinbeck family.

In the early years of the new century, Salinas prospered. Main Street was wide, flanked by shops and restaurants and stables—and soon garages and auto dealerships. Telephone wires ran down both sides of the street, and electric lights dangled above the pavement.

There was an opera house in town, and in 1911 Salinas became the home of the annual California Rodeo. There was a roller-skating rink that was popular. Every evening at 8:00 p.m., the fire station rang its bell signaling curfew for the underaged.

Before Prohibition arrived in 1920, bars and saloons stood on nearly every corner. They stayed open until 2:00 a.m. One, called the Stream, featured a spittoon that was a trough of running water beneath the footrail. Bars were generally for men only, though a few had side rooms where women could be served. There was a Chinatown, its air thick with seductive aromas and its streets lined with gambling houses where the clack of dominoes could be heard from out on the sidewalk. Many of the town's leading men patronized the red-light district on California Street. John heard stories about the "sporting houses" from a classmate who delivered newspapers and would sometimes be invited in to sit and talk with Jenny, a well-liked madam who smoked cigars and kept her girls out of sight when young visitors stopped by.

Despite the family's reversals—John Ernst saw his job at Spreckels as a leveling-off of his stuttering career—the Steinbecks led a comfortable life. In early 1923, with help from friends, John Ernst was appointed Monterey County treasurer after his predecessor committed suicide. The county offices were an easy walk from the Steinbeck home, and the work suited John Ernst. The job paid $250 a month and John Ernst worked to keep it. He won election to a full term and was routinely reelected after that, remaining in the job for the rest of his life. It was the secure dead end he had always feared and always longed for.

The Steinbeck children and their friends gathered at the Central Avenue house to play in the unfinished attic, which was big enough to roller-skate in, or out in the yard behind a white picket fence. John organized a boys' club—Mary was included—that met in the basement, which had a dirt floor. John loved dogs. He owned a terrier named Jiggs that could play dead, and later a shaggy mutt named Omar. There would always be a Steinbeck dog. One named Teddy figured in an incident John long regretted. His parents were entertaining friends one evening when they got out some photos of John as a toddler, naked and in his bath. John's humiliation simmered for days. Finally, when John Ernst and Olive were out, he found the pictures and burned them. When he was discovered, John's punishment was that he could not play with or even speak to Teddy for two weeks. Remembering this as a young man, Steinbeck told a friend that it had been a terrible time—because it was so hard on Teddy.

Ignatius Cooper, who belonged to one of Salinas's few black families, recalled playing marbles with John. He thought John's parents were friendly, but found John himself serious and standoffish. John's childhood friends remembered Mr. Steinbeck as tall, reserved, and well-mannered. He was thin and wore a mustache. He always said something pleasant to John's friends when he met up with them. Olive Steinbeck was nice, too. She seemed in charge of everything, including her husband.

Outgoing and alert to the family's place in Salinas society, Olive was thirty-five when John was born. A joiner, she belonged to the Order of the Eastern Star, an auxiliary of the Masons, in which John Ernst was a member. She was also a founder of the Wanderers, a women's club just thirty-five strong. They maintained a worldly outlook and met to discuss the cultures of other countries. The Wanderers inducted a new member only after someone died or moved away. One of the older Wanderers, Olive was always careful to sit in the back at meetings so she could doze when the speaker bored her. She was convinced that nobody noticed her nodding off, though everyone did. When the town's first women's bridge club was organized, Olive was there. The Steinbecks attended St. Paul's Episcopal Church, as did many of the town's better families. John sometimes carried the cross into the service, though his friends had the impression that he didn't like church and was distracted during the sermons.

A piano stood in the Steinbecks' front parlor—a room that was seldom used. The family and their visitors spent more time in the adjoining living room, which had a fireplace. John's bedroom was upstairs. He rarely showed it to anyone. One friend later recalled that it was austere and had a large dresser against one wall on which

John kept a supposedly real human skull—though where he would have gotten one and why Olive would have tolerated such a thing are unknown.

John's friends liked visiting because although Olive was strict, she often served them something fun to eat. She could make donuts on short notice. One friend of John's thought his mother looked like a Gibson Girl, with "a great, big bosom and a cinched-in waist." A girl who got invited to join the Steinbecks for dinner from time to time recalled how lovely it was—the food was wonderful and the conversation lively. Mr. and Mrs. Steinbeck liked to tell jokes that kept things moving. If you went often, you heard the same jokes more than once.

The Steinbecks were among a number of Salinas families who owned cottages in Pacific Grove and visited them often throughout the year. A tight grid of narrow streets and wind-sculpted trees, the town clung to the peninsula at the southern end of Monterey Bay. Rising from the water's edge in sloping terraces to a high, forested ridge, Pacific Grove was wedged between the towns of Monterey and Carmel. In the late 1800s, the area was a quiet wilderness of woods and grazing lands mostly owned by a rancher named David Jacks. Jacks had come to the peninsula in 1849 from Scotland with an unquenchable thirst for land. Eventually he owned more than 100,000 acres. In 1873, a Methodist minister from the East showed up on doctor's orders to spend time in a moderate climate. Jacks gave the man and his wife a small lot in the pines for a shack, where the minister's health improved so much that he hurried back East and returned with friends looking to settle there, too. This small group grew into a larger idea: a Methodist retreat inspired by the training camp for Sunday-school teachers at Chautauqua Lake, New York. Jacks sold the congregants land for a campground, which they divided into tiny lots, each barely big enough for a tent. Jacks sold more land to the Southern Pacific Railroad. More people came. Eventually, the devout were outnumbered, and Pacific Grove was steadily transformed into a vacation spot and a gathering place for artists and writers who liked the air and water, as well as the more colorful diversions around Cannery Row next door in Monterey. Every fall, clouds of migrating monarch butterflies descended on Pacific Grove to spend the winter there, and each night in all seasons the beam from the Point Pinos lighthouse bore seaward through the gloom, marking the western edge of the continent.

Pacific Grove was fifteen miles from Salinas, out at the end of the old road that ran west from Main Street and skirted the Santa Lucias before heading to the ocean. The Steinbeck cottage, small and square, was on a corner of Eleventh Street in the heart of town. John Ernst kept a garden there, and John inherited his father's passion for growing things. The cottage was just blocks from Lovers Point, a pretty seaside park with a sandy beach for swimming and picnicking, protected from the long Pacific swell that crashed in a tempest of foam and spray against the rocks farther out on the peninsula. Even away from the water, the ocean's presence was carried up the hill on the cries of gulls and the barking of sea lions.

John loved his home in the Salinas Valley, loved living surrounded by mountains that felt like family. The Gabilans, he thought, were friendly and inviting and made you want to climb onto their shoulders, while the Santa Lucias were foreboding—and so in their way, foreign, like another country. He wasn't sure why this was so, but thought maybe it was because the sun rose behind the Gabilans—warming and reanimating the world—and went down beyond the Santa Lucias, leaving him in the dark. And he was afraid of the dark.

In the light of day, the richness of the broad valley was dazzling—especially after a wet spell, when a profusion of grasses and wildflowers burst from the soil. One time, John's father helped drill a well—it may have been down at the Hamilton ranch—and they inspected the changing layers of black dirt, white sand, and coarse gravel that came up as the drill went deeper. There were shells and even a whale bone in a layer of sand from an ancient beach. Farther down they found a hunk of redwood left by a forest that had been there before the ocean. Sometimes at night, in his room, John thought he could feel an echo of the past through the bones of the big house, as if there were nothing but invisible time between his body and the ancient geological layers of sea and forest below. But he loved Pacific Grove, too, a haven by the water that was so close to the valley and yet a million miles away. This was his life, a good one, a life between the mountains and by the sea.

Though he generally preferred his own company, from time to time John assumed the role of leader among a small group of friends. One of the chosen was a neighbor just across Central Avenue from the Steinbecks, a boy named Glenn Graves. The Graves property was big enough for them to keep horses and a chicken coop—a not-uncommon practice in Salinas that was sometimes called a "farm in town." In the spring of 1906, when John was four years old, the chimney on the Graves home toppled during the catastrophic earthquake that hit San Francisco and damaged more than a dozen buildings in Salinas. John came to see himself as a big brother to Glenn, a shy boy who got picked on. Glenn once told his mother that he hoped to grow up to be vice president. When she asked him why only vice president, he answered that John would be president. John told a classmate that he played with Glenn because "somebody has to take care of him." As an adult, John would say that the one thing he could not bear was another human being oppressed, abused, or taken advantage of by anyone more powerful, especially if the motive was greed.

When they were older, John and Glenn owned shotguns and would take Omar out to the Salinas River with them to swim and hunt rabbits. John was a strong swimmer and fearless. But it was a dangerous place, Graves said, as there were patches of quicksand along the banks of the river. They saw a few rattlesnakes, but never shot a rabbit.

Another boy John spent time with was Max Wagner. Wagner had been born in Mexico. His family fled during the Mexican revolution and settled on a farm about seven miles outside Salinas. Because Spanish was his first language, most of the other kids thought Wagner was Mexican. John met him one day when they were playing at the Graves house. John was delighted when he discovered that Max, who would later enjoy a long career onscreen as a bit player in Hollywood, could sing in Spanish. Wagner joined Glenn and John—usually accompanied by Mary—in exploring a nearby section of the slough, pushing their way out to it through the mustard sticks. They built a raft to float around on when there was enough water for it. Other times they would bend the tules flat and build walkways across the marsh. Apparently their parents were unbothered by these activities, except when it rained and the banks of the slough—"dobe," they called it—turned so slick that falling in and being unable to crawl out was a possibility. When the slough dried out, the cattail tops of the tules cracked and burst open, filling the air with their cottony insides that drifted on the wind.

Wagner later remembered that he never saw John doing anything with his father, that they respected each other but were distant. John Ernst did not begrudge his son the life he would have liked for himself—a life of possibility in a burgeoning time—but he disliked being reminded of it and kept to himself. According to Max Wagner, John Ernst always seemed to be at the office. Year after year, John Ernst let the demands of his work close over him. Accepting by increments this self-imposed solitary confinement dulled his senses and made his days somber but easier to tolerate. And by staying out of his son's life, John Ernst shaped that life without meaning to. John was like a shadow cast by his father, a black and moody outline. If John inherited anything from his father it was a milder case of the elder Steinbeck's susceptibility to bleak moods, a ceaseless struggle between contentment and despair that grew more pronounced as he got older. Sometimes the darkness descended on John without warning. More often it sat inside him, feeding a desire to be left undisturbed that would come to border on obsession.

But the family demanded proper appearances, and John was civil, well-behaved, and, apart from the usual childhood malfeasances, never rebellious. And he was protective of Mary. Once, when they were playing with a barrel in the yard at the Graveses' house, Max crawled inside and Mary impulsively jumped in after him. Her skirt caught and was yanked up to her waist. "Hey," John said, his blue eyes blazing, "don't get fresh with my sister." It was the only disagreement he and Max ever had.

Around 1906, John Ernst surprised John with a pony. It was ginger-colored, had a white blaze, and, according to Max Wagner, grew to be a little larger than an ordinary pony, though not as big as a horse. John named her Jill. Max owned a pair of gold-colored chaps that he sometimes loaned to John in exchange for a ride.

Much later, Wagner would remember those days as exciting and filled with surprises because John was a "born storyteller." This more expansive and imaginative side of his personality, which he took pains to hide most of the time, was propelled by visions of faraway lands and ancient times. It was as if there were another person inside John whom his friends glimpsed only when he was in a mood to pull back the curtain. John loved to hear stories and to make them up, and always had a part for Max to play. John was the ringleader, Wagner said, as he conducted his little troupe on one adventure after another. Sometimes they were pirates, other times knights in armor. But always they were part of some tale that John seemed to invent on the spot. "He was a sharpie," Wagner said. "And he was always the captain." Wagner and Glenn Graves were privy to something only a few other kids knew about: John and Mary shared a secret language. They sometimes spoke to each other in words that sounded like English but weren't.

John often visited his neighbors Belle and Jenny Williams, who had never married and lived in a big house with a tennis court. According to Glenn Graves, the sisters "knew everything there was to know" about the early days of Salinas. John was fascinated by all of it. He was a sponge. If you told him a story, he never forgot it. Another childhood friend said John liked talking to a former ranch foreman named Sylvester Carriaga, who lived around the corner from the Steinbecks and whom everyone knew as Joe. Carriaga told Steinbeck stories about Monterey. These might or might not have included information about Flora Woods, Monterey's best-known madam, who ran a brothel near the waterfront called the Lone Star Café.

John, age five, and his sister Mary aboard Jill—
the pony that would live again in one of Steinbeck's greatest stories.
(Martha Heasley Cox Center for Steinbeck Studies, San Jose State University)

Sometimes John got out a small notebook to write down the things Carriaga told him.

John's affinity for stories and his gift for piecing them together from his own imagination had not been apparent at first. For a time, he struggled to read and hated books. Words on a page went blank inside John's brain. Learning to read, he later wrote, had been torture. He regarded books as "printed demons—the tongs and thumbscrews of outrageous persecution." Then, when he was nine, his aunt Molly gave John an unusual book. At first he regarded it grimly. It was *The Boy's King Arthur*, a simplified version of William Caxton's edition of Sir Thomas Malory's *Le Morte Darthur* (more commonly known as *Le Morte d'Arthur*).

But John was beguiled by King Arthur and his mythical court. The Caxton edition, which dates from 1485, is a thicket of perplexing words and mystifying syntax, its archaic vocabulary nearly impenetrable to a contemporary reader. John's children's version was easier, though it retained words and ideas that he found strange and magical. Later, he would develop an affinity for dialects, and he never lost his fascination with the sounds of Malory's ancient language and the mythical place from which it sprang. Other "great books," as he called works such as the Bible or *Paradise Lost*, seemed to him to "belong to everyone." But John believed that Malory was his alone, a story written in a way only he could understand. "I loved the old spelling of the words," Steinbeck later wrote, "and the words no longer used. Perhaps a passionate love of the English language opened to me from this one book." The private language John and his sister Mary spoke was no doubt based on Malory.

John liked to ride Jill out into the fields, Mary at his side, pretending to be on an Arthurian quest. John assumed the role of knight—a stoic, chivalrous protector—while Mary served as squire. She was, he would later say, an excellent one. And every summer, when the Steinbecks made their trip to Pacific Grove, John would beg his father to stop off for their lunch at a pretty valley called Corral de Tierra, with its "castle rock" formation. A high cliff, the fractured and eroded face of castle rock resembles the ramparts of a great fortress. Here, John could imagine Uther Pendragon, the king of England—disguised by Merlin's magic—sleeping with his enemy's wife, who was tricked into believing she lay with her husband. The result of this treachery would be a boy child—Arthur, the future king. Such deeds, such words.

The Steinbecks sometimes took Jill with them to Pacific Grove. One summer John organized a trek into the forest with several vacationing friends from Salinas. John was on foot, with Mary riding Jill. John provided a lively narration of their progress deep into the looming woods. The only sounds were his own voice and Jill's soft tread on the pine needles. Before long they were lost and seemed to be going in circles. Everyone except John and Mary was frightened. After some time wandering among the trees, they found their way home. John always believed there was a parallel spirit world, and the forest impressed him as a place inhabited by things unseen. He kept the memory of it.

Like the other kids in Salinas, John began his education at what everyone called the Baby School, which included first and second grades, and where children getting used to being with one another away from home gathered each day to play beneath the drooping arms of a giant weeping willow. After Baby School, John went to the West End Grammar School, where he impressed his classmates as a bright but stubborn child. Out on the gravel schoolyard, he would go off by himself. Sometimes he pretended not to know the answer when a teacher asked him a question, which seemed deliberately odd. Unlike Mary, who would write "100" on her assignments before showing them to their parents, John was uninterested in what they thought. John Ernst routinely asked if he'd gotten "a licking" at school. Somehow, John was allowed to skip a grade.

His friends learned that if they stopped over after school to see if John wanted to come out and play, they were usually told he was immersed in homework, though they came to suspect that he was just reading and didn't want to be around anyone. John was a puzzle. Occasionally, he'd ask a few kids over, take them up to the attic, and tell ghost stories. One time Max Wagner showed up at the door. Something was going on. Max went in and the veterinarian was there, explaining to John that Jill had died. Recalling this scene sixty years later, Wagner burst into tears.

Salinas High School, a turreted, two-story, red-brick colossus built in 1900, was on Alisal Street, only a couple of blocks from the Steinbeck home and right across the street from the county courthouse where John Ernst worked. The school was known as "the Old Brick Pile." Elvina Iverson, a neighbor who came from one of the oldest families in the valley, remembered walking to school with John every day and never figuring him out. "I don't think anyone ever knew him," she said. "He never, ever talked. He was very shy." John proved an indifferent student in high school—though people noticed how well he did in English. One year the English teacher required a theme every Friday. John looked forward to these assignments, and the teacher often read his aloud to the class.

Another girl who knew John, Dorothy Donohue, was convinced John's reticence hid something going on inside that his friends would have found incomprehensible. "He did things by himself," Donohue said. "He was a deep thinker. People thought he was antisocial. But he was really just thinking."

John never let on what he was thinking about.

John's reading life intensified as a teenager. Besides Malory, he read *The Lives of the Twelve Caesars* by the Roman historian Suetonius, many of the major English poets, Walt Whitman's "Song of Myself," George Bernard Shaw's play *Caesar and Cleopatra*, and rafts of fiction that spoke to youthful exuberance, such as *Treasure Island* by Robert Louis Stevenson. And he read classics: *Crime and Punishment* and *Madame Bovary*. The Steinbeck house was full of books, and as John's sister Beth recalled, "The choice was ours." Some years later Steinbeck

John; his parents, Olive and John Ernst; and younger sister, Mary, reading at home. *(Martha Heasley Cox Center for Steinbeck Studies, San Jose State University)*

reckoned that the books he immersed himself in as a boy were "realer than experience." He didn't remember them as books, but as "something that happened to me."

Almost everybody in the school attended a weekly dance in a warehouse by the railroad tracks in Chinatown. John never went. He didn't like going to ballgames either. If he had a girlfriend, she would have been the only one who knew it, though it was rumored that he and Max Wagner—who was handsome and popular—sometimes sneaked off to visit two girls who lived over on Market Street.

In his senior year, a change came over John and he got involved in school activities he had previously avoided. He became interested in drama and landed a part in the school production of *Mrs. Bumstead-Leigh*. He was associate editor of the yearbook, *El Gabilan*, and contributed a funny essay describing the school, including the English classroom—English, he wrote, being "a kind of high brow idea of the American language." John was no athlete, but he was big and strong and gamely ran track and made the basketball team, though he never got into a game. To everyone's astonishment, John was elected president of the senior class.

In 1895, the California National Guard had formed a cavalry unit called Troop C, headquartered in Salinas. For the next two decades they did nothing but train. Then, in 1916, Troop C was called up to join the Punitive Expedition under the command of General John J. Pershing. President Woodrow Wilson had ordered Pershing into Mexico to pursue and capture the revolutionary Pancho Villa after Villa raided a U.S. Army post in New Mexico, leaving sixteen people dead and the garrison in flames. Troop C was mustered and marched down Main Street in Salinas before a waving crowd. Pershing led 10,000 men south, easily defeating Mexican forces. But they couldn't find Villa and withdrew after a few months. One soldier in Pershing's army was a Harvard-educated, thirty-two-year-old National Guardsman from New York named William Maxwell Evarts Perkins, who spent much of the campaign reading *The Iliad*. Perkins longed to return to his job as an editor at the publishing house Charles Scribner's Sons in New York, where in the coming decade he would find himself at the epicenter of a revolution in American literature.

Troop C came home to Salinas. No one thought they would stay long. Two years earlier, on June 28, 1914, a nineteen-year-old student named Gavrilo Princip had assassinated Archduke Franz Ferdinand, heir to the Austro-Hungarian Empire, and his wife, shooting them dead with a pistol as they passed by in an open car in Sarajevo. The news reached Salinas a day later, and in the coming months the *Salinas Daily Index* reported on preparations for war in Europe. And what a terrible war it was—World War I, the Great War. Bitterly, hopefully, and in the end wrongly, it was called the war to end all wars.

The United States remained on the sidelines of the war until the spring of 1917. Though half a world away, the fighting in Europe threatened to end a civilization thousands of years in the making. The war's horrors broke history in two, obliterating all notions of the glories of armed conflict. Soldiers cowering in filthy, water-filled trenches succumbed to disease and incessant mortar fire. Tanks and poison gas rolled across devastated fields, and airplanes fought in the smoke-smudged skies. Everything died in the war, not just men but ideals such as valor and duty and honor. The human toll was staggering. In one battle that raged for months along the Somme River in France, more than three million had fought, with a million killed or wounded. Ultimately, some two million American soldiers would deploy to Europe, under the command of General Pershing. In Salinas, Troop C was mustered again, and marched once more down Main Street on its way to war. Although many people in Salinas were, like the Steinbecks, of German descent, the troops received a rousing send-off. Salinas was all for the war.

Salinas High School maintained a military training unit called the Cadets. Many of the boys belonged to it, and they expected to join Troop C after graduation and join the fighting in Europe. John was a Cadet and wore the high-collared uniform as they conducted marching drills around town. Glenn Graves remembered a day when he and John were in uniform and encountered a regular army officer. They were thrilled when they saluted and he saluted back. Sometimes the boys went to the gun range to practice marksmanship. The surplus army-issued rifles had a brutal recoil, and one time Glenn's shoulder hurt so much after a session at the range that he could not get out of bed the next day.

In the summers, the Cadets were often put to work on local farms, which were shorthanded because of the war. They called these work parties "bean vacations." One summer, John also did a stint of work at the Spreckels plant, where he was injured when he got a chemical solvent in his eyes. Nearly blinded, John had his eyes heavily bandaged for days, and looked disturbingly like a casualty of war. But he recovered, and it came as a relief and a disappointment when the war ended in the fall of 1918, when John was still a senior at Salinas High. The war was the story of stories, but it would be for others to tell.

Salinas High School 1919 track team.
John is in the back row, far right. *(National Steinbeck Center)*

If his classmates felt they got to know John slightly better as their school days came to a close, what he thought remained a mystery. John was good with his hands and would stay after school to work in the woodshop on his own. Nobody had any idea what he'd do with himself. The prediction for him in the *El Gabilan* yearbook was that he'd be a preacher—an inside joke. Max Wagner, who knew John as well as anyone could, said he read a lot and could quote from books, but never talked about himself unless it was to be seen as different. "John just loved to do the opposite of what a normal person would do," Wagner said. Glenn Graves would sometimes wake up in the middle of the night, notice a light on in John's bedroom across the way, and figure he was reading again. John told him that he always kept paper by his bedside in case he wanted to write something down.

What *was* John's story anyway? The "opposite of what a normal person would do" doesn't explain much. What's clear is that his mind was aflame from an early age, and that certain impulses fell into place and took hold of young John Steinbeck, a boy who would not conform, who could not tolerate a bully, and who believed that somewhere within the solitude he craved there was a world that could be rendered sensible and fair. These tendencies were hard to reconcile and hinted at a difficult but consequential life ahead.

One day after school, John invited a boy named Bill Black up to his bedroom. The house was empty, and the steep, narrow stairway creaked as they climbed to the second floor. Black said the room was plain and dim. Dust floated in shafts of light from two small windows. John walked over to the dresser and motioned for Black to come closer. John knelt and slowly pulled open the bottom drawer. It was full of manuscripts.

— 2 —

LIVE, NOT HOPE TO LIVE

IN October of 1919, John Steinbeck boarded the train in Salinas—his family did not own a car until 1931—for the seventy-five-mile trip north to Palo Alto and Stanford University. At seventeen, Steinbeck was nearly his adult height of six feet. The only other person from Salinas headed to Stanford that fall was Bill Black, a standout athlete who would join the track team as a pole-vaulter. Because he'd gotten a D in Latin, Black had to retake the course to get into Stanford. Black planned to study engineering. He had no idea what Steinbeck was going to college for, but he thought Steinbeck wanted to be a writer. Black never forgot that day in the upstairs bedroom on Central Avenue, when he'd listened as Steinbeck read one story after another. There must have been at least fifty of them, each one handwritten on white paper. Black thought the stories were "grand," packed with action and "easy to follow," and that Steinbeck read them in a way that made them even more compelling. They were all about the Salinas Valley. One story that stayed with Black had been about a pony.

From his earliest efforts, Steinbeck was ambivalent about his writing. He was quick to insist that it was no good, and even after he became one of the world's most successful authors, he continued to doubt that anyone would want to read whatever he was working on. Steinbeck was indifferent about the stories he wrote in high school. He'd sent some of them around to magazines, but nothing came of it. This was due in part to Steinbeck's refusal to include his return address with the manuscripts, which he always sent out under a pen name. Unnerved at the prospect of any direct contact with a magazine, he instead watched to see if any of his stories appeared. None did. Steinbeck said later he was "scared to death," afraid that if an editor contacted him it would be with a rejection—or, worse, Steinbeck said, an acceptance. This was the way it was to be for Steinbeck, craving success and horrified that it might befall him.

Young, shy, uninterested in school, and reluctant to admit to anyone what he hoped to become, Steinbeck was unlikely Stanford material. Opened in 1891—its first student was future U.S. president Herbert Hoover—the university had begun as a monument to Leland Stanford Jr. The only child of Leland and Jane Stanford, Leland Jr. had died of typhus at the age of fifteen. His father, a railroad tycoon and one-term governor of California, believed Leland Jr. had spoken to him in a dream, telling him to "live for humanity." Stanford University was the result.

Public sentiment had been against the university at the outset. It was seen as an unwelcome competitor for the nearby University of California at Berkeley, and a waste of millions of dollars its detractors said would have been better spent augmenting the endowments of existing schools. But by the time of Steinbeck's arrival, Stanford had a student body of nearly 3,000, with graduate programs and a medical school.

Unlike the elite eastern colleges on which it was modeled, Stanford was not a selective training ground for the privileged. Most Stanford students came from working-class families. Admission was essentially open to anyone. Tuition for California residents was free—though that changed after Steinbeck's arrival. In 1920, attending Stanford would cost $40 a quarter.

Stanford occupied nearly 9,000 acres south of San Francisco, near Menlo Park, where Leland Stanford had farmed, kept a vineyard, and raised horses. Stanford students to this day refer to the university as The Farm. In Steinbeck's time the campus was arranged around a Spanish-influenced central quadrangle, red-roofed and flanked by colonnaded arcades; the low-slung buildings and broad lawns lent it a gauzy otherworldliness. Stanford was the warm, egalitarian antithesis of its stony counterparts in the East. Flowers bloomed in February, and on clear days beneath the rapturous Palo Alto sky it always felt like spring.

Steinbeck's first home at Stanford was the men's dormitory, Encina Hall. Inspired by a Swiss resort Leland Stanford had visited, it stood four stories tall, was built of massive limestone blocks, featured long, echoing hallways, and was home to 400 postadolescent males who'd come from mostly small towns or rural areas. In the early years it was bedlam. A favorite prank was "turning up a room"—that is, turning everything in a room upside down while its residents were elsewhere. Freshmen were regularly "tubbed," held underwater until their struggles indicated imminent drowning. Explosions of fireworks and the crash of large objects tossed into the stairwells were common occurrences. Less frequent but more alarming was the discharge of a pistol.

On registration day in October of 1919, a student named George Mors went down to the swimming pool near Encina and saw a "big guy" doing laps. It was Steinbeck. They started talking. Mors was the same age as Steinbeck. He'd grown up in Los Gatos, only twenty miles away, and entered Stanford at the age of sixteen. But he had caught the flu during the 1918 pandemic and missed most of his first year. Mors was lucky. The worldwide flu outbreak infected half a billion people, killing about one in ten—nearly five percent of the world's population. Now Mors was back. He told Steinbeck he planned to live in Encina Hall. Steinbeck suggested they room together.

To Mors, Steinbeck seemed a friendly lug, a "country hick." He had a scar on the side of his chest that he said was from surgery to relieve the pleural pneumonia he'd had as a kid. Steinbeck got a little money from his father each month. His mother sent brandied cherries. One night in the dorm, Steinbeck and Mors gave each other tattoos: small hearts carved with India ink and a razor blade, just above their left elbows. Steinbeck was nervous about the blood and was so timid with the razor that Mors's tattoo soon faded away. But

Steinbeck's got infected and healed into a welt that was still there forty-five years later. He said it had a sharp outline under a full moon.

Mors said that from the moment he met Steinbeck, it was clear that the only thing he cared about was writing. He balked at taking courses that he didn't think would make him a better writer. Steinbeck was warned about this, but "[h]e only took what he wanted to take," said Mors. In a sign of trouble to come, Steinbeck told his friend Glenn Graves that he preferred spending most of his time in the library.

Mors and Steinbeck roomed together off and on for two years. Steinbeck's comings and goings confused several people who knew him at Stanford, and their later accounts of his college days did not always agree as to what happened and when. Since it was clear to Mors that Steinbeck was struggling and cared nothing about school, he asked Bill Black if perhaps he could help. Black had already tried to persuade Steinbeck to come out for track, thinking it would help him fit in. Now he admitted to Mors that he was at a loss. "We both liked John," he said later, but in the end there didn't seem to be anything they could do for him.

In the summer of 1920, Mors and Steinbeck went down to Salinas. Steinbeck's father had a connection in the highway department and had arranged jobs for them on a survey crew laying out the new Highway 1 south of Carmel, along the coast of Big Sur. At the time there was no road on the coast, just an old Indian trail. "You could only travel there on foot or horseback," Mors said. It was wild, forbidding country—steep, crawling with poison oak, and teeming with rattlesnakes. Despite the stunning views of the Pacific Ocean, often from high above, it was said that Big Sur could drive people insane if they stayed there too long. Then there were the "watchers," solitary, wraithlike figures that according to backcountry legend would appear outlined against the sky on a ridgetop and would vanish if approached. Steinbeck admitted he wasn't sure if any of this was true, but allowed that there could still be some Indians roaming the hills. He and Mors carried sidearms—supposedly for rattlers, though they took occasional potshots at seagulls. They worked only a short time before Steinbeck decided they'd be happier and safer at the Spreckels sugar plant. They stayed at Steinbeck's home. Mors was smitten with Steinbeck's sister Mary. She was pretty and had a figure that made him lightheaded. Steinbeck, he thought, treated her like a daughter.

John Ernst asked Mors to "look after" Steinbeck at Stanford. Mors wrote the Steinbecks often—more often than Steinbeck did. It fell to Mors to talk with Steinbeck's parents when he disappeared one weekend. Nobody knew where he was, and the Steinbecks were concerned. John Ernst came up to Stanford and spoke with the dean of men. Eventually they learned that Steinbeck, convinced he was on the verge of flunking out, had gone to San Francisco and gotten a job as a clerk in a department store. He eventually turned up at Mors's house in Los Gatos, asking if he could stay there. Mrs. Mors spent several days "straightening me out," Steinbeck later recalled. She persuaded him to call his mother. Steinbeck returned home and, later, went back to Stanford.

Steinbeck had managed to make another friend at school—Carlton Sheffield, whom everyone called "Dook." They were in two classes together during freshman year, one of which was French. Later, they shared a room in Encina Hall. Sheffield remembered Steinbeck as a "large, rather quiet, impressive individual." He received $50 a month from his parents, which Sheffield said put him in "the plutocrat class." Steinbeck kept his hair short on the sides, which Sheffield said emphasized his high forehead and prominent ears. When he laughed, everyone noticed the fathomless blue of his eyes.

Steinbeck told Sheffield story after story, mostly about his life before Stanford. Some of them might even have been true. There was one about putting his sister Mary onto Jill and then tying her feet together under the pony's belly so she wouldn't fall off. She fell off anyway and was dragged over the ground while Steinbeck struggled to pull her free. That sounded real enough. One of Steinbeck's more dubious claims was that he'd lost his virginity to a one-legged babysitter. Sheffield thought Steinbeck had a knack for vivid narration. Talking about the day-long buggy rides from Salinas to Pacific Grove, Steinbeck remembered those trips in such detail that Sheffield said he could almost feel the plume of grit rising behind the horse on the dusty way to the sea.

According to Sheffield, Steinbeck joined ROTC, but quit almost immediately. It was the same when he went out for the freshman football squad, where they tried, unsuccessfully, to find a place for him on the line. Steinbeck had size and strength but demonstrated no ability. He rowed crew a little longer, but he somehow damaged the veins in his legs as he strained at the oar—an injury that affected him throughout his life. Steinbeck didn't like strangers or crowds, was frightened of public speaking, and tended to keep to himself. Sheffield said Steinbeck worked for a time as a waiter at a Chinese café in Palo Alto where a lot of Stanford students ate because a meal there cost 25 cents. After a few weeks, Steinbeck got into an argument with one of the cooks and had to flee the place. He told Sheffield he had "barely beaten a meat cleaver out the door."

Steinbeck and Sheffield enjoyed boxing with each other, which Sheffield said "usually involved him knocking me down, me getting back up, and him knocking me down again." The taller Steinbeck had a reach and power advantage over Sheffield, but it was the speed of the blows that repeatedly put Sheffield on the floor. While Steinbeck easily cuffed him around, Sheffield always had the feeling that he pulled his punches, not really wanting to hurt him.

In the spring of 1921, Sheffield went to Steinbeck's room, carrying his boxing gloves. George Mors was there alone, reading a note from Steinbeck. It read "Gone to China" and instructed Mors to send his things back to Salinas. Mors later said he had no recollection of such a note. Whether these conflicting memories related to Steinbeck's escape to San Francisco or to some other temporary disappearance isn't clear. Keeping track of Steinbeck grew harder. As his friends finished school and left, Steinbeck slogged on at intervals, making scant progress toward a degree.

Occasionally, Steinbeck made an effort to be more conscientious about school. Early one year—probably 1923—he wrote home to say that he had resisted the temptation to go to San Francisco to celebrate New Year's Eve. In fact, he planned to give up "social activities" in the new quarter to focus on studying. Surprisingly, he had registered for a debating class. He admitted he was afraid of the subject, that he had never been comfortable standing in front of people, never knew what to do with his hands or whether he might "break down." He hoped the class, even if he didn't earn a good grade, would be a valuable experience. But it was a nerve-racking prospect. He said that "every shark in the school is in the class." Steinbeck signed the letter, as he often did then, "Jawn."

Like college students everywhere, Stanford students had a robust and often troubled relationship with alcohol. In the university's early days, students got free samples of wine from the Stanford vineyard on campus. Oddly, Leland Stanford had promoted the idea of making Palo Alto a "dry" city, and over time the faculty and staff of the university became advocates for Prohibition. This did not slow the steady traffic of students between campus and the nearby towns where they could drink, nor did it prevent alcohol from finding its way to Encina Hall—which, along with the houses on fraternity row, was famous for its "beer busts." Administrators' attempts to impede campus drinking went nowhere until 1908, when a Stanford student got drunk in Menlo Park and was shot dead after entering the wrong house in Palo Alto, thinking it was where he lived. The State of California responded by outlawing alcohol sales within a mile and a half of the Stanford campus—a move that only made it a slightly longer walk for a beer.

But Steinbeck had arrived at Stanford just in time for a great national experiment. In 1919, a congressman from Granite Falls, Minnesota, named Andrew Volstead wrote the enabling legislation that led to the adoption of the Eighteenth Amendment in 1920. The era of Prohibition, which outlawed the production, importation, and sale of "intoxicating liquors," had begun—as had the era of ignoring it. Prohibition had scarcely taken effect when people started talking about repealing the amendment, though supporters believed that would never happen. Morris Sheppard, a US senator from Texas who had sponsored the amendment, said, "There is as much chance of repealing the Eighteenth Amendment as there is for a humming-bird to fly to the planet Mars with the Washington Monument tied to its tail."

Prohibition was repealed in 1933.

While it lasted, people made do. Alcohol consumption declined, but according to estimates never fell below 60 percent of pre-Prohibition levels. And binge drinking continued to be a regular fea-ture of college life. At Stanford, alcohol was an essential lubricant for many activities: dates, fraternity hazings, house parties, and espe-cially the Big Game. The Big Game was the annual football matchup between Stanford and Cal—the University of California, Berkeley—which was played following a weeklong series of rallies, bonfires, and parties. The social event of the year, it was one of the few occasions for which Steinbeck could tolerate being part of a crowd. For the 1922 game, Steinbeck arrived in a coat lined with test tubes that were filled with grain alcohol.

Sheffield said that Steinbeck went out with women from time to time, but never had a steady girlfriend. Late one night, he came back to their room drunk. Earlier in the evening they'd been drinking Chinese absinthe with Steinbeck's friend Carl Wilhelmson, a "dark and morose" Finn who spoke with a heavy accent. Wilhelmson was a veteran and struggled to conceal nerves that had been badly jan-gled in battle. The absinthe was "a nasty, yellowish-green color"—and it did not agree with Sheffield, who declined a second shot. He looked on as Steinbeck and Wilhelmson continued to swallow the stuff. They also smoked a little marijuana that Steinbeck had gotten in Salinas. Eventually, Steinbeck said he had a date and left. Sheffield awoke when Steinbeck returned hours later. He sat down unsteadily on Sheffield's bed, landing partly on Sheffield's chest, and began to cry. Steinbeck said he'd gone out with a "wonderful" girl and told her what a sad life he had. She answered him by describing what a sad life *she* had. They'd held each other and sobbed. Now Steinbeck had started up again. After a bit he composed himself, flopped over onto his own bed, and passed out. The next day, Steinbeck was hung over and skipped his classes. That evening, Sheffield found him rigid and unresponsive in bed. Alarmed, Sheffield was about to run for a doctor when Steinbeck went slack and took a heavy breath. They decided it had been some sort of seizure and vowed to avoid Chinese absinthe going forward.

Whether Steinbeck's life then was "sad" is debatable. Certainly he was adrift and unhappy, and he wondered, when he dared to think about it, what in the world he was doing in college. Steinbeck wanted only to write and didn't know if Stanford was helping or getting in his way. On several occasions, Steinbeck came into the dorm room and, without saying a word, took out his revolver and fired it into the wall. "It made quite a noise," Sheffield said, "and left big holes in the wall." Steinbeck never explained himself.

When he wasn't writing, Steinbeck read. One author he admired was the fantasy writer James Branch Cabell, whose most notable book was *Jurgen: A Comedy of Justice*, in which a middle-aged pawnbroker makes an inadvertent deal with the devil and is transported to an imaginary realm in which he is young again and burning with desire. Steinbeck also discovered a prolific Irish novelist, short-story writer, and poet named Donn Byrne, who cranked out book after book. His first novel, published in 1919, was *The Strangers' Banquet*, which told the story of a first-generation Irish-American woman who inherits her father's shipbuilding business and runs it with an unlikely mix of ambition and fair-mindedness. Byrne had a penchant for archaic syntax and sometimes veered briefly into Gaelic, tendencies that charmed Steinbeck.

Sometimes, Sheffield said, Steinbeck would try a course for a week or two and then quit if it didn't suit him. One summer Steinbeck and Mary—who had also enrolled at Stanford—took classes at the Hopkins Marine Station, Stanford's ocean-research facility in Pacific Grove. Steinbeck also made room for some history classes, but he stuck mainly to English courses, often not bothering with final exams. Sheffield said Steinbeck shrugged this off, claiming that he didn't need to prove what he'd gotten from a course, as he was well aware of anything he learned. During his on-again, off-again career at Stanford, Steinbeck managed to earn ninety-five units—slightly more than half of what was needed to graduate. He completed fourteen English classes, earning three As though his grades in the others ranged as low as a D.

In the spring of 1923, Steinbeck and Sheffield enrolled in a poetry-writing class, taught by a gray-maned professor named William Herbert Carruth. When the weather was nice, the class met on the lawn in the shade of an oak tree, its leaves casting wavering shadows on the grass as Carruth gently critiqued their efforts. Sheffield said he and Steinbeck often felt stymied and would take long walks looking for inspiration. One of the poems Steinbeck wrote hinted at a lust for life—and a corresponding distaste for abstract ideas—that would have surprised people who thought him lazy and standoffish. Though written in a self-consciously formal voice, it was good in places, and ended on a note suggesting he wanted to make the most of every minute, and that if he succeeded, then:

I shall have really lived, not hoped to live.

Sheffield graduated in 1923. He went down to Pacific Grove to spend time with Steinbeck. He got in after dark and had trouble finding the little cottage on Eleventh Street. Steinbeck, who'd arrived a few days earlier, took Sheffield over to Monterey for enchiladas and to pick up a couple gallons of bootleg wine. A few days later, after Mary and a Salinas friend named Phyllis joined them, they went back for more wine. Steinbeck thought the bootleg joint—it was in the kitchen of a hotel in a seedy part of town—was too rough for the women. He asked them to wait in the car, and handed Mary his revolver in case anyone tried to bother them. Steinbeck and Sheffield sampled the goods before paying, then returned to the car in what they hoped was a discreet manner, but which looked more like suspicious skulking. Mary mistook them for some other men she'd seen lurking about and warned them she had a gun and to stay back. They managed to identify themselves just before she pulled the trigger. It was a fine vacation. Before Sheffield left, the four of them went dancing and were tossed out of several clubs for "twining legs" and dancing cheek to cheek, which was considered indecent.

That summer, with Sheffield off to a newspaper job in Long Beach, Steinbeck worked again at the sugar plant in Spreckels as a "chemist." This involved performing simple tests on the beet juice as it moved to the crystallization vats. One of his other duties was preventing the plant workers from raiding the lab's stock of grain alcohol. Steinbeck always got along well with working men, Sheffield said. He and Steinbeck wrote to each other often, their letters a mix of essays, short stories, and reports of daily life. Sheffield thought enough of Steinbeck's embryonic literary career that he started saving Steinbeck's letters on the chance they'd be important one day. When they looked at them together years later, Steinbeck was appalled at their indelicacy, and insisted on burning most of them.

Steinbeck never tired of observing his coworkers. There was a group of Filipinos and Mexicans at the plant whom Steinbeck hung out with. They looked up to Steinbeck, who was educated and gave them sound advice on many matters. They taught him how to throw the heavy-bladed knives they used for cutting beets.

The following summer, Steinbeck and Sheffield worked at the new Spreckels plant in Manteca, in the San Joaquin Valley, east of San Francisco. The heat was tremendous, well over 100 degrees in the shade. It was hotter inside the plant. They worked twelve-hour shifts, seven days a week. Their plan was to save up enough money to buy an old car and drive down to Mexico. But Steinbeck was restless, and they lasted less than a month. After going to San Francisco for a couple of days, they went down to Los Angeles to stay with Sheffield's family.

In the fall of 1923, Steinbeck returned to Stanford. With Sheffield and George Mors gone, he grew close to another aspiring writer he'd met the year before. His name was Webster "Toby" Street. Street was a veteran who'd lost an eye in the Great War, and he received $100 a month for his disability. He and Steinbeck attended meetings of English Club, though it was unclear whether Steinbeck was formally a member. One of the club's advisers was a professor named Margery Bailey, a Samuel Johnson scholar who taught a literature survey course that had captivated Steinbeck. Bailey had a house on campus where she put on Sunday-afternoon salons to discuss students' work, serve refreshments, and read aloud from books she found interesting. Steinbeck and Street—who thought he might want to become a playwright—were often invited to attend. Steinbeck was attracted to Bailey's intelligence and love of literature. Bailey, for her part, found Steinbeck prickly, and they quarreled often. After one of these explosions Steinbeck would stay away for a time before going back and starting over.

Steinbeck had an intense fling with a young woman he met in English Club. Her name was Katherine Beswick. She was a year ahead of Steinbeck at Stanford and wrote poetry that everybody, including Steinbeck, thought was good. Beswick would eventually see her work published in *Poetry* magazine. In school, she read Steinbeck's work and made him happy by discussing it with him. In private, they formed a two-person resistance movement to counter Margery Bailey's views on sex. She was against it—they were emphatically in favor.

Toby Street said that when he and Steinbeck got to know each other, Steinbeck was leading a strange life. He lived in a shed attached to a crumbling stable in Palo Alto near San Francisquito Creek. A waterway that once teemed with salmon and sea-run trout, it curled though the heart of the Farm on its way to San Francisco Bay and was one of the features that had inspired Leland Stanford to start buying land there back in 1876. Steinbeck's shed was cramped, barely big enough for the cot, table, and chair that were its only furnishings. But Steinbeck had made it comfortable. He'd managed to find rugs for the floor, and had hung a few pictures and even a curtain. His typewriter was perched on a wooden box. When he needed a bathroom, he was permitted in the adjacent main house. The finishing touch was a little dog Steinbeck adopted that was devoted to him. Toby Street had the impression that Steinbeck didn't pay anything for use of the shed, and also that he was no longer getting money from home. He lived close to the ground at Stanford, yet seemed not to belong there.

At times it was not clear whether Steinbeck was enrolled in school or merely talked his way into a few classes.

Steinbeck liked the shed because it was out of the way and quiet, which was conducive to writing. He'd finished several stories, some better than others. One was about a mechanic who curses God when a machine pulls his arm off. When additional misfortunes befall him, the man assumes they are God's punishment for his blasphemy. Steinbeck thought he'd gotten that one about half right. He also liked a story about a nun, and another inspired by a visit he and Wilhelmson had made to a whorehouse in Salinas—a trip to the seamier side of his hometown that Steinbeck would put to use many years later. As uneven as the stories were, Steinbeck told himself hopefully that they were original. The stories gathered dust in the shed.

Steinbeck did manage to publish a couple of pieces during his time at Stanford. Two stories were accepted by the *Stanford Spectator*, a short-lived journal published in 1923 and 1924 by the English and Press clubs. "Fingers of Cloud: A Satire on College Protervity,"

Katherine Beswick. Steinbeck's Stanford classmate let him tell her anything. *(Martha Heasley Cox Center for Steinbeck Studies, San Jose State University)*

featured an orphan—a dim albino girl of eighteen—who is caught in a storm while walking to a hilltop overlooking a highway near her home. Blinded by the wind and rain, she tumbles down the hill, becomes lost, and eventually finds her way to a ranch and a bunkhouse full of half-drunk Filipino farm workers. Their boss is beguiled by the girl, whose pale skin is a stark contrast to his own. He declares that he will marry her, and does. But the man is cruel and, soon, repulsive to her. She leaves, climbing back to the hilltop overlooking the highway.

The story's meaning wasn't clear, and Steinbeck's use of the obscure Latinate "protervity," in reference to the girl's allure, didn't help—though it suggested Steinbeck thought college taught students to cloak their carnal instincts with fancy words. It may have also indicated that he had come to believe that pretty girls are haunted by trouble, whether unbidden or of their own making. Possibly this sprang from his own experience or only reflected a tacit misogyny of the times, but it solidified into a conviction he would write about often, and a prejudice he would stumble over again and again in his own often messy life.

During his stay on the creek, Steinbeck had an interesting neighbor, a divorced woman with two daughters. Her name was Elizabeth Smith, but she was an aspiring writer and used the pen name John Breck. Toby Street recalled that Breck wrote stories in which animals could speak. Steinbeck thought Breck had technical skill, but that her stories never worked. Breck was among a widening circle of friends, and many of them came by the shed to talk and drink. So Steinbeck didn't think much of it one day when there was a knock at his door. After a few moments and some rustling, a flustered Steinbeck answered. It was Toby Street's future mother-in-law. She was the widow of a Stanford professor named William Whitman Price, who'd built a resort on Fallen Leaf Lake near Lake Tahoe. Mrs. Price lived in Palo Alto and managed the lodge during the season. Street planned to spend the summer there, doing odd jobs and running errands, and had persuaded Mrs. Price to hire Steinbeck as well. Price said she wanted to speak to him about all of this, though he suspected that the real purpose of her visit was to gather information about her soon-to-be son-in-law. Steinbeck invited her in. Price sat on the steel cot explaining the rules of the resort, which included a ban on sexual activity among her employees—unaware of the half-naked coed hiding below her underneath Steinbeck's bed.

This story, which Steinbeck told to Dook Sheffield, was probably at most half true. The improbable part about the young woman under the bed was the kind of detail Steinbeck would have invented to spice things up. As his friends and family learned many times throughout his life, Steinbeck blended fact and fiction in what he wrote and in what he said about himself. He was always his own main character in some kind of story.

In the spring of 1925, Toby Street and Frances Price got married at All Saints Episcopal Church in Palo Alto. Steinbeck was his best man. Street was surprised that Steinbeck agreed to take part, as he doubted that Steinbeck owned a suit. After Street gave Steinbeck the ring on the morning of the ceremony, he wondered if his unpredictable friend would show up at the event itself. But Steinbeck was there, apparently appropriately attired.

Getting married altered Street's thinking about becoming a writer. He switched to law, which in those days one could study as an undergraduate. But he continued to take writing classes, and in 1925 he worked on a play he'd begun two years earlier about a California rancher who is obsessed with the forest on his land. The plot was a complicated exploration of how a physical lust for nature leads to self-annihilation. Street called it *The Green Lady*. He wrote the first and second acts, and started on the third before giving up. Street realized he'd run out of story in the second act, which he said "was never believable." Street worried, too, that his themes of hedonism, incestuous longing, and the main character's death in the never-completed third act might well have been "too violent for the stage." It seems likely that Street would have shared the early drafts of *The Green Lady* with Steinbeck, but later on he wasn't sure when Steinbeck first read it. Whenever Street did show it to him, Steinbeck was impressed and could not stop thinking about the story.

Steinbeck's determination to learn how to write in college was unusual. Few American writers attended college for that purpose—and many skipped college altogether. As an academic discipline, creative writing was unstructured and had no formal recognition until the founding of the Iowa Writers' Workshop in 1936. It wasn't until 1946 that Wallace Stegner started a creative-writing program at Stanford. It may be that Steinbeck, despite years of compulsive writing, still felt that he didn't know where to start and was looking for inspiration outside of himself, some source of ideas beyond what he knew of the world already. This failure to see that what he should write about was already inside him—a mistake other writers of his generation would not make—was to mean a long apprenticeship.

Steinbeck enrolled in a class taught by a popular young Stanford professor—Edith Mirrielees, whose storied career had begun shortly after five o'clock on the morning of April 18, 1906, when a 300-mile segment of the San Andreas fault ruptured somewhere near San Francisco, generating a massive earthquake. The earth heaved up and down the coast and inland to Nevada, leveling or setting on fire 80 percent of the city of San Francisco and killing as many as 3,000 people, a number that did not include uncounted deaths in Chinatown. The coastline itself was altered: In Monterey Bay, the mouth of the Salinas River shifted six miles to the south.

Two people died at Stanford in the quake, and damage on the campus was estimated at $2 million. Edith Mirrielees, a student at the time, wrote a story about the devastation for the *Stanford Alumnus*:

> As the dust settled, ruin after ruin stood out in sharp relief against the blue of the early morning sky—the ragged outline of the Memorial Arch, the pile of broken stone which had been a

chimney, farther off, the gaping front of the Chemistry building, and the big library dome towering up unsupported.

Mirrielees graduated a year later, attended graduate school, and joined the Stanford faculty as an English instructor. Over time, her story-writing class, English 136, became legendary. Slight and unassuming, Mirrielees in 1917 organized the Stanford Women's Unit for Relief Work in France and served there with the Red Cross during the war. More interesting to Steinbeck was that she had published short stories in prominent magazines. He eagerly took her class twice. Miss Mirrielees—he always called her that—was his favorite teacher, and almost certainly the most demanding.

Steinbeck hoped she could teach him the "secret formula" for writing good short stories. But Mirrielees didn't believe such a formula existed, or even, paradoxically, that writing could be taught. At most, she said, writing could be *helped*. Good writing, as Mirrielees explained in a textbook she wrote after Steinbeck's time, depends on the writer having something to say:

> [I]t is by no means necessary to have undergone bizarre experiences. Not many people have had unusual adventures; all people, without exception, have had adventures enough to provide for lifetimes of story writing. Everybody has been a child, grown up, fallen in love, fallen out of love. Everybody has experienced self-pity, self-approval, the anguish of loss by death, the slower anguish of loss by disillusionment. These are the things which make stories. These are the things which make them whether the stories are laid in Turkestan or New Jersey. It is not lack of experience which handicaps any writer. What it is, is the purblindness that prevents his seeing, or his seeing into, the experiences he has had.

Mirrielees was working all of this out at the time Steinbeck took her class. He wrote to Carl Wilhelmson of her kindness. She told him she believed some of his stories ought to be published, though she wasn't sure where.

In his most ambitious piece of writing for Mirrielees, Steinbeck ignored his own experience, trading his childhood and his beloved Salinas Valley for an imagined adventure in a different time and in a place he'd never seen. The story was titled *A Lady in Infa-Red.*

Steinbeck had turned for inspiration to the exploits of a seventeenth-century pirate named Henry Morgan. Born in Wales, Morgan operated out of Jamaica. In 1671, he led a raiding party across the Central American Isthmus and captured Panama City. How Steinbeck came across his story isn't known, though he most likely read about Morgan in a book called *The Buccaneers of America*, by Alexandre Exquemelin, who had sailed with Morgan. Steinbeck's story about Morgan's Panamanian adventure owed some of its clipped melodramatic style to Donn Byrne, the Irish writer whose work he admired. It was clumsy and immature, uninformed by either experience or scholarship. Steinbeck never published it and had to know it was dreadful. But he did not put it aside entirely.

A Lady in Infa-Red was nothing like the kind of new American writing that emerged after World War I—and that was altering the face of literature. In the fall of 1919, a month before Steinbeck arrived at Stanford, Maxwell Perkins of Charles Scribner's Sons had argued for a manuscript he wanted to publish over the objections of the company's senior editors, who thought the book was devoid of "literary value" and "frivolous." The book was called *This Side of Paradise*. Its author, from St. Paul, Minnesota, by way of Princeton, was F. Scott Fitzgerald. After Perkins prevailed and Scribner's agreed to publish the novel, he wrote to Fitzgerald. "This book is so different it is hard to prophesy how it will sell," Perkins said, "but we are all for taking a chance and supporting it with vigor."

This Side of Paradise was about a subject that hadn't been considered until then: the alienation of a generation of young people who'd lived through the Great War and come out the other side. To their elders, the world seemed the same—wounded, but the same. To the man-boys who came home from the war, drained and damaged and quite a few of them shell-shocked—or who, like Steinbeck, had missed the fight by an eyelash—a new culture built on consumerism and thrumming with cars, airplanes, radio, movies, bootleg gin, and casual sex was disorienting. Fitzgerald's hero, Amory Blaine, is a midwesterner who attends Princeton with great expectations, only to find his dreams interrupted by the war, his longings for love and money just out of reach. This was the tragedy—or the irony—of modern life. You could be anything you might imagine, until the world got in your way. Near the close of the novel, Fitzgerald put it this way: "Here was a new generation, shouting the old cries, learning the old creeds, through a revery of long days and nights; destined finally to go out into that dirty gray turmoil to follow love and pride; a new generation dedicated more than the last to the fear of poverty and the worship of success; grown up to find all Gods dead, all wars fought, all faiths in men shaken."

The book was published in March of 1920. Fitzgerald was twenty-four years old. In his review for the literary magazine *Smart Set*, the

Stanford's Edith Mirrielees. The English Department legend said writing could not be taught, only helped. *(Martha Heasley Cox Center for Steinbeck Studies, San Jose State University)*

frequently cutting critic, H. L. Mencken, called it original and brilliant, and deemed it a "truly amazing first novel."

In the fall of 1924, Fitzgerald wrote to Perkins from Paris to tell him about a young expatriate there who had just published a startling collection of experimental fiction pieces. Spare and intense, many of the chapters consisted of only a single paragraph that implied a context that had been stripped away. The book was unlike anything anyone had ever seen. Its crisp, ironic style captured the fatalistic mood shared by young people coming to terms with a newly perplexing world after the war. Published by the Paris-based Three Mountains Press in a limited edition of just 170 copies, it was called *in our time*. The author, Fitzgerald assured his editor, seemed destined for a "brilliant future." His name was Ernest Hemingway.

Perkins wrote some months later to Hemingway—who was off on a skiing vacation and had already agreed to publish an expanded version of *in our time* with another American publisher, Boni & Liveright. For his debut in the States, Hemingway retitled the book *In Our Time* and packed the original vignettes into interstitial breaks between fifteen longer stories, most of which were previously unpublished or had made limited appearances in Paris. These included several about a young Hemingway alter ego named Nick Adams, among them "The Three-Day Blow" and the incomparable two-part masterpiece, "Big Two-Hearted River," stories that would endure and be read for generations to come. The brilliant future Fitzgerald had predicted for Hemingway had arrived ahead of schedule.

Steinbeck was wary of Hemingway, gripped by the hesitancy one writer feels about another that is indistinguishable from envy. He told Dook Sheffield he didn't want to read Hemingway because he was afraid it would influence his style. As it turned out, this would be a widespread and well-deserved concern of American writers for the next forty years.

Steinbeck never forgot an exercise that Edith Mirrielees assigned to her class: Explain the point of a story in a single sentence. If you could do that, it was a start. Steinbeck came to see that what you make of an idea is the difficult terrain over which the "desolate, lonely path of the writer" must travel. The only formula for writing, he said, was the "aching urge" to do it. In the spring of 1925, overcome at last by that urge, Steinbeck left Stanford for good.

— 3 —

THE LONG WINTER

ARLY IN THE new century, the tallest building in the world
was the Woolworth Building in New York City. Designed by
skyscraper pioneer Cass Gilbert using new principles of steel-
frame construction, it was completed in 1912 and rose sixty stories—
nearly 800 feet—to tower over lower Manhattan. John Steinbeck got
his first glimpse of it on a snowy evening in the late fall of 1925, from
a porthole aboard the freighter *Katrina Luckenbach*, as the New York
skyline came into view. He was terrified. Rows of "looming" buildings ablaze with lights stood against the milky sky ominously. When
the ship docked, Steinbeck "crept ashore," waves of panic rising inside
him. Although he had visited San Francisco and Los Angeles, Steinbeck had never lived in a city. Now he was about to live in the most
unforgiving of them all.

Just before his final two quarters at Stanford, Steinbeck had written to Carl Wilhelmson to say that he was finished with school.
"I've had all of the college I deserve," he said. At different times he'd
expressed an interest in traveling somewhere—China, Nicaragua,
Mexico City, maybe Chicago, where his uncle Joe Hamilton, Olive's
brother, had made a fortune with an advertising agency. In November, he went down to Los Angeles to see Dook Sheffield, who was
teaching journalism at Occidental College. Steinbeck was bound for
New York. How he settled on New York isn't known, though both he
and Sheffield had by then acquired sizable piles of rejection slips from

magazine publishers there. Perhaps Steinbeck felt that if he got closer to the heart of the publishing world he'd have better luck, a common impulse that usually ends badly. In Steinbeck's case, he may have also been comforted by the fact that Uncle Joe was well connected in New York and might be able to help him along. And his older sister Beth now lived in Brooklyn. Steinbeck saved a hundred dollars to book passage, and another hundred for when he landed.

The *Katrina Luckenbach* steamed south from Long Beach. Steinbeck watched gray whales and sea turtles. As they passed into the Panama Canal, he gazed in wonder at the lush foliage of the country he'd only imagined in *A Lady in Infa-Red*. He later told Sheffield that he'd gone ashore—Sheffield couldn't remember if it was in Panama or Cuba—and gotten into a fight. In Havana, Steinbeck met a young woman and quickly blew through most of his money showing her the city from a carriage and plying her with rum drinks. He said later he didn't know what he was thinking.

Steinbeck arrived in New York with three dollars and quickly got

Carlton "Dook" Sheffield. Steinbeck believed it was Dook who was destined for greatness. *(Martha Heasley Cox Center for Steinbeck Studies, San Jose State University)*

in touch with Beth. She and her husband, Eugene Ainsworth, lived in a tiny studio apartment, so staying with them was out of the question. But Ainsworth paid for a night in a hotel and loaned Steinbeck $30. He also got Steinbeck a job as a laborer on a project in midtown Manhattan: the construction of Madison Square Garden, which was being rushed to completion before the end of the year. This was the third incarnation of Madison Square Garden, located on Eighth Avenue at Fiftieth Street, and it was being built by the boxing promoter Tex Rickard, who'd made and lost a fortune in the Klondike Gold Rush before turning to boxing. The five fights Rickard promoted for heavyweight champion Jack Dempsey captivated the public, and Dempsey's 1921 title defense against Georges Carpentier—a decorated French aviator in the war—produced boxing's first million-dollar gate. Rickard was paying laborers time and a half every day but Sunday, when it was double time—$2 an hour. Steinbeck was lucky to have a connection that got him work there. He said if anybody didn't show up or walked off the job, fifty men were waiting to take his place.

Steinbeck's job was moving cement up the inside scaffolding with a wheelbarrow, load after aching load. He thought the work might kill him. Although he stood taller and broader than many of the men in the mostly African American crew of cement haulers, he discovered that, despite his size and strength, it was difficult to keep up. The other men fairly skipped up the planking as if their burdens were nothing, talking and singing, never seeming the least fatigued, even at the end of a day that sometimes stretched to eighteen hours. It was cold work. The men warmed their hands over coal grates. Steinbeck pretended to do the same, but it was an act; he couldn't even feel his hands and only stopped to rub them over the fire so he could rest for a few moments. One day, a man fell ninety feet from the scaffolding under the ceiling and landed near where Steinbeck was hauling cement. Steinbeck stared in disbelief. "He was red when he hit," Steinbeck wrote later, "and then the blood in his face drew away like a curtain and he was blue and white under the working lights."

Steinbeck claimed he was on the project for a month or more, but the Garden was completed in time for the start of a six-day bicycle race on November 24. According to Dook Sheffield, Steinbeck spent only about three weeks moving cement. However long it lasted, it was an exhausting time physically and mentally. Days passed in a blur. Steinbeck had rented a third-floor room in a walk-up in the Fort Greene neighborhood of Brooklyn. It had dirty green walls and a big, hissing radiator. At the end of the day, Steinbeck would drag himself home, riding the clattering subway and walking along sidewalks that seemed to sway beneath his feet. He'd fall into bed and then, before he knew it, he was back in the line of wheelbarrows climbing inside the cavern of the Garden. It was like a "fever dream." When the Garden was done, Tex Rickard congratulated everyone on a herculean effort. Decades later, Steinbeck shivered every time he walked by the place.

Steinbeck didn't know what to do next—but fortuitously his rich uncle Joe arrived from Chicago and checked into the Commodore Hotel, where he made a show of ordering room service and firing off telegrams to friends and associates before seeing what he could do for his struggling nephew. Joe Hamilton knew somebody at the *New York American* and ended up getting Steinbeck a one-week tryout as a general-assignment reporter. Steinbeck was to cover human-interest stories in Brooklyn and Queens. The pay was $25 a week—money Steinbeck later admitted the newspaper must have viewed as a complete waste. Steinbeck didn't know anything about reporting, and less about the city. He got lost repeatedly, and was so timid and empathetic that he could hardly bring himself to write stories about murders, divorces, or anyone's misfortune. He was told that whenever a family would not provide a photograph for a story, he should find a way to steal one. But he never did.

Steinbeck liked exploring New York; no two days were the same. The paper's offices were on William Street, in the financial district near the Brooklyn Bridge. The *American*'s city room was so small that reporters had to share typewriters. Steinbeck worried that he was given fewer stories than his coworkers, and was convinced that had he not been hired as a favor to his uncle, the *American* would have let him go after a week. Even at that, he couldn't be certain how long they'd put up with him. His hope was that the paper would not assign him to one of its routine beats, where he'd have to spend every day in the same place. At Christmas he sent home some reproductions of sketches by an artist and illustrator named Mahlon Blaine, whom he had met and befriended onboard the *Katrina Luckenbach*. He told his parents he was doing fine, and, in case they were concerned, that he had plenty of warm clothes.

Unhappily for Steinbeck, the *American* moved him to the federal courts. Most of the reporters there had spent years on the beat. Steinbeck marveled at how well they treated him. They all worked in a single room at the courthouse. The other reporters pretended he knew what he was doing, and when it became clear that he had no idea, they tried to educate him without making a fuss about it. They taught him how to track cases—and also, when it was slow, how to play bridge. Steinbeck later wondered if he would have been so generous with a "young punk" in over his head. "You can't repay that kind of thing," he said. "I never got to know them. Didn't know where they lived, what they did, or how they lived when they left the room."

Steinbeck had moved to a sixth-floor room in an old hotel overlooking Gramercy Park in Manhattan. The rent was a dollar a day. On a gloomy afternoon, Steinbeck wrote to another of his uncles, George Hamilton. Steinbeck said he found the city a strange place that had "grown a helmet of steel and stone." He missed the feel of bare earth under his feet and found no solace in the dismal filaments of sky beyond the skyscraper tops.

Underlining the obvious, Steinbeck said he was lonely that day. As he continued, it became clear that Steinbeck's frame of mind was bleaker than he meant to let on. He told his uncle that his apartment overlooked a park, and looking out the window he could see children at play, bundled against the cold and scurrying around under the watchful eyes of their nurses—women whose "severe" appearances suggested they'd been hired by mothers who did not want their husbands tempted. Other women were in the park exercising dogs. It looked as though it would soon snow, and then everyone would scuttle back to their miserable homes, leaving him with nothing to watch. He wrote that at the courthouse the day before, reporters from the *Times*, the *Sun*, and the *Morning World* had gotten drunk and then begged him to write their stories for them while they continued the bender. He'd agreed. There were three stories that day, and he'd had to write all of them four times, including once for himself, with each slightly different from the others. He thought it was funny that the only paper that cut anything was the *American*.

Steinbeck had moved to Gramercy Park to be near a woman he'd fallen in love with. Her name was Mary Ardath and she had a small part in the *Greenwich Village Follies*, a musical revue that ran on Broadway for five months that winter. She made enough money to take Steinbeck out sometimes to an Italian restaurant, where they drank red wine and she encouraged his hopes of becoming a writer. But she advised him to get some other kind of job in the meantime, maybe in advertising. He was surprised when she abruptly married a banker and moved away, not telling him but only leaving him a note. Two days later, the *American* fired him.

Steinbeck told his parents that he'd been one of several reporters let go as a cost-saving move, and that he was now a freelancer. He could always go back to construction work if he needed the money. He assured them he was fine and would not starve. But he asked them not to mention any of this to anybody. People, he said, prize success. But they also revel in the failures suffered by others. Be patient, he wrote. Maybe in six months he'd have exciting news they would want to share with the world.

Steinbeck was alluding to the possibility—it seemed so real to him—that he would soon be a published author. He had shown half a dozen short stories to an editor named Guy Holt. Holt worked for an adventurous publisher named Robert M. McBride, who had published James Branch Cabell's *Jurgen*. Holt—who was Cabell's editor—was impressed with the stories, and told Steinbeck that if he wrote six more, they would bring out the collection.

Steinbeck eagerly got to work, but he was distracted. The city was beginning to close in on him. He was behind on his rent, and despite what he'd told his parents, he was now often hungry. A friend loaned him a dollar, and he bought some bread and a bag of dried herring, then holed up in his room for a week. He thought he might be too weak to get construction work. He was afraid to go out, anyway. The noise and traffic were unbearable, and he didn't want to risk running into his landlord. Steinbeck maintained that he wasn't even sure if he could climb the stairs back to his room. Somehow he finished six more stories and got himself to McBride's office—only to learn that Guy Holt had moved on to another publishing job. His replacement refused to even read the stories. Steinbeck made a scene and had to be physically removed from the office. Out on the street, he collapsed. He told Dook Sheffield that he had been taken to Bellevue Hospital and admitted for several days—though his family never believed this happened.

Why Steinbeck didn't call on Holt at his new publishing house— or what happened if he did—isn't known.

Steinbeck still insisted to everyone that he was all right. But in May, he wrote a worryingly morose letter to his parents telling them about a trip he'd taken with Mahlon Blaine to Coney Island, a rollicking mecca for New York's immigrants and working class. Steinbeck claimed that he found it a boring blare of lights illuminating throngs of cheerless people. Steinbeck's reaction to Coney Island's diversions betrayed his dark outlook. Unsaid was how bad it was back in the confines of his room with nothing but his own thoughts and four grim walls for company. As would be true throughout much of his life, Steinbeck's sour response to the world around him hinted at a recurring depression—cyclical moods—that he was reluctant to admit.

Steinbeck also wrote to his sister Esther, who lived with her husband in Watsonville, twenty miles north of Salinas. He told her that he didn't know what his plans were. He wanted to come home, but he didn't want to come home broke. He figured he'd need at least "five or ten dollars" in his pocket, an amount puny enough to suggest he no longer cared to pretend his time in New York had been anything but a failure.

Esther probably said something to their parents, because a check from home soon arrived. Steinbeck wrote to thank them for the money, and said he might buy a straw hat. He wished his father good luck in the upcoming election for Monterey County treasurer. He said he was not sure when he would be home, but that he hoped it would be soon.

Spring gave way to summer, and then, in the early fall, Steinbeck talked over his situation with a Stanford classmate named Amasa "Ted" Miller, whom he'd met in English Club. They had both ended up in New York, but their paths diverged. Miller was now practicing law with a firm called Dawes, Abbott & Littlefield. Miller found Steinbeck a "workaway" job on a ship bound for San Francisco. He didn't need any urging. "The city had beaten the pants off me," he wrote later.

Halfway home, Steinbeck wrote to his parents to let them know he was on his way back to California. After twenty-two days at sea, he felt wonderful. Hard work and salt air had refreshed him, and he had lost his "city pallor," which sounded like code for the melancholy that had overwhelmed him near the end. Steinbeck added that he had stories from the voyage that would "make your blood run cold." This might or might not have included one he told Dook Sheffield. Steinbeck said he had gotten into a fight with another member of the crew, an Irish thug who was huge and had everyone cowed—but who turned out to know nothing about boxing. Steinbeck, who detested bullies, cut him up and knocked him out. He spent much of the rest of the trip writing letters for the other crewmen to their girlfriends.

In early November of 1926, John Ernst Steinbeck won reelection as Monterey County treasurer. Steinbeck wrote to congratulate his father. He added that he wished his mother, who had become the assistant treasurer, would give it up and take life more easily. Steinbeck's concern was misplaced, as it was common practice for family members to be on the payroll of county officeholders, and this rarely involved any actual work. The courthouse was sometimes referred to as "the old ladies home." Olive never went there except to pick up her paycheck.

Steinbeck's letter was postmarked Tallac, a village on the southern shore of Lake Tahoe not far from the 10,000-foot peak of Mount Tallac, in the Sierra Nevada range about 190 miles northeast of San Francisco. It was near the Fallen Leaf Lake Lodge owned by Toby Street's mother-in-law, Mrs. Price, where Steinbeck had worked two summers before. Price had found him a new job as a caretaker for one of the oldest families in the area, the Brighams.

In 1882, Dr. Charles Brooks Brigham, a prominent San Francisco surgeon, started buying land on the southeastern corner of Lake Tahoe. Eventually he owned 1,300 acres that surrounded nearby Cascade Lake and included frontage on Lake Tahoe itself. The area was popular with fishermen, but it was the bracing, blue waters of Lake Tahoe that attracted Brigham. He was an avid swimmer and adhered to a regimen of daily plunges into the chilly waters of the lake as a way of promoting his health. Brigham built a sprawling vacation home on high ground overlooking Lake Tahoe. It had a small marina, with a pier that could accommodate a steamer. The naturalist and wilderness advocate John Muir visited the Brighams, as did Mark Twain. After Dr. Brigham died in 1904, his widow Alice and their daughters and their families continued to vacation there each summer.

Steinbeck lived in a bark-sided caretaker's cottage adjacent to the main house. It was small, nearly square, and had two windows overlooking a stone-lined garden pond that in the summer featured a small waterfall. His job included the same sorts of errands and chores he'd done at Fallen Leaf Lake Lodge. He also drove Mrs. Brigham when she went somewhere, and served as a companion-supervisor for the Brigham grandchildren—a part of the job he didn't care for. He was more enthusiastic about the prospect of spending the long winter there after the family was gone for the season and he was snowed in. There would be little to do but write. Between times, when the weather was good, Steinbeck planned to fish and hunt. Soon after he got there, Steinbeck wrote to his parents, telling them about his snug little cabin. He had Omar with him, and he expected that the two of them would have a wonderful time of it. He said he hoped to do some hunting and trapping, and that he'd already seen a coyote the size of a wolf.

Steinbeck spent his first days closing up the main house, shuttering windows, battening the porches. There was a lot of work to do, as the Brighams left everything in disarray when they departed. Ducks were beginning to appear on the lake, and Steinbeck promised to send some down to Salinas. He thought the lake was so blue that if he didn't know the color was natural, he'd have said it was in bad taste. He tried to hunt as often as he could, for himself and also to feed Omar. This was the second Omar, an Airedale. The original Omar had been killed by an automobile while Steinbeck was at Stanford. Steinbeck enjoyed eating snowshoe rabbit; the dog usually got boiled squirrel or sometimes porcupine steak. There was a meat locker where Steinbeck could hang game. He confessed that he had no idea about the hunting seasons, but he'd heard that after the snow came, the game wardens let you shoot whatever you needed to. He'd shot some quail he claimed were as big as chickens.

Once the summer people left, the solitude was tremendous, and the scenery breathtaking. Lake Tahoe sits on the California-Nevada line, at more than 6,000 feet in elevation. It is surrounded by sheer mountains and forests of pine and fir that are entombed in snow in the winter, when the only sound is the shrieking wind. Mark Twain said the air at Lake Tahoe was the air "the angels breathe." Twenty-two miles long north to south and about half as wide east to west, Tahoe is the largest alpine lake in North America. Its azure waters are 1,600 feet at their deepest. The lake's name comes from the name used by the Washoe Indians, who lived in the area for centuries: *Da ow.* The first white man to see it was Lieutenant John C. Fremont of the U.S. Corps of Engineers, during his survey of the West in 1843–44. It was winter. The snow was twenty feet deep in places. Fremont and his men—one member of his party was the mountain man

Kit Carson—were desperately searching for a way through the Sierra Nevadas. They had run out of food and had begun eating their dogs and mules. The horses would be next. On a bitterly cold day in February 1844, Fremont climbed a high ridge and discovered "a beautiful view of a mountain lake at our feet."

Through the first part of November, the weather was fine. Steinbeck liked being out of touch. He told his parents that even if they sent him a telegram, it would be held at the post office in Tallac for the next mail boat or until he retrieved it. Mrs. Brigham regularly sent him the San Francisco papers, but he only glanced at the headlines before using them to get his fire going. He'd been experimenting with his cooking and had come up with a recipe for sweet buns that he roasted over a low fire until they got crisp. They were wonderful with hot chocolate. He mentioned that he'd caught an eighteen-inch trout, which he shared with Omar. Steinbeck also bought eggs at a shop near the post office, and his parents sent him ham and bacon.

Toby Street told Steinbeck that he suspected one reason he took the job at Brigham's was a desire to prove himself in a lonely place. Steinbeck wrote to Street, saying it was true, that he had always been frightened when he was alone. He said he knew that if he ever became a writer, he was likely to spend a lot of time by himself. The long winter at Lake Tahoe would do him good. Steinbeck's fear of the dark was only part of it. At night he could feel the anxiety in the pit of his stomach. There was also the chilling thought that he might not be completely alone. A large animal—there was no moon and Steinbeck couldn't see what it was—had come snuffling around the cabin the night before, and it had scared Steinbeck. Probably, he said, it was only a coyote. But that didn't alter the fact that it had unnerved him. He asked Street not to tell anybody.

Steinbeck was there to write, though the record of his first months at Lake Tahoe is thin, and what he worked on and how it went isn't known. He asked Street to send him a dictionary after he searched Dr. Brigham's library in the main house and was shocked to not find one. He hinted that, unlike most times, when he was juggling different stories, he had now immersed himself in a single project. His manuscript came slowly, but working on it was satisfying. He said that if Street was willing to read it he would soon send him some pages. Steinbeck said the luxury of revising his work over and over reminded him every day of the extravagance of time he had there.

Steinbeck encouraged Street to keep working on his unfinished play, *The Green Lady*. Street was by then well along in law school, and it's doubtful he had the time or the inclination to grapple with a piece of writing he judged hopeless.

Soon, Steinbeck and Omar had company. Carl Wilhelmson, his Finnish friend from Stanford, showed up. Not everyone liked Wilhelmson, who could come across as sullen, but Steinbeck was fond of him. Wilhelmson was also an aspiring writer. One time Wilhelmson had defended one of Steinbeck's stories to another student who'd been critical. Steinbeck was impressed by Wilhelmson's vehemence, especially since he had earlier been skeptical about the piece. Steinbeck told him that he hoped Wilhelmson would be his mentor, as Wilhelmson had an unerring eye for the excesses that cluttered Steinbeck's early writing. After college, Wilhelmson moved to Japan for a time, where he taught English. Steinbeck was glad when he came back.

Wilhelmson was in his element at Lake Tahoe. He had been born close to the Arctic Circle, and the deep snow and biting air agreed with him. Steinbeck wrote home to say that Wilhelmson had found a set of cross-country skis and was now regularly gliding over the deep snow and in general behaving like a kid. Steinbeck tried skiing but could not get the hang of it.

The plan was that Steinbeck and Wilhelmson would support each other's work through the cold dark months. But the cabin, which was comfortable for one, proved crowded with two. Frazzled and anxious, Wilhelmson eventually left. Steinbeck told his parents that Wilhelmson's advice on his manuscript-in-progress had been "invaluable." Carl, he said, was a wonderful critic who saw all of his blunders and the places in his writing where he got carried away and became "ridiculous." One of Wilhelmson's more practical contributions to

Steinbeck's writing had been the nice typewriter he'd brought up and shared during his stay.

In December, the snow continued to pile up, though temperatures remained mild—in the twenties. Steinbeck usually got his mail at nearby Camp Richardson, where the mail steamer stopped a couple of times a week, weather permitting. Other times he would hike to the post office, though now he needed snowshoes even to go to the outhouse. It was hard work getting around. The snow was so powdery that even on snowshoes, he went in to his knees. Omar sank chest-deep and still his feet did not reach solid ground. The dog had to "worm along," swimming through the snow. But he seemed to love it. Steinbeck wrote to his parents asking them to get him a ticket for the Stanford-Alabama football game, which he hoped to come down for.

In March, Steinbeck got a surprise. A new monthly magazine called *The Smoker's Companion* published one of Steinbeck's stories—his first commercial sale. It was titled "The Gifts of Iban." It was a fantasy set in a mythical place populated with not-quite-human creatures. Exactly when Steinbeck wrote the story, and how it came to be submitted to *The Smoker's Companion*, isn't certain. But it seems likely—given its calculated echoes of James Branch Cabell—that it was among the stories Steinbeck had written in a fevered rush for Cabell's editor Guy Holt back in New York. Steinbeck's friend, the well-connected Mahlon Blaine, was friends with the editor of *The Smoker's Companion*, and it may have been that Blaine acted as an intermediary. However it happened, Steinbeck disliked either the story or the magazine—or both. He insisted that the piece be published under a pseudonym: John Stern.

As Steinbeck's first book-length manuscript grew thicker, he became more protective of his time. His sister Mary had become engaged to a man named Bill Dekker. With the wedding approaching that spring, Steinbeck wrote home to say it was unlikely he could attend. He told Mary that if she asked him to come, he would—but it would cost him his job. And that would mean not finishing his book. This was by no means true. He could have finished the book anywhere. What he meant but did not say was that he'd reached a point where an interruption would be intolerable to him.

Part of what was driving Steinbeck harder than ever were words of encouragement from Stanford. He'd sent fifty pages of his manuscript to Miss Mirrielees and was elated when she wrote back that she found it "beautifully done." Shrewdly, Mirrielees told him that his writing was improving because the artful passages no longer stood out so starkly. Steinbeck called this a "bombshell" of praise coming from her. But Steinbeck didn't trust what he was hearing unreservedly. "I don't know whether it will be worth a darn," he said.

The weather improved enough for Steinbeck to do some fishing. He told his parents he'd caught a nine-pound trout. As if to prove his kinship with fishermen everywhere, who practice the purest form of fiction, he said it had put up a tremendous fight and at one point pulled him into the lake.

Summer at Lake Tahoe was pleasant, but Steinbeck found it hard to concentrate even though the Brighams made few demands on him. They went out of their way to make him feel that, although they had five servants, he was different. He took his meals with the family and spent long hours lolling on the beach and cooling off in the lake. His only complaint was that because they treated him like family, he was often included in whatever activities the Brighams undertook. The Brigham grandchildren—there were seven in all—were loud and quarrelsome. Gradually it dawned on Steinbeck that he was kept around mainly because he was big and intelligent and might come in handy in an emergency. He would be glad when everyone was gone again, probably toward the middle of October.

That fall, ahead of his second winter of isolation, Steinbeck asked Carl Wilhelmson to consider coming back to Tahoe. He promised to make sure they were more comfortable and less likely to get on each other's nerves. And this year he'd have a boat they could use to go to Tallac for mail and supplies. Steinbeck assured Wilhelmson they'd eat better, too. He'd gotten to know a couple of workers at the fish hatchery in Tallac, and had learned that they ordered fresh meat and vegetables from Truckee, on the north end of the lake, for $15 a month each. He added that Omar was well and would be joined soon by Jerry, another Airedale that Steinbeck was bringing up from home. They'd make a fine pair but would undoubtedly fight all the time. Steinbeck urged Wilhelmson to talk himself into coming, and in the end Wilhelmson agreed.

While Steinbeck waited for Wilhelmson to arrive, he began a new version of his manuscript. Writers revise, sometimes as they go, sometimes at the end, often both. But Steinbeck's revisions tended to morph into wholesale rewrites. He seemed to be perpetually starting over. He wrote home that he slept soundly after a good day of work. He thanked his parents for some curtains they sent up, which had "transformed" the cabin and made it a place "that wants to be lived in." This was especially nice, as he had been stuck indoors on account of unremitting downpours. Storm after storm swept through, dropping torrents of rain but no snow yet. The wind, meanwhile, moaned ceaselessly. In spite of the onslaught, Steinbeck found his confinement conducive to long spells of writing, when he got lost in his work and the tempest raging outside his door disappeared from his thoughts. The weather was bad enough that Steinbeck wasn't sure when he'd see the mail steamer again. He promised not to use his own boat unless the lake was dead calm, which seemed far from imminent. Every time the wind rose the dogs cowered in a corner.

Steinbeck had let a few people know what he was working on. One was Mahlon Blaine back in New York. Blaine had a contract to illustrate five new books, and he had put out word about a young writer in California at work on one about a pirate named Henry Morgan. Steinbeck called it a "biographical novel," and he told his parents it was a good time to write one, as they were "quite the rage." Where he got this idea isn't certain, but he had no doubt been impressed by Donn Byrne's *Messer Marco Polo* from 1922. In Byrne's imaginative telling, the great merchant and explorer hears of a princess in China and undertakes the long journey there to convert her to Christianity.

The book is brisk and charming at every turn, never bogging down in descriptive passages. It can be read in a couple of hours. And the setting—far away and long ago—appealed to Steinbeck's fondness for legend. Meanwhile, one of the editors Blaine talked with worked at McBride—where they may have vaguely remembered the uncannily similar *A Lady in Infa-Red* as one of the stories Steinbeck had hoped to sell them for a collection.

By December, Steinbeck had finished 150 pages of his latest version of the manuscript. He told his parents that he and Wilhelmson had been working through the nights, sometimes until five in the morning. Just before Christmas, they paused for several days to cut and store ice for the coming summer. They managed to put up 400 blocks, each weighing 150 pounds.

At the end of January, Wilhelmson's anxiety returned and he became "horribly nervous." Steinbeck felt his friend's depressed mood rubbing off on him. Wilhelmson had been gassed in the war, and he could never completely escape the fear that this would somehow harm him years later. Wilhelmson decided to leave for Sacramento. Steinbeck was glad to see him go. He'd soon have a different friend around—a man named Lloyd Shebley, whom he'd met the previous year. Shebley worked for the Fish and Game Commission, and operated the trout hatchery in Tallac. He had hired Steinbeck briefly to help him remove a log jam on the stream that led spawning trout to the hatchery. Shebley was spending the winter in Tahoe City, up on the northwest corner of the lake. Before Wilhelmson left, Shebley invited Steinbeck to come up for a weekend and stay at the Tahoe Tavern, a grand hotel and casino tucked into the woods just south of Tahoe City. It was tempting, but Steinbeck could not bring himself to leave Wilhelmson alone. "He is terrified because he might get sick, and so I shall never ask him to stay alone," Steinbeck told his parents. Steinbeck thought he knew what Wilhelmson was going through, though of course he had no idea what it was like to be gassed, or to return from war emotionally damaged. But he could never look away from someone who was suffering, whether the pain was large or slight.

Almost offhandedly, Steinbeck mentioned in the same letter that he had finished his book. He thought he would stay on at the Brighams' for another few months. He hoped to get a new book started before he left, but was so tired of writing that he needed a break. He was sure the Morgan book was not going to be published—it was possible that he wouldn't even submit it. He called it "pretty crude stuff" and threatened to burn it after Olive urged him to show it around. To cheer himself up, he'd gotten dressed in his best clothes just to see how he looked—which he said was "very well." Perhaps he'd buy some new clothes in the spring and "strut about Salinas for a little while."

It rained and rained. The level of the lake rose nearly two feet. Streams surged and tore at their banks, and swollen creeks appeared where none had been before. A stretch of highway and a stone bridge washed away near Tahoe City. Lloyd Shebley came and stayed for four days during the spawning run at the hatchery, which had been damaged in the flooding. In a few days, he'd have to return to make repairs. Steinbeck wrote home: "Lord how it rains." A week later he wrote again. "Lord how it snows." He added that it was a comfort to be living on a hill and to have a boat to get away in.

Steinbeck didn't say anything this time about his book, but he had other news: He had been offered a job with the Fish and Game Commission at the main fish hatchery in Tahoe City, and he had accepted it. He would work there during the coming summer and fall. He figured it was better than staying on another year with the Brighams. The job would start June 1 and run until the beginning of November. Then he wanted to do nothing but write, either in Salinas or at the family cottage in Pacific Grove.

Steinbeck sent his manuscript to Toby Street, joking that it was the biggest thing in literature since *Beowulf.* He asked Street to read it carefully and tell him in detail what he thought of it. He also told Street to pass it on to Miss Mirrielees when he was done. He was sure Miss Mirrielees would hesitate over the book's "lapses of strict morality," but that she would be more bothered by its "obvious philosophy." This was an interesting way of expressing his reservations about the book—and perhaps a subconscious anticipation of criticism that would come his way in the future concerning the ideas that animated his books.

Steinbeck also sent a copy of the manuscript to his former girlfriend Kate Beswick, who now lived in New York. Beswick offered to type it and forward it to the lawyer Ted Miller, their mutual friend from English Club at Stanford. Miller, in turn, agreed to act as Steinbeck's agent in New York, taking the manuscript around to publishers. When Miller read the manuscript he told Beswick he didn't care for it, but wrote to Steinbeck telling him it was excellent. Steinbeck, who somehow deduced Miller's true feelings, mused that this is the sort of thing you can expect when your friends are your critics.

At some point, the manuscript acquired a title. In his surviving letters, Steinbeck usually referred to the book-in-progress as the "mss," incorrectly using the plural abbreviation for "manuscript." At the end of February, he told Dook Sheffield that he had finished the book, which was called *Cup of Gold*. Right up until the end he believed it was going to be good. It wasn't.

Much as he wanted to begin another book, Steinbeck couldn't work. He felt isolated, preoccupied with the passage of time. This, too, was to become a lifelong theme and obsession. Life was leaking out of him, slipping away into the oblivion waiting for him in death. Each day marked one small subtraction from the whole of life. "Do you realize I am twenty-six now?" he asked Sheffield, as if he had one foot in the grave.

Had his first attempt to write a book killed the thing that had driven him for so long? Steinbeck wondered if the "sharp agony of words" would ever occur to him again. He had been "drunken" on their rhythms. But now his mind had gone silent, and sitting alone with nothing to do in his remote cabin, all seemed lost. The wind rattled at the door. "It is sad," Steinbeck said in closing, "when the snow is falling."

— 4 —

CAROL

*C*UP OF GOLD was a strange book. On the surface, it combined elements of Malory, Exquemelin, and Donn Byrne. At its heart, it concerns the doomed nature of the solitary hero—a man who gets everything he wants, but to the same end as any other man. All but ignored among Steinbeck's books a century later, it was nonetheless the one that prefigured the arc of his own life. In his longing for success, Steinbeck could never shake the feeling that time was running out on him. He could stop time in a book, but not for his own account. Steinbeck was, for all his hard work and discipline and earnest desire, merely mortal. Like anybody else.

The book opens in Wales, where a fifteen-year-old Henry Morgan is desperate to sail for the Indies to make his fortune as a buccaneer—which, after some misfortune and even greater good luck and skill, he does. Fierce and cunning in battle, Morgan seizes prizes across the Spanish Main. Only one thing eludes him: Panama—the Cup of Gold. In addition to its fabled wealth, Panama is also home to *La Santa Roja*—the Red Saint, a woman of surpassing beauty and guile whose name inflames the passions of men in every corner of the Caribbean.

Morgan raises an army of mercenaries and leads them to the isthmus and across. Panama, only a village of grass huts when Balboa first saw it, is now a gleaming city. Morgan captures it easily, looting a vast fortune. But the Red Saint resists his advances. Darkly beautiful, with a sharp tongue and black eyes that seem to laugh at Morgan, she flees after her husband pays a ransom.

Morgan and his men take their treasure back across the isthmus and load it onto his ship, to be divided later. Morgan breaks out kegs of rum, and a great celebration takes place on the beach. In the night, while his men lie passed out on the sand, Morgan steals away with the plunder. Later, back in London, he avoids the hangman and is instead knighted. Sir Henry Morgan returns to the West as lieutenant governor of Jamaica, where he ends his days as a judge, sending men like him to the gallows.

Steinbeck remained ambivalent about *Cup of Gold*. It was a boys' story, a violent one, and yet it was encumbered with a sensuality and a mysticism that would be lost on boys. Steinbeck had loved Malory because he thought he was the only person in the world who understood the legend of Arthur. Perhaps it was the same with *Cup of Gold*. Maybe it was a story that only he cared about.

The urge to write eventually returned. That spring, Steinbeck told a friend he was going to try to turn Toby Street's unfinished play, *The Green Lady*, into a novel. Steinbeck had always been intrigued by Street's play, and after Street abandoned it he told Steinbeck he could have it to do with it as he liked.

Near the end of May, Steinbeck went to San Francisco for his long-anticipated break from self-imposed exile. He wrote to Kate Beswick that he wished he was a Catholic, so he could enjoy confessing his waywardness to a priest. He said his visit to the city had been wonderful, and that he'd gotten his fill of "my two favorite sins." Presumably, drinking was one and women the other—though as the letter made plain, coarseness was another sin that also came naturally to Steinbeck, who routinely featured updates on his sex life in his prolific correspondence with Beswick. Whether she encouraged him or he simply lacked any sense of decency toward his onetime college lover is impossible to say. Perhaps it was a little of both, but as Beswick's letters have not survived we have only Steinbeck's often crude side of the conversation. Luridly, Steinbeck told her that after San Francisco he hoped he had enough sperm left to someday start a family. Celibacy, he speculated, had enhanced his attractiveness to women. Steinbeck's insistence that he'd had liaisons during this interlude might have been more than even Beswick wanted to know, though it could also have been just a lie. Whether the women were many—or any—Steinbeck did not admit to caring about any of them beyond whatever physical release he found in their company. Being young may explain Steinbeck's candor, if that's what it was. But it doesn't excuse his insistence on his own virility—the sort of boast that usually betrays an underlying insecurity.

Work resumed at the fish hatchery, and Steinbeck and Lloyd Shebley were busy—the place was "overcrowded with fishes and undercrowded with help," as Steinbeck put it. He was getting only a couple of hours of sleep at night, and it was unlikely he'd get much writing done over the summer. He reassured himself that winter would return. It was a time of year he now viewed as writing season. Steinbeck's life was taking a new direction. Between shifts at the hatchery, he'd fallen in love.

"I thought I was too old to be stricken," he told Beswick. "I know I am too old to be hasty."

The relationship had taken off like a rocket. Her name was Carol Henning. She and her sister, Idell, had come to Lake Tahoe on vacation and stopped in to see the hatchery. Steinbeck was out feeding the fish when they arrived. He showed them around. The Hennings were originally from San Jose but now lived in San Francisco. Carol worked at the Schilling spice company, where she was personal secretary to its owner. She was twenty-two, stylish, and attractive. She owned her own car and bore a vague resemblance to Ernest Hemingway's wife, Hadley Richardson. Carol was smart and outgoing. Steinbeck, she noticed, was fit and cheerful and had the most disarming blue eyes. He didn't let the sisters leave until they promised to go out with him and Shebley that evening. They got a late start due to car trouble on their way to pick up Carol and Idell, but after dinner and a long night of dancing, Steinbeck and Carol were captivated with each other.

Dook Sheffield, who was back at Stanford for the summer, drove up to Lake Tahoe while the Henning sisters continued their vacation. He found Steinbeck and Carol hopelessly in love. Sheffield was taken aback by Carol's youthful looks—she could have been sixteen, he thought. On the day Sheffield met her, Steinbeck had taken Carol to a rodeo. They'd come back dusty and smiling. Carol had a smudge of dirt on her nose. Sheffield was impressed that Steinbeck was sharing his work with Carol, who—as Kate Beswick had already done in New York—was typing up the handwritten manuscript of *Cup of Gold*. Steinbeck did not hesitate to impose on his friends in this way. He was casual about showing his work around and welcomed small criticisms—though he would not tolerate serious reservations. Anyone who didn't like something Steinbeck had written was not invited to read more. Sheffield, who read the manuscript and the typescript, noticed that Carol was not only a skilled typist, but also a fine, instinctive editor who made many minor but important adjustments. She had an uncanny ear for the way Steinbeck wanted his writing to sound. Sheffield offered a handful of small suggestions, and Steinbeck cheerfully made the changes.

When the sisters went back to San Francisco, Steinbeck bought a dilapidated 1922 Dodge so he could visit Carol. Sheffield figured it cost $50, maybe $100 at most. The car's only redeeming feature, he said, was that it ran. Toward the end of summer, Steinbeck told Kate Beswick he was still in love, if a little less volcanically than he had been at first. He had no plans to get married. "The girl isn't wonderful at all or awfully beautiful at all, or anything, but I'm in love with her. And she is clever." It was a strange way to put it.

Steinbeck had heard nothing from Ted Miller about *Cup of Gold*. He wondered how many publishers had turned it down. He asked Beswick to give Miller a nudge. In September, Miller finally did write. The book had been turned down twice and a third rejection was imminent. Steinbeck figured that there were enough publishers in New York to keep this up for years. He thought that would perhaps be good both for him and for literature.

That same month, Steinbeck decided to leave his job at the hatchery and move to San Francisco, where he planned to live with Carol. He was worried about money. Carol made three times as much as he could hope to earn, and he did not want to embarrass her. He thought maybe he'd buy a pair of corduroys (a fabric Steinbeck loved) so he might be mistaken for a student. Carol was unconcerned about his poverty. Steinbeck planned to start a new book just as soon as he had a table to put his typewriter on.

The urgency of Steinbeck's need to relate details of his love life to Kate Beswick was remarkable. He told her that after his long celibacy at the Brighams', he had somehow acquired a new sexual prowess— though he offered no theory as to how abstinence enhanced performance. He said he could now have an orgasm when he "wanted" one, whether it took thirty seconds or thirty minutes. He reminded Beswick of his poor control in this regard when they were a couple. His new abilities, he said, were much admired and in constant demand—presumably by Carol, since any new conquest would have been unaware of his magnificent staying power until it was demonstrated in the flesh. Disconcertingly, he said he wished Beswick could observe him and Carol. He thought that their simultaneous orgasms were a sign he and Carol were meant for each other. He knew he faced the prospect of intervals of celibacy again because sex somehow drained the well he relied on in his work. He believed fornication and writing were incompatible. But with his new abilities he figured he could always make his way in life as a gigolo. He speculated that Beswick would surely like to experience his lovemaking again for herself.

What a gift to women he fancied himself.

Steinbeck rented his own apartment in San Francisco, apparently because Carol's mother had come to stay with her for a month. He found a job in a jute mill, hauling one-ton bales of jute on a hand truck for eight hours a day. It was grueling work that paid him enough to eat and nothing more. Writing was hopeless under these circumstances. Steinbeck admitted that the jute mill was a scary place to work, but that "one must live." He said that fortunately there was no gas jet in his apartment, or that last proposition might get tested.

Steinbeck's hopes for *Cup of Gold* began to fade. Waiting for news was unnerving. He asked Kate if he should rewrite it, though he doubted that would do any good. Maybe *she* should rewrite it for him. They could publish it under a pen name. If the book had to be changed, he didn't want his name on it anyway. He was too tired to care now what happened to it. If Beswick thought she could make something of it, she was welcome to it. He had just one final request. "I should like this opus to go to McBride's as is," he wrote. He told her the publisher had once been enthusiastic about his work. Steinbeck skipped over the part about his last visit to McBride, when he'd been bodily ejected. If they didn't want *Cup of Gold*, then the book could go to hell.

One weekend Steinbeck went down to Palo Alto to stay with his sister Mary and visit Toby Street. Street insisted that they call on John Breck, who had just sold a novel. Steinbeck thought this sounded unspeakably depressing, but agreed to go. The last word he'd had about Breck came when he was snowed in at Lake Tahoe. Street had written to tell him Breck had been kicked in the head by a horse and was in a coma. Apparently, she'd recovered. Now she was about to be published. Steinbeck confided to Beswick he had hoped never to see her again.

He did not tell Beswick that one reason he wanted to avoid Breck could have been an embarrassing visit that her daughter Polly had made to Tahoe City while Steinbeck was working at the hatchery. Polly and a friend were vacationing and went to see Steinbeck. Polly ended up staying around after Steinbeck finished work. Drinks appeared, and after a while Steinbeck tried to kiss her. Polly pushed him away. Furious, he dragged her upstairs and dangled her out a window by her ankles. Lloyd Shebley heard her screams and intervened before Polly got hurt. After an abject apology from Steinbeck, Polly and her friend agreed to go dancing with him and Shebley the next night. As they spun across the cramped dance floor of a speak-easy, a man with a lit cigarette brushed against Steinbeck's suit jacket, burning a hole in it. Steinbeck whirled around, brandishing a revolver at the stricken man. Shebley quickly stepped in again, and the four of them left in a hurry.

None of this came up when Street and Steinbeck got to Breck's house, though in a way it was worse. Breck came to the door. "Why look who's here," she said. "How are you? Have you sold anything yet?" Steinbeck couldn't get away fast enough. Breck seemed ancient. What if it took him as long to become an author? He said the "cords" on her neck stuck out so much that she looked as though she were "slowly mummifying."

In a letter to Beswick, Steinbeck mentioned in passing that he and Carol had had a scare when she thought she was pregnant. She wasn't. He wished he had a little money so he could quit his job and write full-time, and just before Christmas, Beswick sent Steinbeck $50. Apparently, she wanted to send him more. But Steinbeck insisted that she should not attempt to finance his writing career, which was on the verge of ending before it started. Exhausted by his daily toil at the jute mill, Steinbeck admitted that for probably the first time in years he had stopped writing entirely. Steinbeck thought, as many writers do, that the act of writing did not make one a writer. Rather, writing was a symptom of an inborn compulsion that could not be denied. Writers write because they have to, he believed. And they do so no matter what their circumstances. He felt defeated by the thought that he was too tired to write, exposed as a fraud. Far worse than the failure of his first book was learning that it had been a pose. He told Beswick that if she were rich—or he had talent—he'd gladly take her money. But she wasn't rich, and he had no evidence for any talent on his part.

Steinbeck heard at last from Ted Miller. An editor at McBride had hinted at interest in *Cup of Gold*. Steinbeck was skeptical, and he tried to put it out of his mind. But he couldn't conceal his excitement. He told Beswick he was headed to Pacific Grove and would make her money go as far as he could—though he had already spent $20 of it.

He had no idea what he'd do when the money ran out. Until then he was elated at the prospect of getting back to work. "I shall write and write and write," he said.

Steinbeck kept to himself at the family cottage. On New Year's Eve, he and Toby Street went up to San Francisco to celebrate with Carol. Street got drunk and pulled Carol aside. He told her not to marry Steinbeck. "You are not as important as his work," Street said. The booze must have been strong that night, as Steinbeck's "work" to that point consisted of a single forgettable story in *The Smoker's Companion* and a gaudy pirate saga that was piling up rejections in New York. Carol was "very deeply hurt," though Steinbeck suggested that Street had a point. Carol was upset by what Street told her, but only because he didn't realize that she'd already figured it out for herself.

Ted Miller wrote Steinbeck to say that Mahlon Blaine had resurfaced and was working to find a publisher for *Cup of Gold*. Steinbeck told Beswick that some of the rejections he'd gotten were sufficiently generous for him to hope that his next book would get serious consideration. Apparently that was going to be *The Green Lady*. He didn't want to say anything much about it yet; he thought Street's story was "marvelous," but to make it work, some complex ideas would have to be made convincing. On a different subject, he told Beswick he thought his looks were getting worse. This was offset by his virile physicality. His grim Irish face would never be a good one, he said, but "my body just now is nearly perfect." Why Steinbeck kept telling Beswick things like this can't be explained in any way that make it seem okay. It was simply in his nature.

On January 21, 1929, Robert M. McBride & Company wrote to Ted Miller saying they were accepting *Cup of Gold* and enclosing a contract. Miller wired Steinbeck, asking him to send McBride another copy of the manuscript and a biography of himself that could be used for publicity. Mahlon Blaine, who seemed to have an excellent relationship with McBride and who had surely helped persuade them to accept the book, was going to illustrate the cover.

But Steinbeck would have to wait for a windfall, if there was to be one. It was too late to add *Cup of Gold* to McBride's spring list. It would come out in the fall. Miller hadn't been able to get Steinbeck an advance, but McBride agreed to pay Steinbeck royalties on pre-publication orders as they came in. Miller said they told him the book was "so exceptional" that this might work out to payments of some $400 or so. Miller warned Steinbeck that although the final number could be more, it also could be less. Nobody, he said, could predict how a book would do.

— 5 —

CRASH

At Stanford, Edith Mirrielees had advised Steinbeck to move to Europe if he was serious about becoming a writer. When he asked her why, she said that in Europe poverty was viewed as a misfortune, whereas in America it is a sin. Mirrielees doubted that Steinbeck could stand the humiliation of being poor. This was perceptive, but Mirrielees could not have foreseen that soon the whole country would be overtaken by an economic calamity that was to rescue Steinbeck from shame—ultimately, in more ways than one.

Carol had visited Steinbeck in Pacific Grove a few days after he learned that McBride was going to publish *Cup of Gold*. When they weren't in bed, they spent their time down by the bay catching crabs for salad, cooking chops over an open fire, and playing tennis. If this was being down and out, maybe things were not so bad after all. Steinbeck and Carol learned early in their relationship how to make do, to survive cheerfully with little more than a borrowed cottage and their own ingenuity.

But when Carol left, it was hard for Steinbeck to get back to work. Although he was not proud of *Cup of Gold*, it had a publisher at last and his confidence in his writing was renewed. That didn't make it any easier, however. Writing left him raw and jangled and unpleasant to be around. Sometimes it felt as if a demon inside of him controlled his actions. His parents had come to Pacific Grove planning to stay a few days, but he'd been working on the new book almost around the clock and was so ill-tempered that John Ernst and Olive turned around and went home. That left Steinbeck feeling guilty. He wondered if maybe he should go back up into the mountains and turn fully into the savage he was well on his way to becoming. At least then he would be free to examine his anger from all sides without fear of interruption. Or criticism.

At the same time, Steinbeck thought he should go to New York to put his relationship with McBride on a firmer footing, and perhaps to apologize for trying to bust up their office on his last visit, but not until he had finished at least a draft of *The Green Lady*. That would take him probably until September. He told Kate Beswick he wouldn't come east until the fall. She had agreed to proof the galleys for *Cup of Gold*. Steinbeck had complete trust in her judgment, and he gave her leave to "do anything you damn well please" to them.

A couple of weeks later, Carol came down again. She and Steinbeck were in bed one morning when there was a knock at the door. It was John Ernst and Olive, who of course had a key but found the door bolted from the inside. They came around back and started knocking again while Steinbeck debated what to do. After a few minutes—Olive had found a stick and was beating it against the bedroom window—Steinbeck showed himself, trying to look groggy. While Carol gathered up her clothes, he told his parents to come around front again. He let them in as Carol slipped out the back and headed to the garage to get dressed. Steinbeck told his folks he'd had too much whiskey the night before. Weirdly, this seemed to calm his mother, maybe because she wanted an explanation she could tolerate. Steinbeck thought his father knew he'd had someone in there—and might well have figured out who it was when Carol knocked on the door after a while, pretending she'd just arrived. Carol stayed with the three of them for a few miserable days.

Steinbeck claimed he was having an affair with a neighbor, a woman in her thirties who worked as a secretary in Monterey. He told Kate Beswick he had to do it because Carol was up in San Francisco and he couldn't see her often enough—implying that his need for sexual release outweighed Carol's feelings. Steinbeck didn't think it was a big deal. He said Carol knew all about it and was bothered only that the woman wasn't pretty enough. This miniature portrait of the bohemian life he was leading, and the sexual laissez-faire that went with it, was telling. It could have been true, but was a cruel commentary on Carol even if it wasn't. By now making up things that reflected badly on himself had become second nature for him.

In March, Steinbeck got a look at Mahlon Blaine's illustration for the *Cup of Gold* dust jacket: a garish cartoon of Henry Morgan receiving a gold chalice from two pirates. The primary colors blared. Steinbeck was "a little shocked at the brightness of it." But he told Kate Beswick it didn't make any difference to him and to not tell anyone he didn't like it. He also mentioned that he planned to go up into the high country to work on *The Green Lady*. When Steinbeck finally got the galley proofs for *Cup of Gold*, he admitted that seeing his book in print improved it a little.

By the end of April, *The Green Lady* was progressing rapidly. Steinbeck had never worked like this before. He wrote every day for a few hours in the afternoon, and then for a few more after dinner. Then he went straight to bed and was up early the next morning. He wasn't certain the manuscript was good—he never would be about any of his works-in-progress—but he didn't care. He told Kate Beswick, who was thinking of marrying a fellow poet, that she should go ahead and do it. These days, he said, you could always get out of it in Reno.

Steinbeck would struggle to take full possession of *The Green Lady* for more than a year. Gradually, he turned away from Toby Street's original idea—about a man in love with a forest. An early fragment of the novel's manuscript was attributed to both Steinbeck and Street, though there is no evidence that Street had worked on it. Steinbeck moved the action from Mendocino County to a ranch in Jolon, in Monterey County south of King City—an area he was more familiar with—and expanded the story to include more generations of the family at the center of it. He also experimented with the theme of nature as a living entity. In this version, Anthony (Andy) Wayne seems to be the main character, though much is uncertain, as Andy is just a boy in this only surviving piece of the story. Alert to the forces that live within the landscape of his valley, he thinks the hills around him look like naked people lying alongside one another. He is obsessed with "pretty things," including the trees and sun. By late May, Steinbeck had finished eighty pages. He'd shown it to Toby Street and Carl Wilhelmson, both of whom approved. He couldn't wait to show it to Kate Beswick.

Sometime over the summer, Steinbeck made good on his threat to head into the country and moved to a small cabin in a redwood forest less than twenty miles from Palo Alto—though it might as well have been far away, since nobody knew where he was. He didn't want to see anybody. He was working feverishly and thought he'd soon finish the manuscript, which had grown to more than 240 pages. Steinbeck seemed to be in a semi-manic phase. He'd borrowed $50 a month from his father to live on while he was writing *The Green Lady*. But there was much still to be written, and he'd have to borrow more. He figured he'd owe $400 by the end of the year. Now he thought this book was the best writing he'd ever done. But when he showed part of it to Toby Street—asking him only to read it and say nothing—Street's earlier enthusiasm cooled, and he returned it to Steinbeck covered in suggestions. Street would later insist that he had given *The Green Lady* to Steinbeck with no strings attached. But as Steinbeck reworked the book and it became longer and deeper, perhaps it was less easy for Street to let go of it. Annoyed by Street's criticism, Steinbeck disappeared again. He rented a room in San Francisco without telling Street where he'd gone.

Steinbeck said he had hoped the royalties from prepublication sales of *Cup of Gold* would cover the money he was borrowing. But in the end he got only $180 from his first book. Exactly when Steinbeck received the money, or whether it came in installments, isn't clear. Steinbeck had heard that *Cup of Gold* wasn't selling and had been ignored by critics. This wasn't true, though the trickle of reviews was only starting. Writing in the *New York Herald Tribune*, Will Cuppy said that while the book was "pedestrian" in places, and that its voice sometimes shifted into a modern idiom at odds with the seventeenth-century world of Henry Morgan, Steinbeck nonetheless had a graceful style. And Cuppy—betraying a resentment of the new postwar literature—thought the book was a refreshing alternative to the dreck dominating the current "degenerate age."

A review in the *St. Louis Star* was even kinder. Steinbeck, the reviewer said, had taken a story that naturally appealed to boys and turned it into an adventurous feast for adult readers. And he'd brought Morgan to life as other books about the famed buccaneer had failed to do.

In December, a long, enthusiastic review by Paul Teal appeared in the *San Jose Mercury Herald*. Teal's careful summary of the story suggested a close reading. This was an improvement over the slapdash review that had run in the *Stanford Daily*, which described the book as odd but captivating and claimed the author was a Stanford man, a graduate in the class of 1924 who had spent the last several years traveling abroad.

The *Stanford Daily* was partly right. *Cup of Gold* was different—forgettable and yet compelling in places. It was also easy to get through, even though the brisk action was sometimes stopped in its tracks by windy speeches that passed for dialogue. This gave the book a loopy balance. Despite Steinbeck's lack of technical skill—or maybe it was just his clumsy attempt to make the book sound historical—it somehow hung together. This much was sure: *Cup of Gold* was a false start. The quest at the center of the story and its literal allusions to Malory were pure Steinbeck. But the book was otherwise unlike anything else he was to write. And the smattering of good reviews was hard to interpret. Did other critics ignore the book or did they dislike it and decide against saying so? Few things are less heartening to a writer than a hint of approval, as it leaves open the possibility of wider disappointment.

Will Cuppy was alone among the handful of reviewers in finding Steinbeck's work unfashionable, though he considered this a plus.

Nobody else mentioned the obvious: that it was outside the emerging current of American literature, much of which was being written in Europe.

In April of 1924, F. Scott Fitzgerald had restarted work on a novel tentatively titled *Among Ash Heaps and Millionaires*. The next month, he sailed with his wife, Zelda, and their daughter, Scottie, for France. After a short visit with friends in Paris, the Fitzgeralds went to the Riviera, where everything was a bargain in the off-season, and where Fitzgerald got down to serious work on his novel. By the end of August, he told his editor, Maxwell Perkins, that it was finished—though the manuscript would not reach New York until October. Perkins preferred one of Fitzgerald's earlier titles for the book, and Fitzgerald obliged, changing it to *The Great Gatsby*.

The Great Gatsby sold slowly after its release in early April 1925. The reviews were mixed, but some were sensational. Gilbert Seldes wrote in *The Dial* that Fitzgerald had taken flight, and was "leaving farther behind all the men of his own generation and most of his elders." Scribner's first printing of 21,000 copies was followed by a second, smaller printing that did not sell out. *Gatsby* was decisively outsold by Sinclair Lewis's *Arrowsmith*, the story of a brilliant doctor and public-health researcher. It won the Pulitzer Prize. Lewis, who, like Fitzgerald, was a Minnesotan, had already had successes with *Main Street* in 1920 and *Babbitt in* 1922, and was a towering presence. Before the 1920s ended, he added *Elmer Gantry* and *Dodsworth*, and in 1930, at the age of forty-five, he became the first American to win the Nobel Prize in Literature—a landmark event in that it recognized, at last, that American literature had broken with European traditions and was now firmly on its own.

The new crop of writers wrapped themselves in self-awareness— the source of their inspiration—and a belief that they were reinventing literature after the catastrophe of World War I. In France, Gertrude Stein, presiding over the period from her salon in Paris, had declared postwar writers a "lost generation." What did she mean? Were they ungrounded in the traditions that animated predecessors such as Stephen Crane, Willa Cather, and Sherwood Anderson? Not really. Realism was alive in their writing. And surely they were not lost in the sense of being thwarted, as they were producing bold new work that Stein admired. Were they, rather, the lost souls of a cataclysm, survivors washed up on a beach? Maybe the lost generation was only the first cohort that ever thought of themselves as a generation somehow apart from what had come before. This was the answer put forward by a young poet and critic named Malcolm Cowley.

Cowley, who was from Pittsburgh, had attended Harvard and then gone to France to enlist in the ambulance service as a "gentleman volunteer" while America was still on the sidelines of the war. But there were more ambulance drivers than ambulances, and Cowley ended up driving a munitions transport. American drivers of both kinds were, Cowley later wrote, the "most literary branch of any army" ever. Among them were John Dos Passos, E. E. Cummings, Dashiell Hammett, and, of course, Ernest Hemingway. After the war, Cowley lived for a time in Greenwich Village before going back to France in 1921, where he found Paris crowded with American expat writers, drawn there by exchange rates that made it possible to live on next to nothing, by the fact that you could buy a drink legally, and by the company of others like them grappling with the reality of a world that had been undone. They all faced the same problem, one that had been apparent to Cowley back in high school and that he would write penetratingly about in *Exile's Return* in 1934. American writers were "launching or drifting into a sea of letters with no fixed destination" and with no captain: "Literature, our profession, was living in the shadow of its own great past. The symbols that moved us, the great themes of love and death and parting, had been used and exhausted. Where could we find new themes when everything, so it seemed, had been said already? Having devoured the world, literature was dying for lack of nourishment."

The practitioners of the new American literature seemed to know where they stood in a way that John Steinbeck did not—at least not yet. In 1922, when Steinbeck was twenty, and in and out of college, Proust died—and, with him, what many writers had long recognized as a literary tradition to which they belonged. Besides Fitzgerald, the metaphorical pallbearers include Sinclair Lewis, whose savagely funny novel *Babbitt*, published that same year, drew a hot blade through American consumerism and middle-class striving; and T. S. Eliot, with his poem "The Waste Land," a meditation on a world rendered barren and blasted by war. Crammed with obscure and fragmentary allusions, "The Waste Land" was a kaleidoscopic indictment of a hollowed-out culture.

Through his early writing struggles and with his first book—a story literally centuries out of step with the times—Steinbeck seemed oblivious to the direction American writing had taken, as if he had somehow missed a turn on a long road and come to a dead end. And the so-called lost generation kept producing innovative works of literature. John Dos Passos followed his popular antiwar novel, *Three Soldiers* (1921), with *Manhattan Transfer* (1925), and *The 42nd Parallel*, the first book in his *U.S.A.* Trilogy, published in 1930. And in case anyone had missed it, Ernest Hemingway immortalized the phrase "lost generation" in an epigraph for his youth-defining 1926 novel, *The Sun Also Rises*. It told the story of a group of young friends, expats and others, who travel from France to a bullfight fiesta in Pamplona, Spain. Jake Barnes, Hemingway's protagonist, is a worldly newspaperman who regards his life with cool detachment, except for a searing regret over a war wound that has left him thoroughly male but unmanned. The friends' days and nights are sodden with booze—the drinking never stops—and as they wobble through Parisian dance halls and cafés, strains and rivalries emerge. These conflicts will tax their time together in Spain, where death stalks the bullring in a ritual that offers a counterpoint of clarity and dignity missing from their lives. The book was lean and revelatory, tinged with the anxiety young people felt about their place in a world in pieces. Hemingway's precise depiction of the desire to drown this ambivalence in cheap wine and expensive champagne was at once romantic and heartbreaking— and a thumb in the eye of dull, dry America. As Malcolm Cowley observed decades later, the enormity and pointlessness of the slaughter in the war's grimmest time had nullified thoughts of victory or of the nobility of a just cause, narrowing the soldiers' ambition to only the inevitability of death. Death seemed unavoidable, and no one who had survived that certainty could claim to not be surprised to be alive.

One night during the fiesta, as Jake lays in bed drunk, head spinning and unable to sleep, he considers the many "fine philosophies" of life he has tried out, only to find them wanting. It's possible, he thinks, that the point of living is unknowable. But then he reconsiders:

"Perhaps that wasn't true, though. Perhaps as you went along you did learn something. I did not care what it was all about. All I wanted to know was how to live in it. Maybe if you found out how to live in it you learned from that what it was all about."

Critics were thrilled that Hemingway's novel had lived up to the extravagant promise he'd demonstrated in *In Our Time*. An unsigned review in the *New York Times* praised Hemingway's "weighted, quickening prose" and his "uncanny skill" in portraying the hopeless love affair between Jake Barnes and the alcoholic but beguiling Lady Brett Ashley. *The Sun Also Rises*, said the *Times*, was a major event in an already rich year for books.

Nobody was happier about this reception than Max Perkins, the keen-eyed editor at Scribner's, who, at the urging of F. Scott Fitzgerald and with Hemingway's complicity, had managed to steal *The Sun Also Rises* from Boni & Liveright. Perkins now had charge of the two finest young writers in the world.

Hemingway's breakthrough novel appeared while Steinbeck was going hungry and struggling to write in New York. When *Cup of Gold* came out in 1929, it was the same year that Hemingway published his gripping war book *A Farewell to Arms*. Both of Hemingway's novels from the 1920s would join *Gatsby* in the highest reaches of the American literary canon. Hemingway said that he developed his distinctive style—direct, terse, visual—by studying Impressionist paintings in the Musée du Luxembourg in Paris. He claimed that the lean syntax that gave his stories "dimensions" was inspired by Cézanne, which is a wonderful story even if he made it up. Probably he learned as much or more during his time as a cub reporter for the *Kansas City Star*, where the streamlined declarative sentence ruled.

His style was caricatured as a naked and colorless march of short sentences—though this was far from the case. Hemingway used plain language, but his writing was often dense with rhythms and repetitions linked by his favorite word, "and," as in the arresting opening of *A Farewell to Arms*:

"In the late summer of that year we lived in a house in a village that looked across the river and the plain to the mountains. In the bed of the river there were pebbles and boulders, dry and white in the sun, and the water was clear and swiftly moving and blue in the channels. Troops went by the house and down the road and the dust they raised powdered the leaves of the trees. The trunks of the trees were dusty and the leaves fell early that year and we saw the troops marching along the road and the dust rising and leaves, stirred by the breeze, falling and the soldiers marching and afterward the road bare and white except for the leaves."

Hemingway's reputation came to rest not only on his writing but also on his swaggering persona as a boxer, bullfighting aficionado, big-game hunter, deep-sea fisherman, and war correspondent. Many of these things were still to come, but it was no wonder even then that Steinbeck could not bear to read him. Hemingway was just three years older than Steinbeck. But he had made it to the war, skipped college, worked as a newspaper reporter, and caught the crest of a wave of prose stylists, a wave that eluded Steinbeck as Steinbeck idled away his time at Stanford taking and retaking courses he hoped would teach him how to write. Hemingway was movie-star handsome and heroic—he had carried a wounded soldier from the battlefield despite being wounded himself—and had figured out that the lost generation, far from being bereft of things to write about, was its own best subject. Like Sinclair Lewis, Hemingway would go on to win the Nobel Prize. Nobody reading that irrelevant pirate book *Cup of Gold* could have dreamed that its author would, one day, too.

Cup of Gold was published in August of 1929, coming at the tail end of a party that had seemed like it might never end: the Roaring Twenties. The country rode an unprecedented economic boom. Consumers bought, and, as their appetite for buying ripened, they bought more. Cars, radios, appliances, telephones, tickets to the movies, tickets to travel on airplanes. As Europe struggled to recover from the war, the United States's economy surged. Unemployment was low, wages were up, stock prices soared. Jazz was big. Women could vote. Nobody could drink legally; everyone drank anyway. America's glass was raised in one long toast to its success astride the world.

Then, on Thursday, October 24, a flutter of uncertainty interrupted the fun. Stock prices had been drifting lower since a downturn on the London exchange in September. After a calm opening on the New York Stock Exchange, the volume of stocks being traded shot up, triggering a steep sell-off that cascaded into other markets across the country. The *New York Times* reported that the total losses "cannot be accurately calculated" but were "staggering"—in the billions of dollars. Fear, the paper said, struck big and small investors alike. Bank accounts that were healthy a week ago, the *Times* said, had been "wrecked" in minutes. The volume of shares traded on the New York exchange climbed to nearly 13 million, half again the previous record. The tickers ran for more than four hours after the closing bell. The humorist Will Rogers, who was in New York that day, found dark comedy in what had happened. "When Wall Street took that tail spin," Rogers wrote in his syndicated column the next day, "you had to stand in line to get a window to jump out of." It would take days to dispel the rumors of numerous suicides on Wall Street.

In the middle of that terrible day, five of the nation's most prominent bankers—they controlled some $6 billion in assets—had rushed to a hastily convened noon meeting at the headquarters of J.P. Morgan & Co. This gesture of concern—and its implied promise that things would not get out of hand—had for the moment halted the bloodletting. Share prices recovered through the afternoon. "As word went out in Wall Street that these financiers had met the air of tense anxiety in the financial district was relieved," the *Times* reported. "Almost at once the word was passed around the floor of the Stock Exchange that 'they' were going to support stock prices and the downrush of security quotations was halted." Thomas W. Lamont, senior partner at J.P. Morgan, said after the meeting: "There has been a little distress selling on the Stock Exchange." The group's consensus was that there was nothing to worry about, as the lower prices for stocks did not reflect their actual values. The *Times* said the whole mess was due to a "technical condition."

Things were back to normal on Friday, and the *Times* reported that "the hysteria" had passed as quickly as it had begun. The paper did note that an unusual number of sightseeing buses were making stops in the financial district so tourists could view the place "where all the money was lost." Some people were seen pocketing scraps of ticker tape they picked up from the street in the same way visitors to a battlefield take home spent bullets as souvenirs. Workers at the stock exchange came in on Sunday to clear up some of the backlog and get ready for what everyone assumed would be an uneventful week ahead. All economic indicators were good, and merchants were already excited about what promised to be a strong holiday shopping season.

But on Monday the markets plunged again. The New York Stock Exchange saw $10 billion evaporate. Nationwide, across many smaller exchanges, it was closer to $14 billion. Share prices of many of the country's biggest companies "smashed through their old lows of last Thursday," the *Times* said.

And then came Tuesday.

On October 29, stock prices collapsed in what the *Times* called "the most disastrous day in the stock market's history." As prices crumbled, billions more were erased. Many investors tried to sell their holdings at any price—and found no buyers. The J.P. Morgan group again met through much of the afternoon as the panic deepened. J.P. Morgan's Thomas Lamont told reporters that his group could not hope to maintain stock values, but merely to support the market by slowing its fall. The group stepped in several times to buy large blocks of stock for which there were no other bids. There was a brief rally near the close of trading, partly in response to emergency dividends of $1 a share declared in the afternoon by U.S. Steel and the

American Can Company. But in the end, the day that would come to be known as Black Tuesday had been, as the *Times* put it, "a day of disorganization, confusion and financial impotence." The only good thing to be said was that many investors thought there was no way things could get worse.

And stocks *did* rally the day after Black Tuesday. They were up again on Thursday. Prices wobbled through the following week, then began a slow recovery over the next few months.

Many factors contributed to the Great Depression. Fewer than one in ten Americans even owned stock. But there is no question that the stock-market crash marked its beginning and laid bare the weak foundation of the boom that had preceded it. In Florida, land speculators had created a market for "binders," which guaranteed the right to buy parcels of land. The binders were bought and sold as they climbed in value, even though the land itself was never purchased. Actual ownership of the asset became a fantasy. This was a feature of what the economist John Kenneth Galbraith would later call a "speculative orgy" that was in truth a "mass escape into make-believe." Land binders had an analogue in the stock market: buying on margin. It was a simple idea. You "buy" a stock at its current price, but pay for it later after the price has risen. Since stocks kept going up, so did margin buying.

Some people blamed the banks for reckless lending that enabled excessive speculation in the markets. In his book about the crash, Galbraith argued otherwise. Money, he said, was tight in the late 1920s. Instead, Galbraith believed that what ended the good times were the good times themselves. "Far more important than the rate of interest and the supply of money is the mood," he wrote. "Speculation on a large scale requires a pervasive sense of confidence and optimism and a conviction that ordinary people were meant to be rich."

Steinbeck had shipped the first part of *The Green Lady* to Kate Beswick. He insured it for $500, hoping it might get lost, since he could use the money and the amount was probably more than it would ever be worth. When Beswick received the manuscript a few days later, Steinbeck was sorry to hear it.

Steinbeck's struggle with *The Green Lady* was taking a toll on him. When he heard from Ted Miller that he wouldn't get enough money from *Cup of Gold* to pay off his debts, he was stunned—as if he'd been hit between the eyes and couldn't feel anything. It seemed that his writing career, such as it was, might be at an end. "I see no alternative," he told Kate Beswick, "to going into a trade."

McBride's efforts on behalf of *Cup of Gold* were, in Steinbeck's view, inadequate. This is the usual writer's complaint—when a book fails to find a readership it has to be the publisher's fault. Steinbeck believed that there had been few reviews because no review copies had been issued ahead of publication. But this may not have been true. There *were* reviews, and at least one, in the *New York Herald Tribune*, had appeared in mid-August, suggesting their reviewer, at least, had received an advance copy. Steinbeck also complained that he hadn't received a complimentary copy to give to his parents—and that he couldn't afford to buy one. Reconsidering Mahlon Blaine's cover illustration, Steinbeck decided it, too, was part of the problem with the book. Contradicting himself, Steinbeck complained to Kate Beswick that orders for the book had gone unfulfilled, an indication that readers did want it. In fact, McBride sold most of the 1,500 copies it printed. About the only thing Steinbeck got right was his admission to Beswick that "I know nothing about publishing."

Steinbeck was most upset by a request from McBride that he promote *Cup of Gold* by giving readings. Still terrified of the lectern and a room full of expectant faces, Steinbeck said he would starve before he did that. And there were times when starvation didn't seem far off. He and Carol had gone to the Stanford-USC football game. Stanford lost, but it was a beautiful day, with an armada of planes circling overhead. After the big weekend, Steinbeck had only 50 cents to his name.

It was November of 1929. Steinbeck's work-in-progress sagged, growing duller in his mind the harder he worked on it. He felt as though he'd already written the equivalent of "three long novels" for a draft from which he kept tearing up pages. Steinbeck longed for a change. He still wanted to go to New York, and mused about how lovely it would be to see the city at Christmas, with all the store windows crammed with holiday displays. But, of course, he was broke.

In the late fall of 1929 Steinbeck and Carol abruptly decided to move to Los Angeles. Steinbeck asked Dook Sheffield if he and his wife Maryon could put them up until they got settled. Hard times being what they were—a group effort—Steinbeck and Carol arrived with an entourage: their good friends from Pacific Grove, Ritchie and Tal Lovejoy. Ritchie was a newspaperman and illustrator. His wife Tal—short for Natalya—was one of five sisters named Kashevaroff. Their father was Russian, and at least three of them had moved to the Monterey peninsula from Sitka, Alaska. Smart, beautiful, and uninhibited, the Kashevaroffs were part of the social glue that held together a group of Pacific Grove friends at a time when they were all poor and reminded every day of their predicament—but were young enough not to care much. Steinbeck, who rose each dawn dreaming of greatness, was the exception. Obsessed with the future—his own anyway—Steinbeck seemed often oblivious to the difficulties of lean times. Steinbeck didn't like the present, which was fleeting and always reminded him that time was an enemy.

Steinbeck, Carol, and the Lovejoys had come to Los Angeles planning to start a business they were convinced would make them a fortune—an ambition they must have known was ridiculous, given the sinking economy. It all started with Ritchie, who'd gotten interested in a semi-solid plastic compound synthesized in Switzerland that softened at low heat and could be used to make castings of almost any object—including a human face. They fixed on the idea that this was the formula for untold riches. Being close to Hollywood, they imagined making facial casts of movie stars and other celebrities. Soon Tal's sister Nadja showed up to help. The Russians, Sheffield said, were loud and loved to drink and sing. They had no accents, but were definitely not like most American women. Within

Clockwise from upper left: Ritchie Lovejoy, Steinbeck, and Carol.
(Martha Heasley Cox Center for Steinbeck Studies, San Jose State University)

a few days of their arrival, the beer Sheffield brewed in a small dug-out cellar had been seriously depleted. There was no sign that anyone was lining up to have a facial cast made, and no indication that any of the partners had the remotest idea how to solicit clients. But the celebration rolled on.

When it became clear that the face-casting business was doomed, Ritchie Lovejoy and the Russians—the three of them had briefly moved to a house nearby—went home to Pacific Grove. And then, on January 14, 1930, Steinbeck and Carol were married. The ceremony was performed by the justice of the peace for Los Angeles County, and took place in Glendale. Dook Sheffield was their witness. On the marriage certificate, next to Occupation, Steinbeck had responded "Retired." Afterward the wedding party went out for hamburgers. Celebrating back at the Sheffields', Steinbeck and Carol had to be physically separated after they began arguing.

When he updated Kate Beswick about a week later, Steinbeck said matter-of-factly that he and Carol had been married and were busy painting and making improvements to a "house" they were renting just up the hill from the Sheffields. It was more of a barn, Sheffield said, one that looked as though it had been hit by a cyclone. Obtaining the house had been Carol's condition for going through with the wedding. She saw potential in it, though there were gaps in the siding and roof, and most of the windows were broken. Its main attraction was the rent—$15 a month. After working on it for weeks—Steinbeck managed to install gas and water—the house was remarkably comfortable. It had a thirty-foot-long living room and a big stone fireplace. Carol had scrounged a picture window that Steinbeck installed in the front, giving them light and a view. They painted the place red inside and out, and it looked grand. Steinbeck told Beswick he was ready to go back to work on *The Green Lady* and would soon send her the final installment. Carol was going to try to find work with an advertising agency. It was good there. The warm sun in LA, which was so different from the damp and fog up north, made Steinbeck happy.

The Sheffields liked sunbathing, and they kept a couple of mattresses on a flat area behind their house that was shielded from the neighbors so they could lie out in the nude, bronzing from head to toe. Often they had company—the Steinbecks and other friends— and a raucous, beer-guzzling crowd of naked bodies sprawled on the hillside. Whoever drank the last of the beer had to cover up and go to the house for more.

One day, when it was just the Sheffields and the Steinbecks, Carol and Maryon were bored and decided to bleach their pubic hair blonde. They tried peroxide. Then they tried ammonia. Nothing much happened. They turned to the tangled mat of dark brown hair on the crown of Steinbeck's head. He shrugged. Carol and Maryon began working on Steinbeck in an alternating series of applications: first peroxide then ammonia, then more peroxide, and so on. When they stood back, Steinbeck's hair had turned fluorescent pink. His head looked like it was on fire. Carol insisted they dye it back to normal. But Steinbeck waved them off. He kept it that way for a couple of weeks, and took a trip to Santa Monica to see his sister Mary and her husband, Bill Dekker. The Sheffields and Steinbecks drove there in the Steinbecks' latest jalopy, a topless Chevy that rattled loudly, Steinbeck's flaming hair streaming in the breeze as people gaped. At the beach, Mary refused to sit next to her brother.

When at last Steinbeck agreed to let Carol return his hair to its usual color, it instead came out jet black. Dook Sheffield thought it looked worse than the pink.

When Steinbeck finished *The Green Lady* he gave it a new title: *To the Unknown God*, a phrase he'd found in a Vedic hymn. The title pleased him and seemed a perfect fit. Sometime in early April 1930 he sent it to Ted Miller for submission to McBride. Privately, Steinbeck was still disappointed with McBride; he and Kate Beswick discussed how he might get out of his contract. Beswick suggested submitting something that he didn't care about. But McBride had an option on Steinbeck's next two books, so getting one rejected would not be the end of things. Steinbeck was sure McBride would turn this one down anyway, as it was unlike "the type of stuff they usually print." He thought the story was interesting, but its structure was unconventional, in that there wasn't any.

Time seemed to stand still while Steinbeck waited for news about the book. He was twenty-eight, married, and unmoored. The owners of the ancient house he and Carol had fixed up were so pleased with the renovations that they evicted the Steinbecks so their son and his fiancée could have the place. Steinbeck and Carol moved first to one small, dark house and then another, both of which were farther away from the Sheffields. Money was tight and getting tighter. Steinbeck and Carol split everything fifty-fifty, he said. Steinbeck's father was sending him $25 a month, an allowance no longer pretending to be a loan. Carol had been living off her savings since leaving her job in San Francisco, and that money was almost gone. She'd have to return to work soon.

That spring it seemed to rain constantly. Southern California was gray and cold. When a month passed with no word from Ted Miller or McBride, Steinbeck was miserable. "I'd be happier if I had a rejection than I am waiting for it this way," he said.

McBride finally did reject *To the Unknown God*, and by late summer a second and then a third publisher followed suit. Steinbeck acknowledged there was an "ever increasing throng of people who think it is not a good book," but he kept working. He finished a short manuscript about which he said little, other than that, at 25,000 words, it was too long for a story and too short to be a book. He had a title he liked—*Dissonant Symphony*—but he was otherwise tired of it. He told Kate Beswick he was going to enter it in a contest sponsored by Scribner's, though he was sure the prize offered would attract strong competition. After that he would forward the manuscript to her, and suggested she put it away on the remote chance he'd someday come back to it and turn it into a real novel.

He never did, but maybe he should have. It sounded like an interesting idea. According to Dook Sheffield, the book was about a man based loosely on Steinbeck's father. The story began with the main character's death, followed by accounts of his life given by half a dozen people who knew him. Sheffield believed this format accounted for some of the difficulty Steinbeck had with the story. It also seemed likely that in making his father's life more interesting than it was, Steinbeck must have felt he was in some way betraying him.

The Sheffields liked to have people over, and at one party a shy, eighteen-year-old UCLA freshman named Richard Albee turned up with his older brother, George, who was a writer. Everyone was dancing and drinking, except for a hulking onlooker with flashing blue eyes off by himself in a corner. Richard kept his distance. When George collected him to leave, he mentioned that the "big fellow" was a writer named Steinbeck. Richard was surprised. He thought the man looked like a farmer. When there was another party a few weeks later, Richard Albee worked up the nerve to talk to Steinbeck, and not long after that he was introduced to Carol and the Lovejoys. Like everyone else, he found Carol impressive. She reminded him of a "pioneer woman," tall and raw-boned, not beautiful but handsome and "well built." Her hair was dark and straight, usually pulled back, and she liked to wear pants and work shirts just like Steinbeck. Albee visited Steinbeck and Carol a number of times at the Sheffields'. Richard Albee would later claim that he had invented John Steinbeck.

When the latest house they were renting was sold and they were asked to move out, Steinbeck and Carol decided they'd had enough.

Carol and John Steinbeck on their wedding day, January 14, 1930.
(Martha Heasley Cox Center for Steinbeck Studies, San Jose State University)

Carol had been unable to find work in Los Angeles—jobs were scarce and becoming more so—and the little house on Eleventh Street in Pacific Grove wouldn't cost them anything. Once it was decided, they were surprised that they'd stayed south for so long. Steinbeck said they'd be glad to go home, as they were "sick of the people" in L.A.—though it seemed he meant people like themselves, poor and getting poorer.

Within months of the stock market crash, the US economy itself was in free fall. In 1930, more than 1,300 banks failed. The following year, another 2,300 went under. In the spring of 1931, stocks embarked on another slide, this time one that lasted well over a year. By the summer of 1932, the value of U.S. stocks had fallen by 90 percent. The Dow Jones Industrial Average, which had risen steadily through the 1920s and was nearing 400 before the crash, spiraled downward. It stopped finally, a fraction above 41. Tens of thousands of businesses disappeared. Millions were unemployed, many becoming homeless. Camps of the dispossessed sprang up everywhere, known as "Hoovervilles," on account of the widespread belief that President Herbert Hoover had caused the troubles. One of the biggest was on the banks of the Anacostia River in Washington, D.C., within sight of the U.S. Capitol. It was occupied by the so-called Bonus Army, a group of World War I veterans who had come to collect money Congress had promised them for their service. In July of 1932, under orders from President Hoover, a contingent of regular army cavalry and infantry, under the command of General Douglas MacArthur and Major George Patton, pushed a group of protesting veterans out of the city and back across the river. After evicting everyone from the camp, the soldiers burned it to the ground.

In the heart of the country, as the economy disintegrated, years of drought and cruel spells of extreme heat turned farmland to ash. When the winds came, great, choking dust storms blotted out the sun and buried houses. In 1935, a woman in Kansas wrote to her daughter in California about a dust storm that had raged for days. She said

A dust storm overwhelms Rolla, Kansas, April 14, 1935.
(Franklin D. Roosevelt Presidential Library)

"monster" gusts of wind moved the dirt like "black smoke," leaving behind a landscape that resembled a desert. And there was no escape. In a single day, she said, they'd shoveled 35 pounds of dust out of the house. Two dozen people had died that month, and a similar number the month before. People who ventured out were blinded by the storm and got lost in it, sometimes wandering into the wrong houses. She said she'd seen a woman spitting into the mouth of a little girl who was choking on dust.

Thousands of dusted-out farmers were evicted and lost everything. Many from the Great Plains headed for California, which was not happy to see them. Though they came from many places, including Oklahoma, they were collectively derided as Okies. On they came, a steady stream of creaking and overloaded cars and trucks crawling west on Route 66.

— 6 —

SUCH GOOD
FRIENDS AS THESE

WHEN STEINBECK HEARD nothing from Scribner's about *Dissonant Symphony*, he feared the manuscript had gotten lost in the mail—which he said would be worse than having it rejected. Ted Miller had sent *To the Unknown God* to Little, Brown. Steinbeck convinced himself they had already "bounced" it and he just hadn't found out yet. He was feeling low. Carol's mother had come for a visit and scolded him for not writing for *The Saturday Evening Post* and "making some money." Steinbeck held his tongue but was irate. "Thank God we practically never see her," he told Kate Beswick.

After months of shifting from one temporary home to the next in Los Angeles, it was a relief to be back in the little cottage on Eleventh Street. Pacific Grove was cool and foggy and felt lush compared to southern California, which was a near-desert except when it rained, which was equally unpleasant. They had a new dog, an Airedale named Tillie, and this restored a kind of domesticity that had died with their most recent dog, Bruga. Steinbeck could not be without a dog. He and Carol went to work making things homey, planting flowers and vegetables on every available square inch of the little yard—late-summer planting being one of California's advantages. Steinbeck added a stone barbecue pit and a lily pond with fish in it. His most ambitious project was the addition of a fireplace inside the house. It was set against a wall and featured a cone-shaped copper chimney that Steinbeck fashioned himself. Whenever they built a fire on a murky night, the copper hood filled the room with warmth.

Steinbeck was happy to be near old friends again. He even went into Palo Alto to see John Breck. He found her "still on the verge of a fortune." Some people had all the luck. Toby Street visited Pacific Grove, and they enjoyed a fine weekend. New friends came more slowly—Steinbeck complained of not knowing anybody—but they got acquainted with Jack Calvin and his wife, Sasha, who was another of Tal Lovejoy's sisters. Calvin wrote children's books and was also an illustrator—very much like his brother-in-law, Ritchie Lovejoy, right down to the Russian wife. He and Steinbeck had had a passing acquaintance at Stanford. They weren't close, but the Calvins moved in a circle of writers and artists whose bohemian lifestyle appealed to the Steinbecks, and so they seemed to be the doorway to a new social life. The Calvins lived in Carmel, and Steinbeck and Carol made the trip over to see them when they could. In those days you had to take the long way there from Pacific Grove, going into Monterey and looping up over the hill and back down into Carmel. Gas was expensive, so the Steinbecks had to ration their visits.

There was a short-lived promise of solvency when Carol met a young woman who wrote for the *Monterey Peninsula Herald*. Her name was Beth Ingels. They got on well and decided to open an advertising agency together. There didn't seem to be much competition on the peninsula. They put together a directory of Carmel and sold ad space in its pages. It turned out fine, but they made almost nothing on it and the partnership dissolved after a few months.

By then Steinbeck had resumed work on a story he'd made numerous false starts on. As usual, he was vague with other people about what this project was, though he told Carl Wilhelmson it concerned three generations of men. The book would plumb "the black and sluggish depths of people" in order to show not just what they did but also the psychological motivations behind what they did. This was something new. As he put fantasy and adventure behind him, Steinbeck was beginning to see that sometimes the best stories are in plain sight. He said you could write a novel about a man going to town to buy a blue necktie. While this was undoubtedly true, Steinbeck must have wondered why it was so hard for him to do.

He confided to Wilhelmson that things had not gone well toward the end of his stay in Los Angeles. Apparently it wasn't only homesickness and poverty that had brought him and Carol back to Pacific Grove. He and Dook had grown apart, and he felt his old friend was sinking into a life of ordinariness and petty concerns. Steinbeck thought Maryon was the source of Dook's "inertia." When he wasn't teaching, all Sheffield did was read magazines—which he claimed to not like. Sheffield was wasting away intellectually. Nowadays, he seemed more interested in how crisp his bacon was than in the big ideas that had once been at the center of their conversations. Sheffield's sudden blandness was unbearable. "I don't know if he is shrinking or I am growing," Steinbeck said. Surprisingly, given his own liberal affection for alcohol, Steinbeck also complained about Sheffield's drinking, which he said turned too quickly into intoxication. "There," he said, "that's out."

The move to Pacific Grove made life better, but it had not erased the gnawing doubts Steinbeck harbored about his writing. When he wrote Wilhelmson again a few weeks later Steinbeck was sullen. He and Wilhelmson tended to bring on bleak moods in each other, even by letter. Steinbeck said there was a fog and a wet wind over the peninsula that seemed almost to be coming from inside his head. The night before he'd read through forty pages of the novel he was working on and had promptly torn them up. It probably didn't help that Wilhelmson's novel, *Midsummernight*, had been published by Farrar & Rinehart. Few things are more toxic than one writer's jealousy of another—and if it's a friend, so much the worse.

Steinbeck's anger radiated in all directions, curdling into harsh judgments. He told Wilhelmson he'd been at a party at the Calvins' house in Carmel and was disgusted with Jack Calvin's admission that he only wrote for the money. When Calvin told him that he had long since stopped taking his own writing seriously, Steinbeck snorted that he took everything *he* wrote with the utmost seriousness. He probably sounded out of sorts telling Wilhelmson about this, but he insisted that he really wasn't. He was working, and working always made him feel good.

And things were in fact better. In coming home, the Steinbecks had closed a chapter of their life together that now felt like a desperate prologue. Living in Pacific Grove was easier and cheaper, and for the first time they had a home where they felt moderately secure. They still lived by their wits, of course. They fished and caught crabs and eels, and sometimes went out onto the bay with Italian sardiners. On many days a pot of beans simmered on the stove—the all-purpose, one-ingredient feast of the Depression. Once in a while there was nothing to eat. But life was good again, Steinbeck told Kate Beswick. "We are very happy."

Then McBride informed Steinbeck that they were remaindering *Cup of Gold*, which had been in print for all of a year. Sales had tapered off to nothing. Steinbeck regretted not having had a better publisher. Worse news was the lengthening string of rejections for *To the Unknown God*. Steinbeck said it was being met with such hostility that publishers were competing to see who could turn it down the fastest. He told Kate Beswick that all he needed was another ten or fifteen rejections to be convinced finally that he couldn't write and shouldn't try. "Honestly," he said, "do you think I'm any good at all?" And then, catching himself, Steinbeck switched his tone. Kate Beswick must have pictured him smiling suddenly as he contemplated the future. By age forty, if he still wasn't a writer, he said, "I think I'll take myself for a ride," implying this would not be the kind of ride from which one returned. He wasn't being melodramatic, just "sensible." In the meantime, he would get back to work. Steinbeck ended the letter abruptly, pleading mental exhaustion. He'd been thinking of taking a long hike in the mountains, though he worried the November nights were too cold. But perhaps he should chance it.

Although Steinbeck complained unceasingly about the failure of *To the Unknown God*, which Ted Miller continued to press on one publisher after another, he said little about what he was currently writing.

He just kept grinding away, his doggedness perpetually reinforcing itself. Steinbeck's daily routine varied, but it usually included two stints of writing, one early in the day and another later on. He could not bear interruptions, and his friends learned to stay away when he was working. In December 1930, he surprised Miller with a 60,000-word manuscript that was a kind of surrender. He explained to Miller that he was miserable over a debt he could not repay—presumably the money his father had loaned him, though he wouldn't admit it—and had decided to try something he was sure would make money. Only a few days before he had told Miller that he and Carol could not afford to give anyone presents at Christmas, and joked that their family members might have to make do with having pots of beans dedicated to them. Now he reminded Miller that Joseph Conrad had famously said that only the very best and the very worst writing sold. With evidence accruing that he wasn't capable of the very best, Steinbeck was ready to try for the very worst—and here it was. It was a cheesy detective story called *Murder at Full Moon*.

Steinbeck probably forced himself not to think about the recent talks he'd had with Jack Calvin about dumbing down his writing to make it more commercial. Maybe he felt he was instead taking advice from Conrad. He claimed he'd written *Murder at Full Moon* in just nine days—less than the two weeks it took Carol to type it—and that the one thing he cared about was keeping his name off it. Only Carol, his parents, and now Miller knew he was the author, and he intended to keep it that way. Steinbeck had chosen the pen name Peter Pym, which sounded ridiculous. But he insisted he picked the name because it was simple. He told Miller that any publisher who would take it was free to edit the book in any way they wanted. They could even change the pen name, just as long as no one ever found out he was connected with it.

Steinbeck needn't have worried about being found out. Nobody wanted this book either.

In early January 1931, Steinbeck informed Miller he was determined to rewrite *To the Unknown God*. How many times was he going to say this before he either did it or dropped the whole cursed project? The novel as it stood had a gap of some thirty-five years in the action, and Steinbeck was convinced this needed to be filled in. It had become the book that wouldn't die. Steinbeck had been working on it for nearly three years now. Arguably, it was past time to quit. But Steinbeck could not give up on it; that, he said, would be a tremendous waste. He pleaded with Miller to let him know honestly if he thought the book had a chance. And then he got to his real point: He suggested that it might be a relief to them both if he got an agent.

Steinbeck knew which agent he wanted—Mavis McIntosh, who represented Carl Wilhelmson. She was a partner, along with Elizabeth Otis, at the McIntosh & Otis Literary Agency. The firm was young, and so were they. Both had worked previously at another agency where they were unhappy, and in March of 1928, when Otis was twenty-seven and McIntosh only twenty-five, they struck out on their own—the first women to own a literary agency in New York. They were joined at the outset by a more experienced agent who handled film and dramatic rights, a flamboyant, chain-smoking, thirty-two-year-old Texan named Annie Laurie Williams, who disarmed everyone with her buoyant energy and southwestern twang.

Miller, no doubt pleased at the prospect of being relieved as Steinbeck's representative, sent the manuscripts he had over to McIntosh. Steinbeck waited anxiously. Carl Wilhelmson had finished another novel that was also in McIntosh's hands now, and Steinbeck knew it was good. Maybe his friend's luck would rub off on him—in the same way his moments of despair always did.

Just a couple of months after Steinbeck and Carol returned to Pacific Grove, Steinbeck went to a dentist in Monterey with a toothache. He was in the waiting room, slumped over in pain and wondering if he could afford to be there. An inner door opened, and a short man with a beard emerged, gingerly moving his mouth from side to side. Steinbeck said he didn't notice much about the man on account of the bloody molar he was carrying in his open palm. It appeared to have a hunk of jaw still attached. They stared at it together. "I'm Ed Ricketts," the man said.

That is how Steinbeck told it later on, after their famous friendship had found an exalted place in American literature. Ricketts's sister Frances backed up this version of the event, after hearing an account of their meeting from her brother. But other people who knew them doubted this story, and Carol said flatly that it couldn't have happened that way. She believed it was unlikely that either man would have willingly gone to a dentist; both were like children when faced with even the slightest physical discomfort—especially Steinbeck. This wasn't totally true either—Ricketts had terrible teeth and ultimately had them all pulled and got dentures. Carol's memory was that she and Steinbeck met Ricketts at a party at Jack Calvin's house in Carmel. There was a jug of wine, and when Carol first saw Ricketts he was dancing around a campfire in Calvin's yard. Ricketts was compact—under five feet six inches—and by all accounts was irresistible to women. Remembering Ricketts years later, after both he and Steinbeck were dead, Carol judged him coldly. "He had a neatly trimmed, red-brown-golden beard, which seemed to have deceived a lot of people into seeing him as a Christ-like figure," Carol recalled. "One look into his goatish eyes should have told them better. Ed was a womanizer. He loved women. All women."

This was fair enough, except for the part about people being fooled. Everybody knew that Ricketts was obsessed with women, and that his sexual appetite was insatiable and indiscriminate. But as Steinbeck discovered—and wrote in three books that would immortalize Ricketts—his tireless pursuit of sex was not the most interesting thing about Ed Ricketts.

Edward Flanders Ricketts was born in Chicago in 1897. At eighteen, he briefly attended Illinois State Normal University, but left when he was caught in an affair with a married woman. He worked as an accountant and a surveyor before being drafted into the army. After the war he enrolled at the University of Chicago, where he concentrated on biology, though his academic career was much like

Steinbeck's—intermittent and conducted with little regard for the formal requirements of the program. And Ricketts had his Miss Mirrielees—the zoologist Warder Clyde Allee.

W. C. Allee's groundbreaking work on the behavior of aquatic animals, and their interactions with one another and with their environments—much of it conducted at the Marine Biological Laboratory in Woods Hole, Massachusetts—was revolutionizing biology. Ricketts left the University of Chicago in 1922, a year before Allee began writing a series of essays that would ultimately be published as *Animal Aggregations*, a seminal book on the nature of coexistence among organisms. It was a major leap forward in a field that many people had not even heard of: ecology.

For Ricketts, who as a student was already searching for ways to see beneath the surface of things, the unity of life seemed an inescapable starting point. He roomed for a time with a classmate named Albert Galigher, who was also intrigued with Allee's work. The two of them started a biological supply business. Then Ricketts married Anna "Nan" Maker, and in August of 1923 they had a son, Ed Jr. Galigher had left school and moved to Pacific Grove. Ricketts, inspired by Allee but impatient to investigate marine life for himself, followed Galigher to California. He and Nan and the baby settled in Carmel—just around the corner from Pacific Grove, where the powerful waves surged over a sprawling, rocky tide pool in which every nook and cranny was home to a glittering universe of invertebrates that revealed itself day in and day out as the ocean advanced and retreated. And just a couple of miles closer to town, near the boundary between Pacific Grove and Monterey, was Stanford's Hopkins Marine Station, which had a magnificent library and a faculty who were exploring the budding field of marine ecology and who emphasized direct observation in the field.

Ricketts and Galigher restarted their business as Pacific Biological Laboratories, collecting invertebrate sea life in the nearby tide pools at all hours, depending on the tides and the turbulence of the ocean. They also enlisted a crew of amateurs who caught terrestrial specimens such as cats and frogs and rattlesnakes. The company shipped dissecting specimens and prepared slides to biology classes around the country. Researchers over at the Hopkins station were initially cool toward Ricketts, worried that his collecting might diminish local marine populations. But Ricketts was careful, and in his catalogue he advised customers that the effects of overcollecting were well documented and it should be avoided. He gradually impressed the Hopkins staff with his diligence and encyclopedic knowledge.

Ricketts was a compulsive organizer, and he kept track of his work on index cards. He put the names and addresses of customers in a card file that came to include seemingly every biology instructor in the United States—who were then added to the mailing list for the Pacific Biological catalogue. There were thousands of entries. In another card file Ricketts kept track of colleagues around the world with whom he regularly consulted in identifying new specimens he collected. The specimens themselves were recorded in a vast card file of their own. There were rumors that Ricketts's sexual exploits were also memorialized on index cards—or got randomly included on the backs of specimen cards—but no evidence for this has survived. The company was headquartered in a warehouse in the heart of downtown Pacific Grove, on Fountain Avenue, across the street from Holman's Department Store, a monument to consumption in those hard economic times. Three stories high, Holman's covered an entire block and sold everything from dry goods and groceries to hardware and appliances.

Ricketts and Galigher parted ways in 1924, and Ricketts took over the business. His sister and mother helped, and so did his father, who came west in 1927. In 1928, Ricketts moved Pacific Biological to a less cosmopolitan location to be on the water. The "lab" as everyone called it, was in Monterey, on Ocean View Avenue—more commonly known as Cannery Row on account of the cavernous sardine-processing plants that lined the waterfront.

Monterey Bay was one of the world's most active fisheries, owing in part to its unique subsurface contours. Only a short distance from shore, the Continental Shelf splits, and the bottom plunges to a depth of nearly 12,000 feet in a sheer abyss called the Monterey Bay

Ed Ricketts.
*(Martha Heasley Cox Center
for Steinbeck Studies, San Jose
State University)*

Canyon. In the shallows near land, abalone were abundant, and far-ther out beneath the blue ocean swell was a seemingly inexhaustible wealth of marine life, including squid and, most important, sardines. These were not the bite-sized sardines you buy in a small tin and eat whole on a cracker. This was the California sardine, a relative bruiser of a fish, bullet-shaped and nine inches long. In the 1920s, as bigger, diesel-powered boats began hauling large "purse seines," the sardine harvest increased. The fish had to be cleaned and cooked and packed into cans. This happened in the processing plants at the water's edge in Monterey. The canneries were a jumble of sizes and styles, built variously of tin, stucco, and wood. They were connected to warehouses on the other side of Ocean View Avenue by elevated bridge conveyers called "cross-overs." At one time there were sixteen cross-overs in operation, so that driving down Cannery Row was like driving through an old-time hand-cranked movie scene as sunlight and shadow flickered overhead.

It turned out that the sardines were not limitless. In the early 1920s, there were warnings about overfishing the bay. But with the onset of the Depression, these worries were set aside to keep people working. It was a labor-intensive enterprise. The purse seines were made of cotton thread that required constant maintenance. And some fishermen still pulled nets by hand. Inside the canneries, as demand for fish meal and fertilizer rose, more sardines were processed every year. In the 1934–35 season more than 230,000 tons of sardines were landed at Cannery Row. Nobody wanted it to ever stop. But it did. The reckoning came in the late 1940s, when the sardine industry all but collapsed.

But for years before then, it was all good. Ricketts's lab was in a little house dwarfed by the Del Vista Packing Company next door. The lab was a single-story stucco building on a fifty-foot-wide lot. Ricketts had it jacked up and installed a garage and a shipping and storage area underneath. A flight of stairs climbed diagonally across the front of the building to the main entrance to the office and lab, which were now on the upper floor. There was also a space that at different times served as party room, music conservatory, and living quarters. Out back, on the waterfront, were four concrete tanks for processing sharks and other large species. It was a colorful neighborhood. The Wing Chong Market was just up the street for groceries, and directly across from the lab was Flora Woods's Lone Star Café, the venerable brothel frequented by many of the area's leading men. Visitors to the lab loved its narrow view of the ocean and the sounds of the waves breaking against the pilings and sea lions barking and the distant tolling of bell buoys through the fog late at night as Ricketts and his friends talked and drank beer into the wee hours. Somehow, Ricketts never seemed to notice the acrid yellow smoke curling from the stacks of the canneries, or the rank fish smell that attached itself to everything.

A bookish man who also loved music, Ricketts owned piles of records and a library that occupied walls everywhere in the lab. He left space for a handwritten chart that purported to describe all of human history according to Ricketts's own theory of human progress, which he believed occurred in fits and starts separated by fallow periods when little happened. The graph wended its way through several rooms. You had to stand close to read it; Ricketts's handwriting, though legible enough, was tiny—something he had in common with Steinbeck.

Along with the Calvin and Steinbeck houses, the lab became a gathering place for a group that grew over time. Besides Ricketts and the Calvins, Lovejoys, and Steinbecks, it eventually came to include Carol's former partner, Beth Ingels; the painters Bruce Ariss and Elwood Graham and their wives, Jean and Barbara; and Toby Street, who was now practicing law in Monterey. Richard Albee, the formerly shy student from UCLA, came up from time to time, his head exploding with ideas he was eager to share. And there were Frank and Marjory Lloyd. Frank was a newspaperman from Montreal. The Lloyds had saved enough money for a six-month sabbatical in Carmel and ended up staying a year. Also present was yet another of the spirited Kashevaroff sisters, Xenia, a painter and sculptor who also posed for the photographer Edward Weston. Xenia had lost her virginity as a seventeen-year-old Monterey High School student—to Ed Ricketts, who was thirty-four at the time. She eventually married the composer John Cage.

It was a moveable feast, drifting from house to house, always coming back to the lab, a members-only club of the talented and the impoverished. One rule was that you never showed up without bringing something to share. In the long years since, the lab—which still stands on Cannery Row—has become a shrine to Ricketts. His acolytes, self-described "Edheads," remember Ricketts as a sage and the author of an idiosyncratic metaphysics that to an extent seeped into Steinbeck and figured prominently in the book they coauthored, *Sea of Cortez*. To be sure, Ricketts and Steinbeck grew close and spent hours in deep conversation at the lab. When they let go of serious matters the party erupted again and the music and booze flowed.

Marjory Lloyd, who was only twenty-two when she and her husband, Frank, arrived in Carmel, remembered their introduction to the group: It was at a gathering at the Steinbeck cottage on Eleventh Street. The Lloyds didn't have a babysitter, so they brought their young daughter with them, and she promptly went to sleep in the bedroom. Marjory looked around. The house was spotless and in perfect order. Her first impression of Steinbeck was how tall he was—though she later decided that he seemed larger than he was. With his thick features and powerful shoulders and bad hair, he was not good-looking, though he had the most remarkable blue eyes that made you forget about everything else. Marjory felt magnetized, drawn to Steinbeck. He smoked constantly. And he was quiet in a way that was almost hypnotic. He listened more than he talked. He was "very masculine," but gracious and attentive. He made you feel he cared about what you were saying. Marjory thought nothing could be sexier.

Carol, on the other hand, was "very, very beautiful." Marjory thought Carol was not only one of the prettiest women she'd ever seen, but was charming, witty, and used salty language that was shocking and also a little thrilling. It was clear to Marjory that Carol was the more outgoing of the Steinbecks—and that nobody hung on her every utterance as intently as Steinbeck did. Marjory could see how taken he was with her. He seemed to like showing her off. Carol gave off hints of unsuspected talents. She had painted a funny, well-executed series of fat lady athletes in the nude that hung in the bathroom.

With everyone drinking wine, smoking, and laughing, it was overwhelming. Shy, and unaccustomed to alcohol, Marjory sat down to collect herself. Suddenly, Steinbeck was at her side on the floor, rolling a cigarette. He talked to her in a low voice for a long time. He confided that he was having trouble with his writing, a confession that must have dazzled her. Or maybe it was the wine making her light-headed. When it was time to go, the Lloyds had just gotten out the door when Frank fell into the geraniums. He was in no condition to drive, so Steinbeck took the Lloyds home to Carmel. Marjory had to ask him to stop several times so she could be sick. When they arrived, Steinbeck carried their little girl inside and tucked her into bed. "My first impression of John," Marjory said, "was what a wonderful guy he was."

After that, the Lloyds were in. Marjory said that because nobody had any money—Toby Street did, but was careful not to make a point of it—getting together for food and conversation was the only entertainment they had. Saturday nights were always at the lab, and anyone in the group who found themselves near Monterey made a point of showing up. The celebrating never ended early. They made their own beer, bought wine from a Monterey bootlegger, and hamburgers—ground beef cost 15 cents a pound—were a staple. Sometimes the Steinbecks would talk everyone into playing strip poker. Marjory said later she regretted always having good cards, as getting naked would have been more fun than winning. "I never got past my slip," she admitted.

Marjory found Ed Ricketts quiet and gentle—a compact Steinbeck, only handsome. Carol considered Ricketts introspective to a fault. He liked to have a good time, but he always held something back. It was odd. When Ricketts was amused, he giggled like a schoolgirl. "In all the years I knew Ed," Carol said, "I never saw him throw back his head and really laugh." Ricketts had peculiar superstitions—he hated white flowers, for example—and he was unusually vain. He had fine, lustrous hair that he rarely washed. Rumor had it that he wore a yellow rain hat in the shower.

Carol agreed that the legend that grew up about the lab—that the scene there was a sustained orgy of drunkenness, dancing, and spontaneous sex—had some truth to it. But the stories ignored how disciplined and conscientious Ricketts was. Like Steinbeck, he would not permit anyone to interfere with his work.

After Ricketts and Nan separated, Ricketts moved into the lab. He never wanted for female companionship. One of his most enduring affairs—it went on for at least the better part of a decade—was with

Jean Ariss. It would have been a scandal except for the fact that everyone knew about it, including Jean's husband, Bruce, who was more an accomplice than a cuckold. For a time during Jean's on-and-off relationship with Ricketts, Bruce would walk her to the lab and then leave. When Ed Jr. came to live with his father, Bruce arranged to give him boxing lessons during these visits so that Ricketts and Jean could be alone. At one point, Jean got Bruce to agree to a regular schedule. She could be with Ricketts from 2 to 6 on Mondays and 10 to 6 on Thursdays. While this wasn't as much time as she wanted, at least it would give Ricketts freedom to work. She added that, naturally, she'd sneak down between scheduled appointments whenever she could.

Part of what made Jean's attraction to Ricketts so powerful was that they could never agree where things stood between them. She was left in a near-constant state of anxious longing. Bruce, she said, was good to her, and was wise and kind and tender. Faced with that, being in love with Ricketts was even harder to deny. Even when Ricketts saw other women, she could not bring herself to say it was over. In one anguished letter, she told him she understood why he had recently cheated on her: He'd been under a lot of stress lately, and she knew him well enough to know he had to have an outlet. In case that didn't make Ricketts feel guilty enough, she went on, veering between ambivalence and obsession:

> I've been going through a hard time too. The thought of you with another woman is hard to face. . . . Then clearly, yesterday, I saw that it would be all right. The hot pain of jealousy will be there, but no bitterness or feelings of being repudiated. What we have is not so lightly held that anyone else can affect our deep relationship. I feel sure about it now—so do what seems best with no strings from me to keep you from some—oh damn—don't let her take my place—not yet. . . . Bless you—I love you.

At one party Steinbeck got into an intense conversation with Carol's erstwhile business partner, Beth Ingels. Steinbeck had not liked her much. Ingels had a sharp tongue and could be sarcastic. And she was more Carol's friend anyway. But on this night, as Ingels talked and talked, the way everyone did, Steinbeck became engrossed, almost as if he were memorizing everything she was saying. Ingels had grown up in Corral de Tierra, the pretty valley just off the road halfway between Salinas and Monterey where the Steinbeck family had picnicked on their way to Pacific Grove years ago. There, Ingels said, every family knew every other family, and their lives were entwined, so that whenever something remarkable or tragic or curious befell one member of the community, it was as if it had happened to everybody. The valley was a world unto itself, a set piece—like a stage with a troupe of players who come to life on it. Ingels hoped to write about her experiences growing up in such a place.

For as long as people could remember, Ingels said, everyone in the valley was happy. Disagreements were few and of no consequence. Often the community had parties where everybody got along famously. Life could not have been better. But then, around 1921, a new family came to the valley and—here's the part where Steinbeck leaned in close—they seemed in every way a perfect fit. There was nothing outwardly hostile about them, no hint of malice or misfortune. And yet wherever they went, whatever they touched, whichever civic institution they joined, bad things happened. In their wake, everything fell apart. Hatred and mistrust spread through the community, and an ill wind blew through the valley. A schoolteacher committed suicide; two people were murdered. Families started packing up and leaving. It was the end of everything good that had been taken for granted for so long.

Steinbeck fell on this idea almost at once, setting aside a novel he had been working on. By the spring of 1931, it had become clear to him that the best way to tell it was through a story cycle—similar to Sherwood Anderson's *Winesburg, Ohio*—in which each story is a chapter that stands on its own and at the same time advances the overarching narrative. Characters and places would reappear throughout, linking these independent stories to the pervasive evil that had come to the valley. Each chapter would deal with one family that lived in the valley, which Steinbeck called *Las Pasturas del Cielo*—The Pastures of Heaven—a name he thought was ripe with irony and also a perfect title for the book. What was incredible was that it was all true. Here, it seemed, was a book that could write itself. He asked Ted Miller if he liked the plan. But before he even mailed this letter to Miller, Steinbeck received encouraging news. Mavis McIntosh wrote telling him she liked the things Miller had sent to her—which apparently included the mysterious *Dissonant Symphony*—and looked forward to seeing more. Steinbeck thought that McIntosh had laid it on a little thick and some of her enthusiasm might be "hooey," but it was nice to hear anyway.

Steinbeck wrote a long answer to McIntosh. He told her he didn't have a copy of *Murder at Full Moon* to send her, but would have one typed if she needed an extra to send around. The quicker he could forget about it, the better. McIntosh thought *To the Unknown God* was interesting, but dragged. Steinbeck was surprised to hear this; he thought he knew all of the book's faults, which were many but didn't include tedious pacing. It should have been a play, he said, and had been in the beginning. Giving McIntosh a taste of his endless fixation on the story, he warned her that he wanted to write it again. He also had a few short stories on hand that he could send her, though he doubted any of them would sell. And then he told her about *The Pastures of Heaven*. He'd already finished several chapters and expected he'd have it done by the fall.

While Steinbeck worked on *The Pastures of Heaven* through the summer of 1931, Mavis McIntosh sent the already well-traveled *To the Unknown God* out to a new round of publishers. No takers. Fuming, Steinbeck told her he was going to rewrite it at once. Inexplicably, he started calling it *To AN Unknown God*. He thanked McIntosh again for her interest—and warned her that he was unlikely to make either of them any money.

In August, Dook and Maryon Sheffield visited the Steinbecks, and the four of them went camping for a week in the redwoods near La Honda, southwest of Palo Alto. Sheffield—who later misremembered this trip as having taken place two years earlier—was sure that Steinbeck worked on *The Pastures of Heaven* every day, leaving their campsite to write for a couple of hours in the forest, using a large stump for a desk. Steinbeck didn't recall it that way at all, and complained of getting no work done. He'd gotten into something he was allergic to and spent the week itchy and ill-tempered. When he returned home to find no word from McIntosh & Otis, he assumed they were getting ready to drop him as a client.

Being broke shielded the Steinbecks from the worst of the Depression—they'd never really had anything, so having nothing felt normal. But Steinbeck saw changes taking place around him. He told Carl Wilhelmson he almost wished he could afford to subscribe to a newspaper to keep up with the increasingly dire and surprising events. He noticed that activists had started making Communist speeches to enthusiastic audiences in Pacific Grove, including at several churches. The next thing you know, he said, "Methodists will be dying on barricades in our cities." Steinbeck wanted to know about all of this. The deepening crisis was too interesting to ignore. "The world seems to be crumbling," he observed. "It's about time."

Steinbeck worked steadily on *The Pastures of Heaven*. He'd finished seven stories that fall. He wrote to Wilhelmson that he wished he could be back at Lake Tahoe. He liked the sense of security he always felt there. The only thing that kept him from asking for his old job back was that he was sure Mrs. Brigham would not consider a married couple. What he really missed was Wilhelmson's advice on his work. The stories he was writing were "simple," and he was worried that maybe they were *too* simple. Steinbeck was trying to reinvent his writing. Before, his problem had been the opposite—ornate language and intricate plots. He seemed to be on the right track now, but he just wasn't sure of it yet. He wanted to wait until he was done with the book before he showed Wilhelmson anything.

When he finished *The Pastures of Heaven* in December of 1931, Steinbeck sent it to McIntosh & Otis and then, for the first time in a long time, he took a break while waiting to hear back from them. When word came in February, the news was disappointing. Mavis McIntosh didn't like it—though she added that someone else might, and so it was going out to publishers. In publishing, there are always surprises. Steinbeck assumed the book would get turned down, just like the others. "I'm getting pretty sick of my constant failure," he confessed.

A few days later, Steinbeck was stunned when he received a telegram from Mavis McIntosh. A publisher had accepted *The Pastures of Heaven*. It was his birthday. He was thirty years old.

PART TWO

PHALANX

— 7 —

A UNIT OF
THE GREATER BEAST

AVIS McIntosh and Elizabeth Otis were more impressed with *The Pastures of Heaven* than they let on, not wanting to get Steinbeck's hopes up. They submitted it to only one publishing house, Cape and Smith, where an editor named Robert O. Ballou, a former literary editor for a Chicago newspaper, accepted it within three days. Ballou told Steinbeck how much he liked the book. Steinbeck thought this was inflated praise, but he figured Ballou had to believe he could sell the book or he wouldn't have taken it. There was a brief scramble before Steinbeck got his contract; Cape and Smith was reorganized into Jonathan Cape & Robert Ballou. But when the dust cleared Steinbeck was under contract for this book plus his next two. Mavis McIntosh told him he now had an account with the agency that he could draw against when he needed money. He didn't think he'd take advantage of it, but knowing he could was a wonderful feeling.

Steinbeck got a congratulatory letter from George Albee, the writer he'd met at Dook Sheffield's down in Los Angeles, and who had introduced him to his younger brother, Richard. They'd been writing each other ever since. Albee was impressed that Steinbeck had a book deal. This reminded Steinbeck that almost nobody thought of him as an author—as if *Cup of Gold* had never happened. Steinbeck affected a nonchalance that he surely did not feel. There was nothing magical about being published—it didn't change you unless it was to make you a bigger fool than you already were. He doubted he'd ever see any money from it and he'd be damned if he'd turn himself into a luncheon speaker.

All was well at the cottage on Eleventh Street—though elsewhere the economic malaise that had settled over the country was turning the world bleak. By 1932, US industrial output was half of what it had been before the crash. Farm production had fallen by two thirds, and unemployment was up more than 600 percent. President Hoover had initiated tax cuts in the immediate aftermath of the stock market collapse, but while these reductions were large in percentage terms— many taxpayers saw their rates cut by half or more—tax rates were already so low that the savings for most families amounted to only a few dollars. And on the prairies, where years of careless cultivation had denuded the landscape of its once-heavy mantle of grass, locals said the earth itself had been turned "wrong side up." Then the winter wind began to blow. In late January of 1932, just a month before Steinbeck got his good news—with winds reaching sixty miles an hour in Texas—a strange cloud formed near Amarillo. It was huge and didn't look like any rain cloud anyone had ever seen. Black as night and spewing grit, it moved off to the north—eventually it would reach Kansas—leaving a choking blanket of dust in its wake. In the coming years, there would be more like it.

As the country flew apart—literally—things continued to look up for the Steinbecks. Carol had found a job. Ed Ricketts was paying his sister Frances $100 a month to help at the lab. It was an enormous sum given the times. When Ricketts couldn't afford that anymore, Frances stepped aside, and Carol offered to work half-time for $50 a month. The job involved ordinary clerical duties, though Carol said that Ricketts had his hands in everything—shipping, billing, inventory. But he was patient, and cheerfully explained technical terms and helped her with correct spellings. It was an informal workplace. Kids showed up at the lab all the time. Ricketts loved this, and often took them on collecting expeditions at the tide pool at the tip of the peninsula. Ricketts's father was always there, too. He was a gnomish man who drank Alka-Seltzer constantly. Ricketts had inherited his stature and his bad stomach.

Carol's office was in the reception area by the door at the top of the stairs, and Ricketts's was adjacent. Her desk was beneath a shelf where Ricketts stored a one-gallon jug of cyanide. Whenever a train went by on the tracks just a block up from Cannery Row, Carol could feel the building tremble. She asked Ricketts whether she would make it out the door if the jug ever fell off the shelf and broke. "Nope," Ricketts said.

Ricketts kept three cages of live rattlesnakes along his front wall. Carol said they were small and docile and "hardly ever bit anybody." One day, one of Ricketts's collectors showed up with another rattler and she wondered how he'd managed to catch it, as he was a "half-time collector and a half-time wino." Ricketts fed the snakes white rats, an image Carol didn't like to think about. But one day she made herself watch as a rattler killed and ate one. To her surprise, it wasn't unpleasant and seemed like the most natural thing in the world. She told Steinbeck about this, and he went down to the lab to see for himself.

Carol was thrilled to be working again, and even in hard times she strove to appear fully the "San Francisco working girl" she had been before. She came to the lab in a crisp suit or dress, wearing stockings, heels, and a hat. Getting there was less glamorous—she walked along the railroad tracks. One of the main diversions at the lab was keeping tabs on the comings and goings across the street at Flora Woods's brothel. Carol was disappointed that when the girls went out, they were never "minked up," but instead wore cheap, ill-fitting dresses. They were forbidden to speak to a customer if they ran into him on the street, which must have happened often. Flora was a Cannery Row institution, and she did a brisk business. Carol said they knew that the more prominent clientele parked their cars discreetly behind Flora's, entering and exiting by the back way, and sometimes she and Ricketts would sneak over and check the cars to see who was there.

Steinbeck and Carol liked exploring when they had a little money for gas, often taking trips along the coast as new sections of Highway 1 opened the way into Big Sur. They measured these outings by how many stops for hamburgers and coffee would be needed. Steinbeck loved waypoints, partly for the hamburgers but also for a chance to listen to how other people talked and what they said. One stormy day he and Carol pulled into a café perched on a vertiginous cliff overlooking the raging Pacific. The wind and rain pummeled them as they hustled inside. A young couple owned the place, which was otherwise deserted. When the Steinbecks finished their burgers and started to leave, the couple begged them to linger and have some pie and more coffee. Steinbeck realized they were frightened—not just by the shrieking winds but by the Big Sur country itself. Steinbeck believed there was a kind of madness in the hard stone and blasted sand of Big Sur, a terror that seeped into anyone who spent too much time there. He wondered how the couple in the café would endure. When he and Carol went back a few months later the place was closed up and the people were gone.

One afternoon, Carol's sister, Idell, showed up at the Steinbeck cottage. She had a young man with her, someone she'd met on a cruise from Honolulu a few years earlier. He was from out east but was traveling again and had looked her up. Although they'd exchanged letters, it was clear now that they had nothing in common and Idell seemed to be looking for a way to get rid of him. He was interested in becoming a writer, so when Idell mentioned that her sister was married to a writer, he'd agreed to go see them—and here they were. Idell rushed in and greeted her brother-in-law and Carol. "I'd like you both to meet Joseph Campbell," she said.

Campbell remembered meeting Carol briefly when she'd met the ship from Hawaii. She hadn't made an impression on him at the time. It was different with Steinbeck. Campbell later recalled that as he approached Steinbeck to shake hands, "I thought I was seeing myself." Steinbeck felt the same way. In fact, they were much alike and at the same time completely different. Like Steinbeck, Campbell was six feet tall. Unlike Steinbeck, he was arrestingly handsome, with a flawless complexion, a blinding smile, and perfect hair. A former college track star, Campbell kept in shape, and at just shy of twenty-eight—two years younger than Steinbeck—was lithe and graceful. Steinbeck, who was used to being the most noticeable figure in the room, was for a change physically overmatched. And as he discovered, the gap was even larger intellectually. Campbell had attended Dartmouth and Columbia, and had traveled widely in Europe. He knew anthropology, languages, ethnology, and literature. At Columbia, where he earned his master's degree, Campbell had studied medieval literature and had written his thesis on the Arthurian legend—news that probably delighted and dismayed Steinbeck in the same moment. Campbell was a sun to everyone else's dim planet.

The Steinbecks insisted that Campbell and Idell stay for dinner. It was winter, so they ate in front of the fireplace, getting acquainted. Campbell found Steinbeck "solemn." As for Carol, Campbell wondered how he had failed to notice how bold and beautiful she was when they'd met before. Carol was completely delightful, he thought, straightforward and open. When she smiled, the room lit up. Speaking of her decades later, Campbell said the remarkable thing about the Steinbecks was how different they were. "Carol," he recalled, his voice choked with emotion, "was a lovely woman. *Lovely.* She was resilient and intelligent and sparkling and full of fun."

After dinner and some more talk, Carol and Idell went to bed. Steinbeck and Campbell stayed up drinking coffee. Steinbeck read aloud from the draft of *To an Unknown God.* He asked Campbell what he thought of it and Campbell answered that he felt it lacked "sensuousness" and needed a more visual quality. Steinbeck put it down, got out *The Pastures of Heaven,* and read a few chapters. Campbell was impressed—he said it was "immense," a judgment he never altered. Campbell could tell Steinbeck liked reading his work aloud. It wasn't until later that he discovered that Steinbeck did not enjoy feedback unless it was pleasant. The next morning Steinbeck was up early and revising *To an Unknown God* yet again.

Campbell decided to stay on indefinitely. He fell in easily with the Steinbecks' circle. He found a place in Carmel, and shortly after that a small house next door to Ed Ricketts, who'd moved to Pacific Grove. He liked being near his new friends. Everyone was broke. Campbell said his rent was 50 cents a week. It was wonderful. Naturally, it couldn't last.

Campbell felt he'd found something important that had been missing in his life, which had lately been about books and ideas and the company of tweedy, gray-haired scholars who doted on him. Here he had the bracing company of peers, a rambunctious group of people his own age who were devouring life—eating, drinking, laughing, arguing, making love. On Steinbeck's birthday, the day he heard *The Pastures of Heaven* had sold, they threw a big party to celebrate. Everyone was excited and happy for Steinbeck, as though something great had happened to all of them.

There was always something new to try. One evening when the Steinbecks and Ritchie and Tal Lovejoy were over at Campbell's house, Carol proposed a séance. Steinbeck, who believed in ghosts and was sure one lived in the family house in Salinas, agreed eagerly. They didn't have a Ouija board, so they tried "table tapping." The idea is that emanations from the spirit world tap on or move a table in response to questions. They turned the lights low, and sat down at a small table, putting their hands flat on it. Carol was the medium. They waited. Then—a tap. Carol asked if there was someone there. Another tap. Was there a message? Another tap. One by one, they went around the table asking if the message was for them. It wasn't for Steinbeck or Carol or Tal Lovejoy. They all looked at Ritchie, who appeared uneasy. "Is it for me?" he said. "Is it Grandpa?"

Tap.

The atmosphere grew tense. They urged Ritchie to ask the spirit questions, but he was too frightened. Then the table began to move, pushing itself into Ritchie, inching him backward toward the fireplace. A low cry went up around the table—oooohhhh. Just then, Ed Ricketts walked in and asked what was going on. When he saw the table move, he pushed against it. The table fell over and Ritchie Lovejoy rolled onto the floor and everybody started laughing. But later on, Steinbeck told Campbell he was sure they'd been in contact with the Other Side. He was disappointed the message hadn't been for him.

Though it should have been the other way around, Campbell envied Steinbeck. Campbell was adrift and unfocused. He wanted to teach in a university, but nobody was hiring. Looking for work had become America's top pastime—and not finding any the common lament. Campbell thought he'd stay on the peninsula for a while and think about what to do with his life. Steinbeck, he could see, was serious and had his life sorted out. "I was impressed by Steinbeck's discipline," he said. "No matter what was going on, John was at his desk first thing in the morning. It was a sacred time."

Campbell thought Steinbeck and Ricketts had a special bond, something that separated them from the others. "Steinbeck and Ricketts were very different people," Campbell said. "Ed was a scientist. He'd read Jung. I think Steinbeck got a good deal of his thinking from Ed. In fact, I'm very sure of it. I know he appreciated Ed enor-

Joseph Campbell. He was beautiful, athletic, erudite—and in love with Carol Steinbeck. *(Copyright 2020 by Joseph Campbell Foundation [jcf.org]. Used with permission.)*

mously. I think the presence of a scientist played against John's rather romantic philosophy. And gave him reinforcement. They were a good team, influencing and refreshing and supporting each other in their thinking. It was a philosophical relationship. They liked talking to each other. They were cronies."

Campbell had been in Pacific Grove for a few months when there was a fateful party. It was at Ricketts's house. They were making cocktails from lab alcohol, and it wasn't long before people were blind drunk. Carol careened outside, climbed onto a low tree branch, and started singing. Campbell followed her out and got into a tree next to hers. They looked at each other. Carol told him how beautiful he was. She took his foot in her hands. They were terribly drunk. Campbell said he didn't know why he hadn't been in love with her the moment he first saw her years ago. "That's what I want to know," Carol said. They were both moaning a little, partly from the booze and partly from thinking what might have been. It was too late to do anything about it. They'd missed their chance. Carol dropped her glass. Campbell got down, picked it up, and went over and kissed Carol on the ankle. A door swung open, and Steinbeck leaned out and told them to shut up. Campbell stammered that he was just "getting a lady out of a tree."

After a few minutes, Carol went inside. Steinbeck invited Campbell down to their house for a late-night snack. Carol stayed. Back at his house, Steinbeck produced a leftover veal roast. Campbell, swaying on his feet, told Steinbeck he was very, very drunk.

"I'm not," Steinbeck answered.

Steinbeck explained that he was too agitated to be drunk—the way a man about to be hanged or shot could not get drunk, no matter how much alcohol he was given. "There's something nervousness does to a man," Steinbeck said. Campbell pretended that they were not talking about what had just happened.

Steinbeck went to bed. Campbell wandered back toward his house, but veered over to Ricketts's. It was dark inside. Everyone was asleep. He found Carol in bed in a back room. She had her back to the wall and a blanket pulled tight around her. He leaned down and kissed her on the mouth. Campbell shivered—it was cold—and went into the living room to stand by the radiator for a moment. Then he went back and got under the blanket with Carol and stayed there until morning.

In the journal Campbell kept, he said that they kissed—over and over—but that was all. That might have been true. If it was, perhaps it was a more serious betrayal. Steinbeck claimed—weirdly—that he had no nerve endings in his lips and that he never liked kissing. As Campbell and Carol lay there in the dark, their lips touching, Carol whispered "Jesus Christ" again and again. And then, finally, "I hope that this is hurting you as much as it's hurting me."

The next morning, Campbell staggered home to be sick. Ricketts was up early and puttering in the kitchen as if he hadn't touched a drop the night before. He announced they were going on a collecting expedition, up the shore to the other side of Monterey Bay just past Santa Cruz. Ritchie and Tal Lovejoy came along—there was a magnificent stand of redwoods on the way, and Tal had never seen the big trees. Steinbeck stayed home. In the car, Campbell and Carol sat close, holding hands and staring into each other's eyes. This did not seem to trouble anyone. When they got back they picked up Steinbeck and went for a swim. In his journal, Campbell wrote that he believed "[w]e were all more or less in love with each other." And this left him at a crossroads, though his dilemma was nothing special for someone with ambitions. Betraying his youth and naivete, Campbell told himself that what he was experiencing was *life*, and it was amazing. But it was not the life of the mind he'd always imagined. Could you have both, he wondered. "Life?" he mused, "or thought? Shall I think to live?—or live to think?"

In May, Campbell invited his friends to dinner at his place. It was a feast. They had fruit salad, abalone, peas and potatoes, and, for dessert, strawberries and ice cream. As always, there was plenty of wine. Steinbeck was in a mood and accused Carol of being drunk. A few days later, Steinbeck came to see Campbell. It was just before dark, and it was rainy and cold. He had a paper bag with him, which he set on the table. Campbell asked if it was a gift. No, Steinbeck said, it was something for his dog Tillie. Steinbeck asked for coffee. Campbell thought he knew why Steinbeck was there. At last he came out with it and asked Campbell if he was in love with Carol.

Campbell struggled to answer. They talked awkwardly for a long time. Carol had told Steinbeck everything there was to tell. Steinbeck said he was at least glad that Campbell was as good a man as he was. If that hadn't been the case, Steinbeck said he would have killed him. Steinbeck also said he didn't want any pity. He didn't need it and it couldn't touch him, but he didn't want it anyway.

Steinbeck asked Campbell how much longer he would be on the peninsula. Campbell said a couple of months. Steinbeck allowed that that should be enough time for Campbell and Carol to figure out what they wanted to do. It was a generous thing to say, and it must have made Campbell feel small. Steinbeck asked Campbell if he felt a physical desire for Carol. Campbell, surely lying, said he did not.

"It's worse than I thought," Steinbeck said.

Really? Did Steinbeck simply not believe Campbell? Or did he envy the idea that Campbell could be in love with Carol without wanting to sleep with her—exactly the kind of romantic fantasy that Steinbeck had long found irresistible. Of course, there's another possibility. *It's worse than I thought* is simply a great line, and Steinbeck couldn't help himself. He was always writing.

About a month later, Campbell left on a collecting trip to Alaska with Ricketts and the Calvins. He didn't come back to Pacific Grove. Campbell became a professor of literature at Sarah Lawrence College in New York and the most famous mythologist in the world. In 1949 he published *The Hero with a Thousand Faces*, which examined what he called the "monomyth," his theory that all mythic narratives are actually the same story.

There's another version of the story of Campbell's last confrontation with Steinbeck—a persistent rumor that could be true. It's the same story in every respect save one. In this version, Steinbeck didn't have a paper bag with something for his dog in it. Instead, it was a gun that Steinbeck pulled out and placed on the table when he asked Joseph Campbell if he was in love with Carol.

The Pastures of Heaven was published in the early fall of 1932. Months earlier there'd been yet another shake-up for Steinbeck's editor, Robert Ballou, when his new firm went under while the book was in production. Ballou found a job at another publishing house, Brewer, Warren & Putnam, and implored Steinbeck to join him there. Steinbeck liked Ballou and agreed—subject to the approval of McIntosh & Otis. In June, Ballou had asked Steinbeck for a short biography of himself, plus a photo to use for promotion. Steinbeck—who knew that such things were a routine part of book publishing but had not lost his horror of exposing himself in any way to the public—tried to worm out of it. Ridiculously, he complained to Ballou that he couldn't remember much about his life and wasn't sure which of his few memories were true and which were imagined. As for the photo, the answer was no. Steinbeck had a horror of cameras. A camera, he said, is "so much more sure about everything than I am." It was a clever way to put it, as anyone who has ever looked at a picture of themselves well knows.

About the same time that the book came out, Steinbeck and Carol decided to move back to Los Angeles. They needed another change of scenery and were weary of their little cottage and the endless parties, and perhaps hoped to put the Joseph Campbell episode behind them. They stayed briefly with the Sheffields again before renting a house in Montrose. Steinbeck busied himself with his latest revision of *To an Unknown God* when the reviews of *The Pastures of Heaven* began to appear. They were good, though Steinbeck—ever fearful of any whiff of success—could not bring himself to say so. He told Mavis McIntosh the reviews were "very silly," but he supposed it was a good thing the critics were paying attention to the book. In *The New Yorker*, Robert Coates saw the parallel with Sherwood Anderson. He found the linkages between the stories loose in places, but Steinbeck nonetheless had a fine command of the locale and its citizens.

Proving again the invisibility of *Cup of Gold*, Coates mistakenly referred to *The Pastures of Heaven* as Steinbeck's first novel. It might as well have been. The new book marked the real beginning of Steinbeck's career, the first time anyone heard his true voice. Whatever similarities the book bore to the stories Beth Ingels had told him, they had now been reimagined into a deft, sure-handed depiction of a place where everything is familiar and as it should be, except for an unseen force that guides the destinies of those in the valley.

This powerful influence emanates from a farm with a grim history. Two generations of a family named Battle had lived and died on it, and then, believed by the neighbors to be cursed, the place was deserted and fell into disrepair. Finally, a new family comes to live on the Battle farm—an aged, nearly skeletal old couple and their dour son. The son works day and night to restore the farm, clearing and planting and pruning with a furor that exhausts those watching his progress. He does nothing to fix up the house, and in truth the family lives only in its kitchen. And then, with no sign beforehand, the family disappears. When concerned neighbors finally enter the house to see what happened, they find three breakfasts growing mold on a perfectly set kitchen table. Nobody is there. There is no furniture in any other room. The farm fell quickly back into wildness, "as though practice had made it adept." The land was good, but no one wanted to live there. Time passed. Riotous nature thrived:

"For five years now the old Battle farm had stood vacant. The weeds, with a holiday energy, free of fear of the hoe, grew as large as small trees. In the orchard the fruit trees were knotty and strong and tangled. They increased the quantity of their fruit, and diminished its size. The brambles grew about the roots and swallowed up the windfalls.

"The house itself, a square, well-built, two-story place, had been dignified and handsome when its white paint was fresh, but a singular latter history had left about it an air unbearably lonely. Weeds warped up the boards of the porches, the walls were grey and weathering. Small boys, those lieutenants of time in its warfare against the works of man, had broken out all the windows and carted away every movable thing."

A man named Bert Munroe comes to the valley, looks over the Battle place, and buys it. Rumors spread that he is "one of those people who go about looking for ghosts and writing about them." But the truth is that Bert Munroe himself lives under a shadow, having failed all his life. Farming is his last hope. He spruces up the house, restores the land, and soon his wife and three children join him. As the farm prospers, the people of the valley grow resentful. They secretly liked the Battle farm for the doomed place it had always been.

But Bert Munroe slowly wins over the people. One day they ask him how he defied the Battle curse. Bert says this is what he believes: that he came to the valley with his own curse upon him. When he moved into the Battle place, his curse and the farm's curse struggled against each other and, in the end, "killed each other off." For a moment, everybody has a laugh about that. And then someone offers a different idea. Maybe the two curses had "mated and gone into a gopher hole like a pair of rattlesnakes. Maybe there'll be a lot of baby curses crawling around the Pastures the first thing we know." And everyone laughs even harder at this.

But that is of course what happens. Each chapter of *The Pastures of Heaven* looks at a family and how the many-headed curse that now lives in the valley manifests itself in their lives. This evil takes different forms: sickness, obsession, insanity, morbid preoccupations, grotesque physical afflictions. Steinbeck structured each chapter with varying degrees of complexity and subtle connections to the general theme of the book. In the story of the froglike Tularecito—a deformed idiot savant—the reader meets the local schoolteacher, Miss Morgan. She shows up again in subsequent chapters, including one that flashes back to her arrival in the valley and describes how a catastrophe looms over Miss Morgan when a small lie she tells during her interview for the job threatens to unravel. In the most straight-forward chapter, Steinbeck tells the ironic story of Shark Wicks, who barely gets by in life but has convinced everyone in the valley that he is secretly wealthy. Shark is found out when his determination to preserve his daughter's virginity nearly turns to violence.

Readers who perceived a contest between good and evil in *The Pastures of Heaven* were taking the optimistic view, for in these stories it is never a fair fight between those forces. Steinbeck was more concerned with showing how misfortune attaches itself to certain people and places, how it can contaminate even the most beguiling of settings. Like an infection, it is indiscriminate, sickening the good and the bad alike. This is the book's obvious theme.

But more unifying than the curse are its symptoms—the recurring reversion of the world to its natural state. When a farm or a family is stricken, nature destroys what humankind has made. Houses peel and crumble. Tilled fields are subsumed by weeds and grasses. Well-tended orchards become knotted, spectral forests. The earth, given an opening, always reclaims itself and obliterates order—erasing the outward evidence of an agrarian society. Steinbeck had learned this lesson from his father, who loved to garden, and from his own experience as a laborer in the Salinas Valley. Farming is a ceaseless campaign against nature, which tends toward diversity and chaos, a riot of life-forms that can be suppressed but never defeated. Farming takes luck, but more than that it takes vigilance. Steinbeck's heavenly pastures, like farming country anywhere, are in the best of times a war zone. Let one part of the line fail, and annihilation is at hand. No wonder Steinbeck named the family who brought misery to this pretty valley *Battle*.

Robert Coates in *The New Yorker* called *The Pastures of Heaven* one of the best books he'd read recently. Anita Moffett, the well-regarded critic of the *New York Times*, liked it too, saying there was a genuineness about the tragedies that befell Steinbeck's characters. Moffett lavished praise on Steinbeck's style, which she found vivid and funny. But the most important thing that all the critics noticed was Steinbeck's sure grasp of a place and its people. He was working on native ground.

There's some evidence that Beth Ingels was aggrieved by Steinbeck's use of her memories in his book. Marjory Lloyd said that if

Ingels felt wronged she didn't let on at the time. But long after the fact, Ingels confided to someone who knew her and Steinbeck that she had written out rough drafts of several of the stories she told to Steinbeck—and had shown him this material. She conceded that Steinbeck's version was much the better written. But unlike Toby Street, who had given Steinbeck his play, *The Green Lady*, free of any claim, Ingels felt she'd been cheated. She said Steinbeck "hijacked" her material. Later still, she said much the same to Jack Calvin.

The Pastures of Heaven sold slowly. In January of 1933, Steinbeck got a check from Robert Ballou. He wrote to thank him for it, and also to let him know that Tillie had died. Steinbeck was heartsick about it. He said it would be better for the dog to still be in this world in place of a tycoon like William Randolph Hearst. At least Tillie was housebroken, he said. Steinbeck added—as he had so many times, for so many years—that he expected to soon finish the latest version of *To an Unknown God*. This time, he was sending it in. And it had a new title, something he'd been pondering a long time. The change was small but good: *To a God Unknown*. Ballou had told him that it would be on the spring list. Steinbeck felt he could not stop experimenting with the book and had gotten it to a place where it was either excellent or awful. He couldn't tell which. And then, in February, it really was done, just shy of five years since he'd started on it. Steinbeck sent the manuscript to Mavis McIntosh, telling her it was not a revision of what she'd seen before, but a new book. Steinbeck also wrote to Ballou, who had recently hinted that his relationship with Brewer, Warren & Putnam had become tenuous and that he might strike out on his own. Steinbeck was sympathetic. Publishing sounded like a risky business. And he knew all about struggling. He admitted that he and Carol were in trouble, too. They could not pay their rent, and the power company was ready to cut them off. They'd have to move soon, though he had no idea where. Carol preferred to meet disaster head-on rather than having it sneak up on them.

But disaster got a head start. In March, Olive Steinbeck fell ill and was admitted to the hospital. Steinbeck and Carol rushed back to Salinas and moved into the family house on Central Avenue and began shuttling between it and the cottage in Pacific Grove. All three of Steinbeck's sisters had their own families now and so everything fell to him. Steinbeck spent his days at the hospital, keeping his mother company and even helping with her care. It was awful. His mother faded in and out of consciousness, like a light bulb flickering on and off. For Steinbeck, each passing hour demonstrated the inevitable ravages of old age. Olive wasted away steadily. Nobody told John Ernst how sick she was.

At the end of May, Olive suffered a stroke that left her partially paralyzed. Almost cruelly, her general condition improved slightly and Steinbeck was told she might linger in this way for several years. He'd been writing a little between visits, which usually stretched to eight hours each day. Now he took his work to the hospital, trying to jot down a few lines between bedpan rotations. He was working on a long story about a boy and his pony—perhaps derived from the story he'd shown Bill Black in his bedroom back in high school. In the story, the pony gets distemper—a respiratory infection in horses that is also known as strangles. Steinbeck was experimenting with streamlining the boy's point of view, leaving it up to the reader to figure out what he was thinking. He told George Albee he was writing it for the discipline of working, despite the emotional exhaustion that enveloped him hour after hour at the hospital. Anybody could write when life was calm and comfortable. Steinbeck wanted to prove to himself he could work no matter what was going on around him. He also said he had started to think that someday he'd like to write the story of the Salinas Valley, all of it, and that if he could get it right it would be amazing. But it would take years to get it right.

Hours became days, and days stretched into months. Steinbeck was told that if his mother remained stable, they would send her home, where her care would be entirely up to him. Months could turn into years. He told Dook Sheffield he was at the start of what was likely going to be a lengthy vigil, but he could not leave his mother's side. He said there was no choice in the matter.

Time crawled. Steinbeck had finished the story about the pony. He had no idea what to do with it. It was 10,000 words long—too big for any magazine, and too short for a book on its own. When he couldn't write, Steinbeck thought about many things. One of them was an idea about individuals and groups that had been simmering with him for a few years—and that had more recently been stimulated by conversations with Ed Ricketts and Richard Albee. Albee was still at UCLA but making frequent visits to Pacific Grove. He was studying philosophy and had become obsessed with the teachings of one of his professors, John Elof Boodin. Boodin had published several dense volumes in the early part of the century. One of his main concerns was reconciling metaphysics and science. As science increasingly explained how natural phenomena work, and how such phenomena do not require some external, nonphysical cause, the question was whether science would someday explain everything—including thought. If consciousness is the product of physical chemistry, where does that leave us? Is the universe pure happenstance—a fortuitous creation of itself? Should we worship hydrogen and carbon instead of God?

Boodin, to be fair, was getting ahead of events, often speculating on matters that were unresolved by science at the time but that would have answers in the coming decades. This is one of the complications of a philosophy that balances objectivity and abstraction: Science is always adding to its side of the ledger. Ricketts, who liked to think about such things, was taken with Albee, who also introduced Ricketts to Gregorian chants. These became a regular feature of the daily soundtrack at the lab, their somber monotones floating out over Ocean View Avenue and mixing with the aroma of sardines cooking up and down Cannery Row.

Albee believed that he was a "catalyst" for both Steinbeck and Ricketts, and that the intellectual connections among the three of them reinforced Ricketts's thoughts about science and perception, and Steinbeck's on writing. "I came out of school with my head full of new thinking," Albee said. "I was bringing them all sorts of fresh material. That was my contribution." Albee, in turn, was intrigued by Ricketts's devotion to his mentor, W. C. Allee, which made for a slightly confusing collision of similar last names. All three—Steinbeck, Ricketts, and Albee—came to view the living world as a cooperative endeavor among organisms. Ricketts took things further, exploring the nature of knowledge itself and humankind's search for a higher reality.

Steinbeck melded ideas he got from Ricketts and Albee with the germ of a theory he had been working on for a few years. That summer, with his mother's labored breathing in the background, Steinbeck wrote a long letter to Dook Sheffield in which he tried to explain how groups take on some of the characteristics of individuals. He said that he could use this concept to write about the world more coherently. Seeming to recognize an inescapable banality in his own idea, Steinbeck confessed he was being selfish in sending it along. This wasn't a letter he even expected Dook to read, he said—and if he didn't read it, Steinbeck said he'd never know that, so he was ready to risk being boring. But he needed to do it. Steinbeck began by describing how he'd arrived at his theory. The process involved writing down and thinking about many ideas over a long period of time, until they took on a life of their own and began to lead somewhere. This was exciting, Steinbeck said, especially when these disparate thoughts merged with one another.

Ultimately, Steinbeck said, this is how a novel is born—out of the search for a way to portray what the writer has revealed to himself through all that questioning and probing. Steinbeck then told Sheffield that he had discovered something fundamental about organisms—he called them units. When units form a group, the group acts as a superorganism that has a life of its own greater than the sum of its parts. Corals, Steinbeck said, were an example. Corals are communal organisms. Multiple species associate with one another and over time form a large, diverse structure—a coral reef. Sometimes the process continues, and an atoll is built.

Steinbeck saw similar properties among human populations.

He speculated as to why so many healthy young adults had succumbed during the flu pandemic in 1918 when in other times the same infection had been much less deadly. The germ, he said, was unchanged. Instead, it was the susceptibility of the population that caused so many to die. On a more prosaic note, Steinbeck wondered why so many people would read a bestseller even though they didn't understand it. The group somehow knows better than the individual. Steinbeck admitted this was all confusing.

The "group unit," as Steinbeck called his superorganism, knows the whole history of a species: its genetic profile, every step in its evolution, everything that has ever happened for as long as the species has existed, all of the many experiences of the group of which the individual is unaware. But unlike the individual unit, the group unit doesn't learn or modify its behavior based on what it experiences, so it can overwhelm the choices an individual would make. This explains how an army compels itself to do what the individual soldier cannot.

Group units, Steinbeck wrote, come in all sizes, from a camp meeting singing around a fire to the masses of opposing armies. He realized that his mother was a group unit, composed of cells. Half of them were in rebellion, so the group unit that was Olive Steinbeck suffered and her existence was threatened. Steinbeck said this was all still falling into place for him, but that he would someday be able to write a book based on group-unit theory. What had come clear to him is that men, without thinking about it, are always forming group units, and that these groups differ from their individual constituents. In fact, the larger group is itself a living entity that creates its own history and acts though its own will.

Steinbeck told Sheffield that although this idea was still not fully formed, he could not stop thinking about how it seemed to explain so many otherwise-improbable developments throughout history—from the conquests of Attila the Hun to the recent congressional resolution that would lead to the end of Prohibition later that year. Steinbeck, displaying insight into his limitations, admitted that if he knew more, he'd probably be too timid to propose such a sweeping theory. In one way or another, every living thing, including human beings, had the potential to act like lemmings—agreeably, helplessly, even fatally in concert.

It's difficult to decide whether all of this is baloney—or a perceptive kernel of thought that would breathe life into several of the most-revered books of the twentieth century. The idea that organisms are made of parts, and can also *be* parts of larger groups, is so obvious that it's astonishing Steinbeck would have given it more than a passing thought. And some of his speculation was plainly wrong—the 1918 flu pandemic was lethal because the virus *did* change, picking up genetic material from a bird flu virus. He was, however, partly right, because a group response was involved, too: Older people and the very young—usually the groups most vulnerable to the flu—had been exposed to the bird flu virus and therefore had antibodies for the new strain. Young adults, who were ordinarily more likely to survive the flu, hadn't been exposed to the bird flu virus and lacked antibodies to it.

Steinbeck's observation that group units have their own personalities, for lack of a better term, was more interesting and potentially useful to a writer, as was the idea that the free will of an individual unit is subsumed by the group. For Steinbeck, the group unit is the product of a dynamic transformation that makes a new entity. Whether it's good or bad—a mob, or the cavalry to the rescue—it is a thing capable of independent action and therefore a fitting subject.

Nowhere in his letter to Sheffield did Steinbeck use the word *phalanx*. But it was on his mind. It was a term Richard Albee added to the stew of ideas simmering in Ed Ricketts's lab in the early 1930s. It's from the Greek name for an ancient infantry formation in which soldiers stood shoulder to shoulder in close ranks, eight deep. The front line held their shields tight to one another in an impenetrable wall and advanced behind it. Later, the Romans improved on this, with a formation called the *testudo*, or "tortoise." Like the Greek phalanx, it was slow-moving and nearly invincible. Ranks of tightly bunched soldiers marched ahead behind the front row's forward-facing shields. Soldiers on the flank turned their shields to the side, and soldiers in the middle held theirs aloft, making a roof over the whole group so sturdy it was said that a centurion could run across it. No rain of arrows could halt the *testudo*. Within its protective shell the squad inched forward, looking like and protected in the same way as a tortoise.

Steinbeck eventually came to believe that you could not understand humankind by looking at individuals—any more than you could interpret a human being's behavior by looking at one of their cells. The answers were all in the phalanx, the superorganism, the group unit—that unique, surprising, ceaselessly fascinating thing that is collectively us. "Man," Steinbeck said, "is a unit of the greater beast, the phalanx." And this had been right there in front of him all along. He said he found four instances of the phalanx phenomenon in *To a God Unknown* that he'd put in before he realized what it was. Steinbeck used the term *phalanx* when he wrote to George Albee that summer, explaining that he had come to see that the most important aspect of the phalanx was that it is a repository of knowledge about humanity, of all that it has endured; including "destruction, war, migration, hatred, and fear."

Destruction. Migration. Hatred. Fear. These were the themes to which Steinbeck would soon turn.

— 8 —

GET ME OUT OF
THIS SORT OF THING

O LIVE STEINBECK HOVERED between life and eternity. It was
a bad time in the midst of a bad time. On March 4, 1933, as
President Franklin Roosevelt had taken office, he'd told the
exhausted nation that "the only thing we have to fear is fear itself."
That was the part everyone chose to remember. His next words—
which defined that fear as a "nameless, unreasoning, unjustified terror
which paralyzes needed efforts to convert retreat into advance"—were
less comforting. In his first days in office, Roosevelt asked a special session of Congress, which had been convened to deal with the
banking crisis, to also cut some $500 million in federal spending in
order to keep the government from going bankrupt. Roosevelt was
convinced—incorrectly, most economists now agree—that balancing the federal budget would help lift the economy. Congress was
split on this question, but a coalition of Republicans and conserva-
tive Democrats gave the president what he wanted. Later the same
week, Roosevelt broadcast the first of his "fireside chats." About half
of all American families by then owned radios, and many tuned in.
They heard Roosevelt explain that when the government reopened the
banks after a forced "holiday," those institutions would be sound. The
next day, deposits outpaced withdrawals. The New Deal was underway. To celebrate, Roosevelt ordered the legalization of 3.2 beer ahead
of the expected repeal of Prohibition. As with many of his first mea-
sures, the country could have used something stronger.

That year, about 30 million working-age Americans had no income. During his first month in office, Roosevelt persuaded Congress to establish the Federal Emergency Relief Administration (FERA), and he picked a New Yorker named Harry Hopkins to run it. Ironically, the initial appropriation for the agency was $500 million—the same amount Roosevelt had cut from the budget. Hopkins, who would become the second most powerful man in Washington during the Depression, wasted no time issuing relief grants to the states, spending a then-staggering sum of $5 million during his first two hours in office. When he listened to a relief plan that one of his advisors said would work "in the long run," Hopkins famously snapped back, "People don't eat in the long run—they eat every day." Conservatives railed against FERA as "socialism." Meanwhile, much of America went on the dole. Toward the end of the year, the Roosevelt administration would begin finding ways to make that more palatable, but for now the country had its hands out. Bread lines and soup kitchens appeared in cities everywhere.

For the Steinbeck family, the grim news of the day darkened an already somber time. Once she was moved back home, Steinbeck's mother improved slightly, just enough to convince him that there was no end to her torment—or his—in sight. He bathed Olive and claimed that he changed her bedsheets as often as twelve times a day, though it was mostly Carol who tended to this kind of thing. Carol also continued her indispensable role as Steinbeck's first reader and most incisive editor. Astonishingly, Steinbeck did some of his finest work during Olive's illness. In addition to the suite of stories about a boy and his pony, Steinbeck also wrote an unusually moving short story called "The Chrysanthemums."

In New York, where *To a God Unknown* was supposedly on its way to publication, hard times had hit the book business, too. Robert Ballou was again out of a job and trying to raise money to start his own publishing house. Steinbeck turned down offers for *To a God Unknown* from four other publishers, sticking with Ballou—though it's unlikely that any of those offers involved a large advance. The fact that there *were* other offers suggests that McIntosh and Otis were looking out for Steinbeck's interests as well as their own, shopping the manuscript around. And this might well have been with Steinbeck's blessing. But Steinbeck said he trusted Ballou and none of the others. In the end, Ballou managed to launch his publishing firm and put *To a God Unknown* on his fall list, bringing the total number of titles for his inaugural season to two. In August, Steinbeck corrected and returned the page proofs and waited patiently. As if taking care of his mother weren't enough, Steinbeck had also started helping his father at the county treasurer's office. As accustomed as he was to writing in ledgers—always his preferred medium for composition—keeping actual figures in them was miserable work. He said he now understood why office workers were the way they were.

And still, Steinbeck managed to keep writing. Sometimes he could get down only a few lines before his mother again called out. But he finished the pony story and started on a novel he was calling *Tortilla Flat.* It was set in Monterey and was about a group of *paisanos*, an amiable and proud mixed race descended from the Spanish and indigenous people who had been there for centuries. The *paisanos* lived by their wits and held tight to an ancient moral code, but were disconnected from the social and economic life of Monterey. They were their own country, living high up on the hill above Monterey proper, beyond the paved streets and corner lights of the town, in a place called Tortilla Flat. Many had no fixed address or job. Steinbeck had learned about the *paisanos* from a woman named Susan Gregory, who used to come to parties at the cottage on Eleventh Street.

Gregory taught Spanish at Monterey High School. She was short and thin and elegant, with curly gray hair and a faint Castilian accent. Never married, she was the closest thing to Monterey royalty. Her grandfather was William Hartnell, a British-born merchant who, before statehood, had married a sixteen-year-old Spanish girl, Maria Teresa de la Guerra, with whom he had nineteen children. The de la Guerras were one of the wealthiest and most prominent families in Alta California. Gregory lived on the hill in the heart of Tortilla Flat, where she was an informal mother superior to the *paisanos*. No one knew more about their ways or loved them more unconditionally than Gregory did, and she spent hours telling Steinbeck their stories. Unlike Beth Ingels—who had been one of her students—Gregory never gave any thought to writing about the *paisanos* and did not begrudge Steinbeck's use of the stories she freely gave him. Now, as the bleak days and nights came and went, Steinbeck escaped into the world Gregory had described for him. *Tortilla Flat* was light and funny. He said writing it was a "direct rebellion against all the sorrow of our house."

That fall, John Ernst finally collapsed under the strain of Olive's lingering illness, his frayed nerves leaving him shaking and numb and half-blind. Steinbeck sent him over to Pacific Grove with Carol for a while, where he seemed to get a little better. But Steinbeck thought that if his mother hung on for six more months, she was likely to outlive John Ernst. He told Robert Ballou that his family was falling apart. He said he could handle it better if his father died abruptly rather than by degrees, which was slow torture for both of them. On went the vigil.

To a God Unknown was published in September of 1933, in a meager printing of fewer than 1,500 copies—of which only about 600 were actually bound and sold. Despite Steinbeck's long struggle with the book, and his unfaltering belief in Toby Street's idea, the novel disappeared like a pebble falling into the ocean. Steinbeck had only himself to blame, as there was almost nothing left of Street's original story in his ambitious attempt to find its meaning—except for the vague pantheism that animates the action.

Over the course of countless revisions, Steinbeck had replaced the main character, a Californian named Andy Wayne, with Joseph Wayne, an easterner who comes west to find his fortune in California. In the earliest fragment of the novel—the one that still had Street's name on it next to Steinbeck's—Wayne arrives with the Gold Rush, labors at mining for fifteen years, and then buys a ranch in Jolon, in the southern part of Monterey County.

That earlier draft hinted that Wayne's son, Anthony (Andy), would become the protagonist. But in the final published version, the story is all about Joseph, the patriarch of the Wayne clan, which includes his three younger brothers and their families. Each of the brothers lives by a different code. One is drunken and dissolute, another is pious, and the third is simple and direct and more at ease with the livestock than with people. But it is Joseph and his relationship with the ranch that are the heart of everything.

Back in the fall of 1930, Steinbeck had told Carl Wilhelmson a story about a tree. It was a pine tree that stood in the yard of the Pacific Grove cottage. Steinbeck had planted it years earlier, when it was small and he was still a boy. Ever since, it had been known as "John's tree." He'd watched it grow, and sometimes he imagined it as more than a tree. For a time he let himself think of the tree as the brother he didn't have. Later on, he turned it into something abstract, a totem somehow connected to his own future. This was harmless enough, but there was a problem. The tree had grown tall now, and its lower branches posed a hazard to the cottage and needed to be trimmed away. Steinbeck dreaded even the thought. How could he cut into the living tissue of the tree? Or, worse, what if he killed it? He told Wilhelmson he was afraid of what that could do to him.

What Steinbeck ultimately did with the pine tree isn't known— probably he went ahead and trimmed it and laughed at himself when nothing bad happened. He thought about why he felt the way he did about the tree. The tree was alive, of course, but its hold on him arose from something else. Steinbeck had always considered the tree partly human, and now it seemed it could just as well be partly a god. And then the tree began to change for Steinbeck. Its narrow pyramidal form rearranged itself into the spreading crown of a soaring, heavy-limbed oak. When Steinbeck could see this new tree clearly and feel its greater power, he realized he'd invented it for a reason—so he could put it in *To a God Unknown*.

In the book, a mighty oak stands next to Joseph Wayne's house. Like the nearby glade up in the hills—a hidden and wondrous place where soft green moss blankets the altar of a great stone monolith and a stream flows from a fern-shrouded cave—the tree is holy, consecrated in Joseph's mind. The tree watches over Joseph, protects him and his family and the farm. He talks to the tree, offers it food and wine, confides in it. The tree is not his dead father, but through it, Joseph knows his father, and sees himself as a proper heir to what his father was. The tree is a guide. It permits Joseph to see his life as it is, and comforts him as a savior might if Joseph believed in saviors. When Joseph's wife is expecting, he tells the tree a baby will join them soon, and when it arrives it will be as if they are three generations. Earlier in the day, the local priest had spied on Joseph as he appeared to make an offering to the tree, and warned him that the Devil had been in this country for thousands of years, Christ only a few. Joseph laughed him away, but they understood each other. Later, standing by the heavy, dark trunk in the rain, Joseph spoke reverently to the tree: "'There is to be a baby, sir. I promise that I will put it in your arms when it is born.' He felt the cold, wet bark, drew his fingertips slowly downward. 'The priest knows,' he thought. 'He knows part of it, and he doesn't believe. Or maybe he believes and is fearful.'"

A terrible drought comes to Joseph Wayne's California, a searing parallel with what was happening across the vastness of the American plains. The story unfolds through multiple disasters that appear to be the work of God or Satan—or, more accurately, fearsome natural processes Steinbeck proposed are mistaken for the work of God or Satan. When Joseph's wife dies on the rock in the glade, it seems that the silent stone may have killed her—a question at the center of the novel. This mystery reaches out to Joseph and culminates in his impulsive suicide, a grotesque human sacrifice to all worldly realities and to all of the gods that inhabit them. Joseph dies believing he is one with everything.

The response to the book was puzzlement, and critics were almost unanimous in their use of the word "mystical" to sum it up—not in a good way. After Robert Ballou sent him some of the reviews, Steinbeck predictably snapped that he was delighted that the critics hated the book. He disliked their assertions that the story wasn't real, as he was sure he'd made plain how utterly real it was. He remembered how awful the good reviews of *The Pastures of Heaven* had made him feel—or at least how he'd claimed they did—because alongside the praise was proof that the critics hadn't understood the book, though he was vague about what part of it they had missed. In fact, Steinbeck didn't sound happy or pleased. The critics, he said, were "lice" and "bewildered bastards." Their disapproval only convinced him more firmly that it was a good book. The louder the chorus against him, the better. Forgotten in this tirade was his bitterness about the fact that so few critics had written about *Cup of Gold*. Steinbeck, who said he hated good reviews, loved bad reviews, and was made most miserable over unwritten ones, had nowhere to stand on the issue—a common feeling among all but the most-beloved writers.

Steinbeck's insistence that the critics' voices didn't matter to him—that they only strengthened his resolve whether they loved his books or detested them—of course rings hollow. But it was in keeping with his lifelong defense against his wounds: *I don't care. I don't care if anyone publishes me. I don't care if anyone reads me. I don't care what the reviewers say. I don't care if I never write a great book. I DO NOT CARE.*

It would be remarkable if that were true. Writers write because they do care.

Mysticism did not cloud every judgment of *To a God Unknown*, and some of the more perceptive critics argued that Steinbeck had obscured the book's meaning, if it had one. In a smart review in the *New York Herald Tribune*, Margaret Cheney Dawson wrote that the opposing poles of the great tree and the moss-shrouded rock regulate Joseph Wayne's life, though Steinbeck leaves the reader perplexed as to how. The meaning of Joseph Wayne's life and its sad end, Dawson said, was hard to put into words. But she managed:

"One can only say that he came closer and closer to it in feeling until, when his crops and animals were dead from the dryness of two years and all of his family gone in search of a less treacherous land, he chose to remain behind, living in the shadow of the rock, husbanding the little water that ran from its side to pour over its still-green moss, finally dying with cut wrists on its back, offering his blood to bring back the rain."

Which might be a better line than any in the book itself.

All that work, all those years of living with the conviction that *To a God Unknown* was a story he had to tell, and it now seemed of too little consequence to be noticed. Or, worse, was a curiosity nobody took seriously. It is easier for a writer to be ridiculed than ignored. One reviewer hinted at a small channel of hope for Steinbeck. "C.S." in the *Saturday Review* dismissed *To a God Unknown* as hokum, but allowed that Steinbeck had a nice touch with the region and the people he wrote about. As Steinbeck watched his parents slipping away, he did what he always did. He kept on writing. Being with his mother was like being alone with someone already halfway to the other side he so believed in. He said the house in Salinas was more haunted than ever. "I see things walking at night that it is not good to see," he said.

Olive died early in 1934. Steinbeck grudgingly agreed to be one of her pallbearers. His mother's illness had taken a toll on him that he was only beginning to realize. He could not shake the image of his mother in her sick bed, her eyes rimmed with terror over some unknown thing that hung wordlessly over her for nearly a year. And his father was in some ways even worse off now, an ancient, stumbling reminder of his former self who had become a wraithlike figure in a house growing crowded with the dead and the near-dead. Steinbeck told George Albee that he felt translucent and insubstantial.

Against all evidence, Steinbeck insisted he had no ambition and that he was at his core dull and stupid and slothful. He didn't want much in life. Food. Rest. A roof over his head. Enough intercourse to answer his desire. He didn't care about owning anything. It was not a bad outlook to have in those days, when the country scrabbled in the rubble of lost possessions and ruined ambitions. But having nothing and being nothing were not Steinbeck's destiny, and just then, when all seemed hopeless, his fortunes began to change.

One of the mysteries of writing is how it sometimes happens in spite of everything. Many writers cannot bear distractions. Steinbeck, always brittle and impossible to be around when he was in the middle of a book, had been fiercely protective of his writing time, and nobody who knew him even a little dared interrupt him when he was working. Maybe being alone with his dying mother felt perversely like the kind of isolation he craved. Or perhaps he discovered at last that writing well is impervious to the noise and clamor of everyday life. It happens. Life (or death) taps you on the shoulder, interrupts what you're doing, and suddenly you find that nobody has been bothering you but yourself. Indulgences disappear, instincts take over, mistrust of your own work fades, and the tendency toward self-doubt is carried away. And so it was with Steinbeck in that terrible time. He actually enjoyed himself while writing *Tortilla Flat* and the short stories that fell so easily onto his pages. It did not seem possible that this was the beginning of everything. But it was.

Steinbeck's big, three-part short story now had a title: "The Red Pony." His agents managed to sell the first two parts to a monthly magazine called the *North American Review*, which in the coming months would publish several more of Steinbeck's stories. Unlike his first three books, "The Red Pony" would endure, as alive for readers young and old as if it were—to borrow Steinbeck's own feeling about reading—something that had happened to them.

After *To a God Unknown*, Steinbeck told Carl Wilhelmson that he had abandoned realism forever—an odd claim given the near absence of realism in what he'd written to that point. But in "The Red Pony" he caught up with the world as it is, not as he imagined it to be. The story was as lean and hard as the Salinas Valley hillsides where the action takes place. It's the story of a ten-year-old boy named Jody, an only child whose aimless days on a ranch are forever transformed when he is given a colt—a red pony too small to ride when Jody first sees him standing nervously in a dark stall. Jody names the horse

Gabilan. The pony becomes Jody's day and night, the window through which he sees the sharp, tactile country that is his home. Steinbeck's command of the premise surely stemmed from his memories of Jill, his own red pony, but also revealed a discipline in his prose he hadn't managed before. The story is rich but without ornamentation and absent of gods and curses. One thing happens, and then another, and discovering what it all means is the point. And yet Steinbeck remained alert to the life forces that abound in the world. Every morning Jody is up early and head to the barn to tend his pony:

"In the grey quiet mornings when the land and the brush and the houses and the trees were silver-grey and black like a photograph negative, he stole toward the barn, past the sleeping stones and the sleeping cypress tree. The turkeys, roosting in the tree out of coyotes' reach, clicked drowsily. The fields glowed with a grey frost-like light and in the dew the tracks of rabbits and of field mice stood out sharply."

Jody's trips to the barn feel to him like an extension of a dream he's had in the night. He's frightened by the thought that maybe it *is* a dream, that when he throws open the stall there will be no pony. Each morning, as he comes near the barn, Jody breaks into a run.

Under the guidance of a wise ranch hand named Billy Buck, Jody cares for the pony and begins to train it. Months pass slowly as the time nears when Jody will be able to ride Gabilan. One day he leaves the pony in the corral while he's at school. Billy Buck has told him it won't rain that day, but it does. Gabilan takes a chill, sickens, and, instead of getting better as everyone predicts, suffers and dies. It's a shattering event, more so for Jody's blank, unspoken heartbreak, and it ends part one of the story. In the second section, a strange old man, a *paisano* named Gitano, visits the ranch. He is near the end of his life and has come home to be near the place he was born. In the final section, Jody's father arranges to breed a mare so Jody can have a colt. And in the end, Jody again has his pony—but at the terrible cost of learning even the most wondrous gifts are sometimes impermanent.

At its simplest, "The Red Pony" is a story about a boy discovering—

and being taught—that life has two sides, one clear and warm and embraced by the natural joy of existence, the other a dark heaven from which misfortune falls randomly but inevitably. Jody is receptive to this lesson because he lives close to the ground he shares with other living things. Even at so tender an age, he is aware of the slope of a hill, the texture of the field grasses, the guarded acquaintance of a farm dog, the brightness of the whitewashed farm buildings against the sere landscape. He listens to the squirrels chattering in the trees and watches buzzards riding the thermals overhead, searching for something dead.

Steinbeck eventually wrote a fourth installment with Jody and Billy and the family titled "The Leader of the People." It's about a visit from Jody's grandfather, who is forever retelling the story of how he had long ago led a group of settlers to California—an old man's recurrent monologue that bores everybody but Jody. "The Leader of the People" feels more like a sequel to "The Red Pony" than an integral part of it, and it might have reflected Steinbeck's plan to continue writing about the boy Jody. He hinted at a fifth installment that was never written or did not survive. But "The Leader of the People" does include several lines that seem to sum up everything Steinbeck was trying to say about a boy's introduction to life's complexities. Early in the story, Billy Buck is feeding hay to the livestock. As he pitches the last of a wilted haystack over the fence, Jody speculates that there must be a small army of mice living in the remnants. Billy assures him the hay is "crawling" with mice. Jody wants to call the dogs down and hunt the mice, but Billy makes him wait to ask his father for permission. Later, after the grandfather has arrived, Jody goes out early in the morning to find a stick and launch his attack on the mice. When he pauses by the house, Billy Buck comes over. Jody says the mice cannot know what is coming. "'No, nor you either,' Billy remarked philosophically, 'nor me, nor anyone.'"

Jody is briefly stunned by this revelation. But then his mother calls him to breakfast and half-formed thoughts of fate and mortality vanish as he dashes for the house. And how perfect is that? Jody's innocence is intact, in spite of everything. One minute he's discovered the meaning of life—and in the next it's time to eat.

Steinbeck finished *Tortilla Flat* that winter, along with the later installments of "The Red Pony." He also completed several other short stories—including one that may be his greatest, "The Chrysanthemums." The sure grace and economy of the story was no less remarkable for having sprung from Steinbeck's imagination during the darkest days of his vigil with Olive. It's lovely and painful, and in its most arresting moment does what only the most exquisite writing can do, which is to bring the reader inside the world on the page as if it were more real than reality itself.

"The Chrysanthemums" tells the story of a lonely Salinas Valley ranch housewife named Elisa and her kind but clueless husband, Henry. One day when Henry is out rounding up cattle and Elisa is planting chrysanthemums, a traveling handyman drives up in a rickety, canvas-covered wagon pulled by an old horse and a burro. He's looking for work and falls into conversation with Elisa. She wears a heavy dress, thick gloves, and a man's hat, all of which disguise her youth and beauty. Elisa is astonished—and then fascinated—when she learns that the handyman lives in the wagon and travels up and down the West Coast sharpening knives and pounding dents out of pots. When he mentions that there is a woman on one of his regular stops ahead who would like the kind of flowers she's planting, Elisa—flustered by his interest—impulsively offers to send her some with him.

Elisa wants to make sure the woman knows how to plant the flowers, which are from cuttings and require careful attention. As she kneels and begins to gather the plants, she tries to explain to the handyman what to do with them. Soon Elisa is lost in a cloud of emotion, because what's required is an intuitive feel for the plant, and a touch so gentle it's a caress, a touch that can't be put into words. The handyman, off balance, tries to tell Elisa he understands and mumbles something about nights alone in his wagon. But Elisa's train of thought wanders deep within herself: "Elisa's voice grew husky. She broke in on him, 'I've never lived as you do, but I know what you mean. When the night is dark—why, the stars are sharp-pointed, and there's quiet. Why, you rise up and up! Every pointed star gets driven into your body. It's like that. Hot and sharp and—lovely.'"

The rising pitch of feelings ends abruptly. As Elisa falls silent, she reaches out toward the handyman's leg, but her hand falls before she touches him. Instead, she collects herself, lets him repair a few kitchen pans, and sends him on his way with the chrysanthemum cuttings in a pot of sand. After he leaves, Elisa bathes and admires her body in the mirror. When Henry comes home, they decide to go to dinner in Salinas. On the way she sees the chrysanthemum cuttings lying in the road. She doesn't begrudge the handyman the pot, which he has kept, but why couldn't he have thrown the flowers into the brush off to the side of the road? Had he not realized what had come over her ever so fleetingly? In a short while, they overtake the handyman in his clanging wagon, and when Henry speeds around him Elisa looks away. Tears well in her eyes and Elisa asks Henry if they can have wine with dinner.

When he showed the story to Carol, she told him it was his best. He put it with the others he was saving up.

In Monterey, there is debate about the precise location of the place called Tortilla Flat. It seems to be a term that was applied to several locations where *paisanos* lived, even over in the nearby town of Seaside. When Steinbeck was asked about it years after the book came out, he only tapped a finger against his forehead. But in the book *Tortilla Flat*, the location is explicit: Tortilla Flat was on the hill above the canneries in Monterey, where the town dissolved into the forest and a cluster of ramshackle wooden houses stood in weed-cluttered yards that lined the narrow dirt streets. Remains of this community are still there today. When he sent *Tortilla Flat* to Mavis McIntosh,

Steinbeck thought she would see that his characters—a young *paisano* named Danny and his friends—were based on Malory's Arthurian legend. For Steinbeck, Danny and his friends were, obviously, Arthur, Galahad, Launcelot.

Except that there was nothing obvious about it, and Mavis McIntosh told him so. Steinbeck ended up adding a prologue explaining that Danny's house was like the Round Table and his friends were like the knights who joined it—after which there was no additional discussion of this theme. Readers, having no knowledge of Steinbeck's obsession with the story of King Arthur, no doubt mistook the comparison as a joke, a clever way of suggesting the nobility of an ignoble band of misfits. Steinbeck did write a brief synopsis for the beginning of each chapter suggesting the story that followed was part of a mythical history.

Tortilla Flat is a character study of Danny, a legend among the *paisanos*. But it's a cultural study, too, an episodic excursion to a place where the rhythms of daily life include no visible means of support. The *paisanos* reinvent their lives from one day to the next. They work a little when they must, but mostly enjoy the simplest of pleasures you can imagine. Wine helps, as does a willingness to take what is needed from someone who won't miss it. You can't really call a *paisano* a thief, because that implies dishonesty and treachery, and they are incapable of either. An occasional stay in the Monterey jail is part of their bargain. Scene by scene, the book constructs the loose and yet strangely well-ordered world inhabited by Danny and his friends.

It begins when Danny comes home from the war. At twenty-five he'd gotten drunk and, filled with patriotic fervor, enlisted in the army. He has spent his hitch in Texas breaking mules. He is glad to be home—Danny knew other *paisanos* who had been killed in the fighting—and relieved when he learns that his grandfather has died and left him two small houses in Tortilla Flat. Danny moves into one house and rents the other to his friends, Pilon, Pablo, and Big Joe Portagee. No rent is ever actually paid, and Danny would not think to try to collect it, but the mere idea that rent is owed makes Danny a man of substance. When the friends accidentally burn down the spare house, they are forgiven and move in with Danny. Like any *paisano*, he gets past his troubles quickly.

As in "The Red Pony," Steinbeck showed a control, a restraint in his writing that now featured an accelerated pace and left behind his old awkwardness. Sentence by sentence, *Tortilla Flat* surges forward, pulling the reader along. One challenge—how to capture the *paisanos'* distinct accent and manner of speech, which is a blend of English and Spanish that sounds faintly like one or the other depending on which language you speak—is accomplished by the use of a formal and overly affectionate diction, the vocabulary of the uneducated when they want to sound otherwise. When Danny spots Pilon sneaking along the street with a bottle of brandy hidden inside his coat, he implores him to come to dinner, where he will have to share. "'I looked for thee, dearest of little angelic friends,' Danny says, 'for see, I have here two great steaks from God's own pig, and a sack of sweet white bread. Share my bounty, Pilon, little dumpling.'" When Pilon confesses that he has some brandy to go with the meal, Danny acts surprised.

Of all Steinbeck's books, *Tortilla Flat*, with its light, capering mood, is the pleasantest and most effortless to read. Steinbeck's love of magic and myth wafts through the story, and in one of the finest passages in all of his work, he describes how the *paisanos* spend St. Andrew's Eve. It's a date when some cultures believe supernatural things may occur. According to Monterey legend, buried treasure sends up an eerie glow through the ground on St. Andrew's Eve, and when darkness comes, the *paisanos* search the forest floor above Tortilla Flat, hoping to tread on this uncanny luminescence to reap its riches:

"The night came down as they walked into the forest. Their feet found the pine-needle beds. Now Pilon knew it for a perfect night. A high fog covered the sky, and behind it the moon shone, so that the forest was filled with a gauzelike light. There was none of the sharp outline we think of as reality. The tree trunks were not black columns of wood, but soft and unsubstantial shadows. The patches of brush were formless and shifting in the queer light. Ghosts could walk freely tonight, without fear of the disbelief of men; for this night was haunted, and it would be an insensitive man who did not know it."

Without fear of the disbelief of men: words that describe what every writer longs for.

In the end, Danny's elevated stature in Tortilla Flat is too great a burden for him, and he becomes remote and angry—emotions his friends cannot fathom. Hoping to cheer him up, they throw Danny a party. Everybody who lives in the Flat is there. It is a wild night. Danny becomes superhuman. He drinks three gallons of wine and has sex with every woman there, each bounding out willingly with him to the gulch behind the house, one and then another, as Danny keeps coming back for more. It is an unforgettable scene, and forever after it people will remember how it was. Danny finally goes mad that night, and as his anger increases, so does he. Danny grows huge, larger than anyone, and his eyes are inflamed, like those of a wild animal. Swinging a table leg to make his way through the crowd, Danny charges out of his house, into the night, running toward the gulch to do battle with a nameless demon. Everyone is frightened. Then there is a commotion—followed by silence. When his friends rush out to see what has happened, they learn the truth—that Danny was the same as all of them. He was only a man.

Robert Ballou had repaid Steinbeck's dogged loyalty by rejecting *Tortilla Flat*. He had also remaindered *The Pastures of Heaven* and *To a God Unknown*, and, after asking for a chance to consider publishing a volume of poetry by Carol, had not even acknowledged receiving her manuscript. While McIntosh & Otis searched for a new publisher for Steinbeck, there was one who would soon knock on their door.

The Argus Book Shop, on Dearborn Street in Chicago's Loop,

was a strange, lively outpost of literature. The shop dealt mostly in rare and collectible books, with some contemporary works mixed in. Its owner was a funny, colorful, insatiably curious man named Ben Abramson. The son of a junk peddler, Abramson was born in Lithuania in 1898. He came to America when he was five and lived with his family in the Chicago ghetto. He attended grammar school and then, as a teenager, partnered with a couple of pals in "hoboing" around the country on freight trains, stopping off now and then to earn some money. From an early age Abramson loved books and stayed up long into the night, reading. He started working in a Chicago bookstore in 1916 and by 1920 owned his own shop.

Abramson put out a chatty, informative catalogue called *Along the North Wall*, published limited editions of unusual books he liked, and discretely sold erotica, which led to at least one police raid on the Argus. When Robert McBride remaindered *Cup of Gold*, Abramson bought a few copies and was immediately taken with Steinbeck. He bought up the rest of the remainders as well as the unbound pages of *Pastures of Heaven* from Robert Ballou. Toward the end of 1934, a New York book publisher named Pascal "Pat" Covici—a principal in the firm Covici-Friede—was in Chicago on business when he walked into the Argus. After getting an earful from Abramson— and copies of *Cup of Gold* and *The Pastures of Heaven*—Covici started reading. Covici was impressed but proceeded cautiously. He asked Mavis McIntosh to let him see *Tortilla Flat*, which had been making the rounds and finding no takers. Covici wrote Steinbeck saying that he was interested in his work and hoped he could come to terms with Mavis McIntosh to become his publisher. Steinbeck told George Albee admiringly that Covici was "far from overenthusiastic." He said he liked Covici's restraint, which gave him confidence in the man. By early February, Steinbeck was under contract with Covici. They would remain partners until Covici's death three decades later.

Covici was a burly, opinionated Romanian who stood six feet three and had a snowy mane of white hair. He had previously run his own bookshop and then an artsy publishing house in Chicago before joining Donald Friede when they formed Covici-Friede in New York in

1929. The small firm—just seven employees at first, including Covici and Friede—had offices on West Forty-Fifth Street. Covici was already a minor legend, having published Ben Hecht's depraved *Fantazius Mallare*, the story of a mad, reclusive, phallus-obsessed sculptor, liberally illustrated with explicit drawings by Wallace Smith. All involved were arrested for indecency, a charge Covici wanted to fight in court, though he eventually pleaded no contest and paid a fine.

Soon an advance check for *Tortilla Flat* arrived. Steinbeck was also paid for a new story in the *North American Review*, and Carol—who had taken a job with the State Emergency Relief Administration—had finished typing his new novel, *In Dubious Battle*. He called it "a short life of a Communist," though that term is used judiciously in the book. It is the story of a fruit pickers' strike, and the efforts of officials from a workers' party in leading it. Steinbeck told Mavis McIntosh it was a "brutal" book, and he was sure she would not like it. He said he didn't like it himself.

Everything seemed to be happening at once. Covici-Friede sent Steinbeck a contract for *In Dubious Battle*, sight unseen. They also promised to reissue *The Pastures of Heaven* and *To a God Unknown*. George Albee's novel, *Not in a Day*, had come out, and Steinbeck stayed up until three in the morning reading it. He congratulated his friend and said he couldn't decide if it was high comedy or low—but that it was funny either way.

It's possible that Albee had recommended Steinbeck to his publisher, Alfred A. Knopf, because Steinbeck got three letters from Knopf asking about *In Dubious Battle*. He told Mavis McIntosh he'd also heard that Houghton Mifflin and Random House were eager to publish him. But Steinbeck wanted to stick with Covici-Friede, assuming they accepted *In Dubious Battle*. When he sent off the finished manuscript in mid-February, Steinbeck was under the impression that Covici might decide to rush it to publication ahead of *Tortilla Flat*. He told Mavis McIntosh if that was the case, he would forgo reviewing the galleys, as that would save three weeks. As it turned out, *In Dubious Battle* almost ended his relationship with Covici-Friede before it began.

Steinbeck was already on edge because he'd once again gotten a standard author's questionnaire and a request for a photo from Covici-Friede to use in promotion. He sent the questionnaire—blank—to Mavis McIntosh, begging her to "get me out of this sort of thing." He said it would be better coming from her, as she would be more tactful about it than he would. He said flatly that he always refused to be photographed. He said he understood that the publisher was not being unreasonable, but he didn't care.

In a stew, Steinbeck caught his breath long enough in the same letter to tell McIntosh that he was not upset with his publisher in England, who had cut a sex scene from *To a God Unknown*. "The English," he said, "have successfully denied the existence of carnal relations for some centuries now."

About a week later, he wrote to McIntosh again. To his surprise, she had told him she liked *In Dubious Battle*. Steinbeck quickly forgot about warning her it was "terrible," and instead expressed his impatience for a decision on it. He reminded McIntosh that Covici had a one-month option on the book and owed him $250 if he planned to publish it. The clock was running.

Unbeknownst to Steinbeck, his manuscript had arrived at the offices of Covici-Friede while Pat Covici was out of town. An assistant editor named Harry Bloch, who considered himself an expert on Marxist ideology, read it and decided that Steinbeck knew nothing about Communist organizing tactics. He fired off a three-page rejection letter to Steinbeck explaining the book's shortcomings in excruciating detail—in the process invalidating Steinbeck's contractual arrangement with the firm. Steinbeck, who assumed Covici had approved this answer, was incredulous. He complained to Mavis McIntosh that he was as annoyed as he was disappointed by Covici's attitude, which he said was a fine example of the kind of Communist rigidity he was pointing to in the book. He said he would leave it up to McIntosh & Otis whether to continue with Covici-Friede. He added that he was discouraged, for the moment, but that he wouldn't be tomorrow.

Steinbeck had hoped he and Carol would be able to get away to

Mexico that spring, but the sudden uncertainty around *In Dubious Battle* now made that unlikely. So did his father's deteriorating health. This time Steinbeck got some help from his family when John Ernst moved in with Steinbeck's sister Esther and her family in Watsonville. It was still an ordeal. Steinbeck visited his father often and the forty-mile round trip to Watsonville was a grind.

A month passed. Evidently Elizabeth Otis stepped in to deal with the situation at Covici-Friede, because she now became Steinbeck's main contact at McIntosh & Otis. In early May he told her he'd gotten another author's questionnaire from Covici-Friede. He'd thrown it away. He'd also had a visit in Pacific Grove from an editor with Macmillan who wanted to consider *In Dubious Battle* and asked what was happening with Covici. Steinbeck told him they'd just rejected the book. About the same time, Elizabeth Otis wired Steinbeck to explain that it had all been a regrettable mistake—that Harry Bloch had been dismissed when Covici returned, and they were eager to publish *In Dubious Battle.* Feeling he had the upper hand, Steinbeck wrote to Otis, telling her to advise Mr. Covici that he would not agree to any major changes in the book—and also that they owed him an advance. Within a few days Steinbeck got a letter from Otis and two from Covici setting everything straight. Steinbeck said he was glad to be with Covici-Friede.

All was well, except that Steinbeck's father had suffered a stroke— just like Olive—and was unlikely to recover. Whether he would last only days, or linger for months as she had, no one could say. He died before the month was out. Steinbeck felt a deep sadness, not because his father had died but because John Ernst had told him only months before that his life had been insignificant and that he hadn't done anything he wanted to do. In his dying days he admitted that his time on earth had been wasted. He'd missed everything.

— 9 —

TAKE OFF YOUR HAT, LENNIE

*T*ORTILLA *FLAT* WAS published in May of 1935, to a flood of positive reviews. Lewis Gannett, writing in the *New York Herald Tribune*, declared that John Steinbeck had "fulfilled that promise which some of us so enthusiastically discerned three years ago in his *Pastures of Heaven.*" Most critics appreciated Steinbeck's respectful portrayal of the *paisanos*—though a few reviewers noticed they were a disconcertingly carefree subset of the large portion of the population that the Depression had rendered involuntarily without work. A reviewer for the *San Francisco Chronicle* named Joseph Henry Jackson—with whom Steinbeck would become friends—mistook the book's inspiration by comparing the main characters to the protagonists of Alexandre Dumas's *The Three Musketeers.* But he thought the novel was so good he dared not write about it too closely, for fear of not being up to the task. In the end, he simply implored people to read it.

Steinbeck had dedicated the book to Susan Gregory. He told Elizabeth Otis he was surprised that a book he'd written mainly to take his mind off his mother's illness was causing a stir in Monterey. Hotel clerks were having to tell guests there was no such place as "Tortilla Flat," because tourists were scouring quiet neighborhoods in search of it. Steinbeck said he was politely but firmly turning down all requests for appearances. The publicity was astonishing and frightening. Fame, he said once more, filled him with dread.

Steinbeck instructed his agents to avoid getting him into any deal that promised lofty financial rewards. He didn't want to be trapped into promising anything in exchange for a large check. He'd suffered too much and too long making his work honest. Besides, his father had left him a little money—enough to see them through for a few years, if necessary. Of course, it wouldn't have taken much. Like just about everybody, the Steinbecks got by on next to nothing. Their wardrobe—work pants and sweatshirts for both Carol and him—helped. They were down-and-out twins.

By midsummer, Steinbeck said he was swamped with offers from people wanting to handle his business affairs, which for the time being didn't need much handling. He did agree to one unusual proposition. It came from a local magazine called the *Monterey Beacon*. The magazine, run by Steinbeck's friend Bruce Ariss, was in some way connected to a stable, and they offered Steinbeck the use of a fine riding horse in exchange for a short story they could publish. Steinbeck had one on hand that Elizabeth Otis had sent back, saying it was too salacious to submit to a publisher, so he made the trade. He told Mavis McIntosh that if she wanted her usual ten percent commission, she'd have to come to Monterey and take payment in the form of time on the horse.

The story, which became one of Steinbeck's most famous, was called "The Snake." It was inspired by Carol's account of watching Ed Ricketts feed a white rat to one of his rattlers. Carol had recalled the experience as a demonstration of how an aspect of nature that seemed gruesome really wasn't if you were open-minded about it. Steinbeck saw another layer of meaning. In his story, a severe-looking woman with black, lifeless eyes shows up one evening at a commercial biological lab on Cannery Row in Monterey. She finds Dr. Phillips, the owner—a slight young man with a blond beard—and asks if she can come in and talk to him about something. Phillips isn't happy about the interruption. He has just euthanized a cat that needs to be prepared for shipping, and he is also staging starfish embryos, killing them at twenty-minute intervals to make slides tracking their development—a finicky procedure could go wrong if he gets distracted. Reluctantly, Phillips lets the woman in and gives her an uncomfortable chair he hopes will discourage her from staying long. She promises she won't keep him from his work. Phillips shrugs and explains to her how he's mixing the starfish sperm and ova. When he asks if she'd like to have a closer look, she says no thank you. So he instead begins embalming the cat. The woman sits placidly by, unfazed.

Eventually the woman explains herself. She is interested in Phillips's snakes. She says she wants to see a big male rattler. It must be a male—she has to be sure of that. He points out one, a powerful specimen from Texas more than five feet long. She asks Phillips if she can buy the snake. He's shocked, but then she reminds him that selling specimens is his business. Besides, the woman says she will leave the snake here and only wants to visit him. But it's important that it be hers. They agree on five dollars. At one point, she lifts the lid of the cage and starts to reach in. Phillips pulls her away before she is bitten.

The woman asks Phillips to feed a rat to the snake, and after arguing weakly against it, he does. The snake approaches the rat. It lifts its heavy, wedge-shaped head off the sand and sways. When Phillips looks at the woman as she watches, his knees nearly buckle: She is swaying, too.

The snake bites the rat in a strike too quick to see and retreats. When the rat is dead, the snake returns to it:

"Now the snake came out of its corner again. There was no striking curve in its neck, but it approached the rat gingerly, ready to jump back in case it attacked. It nudged the body gently with its blunt nose, and drew away. Satisfied it was dead, the snake touched the body all over with its chin, from head to tail. It seemed to measure the body and to kiss it. Finally it opened its mouth and unhinged its jaws at the corners."

Appalled by the woman's fascination, Phillips struggles not to look directly at her for fear that her own mouth may be moving in the same way. The snake swallows the rat, pulling in the tail last, just as Carol had described it. Then the woman leaves. Phillips tries to comprehend what he has witnessed, sorting through what he knows about the psycho-sexual imagery—but nothing seems adequate to explain the woman. He waits for her to return, but she never does.

It's easy to see why Elizabeth Otis wouldn't touch "The Snake." Although it has over time acquired a reputation greater than it deserves, "The Snake" struck many critics as obvious and "synthetic," as one wrote. When it appeared in the story collection *The Long Valley* a few years later, even Steinbeck's friend Joseph Henry Jackson at the *San Francisco Chronicle* admitted that he didn't like it. Steinbeck probably felt the same way about "The Snake," given his casual decision to publish it in the local paper, where he could take pleasure in its shock value and not have to bother with fighting over it with his agents and publisher. It's easy to imagine that Steinbeck knocked it off with that very thing in mind. The story—phallic and creepy—is meant to disturb the reader and nothing more. At the *Monterey Beacon*, the barriers to publication were nil. Here was a chance to showcase a previously unpublished story from a now-famous local author. Besides, *Beacon* readers would get a thrill out of reading about the lab and would recognize Dr. Phillips as Ed Ricketts. Maybe this would lead them to wonder if the wild parties they'd been hearing about for years weren't even wilder and weirder than they thought.

Steinbeck had no idea how well *Tortilla Flat* was selling. But in August the *New York Times* reported that the book had topped the sales chart at Covici-Friede, which had its strongest July in two years. George Albee relayed a rumor that the book had sold about 4,000 copies and had gone into a fourth printing. That same month, Pascal Covici visited the Steinbecks in Pacific Grove. He brought Steinbeck a $300 royalty check. In the fall, with *The Pastures of Heaven* and *To a God Unknown* back in print, Elizabeth Otis told Steinbeck that *Tortilla Flat* had crept onto a handful of bestseller lists—which in those days were compiled city by city.

In September, Steinbeck and Carol finally went away to Mexico City. Soon after their arrival, McIntosh and Otis wired Steinbeck to tell him they had sold the film rights to *Tortilla Flat* to Paramount

Pictures for $4,000, a small fortune. He wrote back to both women to thank them. With that kind of financial security, maybe he would write a better book. At least he'd have more time to work on one. He doubted that Hollywood could turn *Tortilla Flat* into a decent movie, but since he had no plans ever to see it, he didn't care. He was more candid with George Albee. He told Albee he wasn't proud of selling his book to the pictures, but he and Carol were going to put the money in government bonds and pretend they didn't have it. And anyway, it wouldn't be the vast sum it sounded like once his publisher and his agents took their shares. Nothing had really changed.

But of course everything had changed.

Although Steinbeck found it hard to work in Mexico, he and Carol loved it there. He said the air was thick and wonderful and coated your skin like liquid. Carol, after the long confinements with Steinbeck's parents and the typing of two books, was in paradise. The local people adored her, and laughter seemed to follow her wherever she went. Carol loved to shop in the markets and proved to be a tenacious bargainer. When she haggled, a crowd gathered. She had been collecting pottery figures, and one day she asked a vendor if he had a bull. But she got her Spanish wrong and instead asked for a stud, which had produced a near riot. They had planned to stay in Mexico until January, but Steinbeck had an idea for a new book and was itchy to get at it. They were back in Pacific Grove before the end of the year.

When he got home, the kind of good news Steinbeck hated was waiting for him: *Tortilla Flat* had won the Commonwealth Club's California Book Award and he was invited to attend the ceremony. Allergic as ever to public appearances, Steinbeck was desperate to stay away from the event. He wrote to Joseph Henry Jackson at the *Chronicle*, begging him to intervene with the awards committee and so he wouldn't have to show up. He had no idea who had nominated *Tortilla Flat*, but if a prize were to be awarded, he felt it should go to the book, not to him. Or it could be handed over to Danny and Pilon and the other denizens of the Flat, to whom it properly belonged— which would have been a neat trick.

Apart from his aversion to any kind of public performance, Steinbeck had an instinct for privacy that bordered on pathological. Though some writers refuse any kind of public performance and instead insist that their work does all the talking, it is unusual for a writer to resist being *known*. Steinbeck was a tireless collector of characters and stories who could not bear the thought that anyone might want to collect him. He took whatever he wanted from the world—and gave back only words, which was not nothing but was less than what the world wanted. Who were these people who would not leave him alone, who pleaded with him to inscribe his name in books, who longed for him to stand up before a crowd and explain himself? They were like the critics who praised his work but didn't understand it—drawn to a flame not for the heat but to be part of the crowd around it. Nothing made him angrier than the expectation that he was obligated to perform for his admirers. He was always happy to enter into the narratives he created on the page—but was forever mad at the one he actually lived in. He told Jackson he prayed he'd never win another award.

The National Industrial Recovery Act, signed into law by President Roosevelt in the summer of 1933, was supposed to help workers by protecting their right to organize and bargain collectively. In California, the Cannery and Agricultural Workers Industrial Union forged ahead. The CAWIU was affiliated with both the Communist Party of the United States and its Trade Union Unity League—which reported to Moscow. Operating through the CAWIU, the Communist Party began sending trained organizers into California's farm fields.

That fall, California was hit by a series of strikes by agricultural workers demanding higher pay. Cotton growers—who had responded to the dire economic times by slashing pay for pickers to less than a third of what it had been in the late 1920s—were hard hit. Cotton production had expanded exponentially in the San Joaquin Valley during the 1920s. By 1933, it was the second-most-profitable crop in the state. Cotton pickers went on strike on October 4, and eventually some 18,000 walked off the job. When state authorities attempted to mediate the dispute, melees broke out in Arvin, Kern, Pixley, and across much of the Tulare County area of the Central Valley east of Salinas. The *New York Times* reported that "pitched battles" between farmers and strikers had resulted in four dead, two critically hurt, and a score of others injured. Lettuce pickers striking in Watsonville and Salinas had narrowly avoided the same fate. To prevent future strikes, bust up picket lines, quell any violence that might again erupt—and hoping to eradicate Communists—the growers organized themselves as the Associated Farmers of California, a powerful and aggressive defender of unfettered capitalism. In essence, the anti-union people had formed a union in furtherance of *their* cause. The Associated Farmers were supported by the California Chamber of Commerce and the State Farm Bureau, both of which helped expand the association to more than two dozen counties. The Associated Farmers distributed anti-union propaganda and maintained files on so-called radical organizers. Most importantly, they organized volunteer militias by committing to act as deputies to local law enforcement whenever labor trouble arose—and they recruited American Legion posts across the state to help. In the summer of 1934, the Associated Farmers staged practice mobilizations, some of them timed to coincide with unionizing efforts in case the workers weren't getting the message. The group's deputies were forbidden to carry guns, and were instead advised to arm themselves with pick handles. Many carried both, and any distinction between deputized law enforcement and vigilantism was slight.

The Communist Party of the United States had been organized in 1919, two years after the Russian Revolution. Its initial membership came from the left wing of the Socialist Party, but from the beginning it was split into factions. John Reed, the reporter and activist who'd covered the Russian Revolution and wrote *Ten Days That Shook the World*, led one group, while the other was composed of mostly eastern European immigrants united by the fact that almost none of them spoke English. In the coming years the party continued to be a coalition of rival groups. Although the 1930s would be remembered as a time of Communist ascendancy—perhaps because of their over-representation among intellectuals and writers—party membership held steady at around 50,000. Turnover was high. In the 1932 presidential election, the Communist Party nominee, William Foster, received 103,000 votes—far fewer than the Socialist Party candidate with nearly 900,000.

With the economy in ruins, American Communists believed their time had come. They initially opposed Roosevelt and the New Deal, which they saw as an attempt to save capitalism in its death throes—the very economic collapse Karl Marx had argued was inevitable. Communists stood ready to assume the vanguard in the "dictatorship of the proletariat." But there was a problem: Roosevelt was popular with workers, many of whom believed the New Deal would restore the economy and put the country back on its feet. Traditional unions proved to be better organizers than the Communists during the economic turmoil of the early 1930s. And with the rise of Hitler in Germany, Communists around the world shifted their focus to antifascism. The faded version of the Communist Party in the United States shifted priorities, too, and eventually supported Roosevelt and the New Deal.

Carol had talked Steinbeck into attending meetings of the John Reed Club in Carmel, where he met Lincoln Steffens, the muckraking journalist and an enthusiastic supporter of the Soviet Union. When Steinbeck learned that two Communist organizers were hiding out in nearby Seaside, he interviewed them. He didn't like Communists, but he hated bullies even more, and it was clear that farm workers were being bullied. Steinbeck wasn't ready to join any party, but he was ready for a fight.

Covici-Friede published *In Dubious Battle*—the title is from a line in Milton's *Paradise Lost* describing Satan's hopeless struggle with God—in February of 1936. This was a scant eight months after *Tortilla Flat*, which was still selling well. Although Pat Covici had assured Steinbeck that their initial rejection of the book had been a clumsy mix-up while he was away from the office, Covici worried that the now-departed Harry Bloch, the editor who had argued against the book, might have had a point. Maybe Steinbeck's depiction of the Red organizers was off. In the spring of 1935 Covici had slipped the manuscript to John Chamberlain, a book reviewer for the *New York Times*, to get his opinion ahead of publication. Chamberlain was a Yale-educated, self-described leftist, and a discerning critic who later in life reversed his politics and wrote for William F. Buckley's *National Review*. Chamberlain also knew Harry Bloch and regarded him as competent, so he must have wondered about being invited to second-guess Bloch's evaluation of the book. Chamberlain told Covici that he wasn't sure Steinbeck had gotten his Communist-style organizers right, but it seemed beside the point. *In Dubious Battle*, he said, was a "dramatic and stirring book."

The action takes place in the pressurized days of an apple-picker's strike organized by two representatives of the "Party." Mac, a seasoned Party insider and skilled organizer, is a mentor to Jim—a fresh recruit to the cause. Jim joins the Party not because of any political conviction, but because he is a victim of the collapsed economy. His father, a slaughterhouse worker and labor agitator, was routinely beaten up by the cops until one day three years before, when he was shot dead as he tried to dynamite the slaughterhouse. More recently, Jim's mother died while he was doing time in jail for vagrancy. When he's asked why he wants to join the Party, Jim says simply, "My whole family has been ruined by this system."

Normally, the Party doesn't send new members into the field. But Mac sees something in Jim and decides to take him on as an apprentice. He tells Jim they're headed for the Torgas Valley—a location invented by Steinbeck, where there are thousands of acres of apples ready to be picked and some 2,000 fruit tramps to do the picking. The Growers Association has announced a pay cut. Mac explains that if they can get a "good ruckus" going, it could well spread to the nearby cotton fields. Like the migrant workers, who move from one crop to the next as the seasons unwind, pay cuts migrate, too. If the workers take less for apples, they are sure to get less for picking cotton. Mac tells Jim he can teach him field tactics that he could never learn except by doing them for real. "I've been out, see?" says Mac. "I'll train you and then you can train new men. Kind of like teaching hunting dogs by running them with the old boys, see?"

Jim is elated at the prospect of finally doing something with his life, which is hollow and meaningless. As he and Mac hustle through a rail yard to jump the freight train that will take them to Torgas, Jim says he feels reborn. "Seems to me I never did much of anything," he admitted. "Everything's new to me." They bound into a boxcar as a train rolls through the yard. This kind of thing used to be dangerous, Mac says—in the old days, train crews would throw guys off moving trains if they caught them. But hard times have changed that, and now the rail workers look the other way.

Mac and Jim organize the apple pickers and launch a strike. When they can't stay on the grower's property, they find a place to set up their own camp. Mac calls in reinforcements, including a physician named Doc Burton. Burton—another of Steinbeck's characters loosely based on Ed Ricketts—is there to handle sanitation in the camp. Mac is glad to have him—they can't afford to run afoul of the health department—but he tells Doc that he's a mystery. The long exchange that follows is undoubtedly one of the passages that Covici's editor stumbled over.

Doc is not a member of the Party, and, as near as Mac can tell, does not even believe in the cause. Doc is amused by this. He tells Mac the problem with causes is that they come to an end, but history does not:

"Nothing stops, Mac. If you were able to put an idea into effect tomorrow, it would start changing right away." Doc says part of the problem is that "good" and "bad" are subjective. He says he wants to "see" things as they actually are. A strike, he says, is like an infection. It starts with a wound.

"Yes. Group-men are always getting some kind of infection. This seems to be a bad one. I want to *see*, Mac. I want to watch these group-men, for they seem to me to be a new individual, not at all like single men. A man in a group isn't himself at all; he's a cell in an organism that isn't like him any more than the cells in your body are like you. I want to watch the group and see what it's like."

Mac doesn't buy it. After all, he's leading a strike, and he is one man, an individual. There may be group-men in the strike, but they're acting at his direction. Mac says Doc's ideas don't have any practical application, that what he calls group-men is a kind of collective beyond what even the Party is for. "The trouble with you, Doc, is you're too Goddamn far left to be a Communist."

Soon the fight Mac is looking for comes, as the strikers are threatened by the growers and their vigilante thugs. Mac shows just how far he's willing to go for the cause when he says that if only a few strikers got shot, things would heat up nicely. As the strike turns more dangerous by the day, Steinbeck draws a gripping portrait of the dynamics behind it—the anger and fear and suspicion that lie just under the surface in the camp. For Steinbeck, this was the part of the human condition he could never abide: the abuse and oppression of anyone by someone more powerful. *In Dubious Battle* may be about Mac and Jim, but it is *for* the workers who are being exploited by the growers. And there is no way to make that story turn out right. It all comes to a tragic conclusion that is—as Steinbeck had warned Mavis McIntosh—not an end at all. Jim has his moment in the sun, learns something in the process, and then it is over.

At the *New York Times*, John Chamberlain's breathless rave confirmed the private judgment he'd offered Covici the previous spring. Chamberlain objected mildly to the setting—he said it was news to him that they grew apples in California—but was otherwise bowled over. He said *In Dubious Battle* was as exciting as *Tortilla Flat* was warming. And what set the book apart from other strike novels was the focus on the organizers rather than the strikers. Whether real Communists would agree with Steinbeck's version of their cause didn't matter, Chamberlain said.

Reviewers across the board noted the stark contrast between *In Dubious Battle* and *Tortilla Flat*. In the *San Francisco Chronicle*, Joseph Henry Jackson, after making this point, argued that the hero of the book was actually the strike and that people on both ends of the political spectrum were sure to find *In Dubious Battle* an objectionable mess. Bourgeois readers would be alarmed by its clear sympathies for the Party, while true Communists would feel that it fell short as a subversive guide to the workers' revolution. Jackson, however, thought those reservations missed the point. *In Dubious Battle* rose above any strict allegiance to ideology. It was a book to be read, not elevated to a manifesto.

A sharp-elbowed dissent came from a recent Vassar graduate named Mary McCarthy. In an annoyed review for *The Nation*, McCarthy overstepped her youth and inexperience—but raised an objection worth consideration. McCarthy wrote that Steinbeck was on solid ground in the way he described working people interacting with one another—how they sound, the way they think, their inherent guardedness. But when he comments on the action, McCarthy said, Steinbeck becomes "ponderous." McCarthy conceded that Steinbeck told a good yarn, but that his obsession with crowds and how they behave was second-rate metaphysics that lacked proof. This was just so much excess weight the novel carried like a rim of fat around its middle. Look closely at this book, she argued, and you'll see the flab.

It was a fair point, but had McCarthy demonstrated more familiarity with, say, "The Red Pony" or *Tortilla Flat*, she might have concluded that Steinbeck was more than capable of unencumbered narrative and might have wondered about his aim in this book rather than simply trashing it. Steinbeck was still working out his phalanx theory as late as 1935, and in an unpublished essay called "Argument of Phalanx" he made many of the same points he did in *In Dubious Battle*—and added an all-important coda that was not in the book. By failing to observe and understand groups, we fail to see how the world actually works and instead find ourselves surrounded by "meaningless, unrelated and destructive phenomena." It's arguable that in *In Dubious Battle* Steinbeck's point about crowds was that the only way to understand them is to watch them and see how they behave—to, as Doc Burton puts it, *see* the superorganism in action. It was Steinbeck's way of saying that whatever the organizers expect to accomplish, the strike group will assume its own identity and in the end will confound their plans.

McCarthy, at the time only twenty-three years old, was sympathetic to the Communist cause and perhaps didn't want to look too hard for Steinbeck's purpose once she had convinced herself he didn't have one. She went on to have quite a life, getting married four times—including once to the literary critic Edmund Wilson, a grudging admirer of Steinbeck, though Steinbeck never felt the same way about McCarthy.

As for Harry Bloch, who had been responsible for *In Dubious Battle*'s near-death experience at Covici-Friede—he landed on his feet after leaving New York some time later. His wife, whom John Chamberlain said "looked like an Aztec princess," was the daughter of Mexico's finance minister. When they moved to Mexico City, she helped Bloch secure a contract to publish the city's telephone directory. Bloch earned a fortune and moderated his enthusiasm for the Communist cause.

Steinbeck considered Bloch the kind of half-hearted fellow traveler that was common back then. "Except for the strikers and the field organizers who were pretty tough monkeys and devoted, most of the so-called Communists I met were middle class, middle-aged people playing a game of dreams. I remember a woman in pretty easy circumstances saying to another even more affluent, 'After the revolution even we will have more, won't we dear?'"

One piece of fallout from *In Dubious Battle* must have convinced Steinbeck that he was on the verge of becoming a prominent author, much as he claimed to disdain that prospect. Out of the blue, Robert McBride resurfaced, threatening a lawsuit over Covici's reissue of *Cup of Gold*, on grounds of copyright infringement. Steinbeck was unfazed by this. At his father's urging he'd earlier clarified that he was the copyright holder. He told Elizabeth Otis to let McBride sue. He doubted he would have the nerve.

.   .   .

As the critics debated the politics of *In Dubious Battle*, Steinbeck told the bookseller Ben Abramson that he was one of the few people who seemed to realize that it was a novel. Abramson replied that his daughter had read and liked it. It was "hardly a book for a child," Steinbeck thought, but he was only slightly surprised. When he was young, he preferred his books "bloody." He wished he could make the world so vivid in his work that adults, who lack the "clear fine judgment of children," would experience it freely and enter into a book without reservation. There were everyday marvels all around us—birds singing in trees, lazy afternoons. Steinbeck claimed that once, in Salinas, he had seen an African lion in the vacant lot across the street. If he told that story well enough, who could say that he hadn't? That was the reason, he said, that he was currently at work on a book for children.

If this was true, no sign of such a book ever came to light. What Steinbeck did next was not a children's book as such—though it would launch countless high school book reports in decades to come. In the spring of 1936, it was apparently well along. He told Elizabeth Otis it would be done by midsummer. He expected to finish it in a new house that he and Carol were building near Los Gatos, in the foothills of the Santa Cruz Mountains, a dozen miles southwest of San Jose. Carol was overseeing the project while Steinbeck kept writing in Pacific Grove. The house was simple but ample, with a large living room under a beamed ceiling, two bedrooms, and a writing room, plus a long porch across the front. Steinbeck had the living room wired for sound and installed a fancy phonograph for his record collection. It would be a glorious retreat from the claustrophobia and hard partying in Pacific Grove. It would also be a relief to escape the oppressive fogs of summer.

For a while, Steinbeck called his short novel-in-progress *Something That Happened*, which was either a dry swipe at a story he didn't trust, or simply a placeholder until he thought of a better title. Eventually, he did—*Of Mice and Men*.

Completion of the new house was delayed until nearer the end of summer, as was the manuscript. And there was a new distraction.

An editor for the *San Francisco News* named George West came to see Steinbeck just after he'd gotten settled in Los Gatos. They'd met sometime earlier at Lincoln Steffens's house. West asked Steinbeck to write a series of stories for the paper on the Dust Bowl migrants pouring into California. Steinbeck agreed to do it. He bought a used bakery delivery truck, outfitted it for roadside camping, and set off for the San Joaquin Valley, accompanied by an official from the Federal Resettlement Administration. The FRA—a year later it would become the Farm Security Administration—was working to set up clean, well-managed camps for migrants who were otherwise living in appalling conditions in ditches and fields.

As you go west from the Mississippi River valley, the land rises steadily and mile by mile becomes drier. Tall-grass prairie gives way to the short grass of the high plains, and farther westward, these scrublands disappear, too—in mountains, and ultimately in a true desert of sage and mesquite where only five inches of rain fall in a year. And because not every newcomer who journeyed west was set on reaching the Pacific Ocean, this hard region gradually became populated—not all of it, certainly not the driest parts, but enough to make problems when things went bad. In 1878, John Wesley Powell— the great explorer of the American West—published his monumental *Report on the Lands of the Arid Region of the United States*, whose title alone should have given pause to anyone thinking this was a place suitable for farming. For a sizable portion of the American West, according to Powell, farming was likely to be a losing proposition. "Many droughts will occur; many seasons in a long series will be fruitless; and it may be doubted whether, on the whole, agriculture will prove remunerative." A dry summation of a dry place.

The settlers came anyway, mostly eastern-born farmers looking for a new chance and bringing with them methods suitable for raising row crops on small acreages in a moderate climate. It was difficult from the start, but now and then the rains came and people were convinced that the good years were the norm. This pattern repeated itself, from boom to bust and back again. And still they tried. They broke the sod of the prairies, tilled their land, and eventually watched it blow away. Russell Lord, of the U.S. Soil Conservation Service, wrote in a remarkable government pamphlet called "To Hold This Soil" that when native vegetation binds the land together, it is sustained by natural replenishment. As the soil wears away slowly, new soil is added in a continual process of destruction and renewal. This was the enduring cycle of the earth left alone, Lord explained:

> But if you take off the cover, rip off trees or sod, pulverize the soil with steel implements, push it too hard, deprive it of its spongy remains of organic growths which help to make soil more absorptive and hold the top of a field together—then you smash the natural balance; and Nature, quite impersonally, starts taking soil away from the top much faster than it grinds, mellows, and builds new soil from below. New soil is chipped and pulverized from parent materials and weathered into being, particle by particle, at the same slow rate as of old. Mature and fertile soil goes off by carload lots with the rain, or leaves on the wind, or both.

The Great Plains had started losing its farm population in the 1920s, and in the 1930s the Depression and extreme heat and drought accelerated the exodus—though hard times and the hostile climate were not the only factors. Increasing mechanization—including the use of tractors—displaced farm workers, and so did government policies that dealt with surpluses by taking land out of production. Even though the total population of the region continued to grow, some 2.5 million people deserted farms in a migration away from both a place and a way of life. In America, people tended to move east to west, following more or less the latitude on which they began. And so the migrants from the northern tier landed in the Pacific Northwest, while people arriving from the southern plains ended up in California. Hailing from Texas, Arkansas, Kansas, Missouri, and Oklahoma—though Okies all—as many as half a million migrants arrived in California in the mid-1930s.

At best slightly educated and having no skills but farming, the new arrivals hired on wherever crops needed harvesting. They were the most recent in a long line of migrants who followed the harvests from one end of the Central Valley to the other. Once it had been the Chinese. Then the Japanese. More recently it was the Mexicans and Filipinos, whom John Steinbeck had worked alongside at Spreckels. What they all had in common was that they had nothing but careers of desperation.

Steinbeck went first to the Gridley Labor Camp, north of Sacramento, before heading south to cotton country. In mid-August, at Arvin, fifteen miles southeast of Bakersfield, he met a dynamic migrant-camp director named Tom Collins. Collins had joined the FRA only the year before—he'd been a teacher and a social worker previously—but was already a force in the government's efforts to provide decent living conditions for the migrants. Gaunt, weathered, and usually dressed in white, Collins stood out in the place they called "Weedpatch." The camp was a project of the Works Progress Administration, the New Deal's biggest agency, which had put millions of people on the government payroll. The WPA did construction projects—buildings and roads—but also underwrote cultural projects by writers and artists.

Housing at Weedpatch consisted of tents on raised wooden platforms; later these were replaced by shacks. There were communal bathrooms and showers. For many residents, it was the first time they'd seen a toilet. More than 400 people were living in the camp in August of 1936, about 170 of them children. Of the eighty-four groups in the camp—families and friends who arrived together—fifty-three were from Oklahoma. Most of the group heads had some kind of work: grape picking, weed pulling, irrigation projects, day labor. Weekly income averaged $15. As the grape season came to an end, many of the workers planned to pick cotton. But rumors circulated that the Associated Farmers would propose a 20 cents per hour wage, and this worried everyone—not because it was so low, but because it was so high that labor would flood into the county and make it harder to find work.

Tom Collins monitored the activities of the Associated Farmers in his weekly camp reports. If anyone doubted the growers' resolve, there was word from Bakersfield that in August the Associated Farmers had held a secret meeting at which they discussed how they would handle a cotton strike if one happened:

> Are we law abiding and liberty loving citizens ready and prepared for a strike? Have we sufficient arms and ammunition?

The migrant camp practiced self-government, which relied on cooperation and common sense, as many of the residents were barely literate. This democracy-on-the-ground made the camps a threat to the growers; the migrants there were easier to organize than in isolated makeshift camps spread across the countryside. Migrants who arrived and requested FRA assistance were interviewed about their situation. One typical respondent, a fifty-eight-year-old man from Oklahoma, gave his profession as "farmer." In 1932, his last good year, he'd earned $2,000. But in the drought years of 1933–35, that had dropped to $600 and then $300. He'd arrived at Weedpatch with five dependents and personal possessions worth a total of $50, including his car. He said he had never gone to school.

Collins found these people remarkable. In the same report, he noted that whenever a destitute family arrived at the camp, the residents cared for them without hesitation. In one case that month, a man had given up his job for a day so a newcomer could earn enough money to buy food for his family. Collins saw it again and again:

> How fine are these people! How truly generous! As a visitor put it this week, "I've never seen so many REAL happy people in my life."

Steinbeck's name appeared in the visitors' log for that report, and he managed to enlist Collins in a tour of the area beyond the camp. Collins and Steinbeck called his truck the "pie wagon," and they drove it from one haphazard encampment to the next. Steinbeck described what he saw in his series of seven stories for the *News* titled "The Harvest Gypsies."

He reported that at least 150,000 homeless migrants were following the harvests in California, a "shifting group of nomadic, poverty-stricken harvesters driven by hunger" to find work as they might—many living unseen in "filthy squatters' camps." The actual numbers varied all the time, but were probably much higher. It was the "unique nature of California agriculture," with its large farms, back-to-back growing seasons, and diversity of crops, that made such a workforce necessary. Being strangers, they met the same insults as outsiders have throughout history: reflexive animus and mistrust. The migrants were believed to be dirty, carriers of disease, and—worst of all—prone to organize and ruin the harvests with their strikes. "Thus in California we find a curious attitude toward a group that makes our agriculture successful," Steinbeck wrote. "The migrants are needed, and they are hated."

A lucky few found their way into the sanitary camps run by the government and compassionate managers like Tom Collins. Many more lived on their own, wherever they could hide their misery, in conditions of surpassing squalor. Steinbeck observed their open latrines in willow clumps and the "absolute terror" of starvation in the faces of once-proud families. He watched as flies collected on the eyes and mouths of malnourished and hookworm-ridden children. This was in America. Horrified, Steinbeck did his best to describe what he'd seen:

"The squatters' camps are located all over California. Let us see what a typical one is like. It is located on the banks of a river, near an irrigation ditch or on a side road where a spring of water is available. From a distance it looks like a city dump, and well it may, for the city dumps are the sources for the material of which it is built. You can see a litter of dirty rags and scrap iron, of houses built of weeds, of flattened cans or of paper. It is only on close approach that it can be seen that these are homes."

Steinbeck let the facts speak for themselves, but the facts were terrible enough that each installment in the series was another stab of cold anger at the systemic oppression of a helpless group of people. When the Associated Growers in one county claimed that they didn't need to deal with strikers through the law or the courtroom—trials cost too much, they said—Steinbeck wrote that their "better way" for dealing with their problems was a "system of terrorism that would be unusual in the Fascist nations of the world."

In the end, Steinbeck—displaying a newfound maturity and a remarkably dispassionate judgment—argued that the best way to deal with the migrant issue was to recognize that in some respects, it was nobody's fault. You could blame the Dust Bowl on bad practices, but you couldn't really lay that at the feet of a starving child. Conceding California's problematic history with nonwhite foreign farm workers, he called this a legacy of abuse that it would be wise to undo; these new American migrants were going to force matters just by being there. Steinbeck thought it was time to do the right thing: "The new migrants to California from the dust bowl are here to stay. They are the best American stock, intelligent, resourceful; and, if given a chance, socially responsible. To attempt to force them into a peonage of starvation and intimidated despair will be unsuccessful. They can be citizens of the highest type, or they can be an army driven by suffering to take what they need. On their future treatment will depend the course they will be forced to take."

When Steinbeck got home, Ted Miller, his old Stanford pal and one-time informal agent, provided a welcome diversion from what Steinbeck had seen by sending him a trove of early rejection letters from publishers. Steinbeck wrote to thank him, though he remembered those days with a shiver. Each rejection had felt like a "little doom." And it hadn't been that long ago. He could only hope that chapter of his life was in the past, though you could never be sure about such things. He told Ted that he and Carol were enjoying life on their two acres in Los Gatos. It wasn't big enough to be called a farm, though Steinbeck hinted at wanting one. But owning more land would have meant either reducing his work—which was out of the question—or hiring help. That wouldn't work, either, Steinbeck said. He was too humbled by hired people to tell them what to do and would end up doing everything himself.

The *San Francisco News* dragged its feet about getting "The Harvest Gypsies" into print. Steinbeck told George Albee they were holding the stories out of fear about the "labor situation." The press in California would write about labor only if its members were depicted as subhuman. When the *News* recovered from its attack of nerves— after all, the paper had *asked* Steinbeck for the series—the stories finally ran in October. Before that, Steinbeck had managed to place a short piece about the migrants in *The Nation*. Steinbeck told Ben Abramson that California was on the brink of a civil war. He hoped that would be averted, but it was clear to him that he'd be writing about what was happening. It figured to be a busy year.

There was bad news from Monterey. On November 25, 1936, an

Tom Collins, director of the federal migrant camp at Arvin, California, known to its residents as Weedpatch. *(Dorothea Lange, National Archives)*

electrical surge on Cannery Row started a fire in the Del Mar Canning Company next door to Ed Ricketts's lab. The lab went up in flames, and Ricketts—who still lived there—lost almost everything but the clothes he was wearing and a few papers. Although he had insurance, Ricketts was able to recoup only a fraction of his losses after the power company convinced investigators that it was blameless for the fire, which was instead attributed to an act of God. Ricketts could forgive God over the lab itself—with help from many friends, he was able to rebuild—but losing his phonograph records and especially his library was harder to take. Steinbeck loaned Ricketts $6,000. That same month, Steinbeck sent a radio to Tom Collins as a present for the migrants, making it a banner week for the residents of Weedpatch. They'd raised enough money to buy a football and a volleyball. Collins said they hoped to find some playing cards and a checkerboard, but that would take time. Patience was one thing they did have plenty of.

George Albee wrote Steinbeck after the *News* series came out, wondering if he was in danger. Steinbeck assured him he was safe. The only risk he faced was going broke. He and Carol planned to start being more frugal, since he didn't think a little book like *Of Mice and Men* would make a penny. But in January the tide of success Steinbeck had been riding for two years turned into a tsunami.

Elizabeth Otis informed Steinbeck that *Of Mice and Men* had been chosen as a Dual Main selection by the Book-of-the-Month Club for March. This meant a large printing and more money than Steinbeck could imagine. He told Otis that any amount of money greater than two dollars was an abstraction to him. None of it seemed real. Maybe he and Carol would finally do some of the traveling they'd always longed to do, but he hedged. They'd decided to do this before and ended up not going. It was always something. He also said his new book—a big one based on his reporting from the migrant camps—was turning out to be harder to write than he'd anticipated. He had no idea when it might be done.

Of Mice and Men was published in late February. It bolted onto the bestseller lists, and before the month was out Joseph Henry Jackson told Steinbeck that Covici-Friede had already sold a staggering 117,000 copies. When Steinbeck wrote to Pat Covici, he couldn't find much to say, other than "that's a hell of a lot of books." A month later, sales were averaging 1,000 copies a day. Steinbeck told Covici that their travel plans were firming up. They would take a slow freighter to New York in April, and then cross over to Europe. He suggested that Covici get on a train to California and join them on the voyage to New York. It would be a peaceful thirty-one days at sea. Covici didn't come.

They started their trip even earlier than planned, sailing on March 23 aboard the *Sagebrush*. In the month since its publication, *Of Mice and Men* had become a sensation. Steinbeck was mortified by the smothering attention, even when it didn't touch him directly. He was, however, pleased by the prospect of seeing the book turned into a play. Annie Laurie Williams, the dramatic rights agent at McIntosh & Otis, had made a deal with the prominent playwright and director George S. Kaufman. *Of Mice and Men* was headed to Broadway in the fall. Steinbeck had thought from the beginning that the story—which broke naturally into a handful of acts—would translate to the stage. Kaufman agreed.

Steinbeck wrote to Williams before he and Carol left to say that he was going to work on the handful of suggestions Kaufman had made for a script and would try to have a draft by the time they reached New York. He also pleaded with her to limit his exposure to the public. He'd already instructed Covici to stop sending out his photograph to the press. He'd been recognized on the street in San Francisco the other day and it made him physically ill. If people demanded to know something about him, they could be told that *Of Mice and Men* was an experiment with a play that could be read as a novel—or a novel that could be played. Steinbeck hoped the press could be thrown off his trail and leave him to tend to his "pack of lumbering dogs," which was evidently an invention of the publicity department at Covici-Friede. Steinbeck had only one dog, at the moment an English setter named Toby.

· · ·

Richard Albee said that Steinbeck was attracted to "big, simple guys." Innocents, Albee called them. Albee remembered that Steinbeck liked to tell a story about one, a strapping farmhand. Whether Steinbeck heard it somewhere or made it up isn't known. As Steinbeck told it, the man would spend all day plowing, and when he finished, he'd comb out his draft horse and then change his clothes and slick down his own hair. Then he'd ride over the ridge, to another farm where two young women lived. He always stopped short of their property. He'd sit there, a silent giant on a big horse, staring at the farmhouse for as long as it took. When one of the women at last came out into the yard, he'd shout at the top of his voice, "*Think you're kind of pretty, don't you?*" And then he'd turn and ride back over the ridge to his house without another word.

In *Of Mice and Men*, Steinbeck imagined a crueler version of the story, one complicated by a partner who looks out for the witless innocent. Barely a hundred pages long, the book tells the darkening story of two men who are less the victims of hard times than they are misplaced on the fringes of society. George Milton and Lennie Small are two bindle stiffs traveling together from one job to the next. Steinbeck introduces them on a sultry evening by the banks of the Salinas River south of Soledad, as they emerge from a grove of willows and sycamores:

"They had walked in single file down the path, and even in the open one stayed behind the other. Both were dressed in denim trousers and in denim coats with brass buttons. Both wore black, shapeless hats and both carried tight blanket rolls slung over their shoulders. The first man was small and quick, dark of face, with restless eyes and sharp, strong features. Every part of him was defined: small, strong hands, slender arms, a thin and bony nose. Behind him walked his opposite, a huge man, shapeless of face, with large, pale eyes, with wide, sloping shoulders; and he walked heavily, dragging his feet a little, the way a bear drags his paws. His arms did not swing at his sides, but hung loosely."

As the two men sit by the river—they're on their way to jobs on a ranch they'll reach the next day—it becomes clear that they have a symbiotic relationship, in which they function as two parts of a single personality. George, the smaller man, is in charge of Lennie, a hulking simpleton who would otherwise be lost in the world, a man so witless and unaware of his own strength that he's an accidental menace. Lennie has trouble with everything—where they are going, where they were before, how they got here. Life unfolds for Lennie minute by minute, with no past and no future other than the one George has imagined for them countless times. Guys like us that work on ranches, George says, are the loneliest guys in the world. They get a job, make a little money, spend it in a night or two in town, and move on. Nobody cares what becomes of them, nobody looks out for them if they get in trouble. But not us, George promises. For us, he says, it's all going to turn out different. They'd save up, buy a piece of land and a little house, a plan that makes Lennie as happy as if it had actually already happened to them.

George and Lennie never get to that promised land. For millions of readers the fleeting story of George and Lennie is a pastoral tragedy, doom in a pretty place. The friendship between George and Lennie is only a brief standoff with a world that has no place for men like them. Or, rather, a world that has one *exact* place for them—the losing end of every situation in which they will ever find themselves. George and Lennie are barely visible. They are men who pass through life with no families and no history, leaving no evidence of having lived at all.

At the ranch, George and Lennie move into the bunkhouse with the other hired men—and soon meet trouble. It's the boss's son, Curley. Curley is small and mean, a former lightweight boxer always looking for a bigger guy he can knock around. Curley wears a glove on his left hand, and the men say that hand is coated in Vaseline to keep it soft for Curley's wife. She is an entirely different kind of trouble. It doesn't take long for Lennie to have problems with both of them, and when Lennie loses control, he and George have to make a run for it. But all is lost this time. Lennie has done something unspeakable. When they meet up at the same place where the story began, George has a gun with him. He knows that if the men hunting them catch up with Lennie, it will be terrible. Like a dog that's too old or too sick to be left alive—and like a dog that doesn't know any of those things—Lennie's life has come to an end. He and George look across the water to the Gabilan Mountains going dark at sundown. The sounds of men shouting drift along the riverbank. The gun is in George's pocket. There is a pleasant breeze. George's voice shakes. "Take your hat off, Lennie. The air feels fine."

Once again, the critics admired Steinbeck's versatility. Here was another book completely different from those he had written before. His ability to render the speech of common men was better than ever. It had achieved a perfect pitch that was making him the voice of the downtrodden. George and Lennie are only two men—I got you an' you got me—but they are emblematic of the legions living in despair. Heywood Broun, in a review placing Steinbeck ahead of his peers, said *Of Mice and Men* was much better than Margaret Mitchell's hugely popular—and much longer—*Gone With the Wind*. Broun was impressed that Steinbeck had hollowed a niche for himself in American literature that placed him between the romantics of the past and the hard-bitten realists of the day. Wilbur Needham, in the *Los Angeles Times*, praised the novel's brevity, saying there was more to it than most books twice its size. Shrewdly, Needham observed that the book's stark pages were either filled with subtexts or were devoid of them. The reader, he said, would have to decide.

As if to prove Needham's point, the First Lady, Eleanor Roosevelt, included a brief mention of the book in her syndicated column, "My Day." Mrs. Roosevelt chose to find an uplifting theme about the importance of friendship in Steinbeck's story, noting how "fortunate we are when we have real friends, people we can count on." It's a reading that grows chilling the more you think about it. What are friends for, if not to stand behind you when trouble comes?

— IO —

THE HUNDRED-DAY SIEGE

As the Great Depression eased, powerful and frightening forces that would fuel a worldwide economic recovery and at the same time lead to an unthinkable conflagration began to appear in faraway places. Fascism took hold in Italy and Germany, and civil war erupted in Spain. Japan, seized by a martial imperialism, invaded and occupied Manchuria. When President Roosevelt tried to send aid to China, Japan resisted—and aligned itself with Hitler and Mussolini. Germany invaded the Rhineland, Italy invaded Ethiopia, and together they provided assistance to Francisco Franco, leader of the fascist side in Spain. The elements of another great war were falling into place. In 1937, CBS sent a twenty-nine-year-old radio producer named Edward R. Murrow to London to line up interviews with European newsmakers. Murrow, who was from Polecat Creek, North Carolina, and had changed his name from Egbert to Edward in college, soon found himself reporting live—often in the middle of the night so as to be heard during evening hours back in the States—on German aggression across Europe, first with the annexation of Austria and later through the Munich Agreement, in which Germany acquired the Sudetenland region of Czechoslovakia. Americans turned up their radios whenever they heard the announcer in New York launch another report with the words "Calling Ed Murrow. Calling Ed Murrow."

As the threat of a wider war grew, Steinbeck remained haunted by what he'd seen in the migrant camps. But his early attempts to write about them stalled. He and Carol traveled to the Soviet Union and Sweden. They sailed to Europe on the Swedish American liner *Drottningholm*, spending much of the crossing in a fog bank—which must have felt like home. They arrived back in New York in August just in time to meet with George Kaufman—who whisked them off to his country place in Bucks County, Pennsylvania, to work on the script for *Of Mice and Men*. Steinbeck was shy around Kaufman and couldn't wait to get back to California. In the meantime, he could scarcely believe that Covici had issued a deluxe, limited edition of *The Red Pony*. It was a handsome volume, but was priced at $10, which Steinbeck found outrageous. "I wouldn't pay ten dollars for a Gutenberg Bible," he said. Maybe not, but the edition was oversubscribed.

Of Mice and Men opened at the Music Box Theatre on Broadway near the end of November. It starred Wallace Ford as George, twenty-five-year-old newcomer Broderick Crawford as Lennie, and Claire Luce as Curley's wife. Luce, a shimmery former Ziegfeld star, had danced with Fred Astaire in the musical *The Gay Divorcee*. Astaire wanted her for the film version but was overruled and was instead paired with Ginger Rogers. But Luce was perfect for Steinbeck's character.

The play was a sensation and ran for more than 200 performances. After the curtain came down on opening night, Elizabeth Otis and Annie Laurie Williams telephoned Steinbeck in Los Gatos—he wouldn't have dreamed of attending the premiere—telling him it had gone splendidly. He and Carol didn't have a phone yet, so they had to drive five miles into town to take the call. Pat Covici had wired after each act, telling Steinbeck the same thing. George Kaufman was more measured. He said the opening had gone fine, but he wasn't sure yet how good the play was.

The critics had few reservations. One of the most enthusiastic was the influential critic for the *New York Times*, Brooks Atkinson. Atkinson had been editor of the *New York Times Book Review* before moving to the drama desk in 1925, where he established himself as a force who could singlehandedly make a play a hit—or close it—overnight.

In his next-day review of the opening, Atkinson liked just about everything—Steinbeck's lean story, Kaufman's "adroit" staging of it, and the performances of a first-rate ensemble. But what really caught Atkinson's attention was the way Steinbeck balanced the story's dark trajectory with appreciative portraits of regular men at work. Clearly, Atkinson wrote, Steinbeck had empathy for his characters. But it was the lean narrative that brought them to life.

After the play was a hit, Atkinson—who had lately complained about the "commercial theatre," with its lack of spontaneity and its overreliance on Shakespeare and revivals of established works—wrote again about *Of Mice and Men* a few weeks later, offering to eat his words. *Of Mice and Men*, he wrote, was commercial to its core—and also a "masterpiece," among the best new plays of the year. Steinbeck's story, Atkinson said, was both a perfect work of art and a shattering emotional experience.

Steinbeck wrote George Kaufman a letter expressing his gratitude and saying that he and Carol could scarcely believe their good fortune in having collaborated with a director of his stature. Who were they to have such luck? Steinbeck said that sometimes when he was writing, his characters became more real to him than he was to himself. That the play managed to do the same thing to an audience for two magical hours was gratifying.

Of Mice and Men won the New York Drama Critics' Circle Award as the best play of the season, beating out Thornton Wilder's *Our Town*.

It was a curious time to be John Steinbeck. Arnold Gingrich published "The Snake" and several other stories in *Esquire*, all of them pieces Gingrich had earlier rejected. Steinbeck told his agents to not charge Gingrich for "The Snake," since he'd already been paid by the *Monterey Beacon* with the use of a horse. Gingrich sent him a watch instead. Steinbeck had to field inquiries from movie people, which he met with hostility. Zeppo Marx called. Steinbeck said he didn't want to know what it was about. Myron Selznick's office offered to manage his Hollywood affairs. Steinbeck answered that he didn't have any such affairs to manage. He and Carol finally got a telephone at the house, so at least he didn't have to drive into town every time something like this came up. He also bought a new typewriter, stepping up from his 1912 model. The new one could type accents and even had the diacritical mark known as a tilde.

In early 1938, Steinbeck reviewed a stage adaptation of *Tortilla Flat*, which was headed to Broadway. He found it funny but riddled with problems. Exasperated, he wired Annie Laurie Williams to see if she could get the playwright to come to California to work on it with him. The next day, he wrote Williams a letter saying he regretted the telegram. The problem was that the more he and Carol read the script out loud, the worse they thought it was. But he knew he had to surrender. If one small scene that he didn't like was dropped, he said he'd sign off on the rest. When the play opened in January— *Of Mice and Men* was still running—Carol went to New York by herself for the opening and to spend time seeing the city with Elizabeth Otis. Carol reported that the play was awful. It closed after four performances. Steinbeck hoped this would dissuade Paramount from making a movie of the book.

Steinbeck felt overwhelmed—by the phone calls, the mail, the success he had always longed for and yet feared more than anything else, and by the demands made of him. A pregnant woman named Alice Kempff, whom he had known years before, hired an attorney to pursue a paternity claim against him. It was a fabrication, and he told Elizabeth Otis he hoped it would go away, but if it didn't, he had any number of identifying marks and scars on his body that Kempff would be unable to describe in court. According to Richard Albee, Steinbeck grew paranoid about his fame. He worried that his friends would no longer like him, and that other people he didn't know were after him. Albee said Steinbeck walked around with steel bolts in his pockets, ready to press them into his fists if he got in a fight.

The most troubling development was a falling-out with Richard Albee's older brother George, his longtime friend and confidant. George now lived on the other side of the country—in upstate New York—but had managed to anger Steinbeck past the breaking point.

Steinbeck and Albee were both represented by McIntosh & Otis, and for some time Steinbeck had been hearing that Albee told their agents lies about him. When he couldn't stand any more of it, Steinbeck wrote to Albee and said he was sick of hearing that Albee had stabbed him in the back again. But he also betrayed a larger and less specific pain that had more to do with his transformation into a well-known author. Steinbeck said his recent days had been hard and unhappy, and that Albee was the only one of his friends who had not tried to help. It was just the opposite. Albee seemed intent on ruining him.

As much as Steinbeck regretted the situation, he was glad to have their disagreement out in the open at last, rather than conducting it by rumor. He ended on a cryptic note, saying that there could be only one reason why Albee hated him at a time when Steinbeck needed his support. Steinbeck seemed to be alluding to envy on Albee's part— which would have been understandable, though not a justification for attacking Steinbeck. But Steinbeck had it all wrong, as it turned out.

Albee had remained a loyal friend and was as much in the dark about what had happened between them as Steinbeck was. The truth was a long time in coming to light. Years after the fact, Richard Albee said his brother was jealous of Steinbeck's talent and success, and that this had caused the rupture. But he later took that back and instead told an astonishing story.

The source of the innuendo about Steinbeck was Anne Albee, George's wife. Anne was an arresting presence, beautiful and nearly six feet tall. She had exquisite taste and worked as a clothing buyer for several department stores. And she was insane. When Steinbeck knew her in Los Angeles, he thought Anne was one of the best storytellers he'd ever met. Nobody realized that she was a pathological liar. Anne said she belonged to a wealthy family that lived in a mansion in the Hudson River Valley. She explained that a small scar on her face was the result of a horrific airplane crash that only she had survived. She'd needed plastic surgery to repair the burns she had suffered to her face as she had tried in vain to rescue other victims from the flaming wreckage. But what a distraction she was. Richard Albee remembered that when Mahlon Blaine was working on sketches for *To a God Unknown*, Steinbeck brought him by the Albee house to use Anne as a model. She was to be "the face and the bosom" of one of the female characters. Anne put on a low-cut black gown that she was repeatedly encouraged to pull farther off her shoulders—until Richard was sent out of the room. He said it was a major disappointment that he never got to see Blaine's drawing.

One of Anne's biggest lies came on the day she married George. She neglected to mention that she'd been previously married to several men—and had never bothered to divorce any of them. After they moved to upstate New York, Anne continued to work as a buyer for stores in the city while doing her best to drive wedges between George and his friends. This included making regular stops at the McIntosh & Otis offices to gossip about Steinbeck. At home, Anne would then report to George that Steinbeck had recently been in to see McIntosh and Otis and had said terrible things about him. Even more deviously, whenever she saw any of Steinbeck's friends in Manhattan, Anne confided to them that George had been saying awful things about Steinbeck.

At some point, Anne confessed to George that she had a daughter from a prior relationship. A pretty eighteen-year-old named Nancy showed up on their doorstep right on the heels of this revelation. She said she'd just gotten away from the orphanage Anne had left her in as a baby. Nancy stayed, and Anne left and got married again. Her new husband, if that's what he was, called George often to ask his advice about how to deal with the crazy lady. Meanwhile, Nancy attended Bard, became a model, and—believe it or not, *this* is the weird part—married George. When George died in 1964, Nancy was disconsolate and never got over it. In the end she killed herself with a handful of pills. She left everything to her psychiatrist.

Steinbeck eventually learned the whole tawdry tale. George's younger brother Richard somehow got the impression that Steinbeck found the story hilarious, though of course there was nothing funny about it and Steinbeck more likely wished he had known the truth and might have helped his friend.

Steinbeck was eager to get back to work. In the winter of 1937–38, California was repeatedly hit by cyclones and heavy rains. Steinbeck wanted to revisit the central valleys to see how the migrants were faring. Word was that thousands of families were starving. But what enraged Steinbeck were the active efforts of the growers and their allies to block relief efforts. He wrote an inflamed letter to Elizabeth Otis, telling her the situation was dire. He said there was smallpox in the camps and that as many as twenty people sometimes had to live in a single tent. The growers, meanwhile, were obsessed by the thought that if living conditions for the migrants were improved, they'd respond by trying to organize against farm interests. Steinbeck was beside himself. He said he had to get to the camps to see firsthand. It was beyond his comprehension that the growers seemed not to realize that without migrant workers for the harvests, their crops would wither in the fields.

Steinbeck planned to head south, perhaps back down to Arvin to see Tom Collins. But within days, an even worse crisis hit closer by—in Visalia, where some 4,000 families had been flooded out of their tents. Once again, local vigilantes were interfering with the government's attempts to assist the migrants. Steinbeck said the Farm Security Administration was pleading with him to report on the disaster. He told Elizabeth Otis the local papers were ignoring what was happening—but would take stories under his byline. Making money off of these desperate people by writing about their plight was out of the question. He planned to spend any money he got for the articles on medical supplies for the migrants. The worst thing was realizing that children were going hungry in California, a land of abundance. Steinbeck said whatever he could do to help he would do.

Life magazine asked him to cover the crisis. *Life* also dispatched a photographer named Horace Bristol to accompany Steinbeck into the camps. Steinbeck returned after a week, devastated. There was water a foot deep in the tents, and children were huddled on beds with nothing to eat and no fire to keep warm. The county had pulled out its medical staff, claiming the situation was hopeless. Steinbeck came back emotionally drained—and broke. He said any notion that one person can't make a difference vanished when he found himself looking at starving children and had money in his pocket.

Life didn't run anything just then. But it would.

Steinbeck wasn't the only one paying attention. The photographer Dorothea Lange was working in the migrant camps. She was interested in photographing strike activities, but these were hard to capture—and sometimes too risky to get in the middle of. She'd tried to photograph a cotton strike in 1938. The Associated Farmers had made the situation toxic by enforcing a low wage rate and rebuffing all attempts by the government to mediate the conflict. The migrants were starving, and they crossed picket lines to work in the fields, effectively breaking their own strike. Lange had wanted to take pictures of the strike breakers, but decided it was too dangerous and went home.

Lange had had better luck two years earlier, near the town of Nipomo north of Santa Barbara, at roughly the same time Steinbeck was making his first visits to the Central Valley. It was in a pea-picking camp on a rainy day. People there were in a bad way—a cold spell had destroyed the pea crop and the migrants were without work and starving. Lange happened upon a lean, worried-looking woman surrounded by her children, and persuaded her to be photographed. Lange took half a dozen shots. The one that the world eventually saw—and that Lange titled *Migrant Mother*—showed the woman with her hand against her jaw, looking blankly to the side, with a child in one arm and another half-hiding behind her shoulder. The woman's name was Florence Thompson. She was from Oklahoma. It was ironic that her image would come to stand for all of the outsiders who had no home, nowhere to be, who worked the land but seemed to not belong there. Thompson was a Native American. *Migrant*

Mother, which captured the anguish and hopelessness at the end of the line for migrants in California, became the most iconic image of the Great Depression.

Later that same year, the *San Francisco News* had used Lange's photos of the migrants to illustrate Steinbeck's series, "The Harvest Gypsies."

Down in Arvin, at the Weedpatch camp in the early months of 1938, another woman was recording what she saw. Sanora Babb had been born in Oklahoma in 1907—but she was no Okie. She'd moved to Los Angeles hoping to become a writer. She worked for the Associated Press and was about to take a job at the *Los Angeles Times* when the stock market crashed and the paper stopped hiring. In 1938 Babb volunteered to work with the Farm Security Administration and traveled to migrant camps in the Central Valley, interviewing relief applicants to determine their eligibility for assistance. Babb was friendly with Tom Collins and shared with him her notes and possibly parts of a novel she'd begun about the migrants. Babb later claimed to have met John Steinbeck a couple of times—presumably when he traveled with Collins to inspect the flood situation during two visits he made to Visalia—but whether Collins shared any of Babb's writing with him isn't known. Her field notes and possibly accounts from her interviews with the migrants, at least some of which ended up in Collins's regular reports, would have been one thing. And Steinbeck did see the reports. But it seems unlikely that Collins, even if he had access to the book she was at work on, would have shown any of it to Steinbeck without Babb's permission. Babb was smart and ambitious and surely would have refused to hand over her work-in-progress to a well-known writer gathering information for his own book.

If Steinbeck had managed to see any of Babb's work, he could not have failed to be impressed. She was good. In a surviving fragment, Babb writes of the beauty of the San Joaquin Valley, and of the catastrophe that befell the migrants who landed there in the 1930s after leaving behind "mortgage-lost farms, bank-claimed machinery and animals, dust-ruined acres." Venturing out among the squatters' camps, Babb saw much the same thing Steinbeck had: "Malnutrition is a subtle disease that few escape. Starvation is a violence close to death. I see it every day, knowing it is the same in another county and another. Measles, scarlet fever, whooping cough, pneumonia are everywhere. Lack of proper care of the eyes of children with measles has left many of them affected. In one crowded trailer where I could hardly breathe for the smell of sickness, seven children were stuffed into two small beds, all ill with measles, one little girl of eight dying with pneumonia squeezed among the others. The mother was sitting on a box in a small path left between the beds and the stove, nursing a baby, also feverish and speckled with measles. They had had no food for two days. The mother was worn out and weak with hunger and the father was out of work. He had walked miles in search of it, and now was too weak to venture away. If this were an exception it might be a little easier to pass over, to remedy, but it is not."

Babb sometimes walked with Tom Collins from one roadside camp to the next. They found people living in abandoned barns and deserted trailers. Everywhere it was the same—sick, starving people, their eyes hollow with fear, yet proud and hospitable if you were friendly to them. And they had a speech that was all their own, she said. One little boy proudly showed her a puppy he'd found. Someone had thrown it from a truck, breaking its legs, but the boy had nursed it and now the dog was healed and plump. "Don't he look like a bar?" the boy said.

Babb wrote that if a family had anything to eat, no matter how meager, they always invited her to share a meal. At one of the government camps, Babb interviewed men who'd run out of money and food after the cotton crop was finished. "We didn't have a man who wasn't weak and pale, lips and hands trembling from real starvation," she said. "They are very proud and try to cover their need. One of the questions is, how much food have you now? The answer was always the same: a pause, and then, 'Well, mister (or missus), we haven't got none.'"

Babb said her long walks among the camps were good for her—

the miles of country road were calming in a way walking in the city was not. But seeing so much suffering took a toll. After her first day in the field, witnessing conditions "worse than I had ever imagined," Babb sat down to dinner back at Weedpatch and began to sob. She had to rush back to her room. Tom Collins told her it had been much the same for John Steinbeck on his first visit. Steinbeck said he could not bear what he was seeing, but that he would tell the whole world about it.

During her trip to New York, Carol had met the documentary filmmaker Pare Lorentz. Lorentz was enthusiastic about the New Deal and had received government support for his films—notably his half-hour exploration of the Dust Bowl, *The Plow That Broke the Plains*, in 1936. Lorentz thought both *In Dubious Battle* and *Of Mice and Men* should be made into movies. He came to see Steinbeck at Los Gatos in February, and the two of them hit it off. Lorentz persuaded Steinbeck to visit Hollywood with him to discuss film possibilities. This went less than well. Steinbeck was introduced to James Cagney, who wanted to play Mac in *In Dubious Battle*, and also to the director-producer Mervyn LeRoy. Still in his thirties, LeRoy was a Hollywood institution—he had directed *Little Caesar*, the 1931 film that made his reputation and also that of its star, Edward G. Robinson. In 1938, LeRoy took over as head of production at MGM and put a film into development that many people doubted could be made. It was *The Wizard of Oz*.

LeRoy wanted to hire Steinbeck, but he said something that killed any possibility Steinbeck would consider it. He told Steinbeck that *Of Mice and Men* would make a better movie if Lennie didn't kill Curley's wife but only got blamed for it. This would make Lennie a more sympathetic character. LeRoy seemed to think this was a brilliant idea, and maybe it was when you think about it. But Steinbeck was insulted. He reminded Elizabeth Otis of how hard he had worked to write *Of Mice and Men*. He said he was not interested in amateurish ideas about how to improve it.

Steinbeck's talk with LeRoy prompted another call from Myron Selznick wanting to manage Steinbeck's film work. Bruised by LeRoy's presumption, Steinbeck again assured Selznick that the rumors he was doing anything in Hollywood were not true, and never would be. Filmmaking involved too much collaboration. Steinbeck said he was satisfied with writing books that his publisher brought out just as they were meant to be.

Steinbeck made at least two attempts at a novel about the migrant problem in the early months of 1938. In March he told Elizabeth Otis he'd already destroyed it more than once. It was frustrating. Steinbeck wondered why it seemed he hadn't learned anything about writing, a question writers routinely put to themselves, though they never get an answer. Whatever the problem was, Steinbeck insisted he had to work through it. He wanted to get things right. He would not be rushed.

That same month Tom Collins wrote to Sanora Babb with a summary of her work that spring. He reported that Babb had visited nearly 500 families living in "tents, shacks, cabins, and houses," and managed to formally interview and register just over 300 of these families for camp settlement. The numbers were remarkable, but Collins was more impressed by the effect Babb had had on the people she met. He told her that she had brought them "happiness and hope," rare things in those days and in those places. Babb, sensing the power of the story that had begun to form in the pages of her daily diary, continued working on a novel about the migrants. Up in Los Gatos, Steinbeck kept searching for a way to begin.

Floundering, Steinbeck promised to let Otis know when he got things on track. But he left out what the real problem was—his fury at the way the migrants were being treated. Steinbeck was simply too angry to get the story right. Yet in May he wrote back to say the book was finished. It was short, just over 60,000 words, and neither he nor Carol liked the title—*L'Affaire Lettuceberg*. They would try to come up with a better one. He said he'd have it revised and sent off with a new title within a month. If Otis didn't like it, he would destroy the manuscript and never think of it again. Steinbeck's temper, coupled with his outrage over the treatment of the migrants, steered the book. The plot centered on the vigilante committees, and how the growers organized anti-union activities, recruiting thugs to do their dirty work. Steinbeck said it was a vulgar book about a vulgar situation, and he'd intentionally made it simple enough for the goons who sided with the growers to understand. He said as vile as the story was, if he could make it even harsher he would.

Richard Albee's claim that Steinbeck had grown paranoid wasn't wrong. Steinbeck felt that a lot of people wanted something from him. Usually it was money, but he'd also gotten a letter from a woman proposing marriage. She said she'd always wanted to live in California. And there were others whom Steinbeck claimed were upset with him for no good reason. Pat Covici had neglected to enter *Of Mice and Men* for the Commonwealth Club award. Steinbeck didn't mind—he remembered how upset he'd been when *Tortilla Flat* had won it—but now there were rumors that he thought he was above such local competitions. Meanwhile, George Kaufman was insulted that Steinbeck had not come to the opening of *Of Mice and Men* and would not see the play before it closed. Steinbeck didn't understand what the big deal was. He said he wouldn't travel across the country to see the Second Coming. And the New York Drama Critics' Circle were annoyed with him, too, after Steinbeck sent a telegram thanking them for their award for the play. In the cable, he mentioned in what he thought was a jocular way that he usually thought of critics as the enemy. And, in any case, he added, the real credit should go to George Kaufman and the cast.

He and Carol thought the wire was just fine, and they were shocked that anyone would take offense. It was getting hard to do or say anything that didn't anger someone. These were petty annoyances, but they happened all the time now. And then, before May was out, Steinbeck did something that set off alarms in New York. He destroyed the vigilante book for the final time and started on something completely different. By the beginning of June, it was coming so fast that he had to hold himself back. Steinbeck envisioned a manuscript of around 200,000 words and he thought he could write it in five months. Most writers can do the math in their heads. That's 2,000 words a day—not impossible but daunting. On any given day, it might not be so much. It's when the days turn into weeks and the weeks turn into months that such a pace becomes hard to keep. Steinbeck told Elizabeth Otis that, at last, after being lost for a long time, he could see the way forward. He was determined—even on such an ambitious schedule—to hold tight to his story lest it seem rushed. Hurrying would be the worst mistake. But it seemed he could do this book, that he *would* do it. Somehow, the vigilante book—which really had been awful—had cleared his mind.

Steinbeck asked Otis to not tell Covici anything about this new project. He couldn't be certain when it would be done. Or even that it would be done. He said 200,000 words was a lot of words, and he might fail yet again. He'd begun keeping a journal in May, and in it he was more concrete about his plan. He wanted to finish by the end of the year, but figured he could do so by the close of October. Even at that, the work would be "leisurely." Keeping a diary would help him stay on track. He was, by nature, a quick worker.

Steinbeck was worried about Pat Covici, who was planning to bring out a collection of his short stories. Steinbeck hoped the book would be out in the fall, but there were two concerns. One was that Ernest Hemingway's new collection, *The Fifth Column and the First Forty-Nine Stories,* was also coming that autumn from Scribner's and promised to be heavy competition. In addition to Hemingway's stories about Michigan and his youthful alter-ego Nick Adams—including the exquisite "Big Two-Hearted River"—the selections would include the more recent African stories, "The Snows of Kilimanjaro" and "The Short Happy Life of Francis Macomber." Steinbeck told Covici he considered Hemingway the "finest writer of our time." He thought it might be bad business to go up against him.

The other concern was that Covici-Friede was in distress. Steinbeck could have been forgiven for wondering why this always happened to him. In late June Covici informed Steinbeck he was short of cash and would be able to send only about a third of the royalties owed him. And the situation was more dire than Covici let on. The company was $170,000 in debt, with over $100,000 of that owed to its printers. *Time* magazine reported that this certainly wasn't Steinbeck's fault—Covici-Friede had made $35,000 on *Of Mice and Men* alone. Steinbeck was owed some $6,000 in royalties—he thought it was only $2,000—and the magazine estimated Steinbeck's total earnings from writing now exceeded $50,000. He was likely to be an expensive acquisition for another publisher. By midsummer it appeared the company might fold. Steinbeck asked McIntosh and Otis to start thinking about a new publisher, just in case. He said he didn't have any preferences—and that his prejudices against a couple of publishers were probably unfounded—so they should use their best judgment. And take the highest offer. Steinbeck stood to lose a year's worth of unpaid royalties if Covici went bankrupt. Going forward he wanted to get the largest advance possible. Why should the publisher hang on to his money when he could just as well invest it? Steinbeck said he wasn't greedy, but also didn't think he should stand in line behind the printers to be paid.

But Covici wasn't like other publishers. Steinbeck would miss him. He assured Elizabeth Otis that he and Carol had plenty of money, more than enough for a good long while. But he complained that there were houses going up all around them in Los Gatos, and they wanted to find a more isolated place farther back in the hills. Financial uncertainties could put this on hold, but he hoped not for long. Steinbeck said he needed fifty acres, not the two they had.

Through the summer Steinbeck counted words and kept track of pages, toting up "days ahead" when it went well and "days lost" when it didn't—the silent psalm of a writer at work. He had to force himself to concentrate on the narrow span of words he wrote each day and to ignore the great mass of work that lay ahead. After only a few weeks, his confidence in what he was doing solidified. In the diary he kept that year, Steinbeck tracked his daily output and marked the battle with himself as to whether he was up to the task. He believed the only way he could overcome his lack of talent was to be as honest on the page as he could be. It was his only hope, since he knew better than anyone how untalented he was. Still, he believed he was winning this endless fight with himself. The book was going well. Time and again, he reminded himself to slow down.

In June, Steinbeck managed to take a whole weekend off. Ed Ricketts came over from Monterey, and together they drove back to the lab to embalm 300 hagfish dripping with slime. A hagfish is an eel-like creature whose ghastly appearance, Steinbeck said, was much improved after it was perfused with formalin. Ritchie and Tal Lovejoy took Steinbeck home to Los Gatos. On the last day of the month, Steinbeck broke his rule and let himself think about the weight of the book remaining to be written—especially the ending, which was clear to him and the object toward which the story inexorably moved. He was convinced he was on the right path and that his theme was a mighty one. It made him feel overmatched but devoted to what he was doing. The characters in his book were alive to him now, and he knew they were better than he was.

Steinbeck relaxed for four days around the Fourth of July. Ritchie and Tal and Ed came over and they drank and danced far into the night. Steinbeck read some of the new book to Ricketts, who approved of it and told Steinbeck it was "moving"—a word far enough outside of Ricketts's usual vocabulary that it must have been true. When Steinbeck wrote about his characters in his diary, it was as if they were actual people. Then, in the middle of the month, during a spell of spectacular weather, he and Carol found a nearby property they wanted. The Biddle Ranch, as it was known locally—a family named Stone owned it now—comprised 47 acres and was perched on a remote ridge. The existing house was unsuitable, but they could build a new one. The asking price, $16,000, was high, but Steinbeck was determined to have it, despite hearing no news from New York as to whether Covici-Friede was insolvent. Negotiations for the ranch proceeded. There were so many distractions, Steinbeck wished he could run away and do nothing but work on the book. The manuscript had reached nearly seventy pages. Steinbeck wrote in a twelve-inch by eighteen-inch ledger, filling its pages edge to edge and top to bottom with his microscopic handwriting—an astonishing and all-but-visually-impenetrable 1,000 words to the page.

On July 18, Steinbeck got a letter from Pat Covici promising him that everything was under control. It was followed a day later by a telegram saying the opposite. Covici-Friede was likely going under. He and Carol could get by without the $2,000 he thought he had coming. Steinbeck confided to his journal that he and Carol would be fine, but that being broke would be hard on Pat. Steinbeck held out the smallest of hopes that Covici might persuade his creditors to stick with him. The short-story collection already had an advance sale of 8,000 copies, which Steinbeck thought ought to count for something. But Steinbeck started getting calls and cables from other publishers who believed he was in play. At the end of the month, Carol spent three days in the hospital recovering from having her tonsils taken out. Then Broderick Crawford showed up for a weekend. Steinbeck liked him, but felt Crawford could not have picked a worse time for a visit. The interruptions were getting on Steinbeck's nerves. He realized he'd been foolish to think he could write the book without stopping. Of course he had to stop now and then. But he wished it didn't make him so frantic. He just had to stay calm and subtract the downtime from the running total. Days ahead, days lost.

In early August Steinbeck decided to take another break and went to San Francisco for a weekend with Ed Ricketts. When he got back, he found that his career had taken another new direction. Viking Press had purchased his contract, paying Covici-Friede's creditors $15,000 and hiring Pat Covici as a senior editor. It was, of course, up to him whether to accept this arrangement and make the move with his trusted publisher and editor, but Steinbeck didn't hesitate and agreed to come aboard at Viking. Covici sent a telegram thanking Steinbeck for his loyalty. He said there was no way he could repay Steinbeck's trust, but to "continue as your honored and happy publisher."

Toward the end of the month, Steinbeck wrote Covici to say how glad he was that things had worked out. Knowing that Covici had come out all right made it easier for him to keep working on the book—though heaven only knew how hard it was. Steinbeck went through his usual enumeration of disclaimers, saying how difficult the book was to write, how it was probably awful, or even if he could finish it. It sounded as if Steinbeck had started looking too far down the road again and was intimidated by what remained to be done. In fact, by any measure the book was coming like an inrushing tide, an irresistible force that would not leave Steinbeck alone. And then, in early September, Carol—who, as usual, was reading and typing the manuscript—came up with a title: *The Grapes of Wrath.*

Everyone loved the title, which was from a line in Julia Ward Howe's "Battle Hymn of the Republic," a martial Civil War–era celebration of that struggle against oppression.

> *Mine eyes have seen the glory of the coming of the Lord*
> *He is trampling out the vintage where the grapes of wrath are stored*

Steinbeck thought it was fitting that the title came from a march, as the book itself was a march of epic proportions, and also because it was an ironic commentary on the helplessness of the migrants in California, whom no god was watching over. Carol's contribution to the book was far greater than giving it a title. As she typed the manuscript from his crabbed handwriting, Carol revised and corrected it as she went. Steinbeck said he was doing the first draft of the book, and Carol was doing the second. The way things were going, they'd finish at just about the same time. He asked Otis to keep all this a secret, but said that Carol's draft was better than his in every way and would be the version he would submit. He couldn't bring himself to think about how far he still had to go, but he thought it was possible that he'd be done in another sixty days. He was desperately tired, but determined to finish.

About this same time, the first copies of Steinbeck's story collection, *The Long Valley*, began showing up in bookstores in California. Steinbeck noted that this happened days ahead of the official publication date. Apparently, nobody could wait. The book was handsomely done and he hoped it would have strong sales, though he worried that the initial printing of 15,000 copies was far too many. On another front, their final offer of $10,000 on the ranch had been accepted, and they began planning their new house there. With all of this going on at once, he and Carol were frantic. Of course, he admitted in the same breath, most people would like to have the kind of problems he lived with. Writing was easier than, say, picking cotton or fighting a vigilante mob, and, in his case at least, far more lucrative. The contrast between the way he lived and the way the characters in his book clung to life was stark.

Crazy things happened seemingly every other day. One time, Steinbeck was at home when a car pulled up and a short man bounded out and knocked on his door. It was Charlie Chaplin—who professed himself a fan. Chaplin and the Steinbecks got on well, though Chaplin was surprised that they had no staff and that Carol did all the housework. Chaplin had a home in Pebble Beach, just by Carmel. In August, Steinbeck and Pare Lorentz went over to the peninsula and spent a night with Chaplin. It was fine, but as time went by Steinbeck's resentment of days lost on his novel intensified. He wished he could be left alone until Christmas.

When Viking Press published *The Long Valley* in September, its reception added to the growing critical assessment that Steinbeck was a writer of talent and promise who was still sifting styles and subjects. The ever-attentive Wilbur Needham at the *Los Angeles Times* offered muted praise. He said Steinbeck never wrote anything that was beneath him—but also never wrote something that fully leveraged his ability. Needham felt that Steinbeck was holding something in reserve. But he liked the fifteen stories published together in *The Long Valley*, and thought the characters in each were different and yet the same. Other reviewers tended to pick and choose among the stories. William Soskin at the *New York Herald Tribune* found the diversity of the material "bewildering." But he loved "The Red Pony" suite, and noted that this was the second time that year that a youngster named

Jody had won readers' hearts—the first being Jody Baxter in Marjo-
rie Kinnan Rawlings's mega-bestseller, *The Yearling*. In general, there
was agreement that "The Red Pony" stories were the best of the lot,
with opinions on the others split. One critic called the book a "sample
room of John Steinbeck."

All but two of the stories had already been published elsewhere,
including "The Chrysanthemums," "The Snake," and "The White
Quail," a stiff, subdued, symbolically leaden story about a mentally
confused housewife whose disapproval of her husband's business leads
him to kill a bird with which she identifies. There was also the new,
fourth installment of the "Red Pony" series, "The Leader of the People." The other previously unpublished story, which some reviewers
admired and others all but skipped over, was the tense "Flight."

"Flight" is set in a place that had long occupied an unforgiving
corner in Steinbeck's memory: the Big Sur country below the Monterey Peninsula. Something about its sere mountains—bone-dry and
scorched by the sun—posed a question he tried to answer for the first
time in "Flight." Years later, he would try again in a different story.
What if, Steinbeck wondered, a boy were forced to flee into such forbidding terrain? This is what happens to Pepe, the oldest son of the
Torres family, after his mother sends him to Monterey on an errand.
Pepe, who is neither a child nor yet quite a man, is skilled with a
knife. While he is in the city, a man who has been drinking insults
him. Pepe reflexively kills the man and dashes home—only just long
enough to gather a few things, including a rifle, before saddling a
fresh horse and fleeing into the mountains. He knows that men will
come after him, that even though there is no sign of anyone yet, they
cannot be far behind. There is no time. As his mother watches him
go, Pepe seems to vanish into another realm. His brother asks their
sister if Pepe is dead. No, she answers. "Not yet."

In the mountains, Pepe runs from his pursuers. They have dogs. It
is easier to ride in the open, but more dangerous, so Pepe retreats into
harder, steeper country, the mountains brittle and broken in places,
but always looming all around him. Once he stops and peers at a

high ridge. The solitary outline of a man is silhouetted against the sky. When Pepe looks away for an instant, the dark shape disappears. Perhaps it is only one of the Watchers.

A day passes. Then another. Pepe is wounded. He loses his horse and his gun. He runs out of water. He climbs higher and higher. When he comes finally to a stony crest and looks down into the next canyon, he sees there is nothing down there but more of the same barren rock and scree, and Pepe, who has learned life's final lesson, knows the end has come. He stands up straight, ready for the mountain to bury him. There is a shot and Pepe staggers backward. Then another shot and he collapses and slides down the rocky slope, down and down, tumbling, until his limp body comes to a rest against a bush.

There was something about the desperation of running away into a forbidding desert—a place empty of hope—that Steinbeck could not shake free of. Usually his writing emptied him of the impulse that led to its creation, and when a story was done he closed the door on it. He claimed he could never think about any of his books but the one he was at work on. But Pepe's story got stuck in Steinbeck's head, and its scenery and mood would resurface in his short novel *The Pearl* a decade later.

The first people who looked at the Steinbecks' house ended up buying it, which meant they had to relocate to the ranch sooner than planned. During the first week of September, they staked off the footprint of the foundation for the new house. A month later they were "camped" in the kitchen of the existing house while their new one was under construction—though Steinbeck would remain in the existing house until the book was finished. In the chaos, Steinbeck caught himself hurrying again. His diary was punctuated by admonitions against the nearly overpowering desire to finish. He wanted to finish, was desperate to finish. And still he told himself again and again, slow down.

Steinbeck could not shut himself off from what was going on in the world, both close at hand and thousands of miles away. The Farm

Security Administration asked him to do a radio interview about the migrant workers' situation, something he wanted to avoid if he could. When Pare Lorentz advised him not to do it, Steinbeck was relieved. Events in Europe were troubling, too. In mid-September, Adolf Hitler closed the annual Nazi rally in Nuremberg with a speech broadcast to Americans by CBS Radio in which he proclaimed Czechoslovakia an outlaw state where millions of Germans were forced to live under foreign rule. The stridency of the Führer's voice was shocking. German claims to the Sudetenland—a region of Czechoslovakia adjacent to Germany and Austria—had not appeared out of thin air. Czechoslovakia had been created in the Treaty of Versailles at the close of World War I. Nearly a quarter of its population was German, and most of them lived in the Sudetenland. Plans for a German invasion of Czechoslovakia had been in place since spring. Steinbeck wrote in his diary that armies were mobilizing and the world could be in shambles by tomorrow. Days later, British Prime Minister Neville Chamberlain traveled to Germany to meet with Hitler about Germany's claim to the Sudetenland. Steinbeck feared the worst. It was plain that England didn't want war; the question that worried Steinbeck was what it would do to avoid one.

Chamberlain went home to London to consult with advisors. More meetings and threats ensued. At the end of the month, negotiators from Britain, Germany, Italy, and France—but not Czechoslovakia—convened in Munich and signed an agreement handing over the Sudetenland to Germany. In the ensuing months, Poland and Hungary would invade Czechoslovakia to enforce their claims over its territory. "Munich" would become synonymous with appeasement, the feckless surrender of principle in the hope of averting war when war is the only right answer.

In Los Gatos, Steinbeck worried about the imminence of war and continued to wrestle with guilt over the size of the new ranch. It was, he thought, far too much for only two people to own. He was exhausted and had been smoking nonstop. Now he had a cough that doubled him over in the mornings. He hoped war could yet be avoided, but it was hard to put it out of his mind. And fame—the dreaded, soul-crushing celebrity—stalked Steinbeck constantly. The Hollywood gossip columnist Louella Parsons reported that Charlie Chaplin was going to visit Steinbeck at Los Gatos, and this meant being on the lookout for the press and curiosity seekers. In the end they had a nice visit. But Steinbeck said he was frightened of "losing this book" in the noise and confusion of his life, and in the deepening mess the rest of the world was sliding into. And still the words kept coming. Carol's typescript reached 400 pages.

October was less hectic. The work went ahead steadily. Steinbeck's sister Mary and her husband, Bill Dekker, came over one Saturday for dinner, and afterward the four of them hiked up in the moonlight to the new house. The roof was on and it was beginning to look like a house. Pat Covici was planning a trip to San Francisco. Steinbeck told himself that if it rained on the weekend, he was going to write a little in case he lost a day when Covici visited. He felt he was getting close to the end of the book. He confided in his journal that he was excited at the prospect of finishing—but would be sad when the book was done and the days ahead and days lost came to a halt.

And then, on October 26, it was over. Steinbeck felt ill—literally. He'd slept much of the day before, and on this last day his stomach churned and he was dizzy. Worried he was coming down with something that might sideline him—and even more worried that he'd driven himself so hard he had nothing left—he pushed through to the end. He concluded the final entry in his journal for the year—it was Day 100—with the same old prayer. "I hope to God it's good."

II

I'LL BE THERE

"To THE RED country and part of the gray country of Oklahoma, the last rains came gently, and they did not cut the scarred earth. . . . The clouds appeared, and went away, and in a while they did not try any more. The weeds grew darker green to protect themselves, and they did not spread any more. The surface of the earth crusted, a thin hard crust, and as the sky became pale, so the earth became pale, pink in the red country and white in the gray country."

So begins Steinbeck's greatest novel—in a drought. It would end in a flood. These are forces of nature, and what happens in between— during one migrant family's arduous journey to California—is the oldest human story: the struggle to survive and hold together. Steinbeck, who had seen the migrants' plight firsthand and knew the odds, had lost the thread in his early attempts to write about what was happening in the verdant but strife-torn fields of California. He'd thought it was a story about the cruelties of the landowners who needed the migrants and also despised them, and of their henchmen, the vigilante thugs who enforced a grievous status quo. But that wasn't the story. Steinbeck's genius lay in realizing that the migrants—faceless, homeless, voiceless—were human beings, and that it was both possible and essential to know them. Their faces betrayed their pain and fear, their homes were lost, and their voices spoke in the plain, brutal diction of the dispossessed. They'd traded one kind of ruin for another. The story of how these people came to this bleak impasse, with no way out other than starvation and death, was *their* story.

Steinbeck's heroes are the Joads. The Joad family are Oklahoma sharecroppers, though they've been on the same forty acres long enough to think of the land as theirs. As the novel opens, Tom Joad, "not more than thirty," is on his way home after a long absence when he meets up with Jim Casy, a onetime local preacher who has lost his calling. They share a bottle and talk. Tom is surprised that Casy doesn't know he's been in prison, doing four years of a seven-year sentence for killing a man. Tom's now on parole. He tells Casy matter-of-factly that the killing didn't bother him. There was a fight, the man had a knife, and Tom was stabbed. So he grabbed a shovel and crushed the man's head. "I'd do what I done—again," he said.

Casy walks with Tom toward the Joad farm. But when they arrive, they see there is nothing to come home to. The house, nearly flattened, is sinking into a field of cotton that has been planted right across the yard, and that has all but swallowed up any sign that Tom's family had once lived there. The Joads have been evicted by the bank that owns the farm. The bank sent in a tractor to plow the land and push down the house to make sure the family got the message. In a couple of years, the cotton would consume what little remained of the soil's former richness and the bank would sell off the land to the next batch of bad-luck yokels coming west.

Tom learns that his family is living over at his uncle John's place, where everyone is picking cotton to earn enough money for a car so they can move west, to California. It's a hard lot—one clean-picked acre of cotton pays 50 cents. But in California everything will be different. They've seen a handbill promising high wages for farm work in a paradise where decent folks can pick grapes and oranges and peaches under the warm sun, and live without fear of being put off the land. Young Tom—that's his father's name, too—has come back just in time to join them. Everyone is going: Ma and Pa; Pa's parents, Granpa and Granma; and Tom's five siblings, Noah, Al, Ruthie, Winfield, and Rose of Sharon. Ruthie and Winfield are children. Rose of Sharon has a husband, Connie, and is pregnant. Uncle John is going, too. Sizing up the situation, the preacher Casy invites himself to come with them.

They plan to get there in a decrepit Hudson Super Six sedan they've modified by chopping off its back half and building a truck bed onto the frame. The truck cost them $75, and they've managed to scrape together another $150. Ma tells Tom it's 2,000 miles to California, some of it over mountains. She wonders how long it will take. Tom reckons two weeks, maybe ten days. Tom learned in prison to take life one day at a time, to never look ahead to when a thing will be done—Steinbeck's own feelings about his work on the book echo through the scene—and Ma agrees. But she can't help letting herself imagine what's at the end of their road west, which in her mind is a place where nice people live in neat, white houses.

Tom doesn't want to pull Ma away from this fantasy, but he says he knew a California man in prison, and it might not be as pretty and perfect as she's hoping. The way he's heard it, there are too many people looking for work in California. Wages are low, and people don't live in sunny little houses, but in filthy camps where they go hungry most of the time. Ma shrugs him off. She reminds Tom of the handbill they've seen—on nice yellow paper, saying fruit pickers were needed. That handbill cost good money to print. Why would anybody go to that trouble if it weren't true?

Why indeed? The answer, which would be incomprehensible to Ma, is that broken dreams are peddled by those who profit from them. Desperation had become a cash crop in California, where the growers understood that as more migrants showed up starved for work they could be paid less. In truth, they could be paid almost nothing. The Joads can't see this—none of the Okies can—but they'll learn it in due course.

Steinbeck built an unusual structure into the book, alternating chapters that told the story of the Joads' trip west and what happened to them in California with shorter interstitial chapters—he called them "general" chapters—that told the real migrants' story as a history and through vignettes in which he tried to put their situation in context. For many readers, and for a fair number of critics, these digressions would be seen as needless interruptions. But it's easy to see why Steinbeck did it—why he could not help himself. The general chapters by turns seethe with anger at the banks and the absentee owners and the corporate farms that choke the life from smaller operators—and they soar with the human spirit of the migrants, who keep moving toward California much as they move doggedly through life—without reflection or regret. They are simple, agrarian people who mostly don't use machines, never saw the danger coming at them until it was too late.

The Joads head west. The road is long and difficult, over mountains and across desert, a way lined with broken cars and broken people. Not everyone makes it. But at last, on a morning when the dawn lies golden on the land, the Joads—the "fambly," as Ma says—stand together looking down into a glorious valley filled with lush green expanses and trees standing in rows, dotted with little towns and larger cities in the distance. Broke and exhausted, they have arrived with nothing.

Early in the book, in a slowly unwinding scene in one of the general chapters, Steinbeck describes a "land turtle"—a tortoise—coming across a field and then climbing up a highway embankment onto the road it must cross to continue on its way. The turtle's progress is implacable. It goes forward, unrelenting and armored against danger by its shell. It moves at a pace determined only by what it must overcome. On the highway, a woman driver swerves to avoid the turtle—but then a man in a truck angles across the pavement to hit it. His tire catches the edge of the turtle's shell, flipping it like a spinning coin to the side of the road, where it lands on its back. After a struggle the turtle rights itself and begins moving off in a new direction—as if that were where it was headed all along.

The symbolism is heavy-handed—Steinbeck could not have pointed to his meaning more plainly—and yet it's perfect. The Joads, like the turtle, move by inches that become miles, move as one within the protective shell of the family. They are a phalanx—one of several in the book—and a *testudo*, the unbreakable tortoise-like formation of ancient Rome. The family is democratic. Everyone has their say, everyone takes their turn, but Ma is always at the center, "the citadel of the family, the strong place that could not be taken." Ma knows that if the family breaks, all is lost.

In California, the Joads find themselves still on a road, one that winds from camp to camp, Hoovervilles and worse. At one point they alight in a government-run sanitary camp called Weedpatch, and for a moment the California Ma dreamed of seems almost real. When Ruthie and Winfield flush a toilet for the first time in their lives they think the rush of water means they've broken it, and they run away. The people are in charge of the whole place, which they care for wisely, and on Saturday nights there's a dance.

But there is no work, and they cannot stay. Soon they are living in semi-imprisonment on a peach farm. Casy has become a strike leader. One night, when a gang of vigilantes comes for him, they find Tom, too. There's a fight. Casy is killed and Tom kills the man who did it. The Joads get away, but Tom is injured and will be easy to identify. They hide out in a cotton-picking camp, living in half of an old boxcar. When Tom realizes he's putting the family at risk and must go away, he talks it over with Ma. She knows he's right, but she cannot bear the thought that she will never know what becomes of him, won't know if he escaped or is dead.

Tom laughs nervously at this. But he thinks he understands now what Casy meant when he talked about one individual being a "piece" of something bigger. He tells Ma that he'll be with her always, an ever-present shadow. And in the same way he'll be wherever people are struggling, anyplace where they're trying to stand up for themselves. The world has come apart, but he will stand with his people at all the broken places. So this is not his goodbye, but a solemn promise. "I'll be there," he says.

The Joads' journey is almost over. Pa thinks the worst is at hand. They have nothing, no food, no way out. Rose of Sharon is about to have her baby. Maybe it's time to just lie down and die. But Ma shushes him, and in one of the most beautiful and perceptive passages in all of Steinbeck, she explains that this is not the end. It's no such thing, she says. The problem with men is that they live their lives in fits and starts, always jarred by events. Women, Ma says, are different. "Woman, it's all one flow, like a stream, little eddies, little waterfalls, but the river, it goes right on. Woman looks at it like that. We ain't gonna die out."

Rose of Sharon's baby comes early, and is stillborn. Then it begins to rain and rain and rain. Water rises around the boxcar. The truck will not start. Pa tries to build a dike in the deluge, but after hours of shoveling it washes away. The water rises. It comes into the boxcar. They build a platform and climb onto it, but the water keeps coming. They have to leave. The family scrambles into the flood up to their waists, half walking, half swimming. They make their way to higher ground and onto the highway, and they follow it, with no idea where it will take them. At times, Rose of Sharon has to be carried. They find a barn and huddle inside. It is dark and dry and they are not alone. A father and son are there. The boy is terrified. The man is starving, on the threshold of death. Already his eyes are vacant. He won't last long. Ma and Rose of Sharon look at each other. And then Rose of Sharon lies down beside the man, bares her breast, and pulls him toward her.

Steinbeck and Carol went over to Pacific Grove when the book was done—they had to get out of the old house, finally. They both felt the strain of the last five months. Carol registered as a member of the Communist Party—impelled, perhaps, by a story that had been as harrowing to absorb as it had been to type and edit. Eleven months later, disillusioned or simply thinking better of it, she again became a Democrat. Word from New York was encouraging enough to upset Steinbeck, whose mistrust of praise remained intact. Pat Covici proposed a large print run for *The Grapes of Wrath*. Steinbeck was against it. He was certain the book would not be popular, and he wanted McIntosh & Otis to warn Viking about going overboard. Better, he said, to print a modest first edition and then make more if it was warranted. But there was a change in Steinbeck. His familiar claim that the latest book would not sell was less insistent than usual. And he hinted at a new openness to working with Hollywood. Paramount wanted to make a movie of "The Red Pony." Steinbeck was willing to be involved, but he wanted a lot of money and specific terms that would guarantee he would have some control over the film. He told Elizabeth Otis to not do any deal until he had all of this worked out.

Steinbeck spent all of November and the first part of December going over the final draft of the manuscript with Carol. And then he sent it off to Elizabeth Otis. He said they were eager for her opinion. Otis had already told him that she and her husband, Larry Kiser, planned to visit the Steinbecks in December. They met in Los Angeles and came up to the new house in Los Gatos, where the visit turned into an editing session. Otis felt that the book's language had to be toned down, and she found an unlikely ally in Carol, whose everyday vocabulary was, to put it mildly, colorful. Carol agreed that there were a handful of places in the book where common obscenities interrupted the flow. Steinbeck grudgingly consented to a few changes, deleting or altering a handful of variants of "fuck" and "shit," though he drew a line at "shitheels," which he insisted on keeping, saying there was no substitute for it. When Otis and Carol phoned Western Union to wire the changes to New York, a flustered operator said she wasn't sure she was allowed to send such language.

Steinbeck explained to Pat Covici that he was trying to be cooperative and was willing to make changes, but that certain things were off limits. Although he had been willing to listen to Carol and Elizabeth Otis when they complained that vulgarities that got in the way of the story should be deleted, he had to draw the line when it came to making cuts just to appease the sensibilities of "delicate ladies."

This was a condescending way to put it. "Delicate ladies" might well take as much offense at being labeled that way as they would over some four-letter words sprinkled through a 600-page novel depicting the most abject human misery imaginable. What was remarkable about the concern over swearing was how utterly unremarkable it should have been. The Joads and their fellow Okies did not talk like people in other books, or like anyone with polite and literate sensibilities, but rather in a patois unique to the hard life they lived. For them language was a blunt instrument, crammed with invented contractions and word approximations. Steinbeck, with his knack for common speech, had listened closely to the migrants he met. And he learned more about their sound from Tom Collins's reports, which included troves of stories about everyday life at Weedpatch that Collins did his best to record exactly as the migrants told them.

Collins wrote that for a time they had a fifteen-year-old girl in the camp who was the "toughest kid" there. She smoked and swore like a sailor, and meted out beatings to boys and girls alike. She didn't seem to have many friends. When the camp council threw her a birthday party, she wept. Another young woman—she was nineteen—had two children and had been divorced three times. A young man a few years older wanted to marry her and move her and her kids into his tent, which already had eleven people in it. Then, after one of the Saturday night dances, he kissed her goodnight and tasted whiskey on her mouth. He didn't approve of strong drink so that was the end of it—and possibly an explanation for the three divorces.

Back in 1935, long before he began to study California's migrants in earnest, Steinbeck had somehow met a man named Mel Thatcher, whose story stuck with him. Thatcher said it was in a migrant camp called Live Oak near San Jose. One day a guy in a bad suit walked up and said he was a writer and could he ask a few questions? It was Steinbeck. Thatcher said sure, they could talk. After a while Thatcher tired of the interrogation and went to his tent. He came back with a diary he'd started the year before. Steinbeck spent an hour poring over the journal and then asked if he could borrow it. Thatcher told him no—but he could come back the next day to read more and ask anything he wanted to. And Steinbeck did come back. A few years later, when Thatcher read *The Grapes of Wrath*, he recognized his own voice in places.

Thatcher had lived mostly on the margins in his young life. He was only twenty-three when Steinbeck met him. He'd been born in New Jersey, but came to California with his family and then left home at the age of seventeen when the Depression set in. He was a hobo for a time, riding freights across the country, earning a little now and then washing dishes and doing farm work and other odd jobs. In 1933, the older hobos were all talking about how easy it was to get work picking fruit in California, so Thatcher decided to try it. He started out picking prunes for 20 cents an hour. You got a bonus if you stayed the whole season—2 cents a box. They went into the field every morning as soon as it was dry and worked for ten hours.

Thatcher bought a car for $11 and drove to Bakersfield, where the car quit and he went to work picking cotton. The pay was 90 cents for every hundred pounds. "Took a lot of doing to pick a hundred pounds of cotton," he said. For a while he dug irrigation ditches for $1.50 a day. The days were twelve hours long. He lived mostly on yams—one big one was a meal—and flour. "Used to say that a teaspoon a day kept the mortician away," he remembered. "We'd mix it with grease and a little salt to make a biscuit." One day he saw something amazing. A long, silver airship flew overhead. It was the USS *Macon*, a rigid dirigible. Nearly as big as the *Hindenburg*, it carried airplanes that could be launched in midair. Later it was caught in a storm off of Big Sur and crashed into the ocean.

Thatcher saw everything. He picked peas sunup to sundown, seven days a week, near Salinas, where the fields were full of stinging nettles. In the Imperial Valley, he picked vegetables and lived in a dirty roadside camp. There were two-hole outhouses at both ends of the camp, and their only water source for drinking and cooking and washing was a mud-choked pit fed by an irrigation ditch. During pea-picking season, the pay was a penny a pound, which Thatcher said nobody could live on. That led to a strike. It ended after some "skull cracking" by sheriff's deputies. Thatcher didn't know anybody who got killed, but he heard that it had happened. They did not get a pay raise.

Every nationality you could think of was working in the fields, Thatcher said. The Okies, who were everywhere, were the most pathetic. They came by the carload. One time a landowner asked Thatcher what a nice young man like him was doing hanging out with Communists. Thatcher answered that he didn't know what a

Communist was, but that hungry people were a problem because, one way or another, they could not stay that way. Once, he was so broke that he lived for a couple of weeks under a bridge near Watsonville. When the hard times ended he moved to Los Angeles and swore he'd never work on a California farm again.

Everyone at Viking was over the moon about *The Grapes of Wrath*. In early January of 1939, Pat Covici told Steinbeck that he, Viking president Harold Guinzburg, and senior editor Marshall Best agreed that the book had left them emotionally spent. When the question of making some minor changes came up, Guinzburg put a quick stop to the discussion. "Right now, as far as I am concerned," Guinzburg said, "I would not change a single comma in the whole book." Viking's sales staff was just as enthusiastic. *The Grapes of Wrath*, a book that had landed unexpectedly in their laps only months earlier when Covici parachuted in, was going to be the most important work of fiction on Viking's spring list. Reading this—and no doubt hating every fawning syllable—Steinbeck must have wondered if there was a catch.

There was.

Covici continued, in the same letter, to say that after they'd had a chance to reflect on their initial reaction, the senior staff had returned to the question of whether any changes might be needed. Although he admitted it was a "sacrilege" to suggest revisions to what was clearly a great book, they felt it would also be a disservice to the novel and to its author if they remained silent about one problem. *The Grapes of Wrath*, he said, was "not quite satisfying as a work of fiction." But it could be. All Steinbeck had to do was change the ending.

If they were bothered by the image itself, Covici didn't let on. Rose of Sharon giving her breast to a starving man was moving, he said. Nobody could deny the power in it. But the ending was so abrupt that it left the reader hanging. Covici said this was at odds with the "vastness" of the book. What the people at Viking thought was needed was more of a build-up to the scene, some context that would establish how the story of the dying man and his son came to intersect with the Joads' saga. And they thought there should be something more *after* that scene that would make the symbolism of Rose of Sharon's gesture more obvious. Covici, who had to know that Steinbeck would never agree to change the ending—that maybe it was the ending of all endings, an ending for the ages—tried to make clear that the idea of changing it was only a suggestion. He told Steinbeck the decision was his alone.

Covici's gentle request was as unwelcome as it was unusual. In their long collaboration, Covici offered endless encouragement and praise, but rarely suggested even slight modifications to Steinbeck's prose. His role as "editor" seemed to include little hands-on editing, and certainly never involved any deep guidance on what to write about or how to do it—advice and direction Steinbeck got more often from Mavis McIntosh and Elizabeth Otis. Covici never let Steinbeck forget how grateful he was to be his editor. Steinbeck was his great discovery, and he tended more to Steinbeck's career than to his prose. Covici once told Steinbeck that in his own "little life" Steinbeck was his "rarest experience." He added that if Steinbeck wanted to be cynical about that he could go ahead—but that it was true. Covici was the father who looked up to the son. Apparently, Steinbeck wasn't the only writer on whom Covici's parental manner worked, as a number of prominent authors eventually signed on with him, including Lionel Trilling, Arthur Miller, and Saul Bellow.

It took a week for Covici's letter about the ending to reach Steinbeck, who was bedridden with sciatica and what was later discovered to be a serious tooth infection. Despite a bad back and paralyzing pains in his leg, Steinbeck wrote back immediately. Vexed less by Covici's tactful request for a change than he was by the fact that everyone at Viking seemed to have missed the point of the ending, Steinbeck did his best to explain things calmly. He said any change to the ending was out of the question. So was adding some kind of background for the starving man that would integrate him into the Joads' story. The fact that he is a total stranger they happen upon by accident was the point. The ending, Steinbeck said, wasn't about anything except survival. He apologized to anyone at Viking who couldn't see that.

This put an end to the discussion about the ending. Steinbeck, of course, was right about everything—well, everything except the part about his being sorry.

By the end of January, the Steinbecks were well along with reading the galleys. Steinbeck told Covici that Carol was going through them carefully. "It's her book and she wants it right," he said. For him, it was different. He had to force himself to read it. "It's like unburying the dead," he said.

In late March, Covici told Steinbeck that Viking expected to ship more than 40,000 copies of *The Grapes of Wrath* by its publication date on April 14. Steinbeck was still convinced that that was too ambitious, but he was becoming less adamant about it. Covici was worried about Steinbeck's lingering illness, which he incorrectly thought was arthritis. Steinbeck was getting better now, though he was trying to keep that a secret. Being sick had discouraged people from visiting or asking him to do things, which was a pleasant change. But before

Steinbeck, circa 1939, the year *The Grapes of Wrath* was published. *(Bettmann via Getty Images)*

long the world would be outside his doorstep to stay. That spring, *The Grapes of Wrath* surged to the top of the bestseller lists. Sales would soon approach half a million copies.

Once more, the critics celebrated what they said was Steinbeck's best book so far. This had become a pattern and the conventional view—that Steinbeck's career was on a trajectory, an arc, that had begun in the clumsy escapism of *Cup of Gold*, surged upward in ever more subtle and penetrating works like *In Dubious Battle* and *Of Mice and Men*, and had now sailed free in a powerful, massive, and brutally realistic depiction of a social and economic disaster that more than any other was emblematic of the times. Steinbeck's writing had merged with history. Finally, it was built to last.

In a thoughtful and balanced review for the *New York Times Book Review*, Peter Monro Jack called *The Grapes of Wrath* "as pitiful and angry a novel ever to be written about America." Jack said he could not judge the veracity of the book—though it lined up with other reports about California's migrant-worker problems, including Steinbeck's own earlier books. Jack wasn't sold on the ending. He found it pandering and said it was justified only to the extent that such a long book has to stop somewhere—a strange objection even though it is indisputably true. Books have to end. But Jack said any reservations he had about the novel were small alongside Steinbeck's heart and sincerity, which he said had few equals in literature.

Malcolm Cowley, writing in the *New Republic*, declined to rate *The Grapes of Wrath* as highly as other critics who were calling it the book of the decade—but he admired it intensely, especially its fury, which he said jumped off the page in its vivid characters. Cowley sensed the feverishness with which Steinbeck had been consumed during the five months he worked on the book. Steinbeck's novel, he wrote, was propelled by a "headlong anger" from beginning to end. He said he could almost imagine Steinbeck writing it without stopping.

Whatever faults the book had—Cowley added his voice to the

complaints about the "general chapters"—he said they disappeared beneath Steinbeck's compassion and respect for the migrants, whom he was careful not to pity.

A few reviewers found the book alarmingly radical. An unsigned review in *Colliers* labeled it Communist "propaganda," a call to swap the American way for the "Russian system." In *The Nation*, Louis Kronenberger wrote that of course the book was radical—how could it not be, given its subject? Kronenberger thought it burned like a torch and possessed the two qualities that were essential to a work of social protest: indignation and compassion. Clifton Fadiman, in *The New Yorker*, detected a similar political tone but said it was far outweighed by Steinbeck's gnawing portrayal of people falling away from their already precarious place in society. *The Grapes of Wrath* might well be the prototype for the Great American Novel, Fadiman said—a backhanded way of suggesting that was what he was almost ready to call it. Fadiman thought Steinbeck's ability to portray ordinary people made the book a kind of folktale—so authentic that it was like a story you overheard on the street. Or by a campfire along the roadside of Highway 66. Fadiman said the book delivered a potent message without becoming a sermon. It wasn't subtle, but it didn't hit you over the head. It got inside you.

In the weeks leading up to the publication of *The Grapes of Wrath*, with his recent books still selling and the play version of *Of Mice and Men* now on tour and headed to film, one huge check after another arrived from McIntosh & Otis. Steinbeck said he and Carol were putting it all aside for the lean years to come—though they ended up treating themselves to a few things, including his-and-hers Packards and a milk cow to pasture at the ranch. Bookstores in California again jumped the official publication date by a few days and put the book on sale in early April. It flew off the shelves. Meanwhile, *Of Mice and Men* had been sold to Hollywood. Lewis Milestone was set to direct. Steinbeck liked the script, but felt badly that none of the Broadway cast were going to be in the picture. He told Elizabeth Otis that Wallace Ford and Claire Luce were fine stage actors, but that Milestone didn't think they'd photograph well in close-ups. Broderick Crawford was out, too, in his case for getting fat and becoming difficult.

More than a month before *The Grapes of Wrath* came out, Steinbeck began hearing rumors of a smear campaign by the Associated Farmers. Because they were well-connected with California law enforcement, Steinbeck thought he might be falsely charged with some kind of crime—drunk driving, or sexual assault. Toby Street warned him to be careful, and to keep a record of whom he was with at all times in case he needed an alibi. There was more. He'd learned of an episode at a bookstore in Monterey. Several well-dressed people had come in and started asking questions about Steinbeck. When the store owner wanted to know what it was all about, they claimed they were investigating Steinbeck for J. Edgar Hoover at the FBI. This wasn't true—there was no FBI investigation—and that made the story all the more disturbing. In the coming months, *The Grapes of Wrath* was banned in a handful of libraries in California and as far away as New Jersey and Kansas City. Three copies were burned in St. Louis, and one in Bakersfield, where the Kern County Board of Supervisors also adopted a resolution banning the use, possession, or circulation of the novel in schools and libraries. The formal resolution denounced *The Grapes of Wrath* for its portrayal of "our citizenry" as "low, ignorant, profane and blasphemous," and for characterizing local officials and growers as "inhumane vigilantes, breathing class hatred and divested of sympathy or human decency or understanding toward a great, and to us unwelcome, economic problem brought about by an astounding influx of refugees." These refugees, the resolution continued, were indigent farmers who had been "dusted or tractored or foreclosed out" of their homes elsewhere and were now pouring into California. They probably didn't mean to, but the Kern County supervisors seemed to understand *The Grapes of Wrath* in a way few critics would.

Steinbeck tried to reconnect with a couple of old friends that spring. He'd heard from Carl Wilhelmson, who was married now. Steinbeck invited him to the ranch. He also wrote to Dook Sheffield about certain misunderstandings they'd had. One concerned their recent move to the new place, where Sheffield thought he might not be welcome. In truth, they'd been estranged for a couple of years. Sheffield had split with Maryon, and Steinbeck offered to pay Sheffield's way at any university he chose if he would go back to graduate school. Sheffield, who had left Occidental and was now working as a reporter on a small paper in Marysville, was tempted—but said no. Steinbeck tried to be understanding, but thought Sheffield was settling into a much smaller life.

The real problem between them was still Sheffield's drinking. Steinbeck told him that when he drank too much, Sheffield reminded him of his mother after her stroke. Alcohol changed his eyes and his expression in ways that were frightening, that made him suddenly unrecognizable—and unpleasant. Sheffield claimed that Steinbeck's bluntness had a "salutary" effect on him. After this, his drinking never came up between them again.

Some months later, Sheffield visited the Steinbecks at the ranch. It was an impressive place. The house was similar to their first Los Gatos house, but bigger, with a large fireplace and many windows in the living room. They'd also fixed up the old Biddle farmhouse for guests. And there was a delightful, narrow swimming pool. Steinbeck had saved a fortune on it by eliminating a pump and filter system and instead feeding it directly from a spring. After the success of *The Grapes of Wrath*, they hired a Japanese cook-gardener, and an "Okie boy" to do odd jobs. Steinbeck said the hired man wasn't really necessary, but he needed the work. Sheffield thought the location of the ranch was by far its best feature. It was surrounded by a forest, and there was a small lake fringed with green. Steinbeck seemed to enjoy milking the cow, and they planned to do some canning in the fall. When Steinbeck's dog, Toby, went out one day and didn't come back, Steinbeck didn't know if some accident had befallen him or Toby had simply decided to explore the world—but he settled on the latter. That dog was always thinking too much. Next, Steinbeck had a strapping, long-legged Doberman, which he sentimentally named Bruga, after a dog he'd had down in Los Angeles that had died.

Bruga no doubt discouraged trespassers. But then Bruga bit Steinbeck on the hand, and Steinbeck moved on to another dog. There was always another dog.

Steinbeck loved it at the ranch, but he decided to go to Chicago, to work with Pare Lorentz on a movie financed by the United States Film Service. A documentary and feature-film unit Lorentz created for FDR's Resettlement Administration, the film service made movies for various government agencies. The film Steinbeck was summoned to help write was a medical drama called *The Fight for Life*, which Roosevelt hoped would spur Congress to pass a public health bill. Steinbeck kept his involvement a secret. He didn't want anybody to know where he was or what he was doing. He believed Hollywood was changing and he wanted to learn everything he could about making pictures. When he got home a couple of months later, he said he'd been all over—to Chicago, New York, Washington, and down into the Deep South. Next he headed to Hollywood to work at a sound studio. Hollywood scared him because so many people there

Pascal Covici. The publisher-turned-editor called Steinbeck his "rarest experience." *(Bettmann via Getty Images)*

hated what the industry did to them. They were like ghosts, though many of them seemed nice and some were even beginning to wake up politically. It was around this time that Annie Laurie Williams at McIntosh & Otis sold the film rights to *The Grapes of Wrath* to Hollywood studio mogul Darryl Zanuck for $75,000.

In June *Life* magazine ran its photo spread from the migrant camps, with captions excerpted from *The Grapes of Wrath*, plus a few written by Steinbeck specifically for the feature. Horace Bristol's photos, from his expedition with Steinbeck to the flooded camps near Visalia, captured the images that became the book—the leaky tents and the rattletrap cars, a Ma Joad figure wringing her hands, children splashing through a flood alongside a line of boxcar houses. The brief text highlighted the depths of the problem, which the magazine identified as a cruel subset of the Great Depression writ large:

> Migrants are still in California, squatting in hideous poverty and squalor on the thin margins of the world's richest land. Of the one-third of the nation that is ill-housed, ill-clad, ill-nourished these are the bitterest dregs.

Steinbeck told Dook Sheffield that the Associated Farmers were attacking him and *The Grapes of Wrath*, but to no avail, as all of his claims in the book were well documented. He turned over materials to the FBI in case something happened to him. These might have included Tom Collins's reports, which Steinbeck had briefly worked on in hopes of getting them published. His worry for his own safety wasn't imaginary. Some years later Steinbeck related to a friend that a deputy sheriff in Santa Clara County had warned him to be careful traveling in California—in particular to avoid being in any hotel room by himself. The deputy claimed there was a plot afoot to frame Steinbeck on a rape charge—the very sort of thing he'd discussed with Toby Street. The way it would work is that after Steinbeck checked in, a woman would come to his room, rip off her clothes, and scream rape.

Steinbeck also gave materials on the migrant situation to the

La Follette Committee. Robert La Follette Jr. was a progressive U.S. senator from Wisconsin who chaired a subcommittee looking into the problems of rural migration in California and across the country. The subcommittee found that one reason the government had been slow to react to the migrants was that rural populations had never before needed relief on such a scale. During the Depression, soup kitchens and bread lines were common in cities but not in the countryside, where people lived on the land and were used to feeding themselves. Once displaced from the land, however, the migrants—who had little hope of finding employment in industry—were parted from the only way of living that they knew. The subcommittee heard testimony that in the long run these people needed productive land they could farm, but that it could take fifteen or even twenty-five years to find a way to provide it for them. The government was thought to be all but incapable of that kind of foresight, even though finding land for people who'd been deprived of it seemed the most obvious thing in the world. In the interim, part of the basic fabric of the country was coming undone. As W. W. Alexander, head of the Farm Security Administration testified:

> I do not believe that America can continue to be the kind of place it is now and has been in the past with these migrant families floating around. There is something to be conserved that is of very great value to the nation and I think we have not yet taken seriously enough the value of farm ownership and making these people secure in their ownership.

Steinbeck had come to the end of perhaps the most productive and acclaimed five-year stretch of work by any author ever. Starting with *Tortilla Flat* in 1935, Steinbeck had had one breakthrough after another. Year to year, one book to the next, he had become a major force in American literature at the age of thirty-seven—or, in about the same length of time that he had grappled with *To a God Unknown*. In a probing examination of Steinbeck's work published in his collection *The Boys in the Back Room*, Edmund Wilson offered a judicious summing up of a career he thought was at a vibrant midpoint but was complicated by Steinbeck's preoccupation with natural forces and "animal" behavior. More so than any other critic, Wilson saw biology as the framework in all of Steinbeck's writing. He noticed that in addition to prefiguring the Joads' journey west in the progress of a turtle, Steinbeck had them travel through *The Grapes of Wrath* "accompanied and parodied all the way by animals, insects, and birds."

Steinbeck, Wilson said, had a technical skill—he called it virtuosity—that tended to obscure his meaning. He thought Steinbeck's body of work represented a searching exploration of California that was unmatched, except by William Faulkner's "exhaustive study" of Mississippi. But while Steinbeck's gaze was fixed on California, he never saw it the same way twice, Wilson said. No two of his books were alike. "Thus attention has been diverted from the content of Mr. Steinbeck's work by the fact that when his curtain goes up, he always put on a different kind of show."

And the "content" that sprang from this kaleidoscope of story and form was, for Wilson, Steinbeck's conviction that all living things, including human beings, inhabit a natural narrative that is based on biological principles. Wilson thought this was a hidden asset of Steinbeck's work:

"Yet there is in Mr. Steinbeck's fiction a substratum which remains constant and which gives it a certain weight. What is constant in Mr. Steinbeck is his preoccupation with biology. He is a biologist in the literal sense that he interests himself in biological research. The biological laboratory in the short story called 'The Snake' is obviously something which he knows at first hand and for which he has a strong special feeling; and it is one of the peculiarities of his vocabulary that it runs to biological terms. But the laboratory described in 'The Snake,' the tight little building above the water, where the scientist feeds white rats to rattlesnakes and fertilizes starfish ova, is also one of the key images of his fiction. It is the symbol of Mr. Steinbeck's tendency to present human life in animal terms."

The tight little building above the water. Wilson's recognition that Ed Ricketts's lab was hallowed ground for Steinbeck was a critical bull's-eye. But he admitted to ambivalence about the way Steinbeck's biological perspective worked in constructing believable characters. In *The Grapes of Wrath*, Wilson said, Steinbeck "summoned all his resources" to make the reader feel a connection to the Joads as human beings. But he thought the result was "not quite real." Steinbeck turned the family into players on a stage, giving them authentic-sounding dialogue but not credible personalities. This was all too theatrical, Wilson said—as if the Okies did not exist for Steinbeck as actual people. It was an odd objection considering the source—a bookish, neatly tailored man who could be seen as a bit of a fiction himself. What, we can only wonder, would a real Okie make of the erudite, Princeton-educated Mr. Wilson? Surely a hardened and world-weary tenant farmer would doubt that any such person could exist.

For Wilson, biological realism was Steinbeck's "natural habit of mind," and it translated in his books to an "irreducible faith in life" that Wilson found appealing. Even though he didn't think any of Steinbeck's books so far could be called first-rate—a harsh conclusion given the otherwise laudatory tone of the essay—Steinbeck himself had a talent and a mind that were indeed first-rate. What Wilson could not discount was what he called Steinbeck's "unpanicky scrutiny of life." Wilson was stuck on the word "life" when writing about Steinbeck. And no wonder. In biology, life finds a way. The great, diverse multitudes of species evolve and survive through eons of tumult, crowding into every corner of the earth. Life is fraught, but living things do not give up. Which was another way of saying that whatever else Steinbeck put into his books, the most important was hope.

In the summer of 1939, *The Grapes of Wrath* soared. It had landed in third place on the *New York Times* bestseller list in its first month of publication, and rose to number one by the start of May, where it stayed for the next five months. More dazed than elated, Steinbeck was bewildered by the book's success—and he may or may not have heard what only a handful of editors in New York knew. It was by the slimmest of chances that *The Grapes of Wrath* had even been published.

Early in 1939, before Steinbeck's book came out, Sanora Babb blindly sent four chapters of her novel about the California migrants to a rising young publishing executive in Manhattan named Bennett Cerf, president and cofounder of Random House. Cerf was impressed. He sent Babb a check and told her he would expect the completed work sometime in the summer. And in August, Babb delivered. The book was short and was titled *Whose Names Are Unknown*, a phrase she'd found on an eviction notice. Cerf concurred with the Random House editors who read Babb's manuscript and found it less visceral and authentic-sounding than *The Grapes of Wrath*, to which it bore similarities, but thought it more rewarding in its portrait of the land and the people on it. The editors also said—interestingly—that Babb's book had a stronger ending, one that was "solid" and not a "trick." The only problem, of course, was that *The Grapes of Wrath* was by then the book of the year. Cert ruefully wrote to Babb telling her that publishing her book now was out of the question. "What rotten luck," he said.

Cerf urged Babb to sign on with Random House anyway, and sent her a contract for her next book. He also generously sent *Whose Names Are Unknown* around to several other publishers, all of whom turned it down for the same reason Cerf had. One of the editors who sent Babb a polite rejection was Pascal Covici. Cerf never got Babb's next book—a novel called *The Lost Traveler*, which came out in 1958 and was followed in 1970 by her memoir, *An Owl on Every Post*. Babb died in 2005, at the age of ninety-eight. *Whose Names Are Unknown* had finally been published the year before that, sixty-five years after it was written. The publisher, fittingly, was the University of Oklahoma Press.

Had Babb been quicker—or if Steinbeck had listened to his own repeated warnings to himself to slow down—their books might have been finished in a different order, and *The Grapes of Wrath* could have been the one everybody liked and nobody wanted.

The world frayed as 1939 hurtled by. War in Europe seemed inevitable. Poland, like Czechoslovakia, had been assembled from a jigsaw puzzle of territories in the 1919 Treaty of Versailles. Germany disputed the western region of Poland along its border, home to many Germans, and the Soviet Union had designs on the eastern region. In August, Germany and the Soviet Union signed the German-Soviet Nonaggression Pact, which declared their peaceful intentions toward each other and included a secret provision that would allow them to partition Poland and claim the parts of it each wanted. Hitler intended to proceed immediately with an invasion, and after a brief delay, Germany attacked at the beginning of September. Earlier that year, Britain and France had signed treaties promising to come to the aid of Poland if it was attacked, but in the intervening months they had urged Poland not to fully mobilize its large army for fear it would ignite a conflict. Germany's invasion was swift and deadly—especially the coordinated *blitzkrieg* of fast-moving tank and air attacks. Warsaw and other targets were shelled and bombed and strafed into submission. On September 3, Britain and France declared war on Germany—and World War II began. In London, air-raid sirens went off only moments after Neville Chamberlain broadcast the declaration of war. It turned out to be a false alarm—but a preview of things to come.

In mid-September, as the Poles waited for France to come to their rescue on the western border, Soviet forces invaded Poland from the east. This was confusing, because no one was sure how the British and French would respond. Would they now declare war on the Soviet Union? They didn't, and by the end of the month the German invasion had succeeded. On October 5, Hitler toured Warsaw in triumph. Europe waited to see what would happen next, while in Washington

President Roosevelt had to reconcile the isolationist instinct that was widespread in the country with his belief that war was likely to come whether America wanted it or not.

Roosevelt wrote to Joseph Kennedy, the U.S. ambassador to Britain, telling him that Americans did not yet appreciate the fact that the world was shrinking, that mere geography could no longer protect us, and that we were experiencing "the rapid annihilation of distance and purely local economies." America and Europe were inherently linked, and Europe's problems, he believed, would likely become ours. Roosevelt chose a middle way as his public position, doing his best to sound neutral while preparing for war. Earlier that year he'd authorized a massive build-up of the navy. After the German attack on Poland, Roosevelt asked Congress to authorize the Selective Service in case a draft was needed, and added another $15 billion for a general rearmament. In the fall of 1939, as the bombs fell on Warsaw, the total U.S. armed forces numbered 140,000 troops. Within two years, that would climb to 1.25 million. Perhaps the biggest hint about Roosevelt's intentions came in 1940, when he decided to seek a third term—something he'd said he would do only in the event of a worldwide crisis.

Steinbeck kept track of these developments while dealing with his own miseries. His sciatica had recurred, and for a while his leg hurt worse than before. In June he'd pleaded with McIntosh & Otis to take over the crush of mail he was receiving—as many as seventy-five letters a day. Some of it, he said, was plainly from the insane. One woman named Irma wrote to him every day. And he said the phone never stopped ringing. So many people wanted something from him now—signed copies, appearances, prefaces for other books. He could not stand it. Something had to be worked out, or "I am finished writing."

Not long after this, Steinbeck started throwing away letters without reading them. One day, one person and then another came up to the door of the ranch before eleven in the morning—after ignoring the locked gate—wanting to meet him. He told Elizabeth Otis he was thinking of bailing out of the film project with Pare Lorentz so he could escape to Mexico. It was hard to say which was worse: the adulation of his legions of readers or the hatred directed at him by the growers and their allies. He suspected it was the former. He'd anticipated that he would be attacked by the big farm interests, but being besieged by so many adoring fans who wanted some piece of him was unsettling. Jack Benny mentioned the book on his radio program, and made things worse. Steinbeck said the sheer momentum of the book scared him. The public's obsession with it was, he said, unhealthy. When it dropped from first place to second on the local bestseller list, Steinbeck was elated. He said he took comfort in dreams of obscurity. With any luck, he said, *The Grapes of Wrath* would fall from the bestseller lists everywhere, and in six months he would be forgotten.

Steinbeck said his vilification at the hands of the large landowners seemed without limits. Lately they'd spread a rumor that the Okies hated him and had threatened to kill him for lying about them. Tom Collins reported that when the residents at Weedpatch heard about this, they wanted to "burn something down." Steinbeck believed the campaign against him by the Associated Farmers only sold more

Elizabeth Otis, Steinbeck's agent and confidante. *(Martha Heasley Cox Center for Steinbeck Studies, San Jose State University)*

copies of the book. People who wrote articles against him routinely said they hadn't read *The Grapes of Wrath*, as they wouldn't dirty their minds with it. And still the vigilantes patrolled the camps. Steinbeck figured it was going to be a bloody year.

And in so many ways, it was. In Europe. In the farm fields of California. And even right at home, where the biggest trouble didn't come from the outside but from inside the pretty house on the pretty hill. Here there was no actual bloodshed. It was worse than that.

— 12 —

AT SEA

BOOK HAS TWO LIVES. The first is with the author, when it is like a difficult child being coaxed to behave. In the second, it leaves home and makes its way in an uncertain world as the author watches and hopes for the best. Some writers have two lives as well, one a time of apprenticeship and struggle, and the next in company with the consequences of success. Nothing is harder to live up to than your own finest moment, and when it comes early—as it did to John Steinbeck with *The Grapes of Wrath*—the way forward can be long and difficult. In the summer of 1939, Steinbeck embarked on his second life. Having become the writer he longed to be since childhood, he now set sail on the sea of fame. He would not be the same man. Almost inevitably, it started with a woman who wanted to meet the writer.

She was a nineteen-year-old lit fuse named Gwen Conger. Conger was a contract performer for CBS Radio in Los Angeles and also worked as a lounge singer at Brittingham's, a restaurant and watering hole adjacent to the CBS studios on Sunset Boulevard. It was popular with show people. Steinbeck met her in June of 1939 while he was in Los Angeles, supposedly learning the movie business—though it was notable that after months of intense collaboration with Carol on *The Grapes of Wrath*, he was now finding reasons to be away from her.

As had happened with Ed Ricketts, there were multiple versions of the story of how Steinbeck and Gwen met. Steinbeck was introduced to Conger by his childhood friend Max Wagner. Wagner had moved to Hollywood in 1924 and had become a bit player in the movies—he had a small part in *Tortilla Flat* and decades later made a number of appearances on popular TV Westerns such as *Gunsmoke* and *The Rifleman*. Both of his brothers were in the film business. Jack Wagner was a screenwriter, and Blake Wagner a cinematographer. The three of them shared an apartment not far from Brittingham's, and they sometimes said hello when Gwen walked by on her way to work. When Max finally went down and heard her sing, he was smitten. Gwen said Max fell in love with her and took her everywhere, but she wouldn't sleep with him. She said that when he had a few drinks—which was often—Max liked to reminisce about his "friend from Salinas," the writer John Steinbeck. Gwen was impressed. Everybody knew who John Steinbeck was that summer. Max had last seen Steinbeck in 1929, when the Steinbecks were living at Dook Sheffield's place near Los Angeles. Carol had been cool toward him, and maybe that's why he decided to introduce Steinbeck to another woman when he got the chance.

According to Wagner, he took Steinbeck to Brittingham's, telling him "there was a girl there who sings out of this world." They listened as Gwen did a few numbers, and after a while she came over. Wagner introduced them and put Gwen next to Steinbeck when she sat down. She had reddish-blonde hair, a flawless complexion that everyone noticed, and a shape that caused one friend to say "she was made for the bedroom." As Gwen herself told it, she'd developed a thirty-six-inch bust at the age of twelve and was used to male attention. Gwen was beautiful and smart and very funny, and it didn't take long for Steinbeck to see all of that.

A couple of days later, again according to Wagner, Steinbeck fell ill and holed up at the Aloha Arms Apartments, where Wagner was staying. When Gwen asked about him, Max suggested she take him some chicken soup. When she got there, Gwen propped Steinbeck up on some pillows. Soon he was better, so she suggested they go for a ride in her car. The three of them drove up to Laurel Canyon to see a friend of Gwen's. By the time they got there, Steinbeck seemed to be cured. "I think he would have stayed there," Wagner said. "He was a peculiar guy." After that, Steinbeck and Gwen started spending a lot of time together.

Gwen's version of the story was better—though it's a stretch to believe all of it. She said they did not meet at Brittingham's, but at the Aloha Arms, where Steinbeck seemed to be quite sick. Gwen was working on a picture that starred Irene Dunne, and somebody on the set had given her a copy of *The Pastures of Heaven*. She read it and told Max Wagner she wanted to meet Steinbeck. Wagner explained that Steinbeck was in town, but was under the weather. Maybe he could use some chicken soup. Gwen went to Steinbeck's apartment with the soup—Steinbeck detested chicken soup—and when she arrived, it was a miserable scene. The apartment was in disarray, with Steinbeck sitting up in an old Murphy bed, smoking and sharing a bottle of Scotch with Wagner. Gwen said Steinbeck had trouble walking—she thought at first because of the Scotch, though it later became apparent that he was having trouble with his leg. The place reeked of cigarettes and booze and fevered sweat. There was nothing to do but have a couple of drinks with Steinbeck and Wagner. At some point, Gwen said, Steinbeck fixed his "cold, blue eyes" on her and she really looked at him. Before she knew what happened, Wagner had gone home, and she and Steinbeck sat up all through the night.

Gwen decided that what Steinbeck needed was a hot bath. She drew one and had him get in. As she washed his back and massaged his legs she noticed that he had prominent varicose veins in his thighs and up into his groin—these might have had something to do with his difficulty on the rowing team back at Stanford. Steinbeck had, Gwen said, "a magnificent physique," a phrase open to interpretation but suggestive of what Gwen might have seen in him that helped her get past their eighteen-year age difference. Gwen never said exactly what happened between them that night—she insisted they didn't sleep together until later—but she claimed that it was "pure chemistry," and that because Steinbeck was in such pain, her "maternal instincts" were aroused. "Whatever I was able to provide," she said, "was something he needed."

One of the things Steinbeck talked about that night was his fear of being used by people, of no longer trusting anyone who wanted to be his friend. The frenzied reception of *The Grapes of Wrath* was only part of it. Gwen thought he'd felt that way his whole life. When the sun came up and Gwen said she had to go to work, Steinbeck promised he'd come to Brittingham's that night to hear her sing.

But Steinbeck did not show up. When he did come the following evening, he hobbled in with a cane. Gwen thought he looked crippled. They had a few drinks. She didn't tell anybody who he was. It went on that way every night for a few days, until Gwen had a night off and Steinbeck took her to dinner. They went to a funny little place that served Swedish food, of all things. Gwen felt she was being seduced. Steinbeck, she learned, was supremely confident about his sex appeal. Steinbeck rubbed his knees against hers under the table and held her hand. He used his free hand to partially hide his face. Gwen had the impression he was afraid someone would recognize him, and it was clear that he hated even the thought of that. He asked Gwen endless

Gwen Conger. *(Photograph by Maurice Seymour, courtesy Ronald Seymour)*

questions—where was she from? What had her life been like? What did she like to read? Whom, if anyone, was she in love with? Gwen was flattered, but nervous at his close inspection of her.

Gwen told Steinbeck she was born in Chicago. Her mother's side of the family had once owned a lot of land in Wisconsin. Her father deserted the family when she was three, but her mother—a woman Steinbeck took to calling "Bird Eyes" after he'd met her—quickly remarried. Gwen's stepfather was a nice man, and they spent time in the country, where Gwen learned to swim and hunt and fish—a part of her story Steinbeck had to find endearing. She also admitted that she'd been taunted by other kids about her body. Sometimes they threw snowballs at her chest. Now it was just Gwen and her mother sharing an apartment in Los Angeles with Gwen's aunt Fann. Gwen was the breadwinner and it was a lean time for them, as it was for most people.

When the check arrived, Steinbeck discovered his wallet was empty. He explained to Gwen that Carol handled all their money and that he got an allowance of $35 a week. Somehow, it was gone. Gwen had just enough to cover the bill. Steinbeck said he'd pay her back the next day.

Steinbeck headed back to Los Gatos after that, and for a time Gwen only got letters from him. And books. At one point, when Steinbeck thought he might not see her again, he sent Gwen a book about Petrarch, the fourteenth-century Italian priest and poet who surrendered his calling to pursue—unsuccessfully—a woman named Laura. Steinbeck also wrote Gwen twenty-five love poems crowded with references to her red hair and pure, sweet-smelling skin, and with allusions to the way his cares melted away when they were together. She made him feel insulated against the world. The poems were lousy, but one bit jumped out:

> *I have known girls more beautiful than you*
> *Who were not as beautiful as you*
> *I have known women, red haired*
> *Milk skinned who were yet not red haired,*

Not with the good smell of a girl and they
Were girls too, and red haired.

The transition from struggling writer to Great Man of Letters, which had begun in what felt like the blink of an eye, was an unhappy time for Steinbeck. There was a chill between him and Carol that had preceded his infatuation with Gwen Conger, and even worse was not knowing what to do next. He told his old friend Toby Street—who so long ago had given Steinbeck *The Green Lady* in the belief that he was destined to be a writer—that he was by nature a neurotic person, and that he survived by pushing all of his neuroses into his books. Steinbeck said writing literally took something out of him—made him smaller. And yet he could not stop writing. Not working was like suffocating. When he finished a book and knew it wasn't good that wasn't what bothered him. What bothered him was knowing that he couldn't have made it better.

This echoed the complaint of another American writer who felt himself staring into a dim future after the strain of completing the book he knew he could never improve on—Herman Melville. Melville was thirty-two years old when *Moby-Dick* was published in the fall of 1851. During the time he worked on it, Melville realized both how good it was and how powerless he would be when it was done to live up to the many ideas for more books that filled his head. He claimed to have fifty of them he could write at once if he only had enough quick-witted assistants. But before he was done with the whale he began to feel differently, writing to his friend Nathaniel Hawthorne that *Moby-Dick* had come to him insistently—he spent just over a year writing it—now he feared that kind of creative fire would never again burn as brightly for him, that he was more likely to fade back into anonymity. "I feel that I am now come to the inmost leaf of the bulb," he wrote, "and that shortly the flower must fall to the mould."

Things between Steinbeck and Carol worsened that summer. Both were in a state of constant agitation. Dorothea Lange had promised her publisher that Steinbeck was going to write a preface for her book of migrant photographs. But he'd refused, and now she was angry with him. He was going to get away from these sorts of distractions for two weeks back down in Hollywood. He was probably tempted to make this a visit to Gwen, but ended up persuading Carol to come with him. They stayed at the Garden of Allah Apartments. It did not go well. Offering few specifics, Steinbeck told Elizabeth Otis that Carol had become "hysterical" and abruptly went home. Steinbeck, who was sick again, stayed on in Los Angeles for two weeks and then, rather than going home, went to Pacific Grove and stayed at Ricketts's lab. He said he had no doubt he was to blame for everything. He didn't hear a word from Carol and knew only that she was at the ranch. He'd never questioned Carol's dedication to him the year before, when she was his partner in writing *The Grapes of Wrath* and served as his faithful bulwark against distractions. Now he told Otis that Carol no longer loved him. He could feel it at all times, but it was worse when she drank and told him so.

He added that he wanted Carol to be happy and knew that he was not the answer. He said nobody could help him. But a few days later, he said he was back at the ranch and that he and Carol had patched things up—or had at least achieved a truce. This was to become their pattern—on the rocks one minute and in love again the next. Only days after this update, Steinbeck wrote to Otis once more to say that Carol was losing her mind, if she hadn't already. Or maybe, he said, it was "premature menopause," a stupid suggestion that proved the meanness was not all on Carol's side. It seemed that Steinbeck was surrounded by hysterical people, as that is how he now referred to the Associated Farmers—who, unlike Carol, deserved the label. He said they continued to savage him in the papers, and also in a whispering campaign of personal attacks. Rumors were spread that he was Jewish—an awful thing, apparently—also that he was a sexual pervert, a drunk, and a dope fiend.

Elizabeth Otis kept sending him checks, mostly royalties and rights fees from *Of Mice and Men*, which would soon be released as a movie. The gush of money would grow as proceeds from *The Grapes of*

Wrath added to his steadily swelling income. In September Steinbeck and Carol took a two-week driving trip up to Vancouver. Steinbeck said they'd succeeded in "losing touch" with the craziness around the book. He said if they ever got forced out of California, Vancouver was where they'd go.

In October of 1939, one year after he finished *The Grapes of Wrath*, Steinbeck resumed the journal he'd kept while he worked on the book. Having gone a year without writing—the longest time he'd ever done so—he now had to put his life back on track. He'd become a "public domain," which he still tried to fight off as best he could, but admitted to no regrets about the wealth that had come in the bargain. "[W]e are rich as riches go," he said. "We have enough money to keep us for many years. We have this pleasant ranch which is everything one could desire." He was surprised that the book kept selling even after the war broke out in Europe. He called it a "curious kind of war," and predicted that its true nature had not yet emerged. A few days later, Steinbeck was overcome with foreboding and "strong death premonitions." This was his old complaint that life rushed by and each year brought him closer to the end. It wasn't that he felt death was imminent. The trouble was that it was inevitable. To be ready whenever death should come, Steinbeck dug out every scrap of correspondence he could find and burned it all. "I have a horror of people going through it," he said, "messing around in my past, such as it is."

Another big check—this one for $13,000—arrived from McIntosh & Otis. When Steinbeck wrote to say thanks, he reminded Elizabeth Otis of how excited they'd been with the $90 they'd gotten from the *North American Review* for "The Red Pony" not so long ago. Sadly, such excitement would never come again. Was there anything left of that writer or even of that man? He wasn't sure what the answer was. "But I know it will be found in the tide pools and on a microscope slide rather than in men."

Steinbeck wrote to Dook Sheffield in a similar vein, betraying a tectonic shift in his thinking about what to do with his life. He admitted that he had never thought much of the novel as an art form and felt that he'd done everything he could with it. It was time for something different. He regretted not being better educated, especially in math and science, fields he now deemed more important to understanding the human condition than fiction writing. But he admitted that the whole idea of launching some new career had come to him at a time of personal and professional stress. Maybe he couldn't trust his instincts. It was a confusing time for him. He wondered what Dook thought. It seemed to Steinbeck that the unease jangling in Europe was rattling his nerves.

Ed Ricketts had spent much of the 1930s at work on a field guide to the intertidal zone on the Monterey Peninsula, which he hoped to publish with Stanford University Press. When his lab burned down in 1936, the manuscript was the only thing Ricketts saved from the flames. Stanford had to overcome its concerns about Ricketts's lack of formal training—though his friends at Stanford's Hopkins Marine Station in Pacific Grove were in awe of his extensive knowledge—and also the book's unusual format. Rather than organize his survey of life forms taxonomically, by genus and species, Ricketts had followed an ecological outline, placing his invertebrates where they lived. Ricketts broke down the intertidal region into specific shore types, and within those broad categories he narrowed each ecosystem within its vertical strata—from the lowest parts, which are always underwater, to a middle zone, which by turns is dry or wet as the tides rise and fall, to the upper reaches, touched only by intermittent spray. Essentially, Ricketts had devised a way of seeing the living components of the seashore environment in exactly the way you would encounter them in the field. It was a radical departure—and an inspired one. Stanford finally published *Between Pacific Tides* in April of 1939, the same month *The Grapes of Wrath* came out. Some years later, Rachel Carson—prose-poet of the oceans and godmother of the environmental movement—would base her best-selling guide to the Atlantic shoreline, *The Edge of the Sea*, on Ricketts's book.

Stanford wanted Ricketts to do another guidebook, this time about the shoreline of San Francisco Bay. Steinbeck thought it was an excellent idea. After he'd loaned Ricketts money to help in the recovery from the fire, Steinbeck joined the management of Pacific Biological Laboratories—though his job as vice president amounted to little more than hanging out with Ricketts at the lab and making the occasional beer run. Steinbeck suggested they write the San Francisco Bay book together and sell it to either Stanford or Viking, depending on which made them the better offer.

Steinbeck and Ricketts made a collecting trip to the bay on Christmas Day of 1939. Carol went with them. In the weeks that followed, both Ricketts and Steinbeck drafted sections of the book—and both took a stab at an introduction. Steinbeck went over to Monterey to work on his introduction at the lab. He couldn't get it right. He realized the book was going to be hard for him to do in his current state of mind. He experienced a "crash within myself"; everything felt finished. He had no plans that seemed to matter. Carol, who'd gone back to the ranch, seemed only half in the picture. After about ten days she came over to Monterey. Steinbeck thought maybe they'd get a hotel room.

In fact, Steinbeck did have a plan—it just hadn't completely formed yet. While he and Ricketts were tentatively beginning to work on the bay guidebook they'd started thinking about a more ambitious project, a survey of the intertidal region on the coasts of the Sea of Cortez, also known as the Gulf of California. The "Mexican book," as Steinbeck called it, would be for a general audience and would definitely be published by Viking. They were going to drive, and they got as far as buying a truck and beginning to outfit it for collecting. Steinbeck bought a fancy microscope and consulted with a company in Berkeley about building a refrigeration unit for the truck.

Steinbeck was everywhere that winter, in bookstores and in theaters. The movie version of *Of Mice and Men*—with Burgess Meredith as George and Lon Chaney Jr. as Lennie—opened in Hollywood in December. Steinbeck and Carol went down to see it and were also given a preview screening of *The Grapes of Wrath*, which was set to open in January. Steinbeck loved the picture. He said it looked almost like a documentary. He thought the cast—which included Henry Fonda as Tom Joad, Jane Darwell as Ma, and John Carradine as Casy—was terrific. None of the material from the general chapters was in the movie, and Steinbeck thought this smart decision had made the film grittier than the book.

Steinbeck's fondness for the film must have shocked Elizabeth Otis and Pascal Covici, since director John Ford and screenwriter Nunnally Johnson had moved around key episodes and dispensed with the book's elegiac ending altogether. The movie finished instead on an uplifting note, in an expansive rewrite of Ma's speech about how women move through life as a river flows between its banks. The Joads and their kind won't die out, Ma says—they'll go on because "We're the people that live." This is at considerable odds with the message of the book—not to mention the realities of what Steinbeck had seen in the migrant camps—but it gave audiences the happy ending they were thought to need.

The movie has not aged nearly so well as the book. Johnson turned Steinbeck's clipped, earthy rendering of the Okies' speech into solemn, plainspoken wisdom without the truncations and faulty vocabulary—though he did retain their wariness and reserve. This helped keep Tom Joad from disappearing in Henry Fonda's matinee-idol presence—which Fonda admirably tried to downplay—but it left Ma and Casy too often staring wide-eyed into infinity as they make quaking speeches declaring that life is mysterious and deep. Melodrama succumbed to hokum.

But what a look. John Ford was friends with the Irish writer Liam O'Flaherty, and Ford saw parallels between the migration of Steinbeck's Okies and the journey to America of the evicted Irish tenant farmers in O'Flaherty's *Famine*. Ford's cameraman, Gregg Toland—who shot *Citizen Kane* the following year—evoked Ireland's devastated countryside in the burned-out and tractored-over Oklahoma landscape. In one exquisite shot, he even captured the small plumes of dust rising from Tom Joad's footfalls as he walks across a field. In another, when the Joads drive into their first migrant camp and the raggedy, starving residents make way for the overloaded truck as it rocks forward unsteadily, he created a hellish and mesmerizing scene.

In February, Steinbeck and Carol were at work on their income tax returns when another huge check arrived from New York. They figured they owed something like $40,000 for the previous year. Steinbeck said they were saving every penny that came in, as they expected they'd have to live on it for the rest of their lives. Or maybe not. Steinbeck had an idea now for a series of articles based on the Gulf of California expedition. He and Ricketts had set aside the San Francisco Bay guidebook—in the end it never happened—and were now getting ready for the Mexican trip. After considering the ruggedness of the remote areas they wanted to visit along both sides of the gulf—700 miles long and anywhere from 30 to 150 miles across between Baja and the Mexican mainland—Steinbeck and Ricketts dropped the idea of driving down in a truck and instead leased a seventy-six-foot-long purse seiner to go by sea, skirting the coast and stopping in at intervals to explore the tide pools. The boat was named the *Western Flyer*. The cost of the six-week charter was $2,500, not counting provisions. Steinbeck was paying, so he asked Elizabeth Otis to see if she could sell a package of reports on the trip based on the ship's daily log.

Finding a boat had been harder than Steinbeck and Ricketts expected. It turned out that many of the boat owners in Monterey thought Steinbeck was a radical, or worse, and might have been involved in organizing the longshoremen who had staged a strike the year before. After being turned down by several owners, they asked Toby Street—whose Monterey law firm was counsel to the Boat Owners Association—for help. Street introduced them to Tony Berry, captain and co-owner of the *Western Flyer*.

She was a handsome vessel, long and lean and well kept. Steinbeck inspected the engine room and found it spotless. The 165-horsepower Atlas diesel was gleaming and the tools were polished and hung in their proper places. There was room for people and gear. In addition to

Steinbeck, Ricketts, and Captain Berry, the crew would include Hal "Tex" Travis, the engineer, plus two deckhands, Tiny Colletto and Sparky Enea. Tiny and Sparky had known each other since grammar school in Monterey. Tiny, at five feet two inches and 118 pounds, was a compact block of muscle who joined the expedition on a lark. An undefeated former bantamweight boxer and a navy veteran, he was also a locally legendary ladies' man who was dating one of Flora Woods's girls from the Lone Star Café. Sparky was an inch shorter than Tiny and, like all Sicilians, loved to tell stories. Steinbeck had tried to say no when Carol asked to come along as the ship's cook, but she made it clear she wasn't really asking. And so she came, although once at sea she declined to do any cooking. The crew found it strange that Steinbeck and Carol said no to Captain Berry's stateroom when he offered it. Instead, Carol would sleep in the wheelhouse, and the rest, including Steinbeck, in the forward crew quarters.

They outfitted the *Western Flyer* for the trip with collecting gear and makeshift work areas above and below decks, stocks of alcohol and formaldehyde, microscopes and cameras, plus a scientific library that had to be lashed down topside. They also loaded cigarettes, whiskey, brandy, wine, and a little beer, though they planned to buy beer as they went in Mexico. Ricketts and Steinbeck were both fond of Carta Blanca. Anticipating the heat, they installed a small refrigeration unit meant to cool seawater for keeping specimens alive, though in the end it was used mostly to chill the beer.

The *Western Flyer* sailed from Monterey on March 11, 1940. There was a send-off party onboard that delayed their departure for several hours. The *Monterey Peninsula Herald* sent a photographer down the pier. Steinbeck ducked behind Carol when a group photo was taken. He later gave orders to the entire crew that at no point on the trip should anybody take his picture. They finally sent their guests home and got underway.

Carol, who had continued drinking on their way out, became sick in the rolling seas and went to sleep. When Captain Berry asked about dinner, Sparky Enea—who'd learned to cook on his father's tuna boat—volunteered to take charge of the galley, a job he retained throughout the trip. Steinbeck said that first night they ate the "cold wreckage" of the snacks they'd served earlier that day back in port.

The book Steinbeck and Ricketts envisioned as an account of the trip was to be similar to *Between Pacific Tides*, but with the addition of the story behind the research. The Gulf of California is one of the richest and most diverse marine ecosystems on the planet—home to thousands of invertebrate species, many fishes and marine mammals, including the largest living creature on earth, the blue whale. The gulf is known for its abundance of giant manta rays, which often jump clear of the water and momentarily appear to take flight on their outstretched wings before crashing back into the sea. Jacques Cousteau called the Gulf of California "the world's aquarium." In 1940, the gulf had been thinly investigated, and mostly by specialists who collected only certain species. Steinbeck and Ricketts wanted to study the bigger picture, to work on everything in the tradition of the great naturalist Charles Darwin. The one thing that set their expedition apart from the famed voyage of the *Beagle* was that Darwin had years to work. Steinbeck and Ricketts would have six weeks.

When or even if Steinbeck's idea for a series of articles disappeared into the book project isn't clear. By the time they got underway, Steinbeck and Ricketts had agreed that each of them would keep a journal, and that Steinbeck would rely on both diaries in writing his portion of the book. Ricketts would, of course, be in charge of the phyletic catalogue at the end—the formal scientific inventory and discussion of invertebrates surveyed and collected at a series of stopping-in places along the coast. But in the end, only Ricketts kept a daily journal, and Steinbeck used that and his memory to reconstruct what happened. Sensing that readers would find their trip as much a pleasure excursion as work, Steinbeck kept it light, reporting on the collecting places and what they saw and did at each, recalling the color and shape of the sea and the land, recounting the ways they were charmed by the Mexicans and the local Indians they encountered, keeping time by the steady rhythm of the tides. He also included portraits of the captain and crew and mused on all that befell them at various ports of call. The title they settled on was *Sea of Cortez: A Leisurely Journal of Travel and Research*. Although Steinbeck wrote of how hard they drove themselves to collect as much as they could wherever they could, he merrily played up the "leisurely" aspects of the expedition.

Toby Street went with them as far as San Diego, where they saw the U.S. Navy in a frenzy of war preparation. Munitions and explosives were stacked everywhere, squadrons of airplanes flew over in tight formation, and submarines lay ominously alongside the wharf. Steinbeck talked with a gunnery officer, and wondered if the man could do his job if he ever saw the results of one of his shells falling among civilians miles away. News reports from Europe, coming in via shortwave radio, described a continent on the threshold of war. That spring, Germany would invade Denmark and Norway before taking Belgium and the Netherlands. By May, British forces would be surrounded at Dunkirk. America hung on the words of Ed Murrow, who now prefaced his reports with three somber words: "This is London." Steinbeck wrote that, whether you were for or against the war that everyone feared was coming, the men getting ready for it were the "true realists."

Back at sea, the crew got used to one another. Everyone noticed that Steinbeck and Carol observed a cool détente. They rarely quarreled and just as rarely displayed any affection for each other. When Carol removed her top to sun herself on the deck, the crew stared, while Steinbeck looked out blankly at the ocean. Sparky Enea thought Carol was unhappy and amused herself on the trip by flirting with Ricketts and Tiny Colletto. In fact, it seems likely that Carol took turns sleeping with both of them—and never with Steinbeck. But sometimes, on sultry nights when the *Western Flyer* lay at anchor under a spray of stars that included the Southern Cross, Steinbeck and Ricketts and Carol would go up on the bridge with brandies and talk for hours. It was almost like old times.

The six men divided themselves into three watches, taking their turns at the helm—Steinbeck and Tex, Sparky and Tiny, Captain Berry and Ricketts. Berry probably insisted on pairing up with Ricketts because he didn't like him. He thought Ricketts was lazy and drunk most of the time, more burden than he was help, except during collecting trips ashore. Ricketts's habit of stripping naked and soaking in a tub on the deck for hours at a time annoyed the crew.

As they passed south of the border with Mexico, the ocean turned a deeper blue. The crew was dazzled. "Tuna water" they called it. The *Western Flyer*, which had a cruising speed of about 11 miles per hour, knifed forward through the calm and oily-looking seas, trailing a narrow wake of foam. Captain Berry, a cautious skipper, kept her well offshore. On March 16, five days out of port, they passed through a sprawling mass of small red pelagic crabs swimming on the surface. It was like a crimson carpet spread across an ocean the color of lapis lazuli. Continuing to run day and night, they reached the tip of the Baja Peninsula two days later, and made their first collecting stop at Cabo San Lucas, threading their way into the unfamiliar harbor in the middle of the night and then meeting with a contingent of friendly local officials the next day before pulling on their rubber boots and going ashore to explore the rocky extremity of the land they'd sailed along the preceding week. Their equipment was simple: pry bars, buckets, assorted jars and glass tubes for collecting small specimens. And they were not disappointed on their first outing. Among the rocks was a fierce profusion of life—urchins and starfish and univalves clinging to the sharp edge of an ecosystem pummeled by the surf.

They hurried ahead of the tide, eager to see everything before the sea returned and submerged the brilliantly colored field of starfish, worms, snails, and hermit crabs. When it was time to go back to the *Western Flyer*, they climbed back into the *Baby Flyer*, the ship's short, heavy-bodied landing skiff that was "powered" by a notoriously unreliable outboard motor Steinbeck dubbed the "Hansen Sea-Cow." Outboard motors were small and primitive in those days. The Sea-Cow became a humorous bit player in the book. Seemingly with a mind of its own—the Sea-Cow liked some of the crew better than others—it ran only when it wanted to, which was rarely. Among its idiosyncrasies: it somehow used the same amount of gas whether it started or not. Where the fuel went when the motor refused to run was anybody's guess. Steinbeck said the motor also possessed clairvoyance, and that on a handful of occasions when they were ready to pitch it overboard, the Sea-Cow spluttered to life and ran perfectly, saving itself from a watery grave.

On that first day, they had to row back to the ship.

After sorting and recording the specimens, they cleaned up and went ashore, stopping at a small cantina that was infested with giant cockroaches but served Carta Blanca beer, which was warm but still good. Steinbeck bought a bottle of a native liquor called *damiana* that was infused with a local herb claimed to be an aphrodisiac. He said they planned to "test" it later, but never got around to trying the stuff. In the end it was seized by customs on their return.

From Cabo San Lucas onward, the voyage included a handful of predetermined collecting stops as they worked their way up the western edge of the gulf and then back down on the eastern side. In between they would go ashore wherever it looked interesting and approachable in the skiff. At Pulmo Reef, the falling tide revealed a flat coral plateau notched with crevices and dotted with limpid pools glittering with life under the tropical sun. They loaded the skiff and were pushed for a short distance toward the reef by the Sea-Cow, though they had to row the last part. The intertidal zone teems with things that bite or sting or poke, so they always wore their rubber boots and took care where they put their hands. As the ocean stood low, the company filled and refilled their buckets and vials.

Much of the Gulf of California is flanked by hot, arid landmasses, and this produces atmospheric conditions over the temperate sea that often create the mirages for which the gulf is famous. For example, it is sometimes possible along the Sonoran coast on the gulf's eastern side to see mountains over on the Baja Peninsula on the western side—even though they are below the horizon. The crew of the *Western Flyer* encountered this phenomenon repeatedly as they moved north. They would pass by a headland that suddenly seemed to shear

away from the mainland and stand apart, like an island, before separating itself from the water and floating into the sky. Even close to
shore, it was difficult to tell what the land looked like. Some islands,
clearly marked on the map but nowhere to be seen, spontaneously
appeared close by long after they should have been sighted, while
others were sometimes visible at distances far beyond what should
have been possible. The mirages made Captain Berry nervous, as he
had fixed ideas about how to handle the ship that depended on always
knowing exactly where danger lay. He didn't like thinking that his
eyes might be deceiving him.

They fell into a pattern, searching out collecting places, working
hard through low tide, fighting pitched battles with the Sea-Cow,
getting underway again, and then finding that evening's anchorage,
where they relaxed and drank and talked under the southern night.
Sometimes they read—Steinbeck had brought along copies of *The
Grapes of Wrath* and *Studs Lonigan*, which proved popular with Tiny
and Sparky. Many times they felt powerfully isolated. Oddly, given
the heat and the ceaseless movement, it must have reminded Steinbeck of those dark winters at Lake Tahoe, when the very thought of
any larger world seemed improbable. As they lay at anchor at night,
a heavy dew soaked the deck, and when the engine shut down it
grew still except for the occasional splash of a fish or ray breaking
the surface. Steinbeck said the silence made the crew nervous. They
were glad when they heard the barking of a dog or some other proof
of life onshore.

Apart from his eagerness to finance Ricketts's scientific studies
and to work on a book with his closest friend, Steinbeck went on
this trip to escape the crush of notoriety and hostility that had overwhelmed him with the publication of *The Grapes of Wrath* and the
back-to-back releases of two major Hollywood films based on his
work. Uncomfortable with being the writer of the moment, and then
disoriented by his affair with Gwen, Steinbeck had taken leave of
the life he'd known, and for him, the expedition to the gulf was a
voyage of departure. He was embarked on a new phase, this time
with no plan and with a different struggle ahead. Each day was an

incremental goodbye to the anxious thrill of becoming a writer and a deeper stride into the mire of being one. Having Carol close at hand reminded him of all this, kept the tension from fully dissipating. He could not have failed to notice her unhappiness with him as she shifted her gaze between Tiny Colletto and Ed Ricketts. Back in the summer, Joseph Campbell had turned up in Monterey. Campbell had gotten married, and he stopped in California on his way home from a honeymoon in Hawaii. He steered clear of Steinbeck, but did visit Ricketts—something Steinbeck no doubt heard about. So there was that old wound aboard the *Western Flyer*, too.

They spent March 22, which was Good Friday, in the port city of La Paz, a splendid old colonial settlement nestled on the southern rim of a broad bay on the western shore of the gulf. The place was not unlike Monterey and reminded them all of home.

The crew cleaned up, put on decent clothes, and went to church. Later in the day, Sparky and Tiny found a bordello that was closed in observance of the religious occasion and bought enough tequila for two of the girls to open the place up. Two days later, after proceeding north, they were anchored off San Jose Island. It was Easter Sunday. The night before, the crew had been attacked by hordes of black flies and got no sleep. Instead, they lay awake listening to Tiny Colletto tell the story of his life. Steinbeck said it was a "disreputable" saga of behavior so indelicate that it defied biological probabilities, not to mention the postal codes respecting obscene material if Tiny were foolish enough to ever write any of it down.

Easter was hot, the beach bright yellow. They swam and walked along the sandy edge of a lagoon, half-heartedly collecting a few specimens before going back to the *Western Flyer* to nap and later talk about the nature of all things, of how the universe works, and of why we lose our way whenever we ask "Why?" Steinbeck turned this informal afternoon symposium into a rambling monologue that afterward came to be known as the Easter Sunday Sermon, and has long since been attributed to Ricketts. The signature episode in *Sea of*

Cortez, it was an attempt to distill ideas that Steinbeck and Ricketts had been discussing for years, about the interplay between metaphysics and the concrete endeavors of literature and science. At its core was a concept Ricketts called "nonteleological thinking," which he believed was essential to seeing everything clearly.

Teleology is a branch of metaphysics that figured in Greek philosophy and proposed that everything in the physical universe, including all living things, have both a purpose and a cause that are inseparable. In plain language, it's the idea that everything happens for a reason. The universe does not merely evolve—it *strives* to become what it is. As a working philosophy, teleology was already dead and buried when Steinbeck and Ricketts challenged it, though its main underpinning of cause-and-effect was then—and still is—common enough in the way people look at the everyday world. On moral and social questions, teleological thinking searches for solutions, often where there are none.

Alternatively, nonteleological thinking allows one to see the world as it is, and to understand that nature is not driven by some external imperative but simply exists.

Much of this was a muddle—a load of proto-existential gibberish. For Ed Ricketts, nonteleological thinking had practical advantages in that it excused any kind of behavior and overlooked most kinds of misfortune. Not that Ricketts felt anything he did needed excusing. Everybody loved Ed Ricketts. Women just loved him more. Why Steinbeck—who'd made a career of railing against misfortune and injustice—went along with a concept that offered no comfort to the disadvantaged is a mystery.

Toward the end of this passage, Steinbeck veered into the more generalized effects of nonteleological thinking; specifically, that it allows one to perceive the "underlying pattern" of the universe, to see everything as a unified whole that is not the result of anything, that only exists and is discoverable for those open to it. In this realm of understanding, one comes to perceive the ultimate truth, what Ricketts called "the deep thing." In this complete picture of reality, the experience of being simply *is*. The search for reasons is pointless.

This section of the book would have been more entertaining if it had actually happened the way Steinbeck hinted—if it really had been Ed Ricketts pontificating, Carta Blanca in hand and half in the bag, while the bored crew kept a casual eye on Carol sunning her torso. No doubt Steinbeck and Ricketts talked about these ideas during the trip—they were *always* discussing such things—but Ricketts makes no mention in his diary of any special discussion on Easter Sunday. Neither did Sparky Enea, who also kept a journal of sorts and later published a slim book about the trip—though to be fair Sparky didn't seem to correctly remember exactly where they were or what they did on Easter weekend. The point is, there was no Easter Sunday Sermon.

Instead, Steinbeck invented this session, inspired by an unpublished essay by Ricketts on the subject of nonteleological thinking. And it's telling that in the most collaborative section of a book that in many other respects belonged to Steinbeck, it was all Ricketts. Ricketts had a fresh draft of his essay typed up so that Steinbeck could incorporate it nearly verbatim into *Sea of Cortez*. They could as easily have chosen a different essay by Ricketts—one of several that he had tried, without success, to have published and that he had shared with Joseph Campbell. It was called "The Philosophy of Breaking Through." Inspired by many sources—the poetry of Robinson Jeffers, the writings of Lao Tzu, but mainly by his own experiences of life's ups and downs—the essay is a perceptive contemplation of the idea that beyond the realm of everyday events and emotions, there is a plane of perception in which all is of a piece. In common parlance, to break through is to become one with the universe. To borrow the language Ricketts used in both essays, breaking through means seeing at last the great connective pattern in all things. It seems likely that although Steinbeck stuck to the script from "Nonteleological Thinking," in his own mind and in his private experience of the gulf expedition, he conflated both of Ricketts's theories. After all, one led to the other—though it sounds teleological to put it that way.

Years later, the literary critic Alfred Kazin—Steinbeck's most perceptive interpreter—dismissed the Easter Sunday Sermon, and everything that Steinbeck and Ricketts had fed into it, as nonsense.

It betrayed, Kazin said, second-rate minds at work, and showed that Steinbeck was naive in thinking that these ideas added gravitas to his writing:

> Characteristically, Steinbeck's thought has been a vaguely "nonteleological" biologism which in itself (apart from the beautiful descriptions of the natural world in which it usually comes) is not so much a philosophy as an excuse for not having one— philosophy on the undergraduate bull-session level that shades out all real distinctions in the world and destroys the heroic sense of history, of the human aspiration toward meaning and truth, that is the positive content of the great Western tradition.

That's where the biology came in, Kazin believed, as a substitute "creed," though it offends science to call it a form of religion. Kazin argued that *The Grapes of Wrath*—a book he admired—was outside Steinbeck's natural territory as a writer and was also at odds with his political beliefs, which were nil. He believed that Steinbeck had been compelled to write about the migrants because he could not bear doing nothing. But he was better off in a lyric adventure like *Sea of Cortez*, which Kazin considered a delightful book.

Steinbeck wrote that as the trip went on, they became more in tune with the narrow space where the sea met the land, and less connected to the conventions of regular human society. They dispensed with their clothes, living in swim trunks and walking around barefoot under broad straw hats to protect themselves from the sun. When they were hot or dirty, they simply dropped over the side and were rejuvenated. They ate fish every day, gorged themselves on huge, fattening biscuits, and made lemon pies that they fell on and fought over like a pack of dogs.

Steinbeck posted letters to McIntosh & Otis from Loreto, halfway up the Baja Peninsula, and from Guaymas, halfway down the eastern side of the gulf. He was tired and sunburned, but the collecting was wonderful. It would probably take years to identify all of the specimens. He reported that they had had no word about what was happening in Europe and were glad of it.

From Guaymas, the only town of any size they visited, Steinbeck wrote that the crew had gone on a bender that left everyone badly hung over. Tex Travis hadn't returned to the ship in the morning and was presumed to be in jail. Steinbeck would retrieve him eventually. The evening before, Tiny Colletto had challenged a local boxer to an exhibition match. He'd prepared for the fight by drinking rum with Sparky Enea all afternoon and was in danger of toppling before the first punch was thrown. Enea, who must have heard it wrong, said the local fighter went by the nickname "Kid Senorita." Tiny held his own for a few rounds before getting knocked out. They weren't in a regular ring with a mat, and Tiny's head hit the floor hard. Enea was relieved when Tiny came to and suggested they visit the nearest brothel.

They spent three days at Guaymas, departing on April 8 "a little tattered and a little tired." The next day, they came upon a Japanese shrimping fleet, an operation they were keen to inspect. The fleet consisted of a large mother ship, where the shrimp were processed, and eleven smaller "dredging" boats, each of them more than twice the size of the *Western Flyer*. They got into the dingy and pulled it alongside one of the dredging ships. The Japanese crew frowned down on them until their papers were inspected and found to be in order, at which point they were welcomed aboard. What they observed was the kind of cruelly efficient destruction of an ecosystem that has long since imperiled the oceans.

The dredging ships pulled immense bottom-dragging nets that caught shrimp by the ton—as well as anything else lying along or near the bottom. This included sharks, pompano, small tunas, rays, and catfish, and also various marine plants that were uprooted as the net swept up every living thing in its path. All but the shrimp were tossed over the side leaving a long line of dead and dying fish trailing off behind the ship. It was clear that as the fleet moved over the water, it was scraping the ocean floor clean. In his later account of this rapacious harvest, Steinbeck urged the Mexican authorities to undertake a study of the gulf's fishing stocks and to set catch limits that could stabilize the ecosystem against such exploitation, which was plainly unsustainable.

Managing wildlife populations for both commercial and recreational uses was still a new idea then. In 1939, the same year *The Grapes of Wrath* and *Between Pacific Tides* came out, Aldo Leopold published *Game Management*, one of the pillars of the emerging field of conservation biology. It was based on a series of lectures Leopold had given a decade earlier at the University of Wisconsin. A Yale-educated former employee of the U.S. Forest Service, Leopold proposed that along with traditional methods of maintaining wildlife populations—such as established hunting seasons and limits—it was becoming more important to understand and sustain complex interactions between humans, animals, and the total environment. This more holistic approach was a hallmark of the Roosevelt administration's efforts to restore game populations, especially waterfowl, which in the coming decade would lead to the establishment of a system of wildlife sanctuaries closed to hunting, and to scientifically regulated hunting seasons and bag limits everywhere else. In 1940, Roosevelt folded two existing federal agencies into one, creating the U.S. Fish and Wildlife Service to further these efforts. This was essentially the same approach that Steinbeck and Ricketts believed was needed in the gulf. Not unlike the situation with the migrants, this problem in the gulf did not originate with the underclass doing the actual work, but with corporate interests far away. Steinbeck wrote that they liked the Japanese crew, but that they were "good men doing a bad thing." And he worried that the gulf's ecosystem would never recover.

Around three in the morning on April 13, the *Western Flyer* rounded the tip of Baja, reentering the Pacific and turning north. Soon they encountered the only bad weather on the trip. The steep seas built steadily and the wind shrieked in the rigging as they crashed ahead into one wall of dark, foam-flecked water after the next. No one got sick, except for Ricketts, who climbed into his bunk and stayed there. The crew could not take a step without hanging onto something, but strangely the wild ride seemed to settle everyone's mood.

Steinbeck let the story stop there, with the *Western Flyer* fighting her way back to port. When they stopped in at San Diego and turned on the radio, they were stunned to learn that Germany had invaded Norway. Steinbeck insisted they keep the radio on, and he made notes about what had happened in the world while they were away from everything. They went out for dinner ashore and then Ricketts—who was weary of being seasick—decided to drive back to Monterey with Tiny Colletto's girlfriend, who'd come down to meet them. For some reason, this enraged Carol, who stayed away from everybody for the rest of the trip.

They arrived back in Monterey on the morning of April 21 and were greeted by a crowd that included—according to Carol—a pretty, young strawberry blonde named Gwen. Everyone was sad the trip was over. "Nothing lasts," Tiny Colletto said philosophically. "Everything has to end." And so they were home, everybody but Steinbeck, who in so many ways would never be home again.

The fight for Norway was bloody—ultimately nearly 5,300 Germans were killed and about 4,500 British died, most of them sailors on ships sunk by the Nazis. The Allies' attempt to land a large force and repel the German invasion had been haphazard and half-hearted. England's first lord of the admiralty, Winston Churchill, was partly to blame for the poorly executed British naval operation, though that did not stop King George VI from inviting Churchill to replace Neville Chamberlain as prime minister in early May. Britons liked Churchill's bellicosity. He talked a tough game of war. By the end of May, stranded British troops were being evacuated from Dunkirk in a massive civilian boatlift across the English Channel. And by the end of June, the German army was parading down the Champs-Élysées in Paris.

On June 18, Churchill spoke in the House of Commons, saying

that once the conquest of France was complete, Britain would be next in line for the Germans. He said that if Britain fell, so would the world. But he promised they would not fall, that the coming fight would prove to be England's "finest hour." That summer, British and German airplanes began to engage over the channel, and in August the Germans bombed military installations in Britain. By the end of August the first bombs were falling on London. More than 400 Londoners were killed in a raid one night in early September. Edward R. Murrow—in a broadcast notable for his rendering of the fearsome beauty of war—described the scene in Britain's capital:

"The fires up the river had turned the moon blood red. The smoke had drifted on till it formed a canopy over the Thames; the guns were working all around us, the bursts looking like fireflies in a southern summer night. The Germans were sending in two or three planes at a time, sometimes only one, in relays. They would pass overhead. The guns and lights would follow them and in about five minutes we could hear the hollow grunt of the bombs. Huge pear-shaped bursts of flame would rise up into the smoke and disappear. The world was upside down."

Like many Americans, Steinbeck was appalled at the rapid expansion of the war across Europe and assumed that soon America would have to step in. When he began to think of writing about the war isn't certain, but given that he rarely stopped thinking about writing it seems likely that the war was a subject already churning in his mind.

On returning from the gulf, Steinbeck was pleased to learn that the First Lady had toured migrant camps in the San Joaquin Valley, from Bakersfield to Visalia, in early April. Mrs. Roosevelt looked in on several wretched squatters' camps and also the sanitary camps set up by the Farm Security Administration, the latter of which were vital to relieving migrant suffering. A reporter following her asked if she thought Steinbeck had exaggerated the migrants' situation. "I never have thought *The Grapes of Wrath* was exaggerated," she replied.

Steinbeck wrote to Mrs. Roosevelt saying he was sorry not to have met her during her visit to California. And he thanked her for endorsing his book. He said it was good to have her opinion, since he'd been called a liar so often he was sometimes tempted to believe it.

That spring *The Grapes of Wrath* won the Pulitzer Prize for fiction. Steinbeck and Carol were in Monterey and managed to miss some of the excitement. Their houseboy at the ranch said the phone rang all night. The Pulitzer was embroiled in controversy that year because William Saroyan had refused the award for his play *The Time of Your Life* on the grounds that art should not be a competition. Reporters across the country were eager to get a comment from Steinbeck—who was probably sympathetic to Saroyan's stand, but suspected that he was also doing it for publicity, something Steinbeck did not want. He figured that Saroyan would be forever remembered for turning it down, but if he accepted the award he would be forgotten in six months. Steinbeck admitted to having disparaged the Pulitzer, but said he was "pleased and flattered" to have received the prize.

Steinbeck was so used to getting checks in the mail that when the $1,000 Pulitzer award arrived, he thought he should do something constructive with it. He signed it over to his friend Ritchie Lovejoy so he could work full-time on a novel he was writing. Steinbeck also offered the Lovejoys use of the Eleventh Street cottage. Lovejoy quit his job in the ad department at Holman's Department Store; produced a 618-page manuscript titled *Taku Wind*, a complex, multitrack story set in Alaska; and had a son with Tal, whom they named John. How long Ritchie worked on the book isn't known, though it appears he needed two different typewriters to finish it. The book was never published.

Steinbeck did not start in on *Sea of Cortez* right away. In May he and Carol went to Mexico City, where Steinbeck was to begin work as the screenwriter on a documentary, *The Forgotten Village*. It was good to be away again. He wrote to Elizabeth Otis from Mexico that nobody knew or cared anything about the Pulitzer Prize down there, which was a relief. The film, which Steinbeck was to write on the fly, told the story of how modern medicines were being used to counter illnesses caused by the town's contaminated water.

Gwen—whose recollections of this time were confusing—later insisted that she and Steinbeck had not yet slept together. In fact, she was pregnant by another man at the time. But Steinbeck pressed the issue when he got back from Mexico. After they finally did make love—it happened on a rainy weekend at Oceanside, where Steinbeck spent hours on the phone with McIntosh & Otis—Steinbeck told her he was going to try to make things work with Carol. Gwen wanted an abortion, but said nothing to Steinbeck about it and instead claimed that she had tried to kill herself by drinking a bottle of iodine. It didn't work—iodine is only mildly toxic—though she had to have her stomach pumped.

Distracted by troubles with his wife and his mistress, and worried about the war in Europe and when it would come to America, Steinbeck put off getting to work on *Sea of Cortez*. He made several trips to Mexico for *The Forgotten Village*, and back at the ranch in Los Gatos he started writing a comic play about life on Cannery Row called *God in the Pipes*. He bought himself a new pen he planned to use for *Sea of Cortez*. In January 1941, he was in Hollywood for two weeks finishing up the film and staying at the Aloha Arms, where Gwen joined him when she could. He thought maybe he was getting her out of his system. "Just a feeling," he wrote in his journal, "and I hope it is true, really, deeply, I hope so. Can't really see anything good in it in any future." He returned to the ranch, where it was raining. Carol was morose and kept her distance.

Germany's cold-blooded prosecution of the war in Europe seemed to Steinbeck likely to succeed in the short term—and offered the promise of disaster in the long run. He told Pat Covici that humankind was at its best in a state of "semi-anarchy." Maybe he had absorbed some of Ed Ricketts's ideas about primitive people being better off than the civilized version. Steinbeck thought a regime as brutal and as controlled as the Nazis was "suicidal." But he insisted he had not lost hope. He said that evil appears from time to time and is invariably vanquished by the indomitable heroism of the human race. And so, Steinbeck was convinced, war would come again for us as it already had for Europe. This was our destiny, though our fate would be to overcome it.

Toward the end of the month, Steinbeck went over to Pacific Grove and stayed in a cottage his sister Esther owned at the end of the peninsula. He met up with Ed Ricketts and Toby Street, and the three of them got drunk. For some reason, he didn't feel hungover the next morning and impulsively started writing *Sea of Cortez*. Steinbeck wrote that, having been to the gulf and waded its intertidal zone, taking specimens, leaving their boot prints in the sand until the next tide, the crew of the *Western Flyer* had become a permanent fixture of "the ecology of the region." Nothing is fixed in the world, yet everything that happens leaves a trace and remains forever. Their journey had been so peaceful, so in tune with the sea and the sunburned landscape that stood beside the blue water, that a civilization in flames far away scarcely seemed possible. But it was all of a piece: "And if we seem a small factor in a huge pattern, nevertheless it is of relative importance. We take a tiny colony of soft corals from a rock in a little water world. And that isn't terribly important to the tide pool. Fifty miles away the Japanese shrimp boats are dredging with overlapping scoops, bringing up tons of shrimps, rapidly destroying the species so that it may never come back, and with the species destroying the ecological balance of the whole region. That isn't very important in the world. And six thousand miles away the great bombs are falling on London and the stars are not moved thereby. None of it is important or all of it is."

PART THREE

TRAVELS

— 13 —

CONCEIVED IN ADVENTURE
AND DEDICATED TO PROGRESS

Alone in Pacific Grove at the beginning of 1941, Steinbeck thought he'd gotten off to a good start on *Sea of Cortez*—Ricketts agreed—but within days he doubted everything. Steinbeck claimed he was "ill in the mind," overwhelmed by his cares and lost in a morass of gray, meandering thoughts. It was frustrating because he knew the book could be good. "I don't seem to have the knack of living any more," he wrote in his journal. "The clock is running down, my clock." He wondered how Carol was doing. He knew how low she'd been feeling but he hadn't heard from her. And that was the last entry he made.

Steinbeck had given up on *God in the Pipes*, which had convinced him that he could not write a play. But he looked forward to having the winter to work on *Sea of Cortez* and for coordinating several projects in Hollywood, including *The Forgotten Village* and adaptations of *Tortilla Flat* and "The Red Pony." After working a couple of weeks in Pacific Grove, he went up to the ranch in late January and found Carol depressed and losing weight. He bought her a ticket to Honolulu for a six-week vacation—a trip that would be restorative for Carol and also give Steinbeck a chance to rendezvous with Gwen, who was not at all out of the picture. He resumed his work on *Sea of Cortez* and made good progress. He counseled Elizabeth Otis to stay calm about the Japanese threat in the Pacific. It was, Steinbeck said, nothing but a bluff, as Japan had far too much to lose by going to war against the United States. There wasn't any doubt about the overwhelming superiority of America's navy, which he had seen firsthand as being ready for trouble.

Gwen came up to Pacific Grove, and for a time she and Steinbeck stayed at Esther's cottage. Gwen liked to sleep late. Each day, Steinbeck would get up at dawn, build a fire, and work until noon on *Sea of Cortez*. His work sustained him, though he wondered what would happen when Carol got home. The explosion came in April, when Carol returned, this time not to the ranch, which they had abruptly sold. Carol and Steinbeck had moved to a cramped, decrepit house they'd bought on Eardley Street in Pacific Grove. Gwen later gave varying accounts of what happened when she got there.

In what seems the more truthful version, Steinbeck called Gwen and asked her to come to Pacific Grove. He needed to see her, though he said he hoped to reconcile with Carol. He did not mention that he had told Carol everything. Steinbeck confided to Mavis McIntosh that Carol said she would not be pushed aside, that she would fight to keep him. Steinbeck felt he had to stay with Carol—but could not bear the thought of giving up Gwen. It was an unresolvable mess that would turn into an ambush.

When Gwen arrived at the Eardley Street house thinking she would have a private conversation with Steinbeck, she found the place surrounded by a tall, vine-covered fence. It was a gray day, with fog beginning to settle in, making the house look dark. Gwen walked in through the narrow gate and entered the house by the open front door. The inside was dismal, filled with old, smelly furniture. Steinbeck was there, sitting on a vegetable crate.

Carol was there, too.

There were several empty wine bottles lying about, and Steinbeck and Carol seemed woozy. According to Gwen, Steinbeck explained what was going on. "I know you both love me," he said, "but I've just decided that I think we need to have a confrontation. Whichever of you ladies needs me the most—that's the woman I'm going to have." Steinbeck rose unsteadily after this preposterous announcement and walked out the door and down the street to a bar. As Gwen explained her reaction years later, "I was not ready for that kind of shit."

It did not figure to be a fair fight. Carol was mature, profane, desperate, and tough—not to mention half of the creative team that had given the world several books that would last forever. Steinbeck would be lost without her. Carol knew the score and was determined to come out on top. But she never had a chance. Gwen sat down and waited.

Carol went first. "You don't want him," she said. "You don't love him. I love him terribly, but he hasn't slept with me in three years. I have to masturbate all the time, and that's why I sleep with lesbians." Gwen—who at this point was still only twenty-one and no doubt intimidated—claimed to have never heard such things before, even though she mentioned that she'd been "raised in the theater," whatever that meant.

Carol told Gwen that Steinbeck's sisters, a "bunch of clannish bitches," would never accept her. Gwen later said this turned out to be true. Carol warned her that Steinbeck would be unfaithful to her. This also proved true. "He's a jealous, nasty man," Carol said, "and if you get him, I am going to take him for every goddamn, fucking cent. I'll kill you if I can, because I want him, and I know he is going to be famous. After all the years I've lived with him, I won't let that happen."

Reeling, Gwen suggested they have a drink. Three bottles of expensive champagne later, Gwen called a cab. They'd had a nice talk. Steinbeck decided to stay with Carol. But ten days later they separated. For Carol, it was the end of it. Gwen had won. As for Steinbeck, well, he was already famous.

By midsummer, Steinbeck and Ricketts were revising the manuscript of *Sea of Cortez*. At Viking, where the book was scheduled for fall publication, Pascal Covici was impatient. He told Steinbeck to skip a third draft—he could make final corrections on the galleys—and to send each chapter as it was finished. Covici said everyone in New York was "keyed up" about the book and that it figured prominently in their sales plans. If for any reason the book would be delayed, the sooner they knew that the better. But he did not want any delays.

Steinbeck had persuaded Gwen to move to Monterey once Carol was out of the house, despite a warning from Toby Street to Gwen's mother. It was reminiscent of Street's attempt to scare off Carol years before, when he'd told her she would always come in second to writing in Steinbeck's affections. And perhaps Street thought that the breakup of Steinbeck's marriage had happened just as he had predicted it would. Street was a sometimes strange friend to Steinbeck. He told Gwen's mother that Carol, too, had once been a "sweet girl," and that Steinbeck had turned her into a "monster." If he gets Gwen, Street said, he'll do the same to her.

Covici, who by this time knew about the breakup of Steinbeck's marriage, offered him perspective on the upheaval in his personal life—though it was more a calculated plea that Steinbeck continue working all-out on *Sea of Cortez*. Covici said he wasn't worried about Steinbeck. The truth was, Covici was in awe of Steinbeck's talent, and if anything, was jealous of him. Everyone has regrets as they get older, he advised. And yet we keep living. "What I do positively know," Covici wrote, "is that I want you to go on."

Unspoken, but on both men's minds, was how the prospect of war figured in the urgency around *Sea of Cortez*. If America were pulled into the conflict, would readers care about a ragtag group of pseudo-philosophers drinking beer and chasing snails and starfish at low tide in the Gulf of California? The mood in the country was still intensely isolationist, though the public was increasingly resigned to the near certainty of war. A poll the day before the election in 1940—an election Franklin Roosevelt feared he might lose because of his insistence on aid to Europe and an aggressive military buildup at home—showed that less than 16 percent of the country favored war, but 70 percent put the odds at even that we'd end up in one. Roosevelt had done what he could to stem this pessimism, promising the country: "Your boys are not going to be sent into any foreign wars." But this was campaign rhetoric, and when Roosevelt won the election, there was elation in Britain. Surely, American help was on the way.

At the start of 1941, in a stirring essay for *Life*, the magazine's publisher, Henry Luce, had argued for a more muscular response to world events. America, Luce wrote, was no longer a second-rate, postcolonial bystander on the international stage. It was now the most powerful and most morally upright country in the world—and therefore obliged to lead in all things and in all places. The twentieth century was our moment, Luce claimed. The title of the piece was "The American Century."

Luce wrote that while America could never ensure "good behavior" everywhere in the world, America was nonetheless responsible "to herself as well as to history" to do what it could to keep the world safe for American values and interests. Like any noble claim for the homeland and its rightful place atop the world order, this argument had jingoistic undertones. Luce was a partisan—he wanted to ensure that Franklin Roosevelt would be remembered as our greatest president, and he insisted that if Republicans maintained their isolationist ideology, they would be irrelevant. But Luce's main point—that isolationism was unfathomable in light of events—was hard to ignore. America enjoyed the privilege of wealth. As the deepest gloom of the Great Depression lifted, Luce reminded Americans that they were indescribably fortunate compared to the rest of humankind, far richer in every way than other countries. By what right could we, as "the most powerful and vital nation in the world," decline to play our role as its leader?

Luce believed that once Americans set aside their isolationism, they would see how broadly American culture already pervaded the rest of the world, whether it were jazz, movies, or modern machines and technologies. More important, however, was that America had become the world's "powerhouse of the ideals of Freedom and Justice," and it was now our duty to commit fully to the expansion and preservation of those principles. America had become powerful, but it also had a higher calling:

Other nations can survive simply because they have endured so long—sometimes with more and sometimes with less significance. But this nation, conceived in adventure and dedicated to the progress of man—this nation cannot truly endure unless there courses strongly through its veins from Maine to California the blood of purpose and enterprise and high resolve. Throughout the 17th Century and the 18th Century and the 19th Century, this continent teemed with manifold projects and magnificent purposes. Above them all and weaving them all together into the most exciting flag of all the world and of all history was the triumphal purpose of freedom. It is in this spirit that all of us are called, each to his own measure of capacity, and each in the widest horizon of his vision, to create the first great American Century.

Steinbeck felt guilty about Carol—partly from a fondness that survived their breakup. Partly, too, it was because he knew she'd helped him when he needed help, and he'd pushed her away when it was the other way around. But he admitted to feeling free at last of a thousand small annoyances. These were the sorts of minor daily interferences that pass between every wife and husband, but in a long confessional letter to Mavis McIntosh, Steinbeck said escaping Carol's hectoring was like being able to breathe again. It was wonderful to simply take out the trash and not be accused of inadvertently throwing away a spoon. Either he'd stopped snoring, or Gwen, unlike Carol, didn't mind or notice it. He'd discovered he was not an idiot about money. And he was thrilled that he could once again take a drink and not worry that it would lead to a fight. Drinking, he said, made Gwen affectionate—whereas alcohol made Carol mad, and if she had enough there were often unpleasant consequences. Mostly he was relieved at being relieved. The house was "easy" now, he said, something he hadn't felt in a long time. It was wonderful to at last not be living in a state of perpetual conflict. Carol used to say he was ugly. Gwen liked to declare him "the prettiest thing I ever saw," and then collapse laughing.

Steinbeck was working on the galleys for *Sea of Cortez* by late September. Then, in October, he and Gwen moved east—another sign that when Steinbeck stepped off the *Western Flyer* the year before, California no longer seemed like home. Mavis McIntosh had suggested they come to New York, and Steinbeck admitted that he needed to get away from Carol. There was no point, he said, in staying put and taking her abuse. And he hoped his moving away might make things better for Carol. He said one regret was that all of his friends and even his sisters liked Gwen—something Gwen privately doubted.

Steinbeck had remained friendly with Burgess Meredith after *Of Mice and Men*, and he and Gwen stayed for a time with Meredith at his country place in Rockland County just outside New York City. Eventually they moved into the city to the Bedford, a residential hotel where Annie Laurie Williams lived. Toby Street was left to deal with Carol and to begin negotiating a divorce, no doubt thinking to himself it had come to pass just as he had predicted. Gwen decided she didn't like her name and changed it to Gwyn, short for Gwyndolyn. Nothing was the same.

Once *Sea of Cortez* was finished and in Viking's hands, Steinbeck put aside the idea that he couldn't write a play and began one about an imaginary town in Europe invaded and occupied by an unnamed army. Artful propaganda, it was called *The Moon Is Down*, and its smart premise was that the invaders would, over time, be undone by the silent hatred directed at them by their captives. It would eventually make it to Broadway. Meanwhile, *The Forgotten Village* had run afoul of the New York State Board of Censors because of a childbirth scene, although there was nothing explicit in it. Steinbeck feared that if they couldn't show the film in New York, there was no hope for it.

Sea of Cortez was published at the beginning of December. The reviews were again wonderful. Many critics called it an "unusual" book, and they also took an interest in trying to determine which passages belonged more to Ricketts or to Steinbeck—though Charles Poore of the *New York Times* chose to describe the coauthors as a "joint personality" with a gift for the written word. One of the better reviews was by Steinbeck's friend Beth Ingels, who had apparently forgiven Steinbeck for stealing her stories in *The Pastures of Heaven*. Writing in the *Monterey Peninsula Herald*, Ingels said *Sea of Cortez* revealed a lot about Steinbeck as a man and why he had become a major figure in American literature. The trip, she said, was entertainingly described, but was a pretext for a serious discussion of ideas that Steinbeck and Ricketts had been ruminating on for years. The result, she said, was among the more compelling books ever published in America.

As the accolades poured in, nobody detected a curious discrepancy in the book. Early on, as Steinbeck detailed preparations for the trip, he discussed the matter of provisions. "It is amazing," he wrote, "how much food seven people need to exist for six weeks." But anyone reading *Sea of Cortez* could count only six people aboard the *Western Flyer*. The missing seventh member of the crew was Carol, who was nowhere mentioned in the book.

Sea of Cortez seemed likely to prove Steinbeck wrong, once again, for having low expectations for a new book. But then, almost before anyone had seen *Sea of Cortez*, a dark smudge appeared on the western horizon near Hawaii just before 8:00 a.m. on Sunday, December 7. The shadow grew larger. It was the first wave of an attack by more than 300 Japanese aircraft operating from six carriers. Their target was the U.S. naval fleet, which had been stationed at Pearl Harbor in Honolulu for a year and a half in hopes of discouraging Japanese expansion in the Pacific. The sneak attack devastated much of the Pacific fleet and outraged the country. A day later, President Roosevelt told a joint session of Congress that December 7 was now a date that would "live in infamy," and he asked for and got a declaration of war against Japan. This was answered by a declaration of war against the United States by Germany and Italy. Now, nearly every corner of the world was in conflict. In the Soviet Union, the German army continued the siege of Leningrad that had begun earlier in the fall. Surrounded and cut off, the city's two and a half million citizens were starving and freezing to death in the Russian winter, while in London the bombs kept falling. At home and around the world, the sun-drenched, carefree voyage of the *Western Flyer* suddenly seemed of slight interest.

Within hours of the attack on Pearl Harbor, Steinbeck finished the script for *The Moon Is Down*. A month later he was making revisions with the play's director, Lee Strasberg. He wasn't sure they could do much with it, and he told Toby Street he was tired of the whole thing. The good news was that he'd turned the play into a short novel that Viking planned to publish no later than March. They assured Steinbeck it was going to do well. This was a relief, as with the war on, *Sea of Cortez* had all but died at the bookstores. Steinbeck told Toby Street he wished he could be back in California, though that would probably have to wait until the war was over and Carol's ill will had cooled. He envied Street, who had run into his own marital problems and was living in Steinbeck's cottage on Eleventh Street— the little house that so often had been the refuge of last resort for so many. He told Street he was glad he was there. It was a pleasant place to think in. In a faint echo of the dream George and Lenny had in *Of Mice and Men*, Steinbeck said he could be happy with the simple, quiet life. He said when the war was over he'd like to find some land near Monterey where he could keep some animals and start a family with Gwyn. But he admitted that it was doubtful things would work out that way.

Steinbeck's uncertainty was due partly to the ongoing discussion with Carol over a divorce settlement. Steinbeck insisted that he would not "chisel" her in any way, that he would give Carol everything he could afford to give. He told Toby Street that she was beautiful, and with money she'd have no trouble finding a new husband. In the end, Street negotiated an agreement that ended any claim Carol had on Steinbeck's future earnings. In return, Steinbeck would pay her $100,000—an enormous sum in those days. Steinbeck was sure Carol could live on that for the rest of her life, and knowing how frugal she was, he figured she'd die with more than that.

Steinbeck's financial situation previewed how it would be for him going forward—always spending most of what he made and forever needing to make more to sustain his lifestyle. It was funny, in a way. When he'd had no money—when nobody had money—Steinbeck rarely complained of his poverty. Once he became a highly paid author, money was a constant vexation. This was especially true at tax time, when the sums he owed the government proved year-in and year-out that he was inarguably rich, but usually strapped. Toby Street, who handled legal and financial matters for him, informed Steinbeck that, at the moment, he was not broke. But he was close. Steinbeck had $140,000 in cash, plus property worth $35,000—impressive wealth at a time when the country was still climbing out of the Depression. But after he gave Carol $100,000 and paid a $35,000 tax bill, the most successful writer in America would have around $5,000 in the bank.

Even so, life was better than he'd imagined for a long time it could be. Gwyn, he said, worked at their relationship, and this was something new to Steinbeck. She seemed happy, too. Still, he could not shake the feeling that part of him had died, that he was on a new, uncertain path. And he was sad that his marriage to Carol had failed. But, surveying his situation, it seemed generally okay, if not perfect. As life so rarely is. Steinbeck had just turned forty. He had money, fame, a soon-to-be ex-wife, and a gorgeous, amiable young girlfriend. Steinbeck had become a bundle of midlife clichés, and he lived now as an uprooted happy man still haunted by unhappiness.

The novel version of *The Moon Is Down* was published in March of 1942. It was a parable, set in a place with no name, where characters without nationalities or histories grapple with one another after a town is taken by force. There are allusions that suggest the invaders are Nazis, and that the town they occupy could be a town on the coast of Norway. But the story is blankly universal, the terse dialogue familiar. The occupation happens swiftly and cruelly. The invaders enjoy an overwhelming military advantage. But as the occupation wears on month after month, the conquerors succumb to the knowledge that they are despised, that the townspeople would kill them if they could. Away from home, they begin to doubt whether they know the truth about what is happening there. They must be winning the war, for that is the news. But what if the news is not the truth? Gradually, the tables turn:

"Thus it came about that the conquerors grew afraid of the conquered and their nerves wore thin and they shot at shadows in the night. The cold, sullen silence was with them always. Then three soldiers went insane in a week and cried all night and all day until they were sent away home. And others might have gone insane if they had not heard that mercy deaths awaited the insane at home, and a mercy death is a terrible thing to think of. Fear crept in on the men in their billets and it made them sad, and it crept into the patrols and made them cruel."

At its simplest, *The Moon Is Down* was meant to show that the harsher and more unjust an oppression is, the more hostility is reflected back at the oppressors. But there are deeper, complex themes playing through the book. In a wrenching sequence, one of the young occupiers calls on the town's beauty. Her name is Molly, and the soldier—lonely, afraid, but overcome by the thought that perhaps she will show him even a small tenderness—at first doesn't realize that he'd commanded the firing squad that executed her husband. Molly talks with the soldier, by turns warmly and then icily, and ultimately in vulgar terms, daring him to say what it is he wants her to do. The soldier is confused and helpless against what he perceives as a flicker of compassion in Molly. When he leaves, he asks if he can come back later. Molly doesn't answer directly. And when he does come back, she meets him at the door with a heavy scissors hidden in her dress, having first tested them in the air to satisfy herself that they will work as well as a knife.

The Moon Is Down stumped the critics, who were split, but sales were sensational. Some 85,000 copies were sold ahead of publication, and the Book-of-the-Month Club ordered a printing of 200,000. It was much the same when the play opened a month later. The reviewers ran hot and cold, but the audiences kept lining up for tickets. Annie Laurie Williams sold the film rights for a breathtaking $300,000. The "problem" many critics had with both the book and the play was its subtlety, something that in hindsight seems its greatest strength. Those who didn't like the book complained that it casually normalized the Nazis, and that encouraging the conquered to heedlessly push back against the invaders could be dangerous. Decades after it was conceived as propaganda for the European resistance movement, *The Moon Is Down* today instead reads as a taut, concise study of the dehumanizing cost of evil—the price paid by those who suffer it as well as those who perpetrate it.

Steinbeck's mix of propaganda and literature, however soft and slight it seemed to some American readers, caused a stir in occupied Europe, where it struck a chord of hope. The book was outlawed by the German occupation—and eagerly translated and secretly printed and distributed to resistance movements across the continent. It was smuggled over borders, mimeographed by lantern light in the dead of night, passed around secretly by book dealers and local officials who knew whom they could trust. Sales of illegal copies helped fund resistance operations in France, Denmark, and Holland.

Steinbeck wanted to go to war. Carol had filed for divorce on grounds of mental cruelty—Steinbeck did not contest the point—and this meant a one-year wait for a final decree. Steinbeck spent the time trying to secure a commission in the army. He'd already done some unpaid work as a consultant to the Office of War Information, where he had submitted an early draft of *The Moon Is Down* that was set in what could be seen as an American town. The OWI rejected it for being defeatist—nobody wanted to contemplate the prospect of America being occupied.

In March of 1942, Steinbeck accepted an unpaid job as special consultant to the secretary of war. Steinbeck was assigned to the air force and spent time flying in various kinds of military planes before being sent to an air base at Sherman Oaks, California, where he worked on a film about the training of a bomber crew. He turned that project into a slim book called *Bombs Away* that Viking published in the fall as a recruiting tool for the war effort. That spring, while still waiting to hear about an active-duty commission, Steinbeck had written to Francis Biddle, the U.S. attorney general, asking him to stop an FBI investigation of him. He said "Edgar's boys" were under the mistaken impression that he was an "enemy alien," which seemed easily disprovable given the public record of his Salinas childhood.

Steinbeck was wrong. The FBI maintained at the time, and forever afterward, that it had never investigated Steinbeck. But the Bureau did eventually obtain a file on Steinbeck. It had been put together by the Military Intelligence Service in the War Department and ran to more than 100 pages. This is apparently what Steinbeck mistook for an FBI inquiry. The report's purpose was to determine Steinbeck's suitability for a commission, and the focus was on whether his radical tendencies in the 1930s were disqualifying. In plain language, the government wanted to know if he was, or had been, a Communist—ironic in that the Soviet Union was our ally in the war and was, at that moment, suffering massive military and civilian losses on the Eastern Front.

This file contained personal information and summaries of interviews with many of Steinbeck's friends and associates, including Carol, who was not happy being talked to about her estranged husband. Most people vouched for Steinbeck's honesty, integrity, and loyalty to the United States. The report gave his height at a precise 5 feet 11 1/3 inches and said he had no police record and that his credit history was "satisfactory." It also listed him as a vice president of Pacific Biological Laboratories Inc. Under "adverse" findings was his association with "individuals who are known to have a radical political and economic philosophy, and with some members of the Communist Party." Steinbeck also owned a "large volume" of Communist literature and many books that expressed radical political views. The file duly noted that Carol had registered in Santa Clara County as a member of the Communist Party in 1935. She told the investigators that Steinbeck had no fixed political beliefs—but if he was anything he was a New Deal Democrat. She said he was not and had never been a member of the Communist Party.

The investigator in charge, a Lieutenant Colonel Boris Pash, recommended that Steinbeck be given a commission. Pash called him a "candid and powerful writer" who may have exercised "poor judgment" early in his career by associating with members of the Communist Party, but Pash believed this was only for the purpose of gathering material for his writing. Pash thought Steinbeck was honest and loyal, and should be awarded an assignment in which his writing abilities could be used. But Pash's commanding officer disagreed, and believed there was "substantial doubt" as to Steinbeck's loyalty and discretion. And with that, the case was closed. Steinbeck did not receive a commission.

Instead, he was assigned to the Office of War Information in New York at a salary of $3,600 a year. Steinbeck was to be a foreign news editor and would make it to the war that way. He told Toby Street he hoped to sign on as a correspondent with a "big reactionary paper" like the *New York Herald Tribune*. From what he'd seen of the army so far, he thought if he'd ever gotten in he would have preferred to be a private.

In January of 1943, 20th Century Fox asked Steinbeck if he'd consider writing a film about the merchant marine, to be directed by Alfred Hitchcock. Steinbeck wrote a screenplay—the movie was *Lifeboat*—and with a number of changes that made Steinbeck unhappy, it came out a year later. Steinbeck was sufficiently annoyed that he demanded his name be dropped from the credits. It wasn't.

In mid-March, Toby Street informed Steinbeck that his divorce from Carol was final. At the end of the month, Steinbeck and Gwyn went down to New Orleans and were married. Throughout his life, Steinbeck—like many writers—consumed alcohol regularly and with pleasure. Most days ended with a drink. Or a few. And as he aged and became more social he drank more. Though his habit of rising to write was sturdy, as he got older he more often complained of being hungover, suggesting that those mornings were not always as productive as they might have been. But his friends were impressed at Steinbeck's ability to hold his liquor. He was rarely drunk. He paced himself even when everyone around him was far gone. His friend

Richard Albee said that in fact he had never seen Steinbeck inebriated, though they spent many times together bending elbows.

But Steinbeck *was* drunk in New Orleans that spring, a sign, perhaps, of an underlying ambivalence about embarking on another marriage. He and Gwyn drank themselves silly the day before the big event. Steinbeck treated his hangover on their wedding day by continuing to drink right up to the ceremony. Gwyn dealt with hers by crying all day, surrounded by a wedding party she described as "pie-eyed." The wedding took place in an outdoor courtyard, and the happy couple looked as sick as they felt. Somebody put the wrong music on the phonograph as Gwyn started down the aisle and Steinbeck burst out laughing. Steinbeck had given her the rings for safekeeping, and she'd managed to lose hers. At the altar, they took turns putting the one that remained on each other's finger. The officiant was a local magistrate, and for some reason the beginning of the ceremony was in French. Gwyn didn't remember the day clearly, but she did later recall yelling "Oui!" at the judge over and over again. Gwyn, concerned about their age difference—something that would always bother Steinbeck—told everyone she was twenty-seven, even though she later admitted she was twenty-five. In truth, she was twenty-three.

At the reception, the party got wilder. Gwyn said Steinbeck was "plastered." Suddenly the police arrived and informed Steinbeck he was the subject of a paternity suit. Everyone fell silent. Steinbeck gaped at the summons, swaying slightly. And then everybody started laughing. The whole thing was a gag arranged by one of Steinbeck's friends. Everyone but Steinbeck and Gwyn thought it was hilarious. Steinbeck sulked and Gwyn went back to their room and cried some more. Two days later, Steinbeck wrote to Toby Street, telling him the wedding had been "nice and sentimental."

Steinbeck then got word that he'd been hired by the *Herald Tribune*. He arrived in London in June, his first stop on the way to the war.

Steinbeck wrote melancholy letters to Gwyn—sometimes it was to Gwyndolyn, sometimes to My Darling—telling her how homesick he was, how he hoped she could stand the long wait until he came home. It was hot and cloudy in London, but the city was beautiful against a panorama of big clouds. He worked hard but said nothing about what he was doing. He thought about her constantly.

In August, after not writing for a few days, he told Gwyn he'd been on the move and was now on the Mediterranean coast in Algiers, where there had been heavy fighting. He was embarrassed by his circumstances. Instead of asking to be quartered with the troops, and not knowing better, he'd gone to a hotel when he got in and asked for a room. Even though its windows were boarded up and bombing had loosened the wallpaper, he was in nicer living quarters than the generals he was covering. It was suffocatingly hot—he had to write lying down so as not to drip sweat onto the paper. In a story he filed with the *Herald Tribune*, Steinbeck wrote about how white the city was under the torrid African sun, and of the sounds of countless languages and dialects blending together on the streets. In addition to the usual exotic mix, this now included American and British accents and the steady rumble of equipment. He said he'd probably be back in London in three weeks. Northern Africa reminded him of California. The blue of the Mediterranean was like Monterey Bay. He traveled every day with a photographer and an enlisted man. One night he visited a monastery with a group of naval officers and listened to the monks' Gregorian chant at evening prayer. It was lovely, like being down at the lab with Ricketts. The war was tolerable. His loneliness was the hard part. Toward the end of the month a cable Gwyn had sent to him in London finally found him. His sister Mary was worried about her husband, Bill Dekker. When Steinbeck looked into it, he learned that Dekker, who had been promoted to lieutenant colonel, was missing in Sicily. He wrote to Gwyn to tell Mary he was sure Bill was not dead.

Steinbeck was not back in London the following month after all. Instead, he accompanied the invasion to Salerno, south of Naples, on September 9. The Italian government had just surrendered, but German resistance remained fierce. Steinbeck hurt his knee but was otherwise uninjured during the landing, though he suffered a temporary hearing loss from the heavy gunfire. The troops he went in with were green but well trained and outwardly confident. On the iron floors of the landing craft, they laughed and teased one another until they came near the beach. Then, Steinbeck wrote, a silence settled over everyone and fate was left to take its course: "Not one of these men is to be killed. That is impossible, and it is no contradiction that every one of them is to be killed. Every one is in a way dead already."

Steinbeck was only briefly attached to the landing force. He'd sped over from North Africa on an American PT boat before joining up with a special-operations group of light watercraft operating with a destroyer, the USS *Knight*. He returned to the *Knight* after the action at Salerno. Their mission was mainly diversionary, conducting guerrilla raids up and down the coast to confuse the Germans about where the Allies were operating, blocking radar installations, and sometimes tricking the enemy into believing they were part of a large invasion force. Everyone noticed Steinbeck's courage under fire. On one operation he removed his press insignia and armed himself with a Thompson submachine gun—a violation of international law that could have gotten him executed had he been captured and identified. Steinbeck became an object of fascination when word spread that Warner Bros. had bought the film rights to *The Moon Is Down* for $300,000—though the men were already used to being around a celebrity. One of the group's commanders was an unusually handsome American naval lieutenant—the actor Douglas Fairbanks Jr.

Fairbanks was fond of Steinbeck. One dark night when the group was ordered ashore to accept the surrender of a small island off of Naples called Ventotene, Fairbanks volunteered as soon as he saw Steinbeck get into one of the small boats. Clambering onto a wharf in the harbor, they came under fire, but learned that the Italian locals wanted to surrender, as they believed there was a large "fleet" just offshore. It was a different story with a garrison of nearly ninety Germans holed up in the hills above the harbor and determined to fight. Although woefully outnumbered, the landing party and a handful of reinforcements advanced on the German position under a white flag and demanded their surrender. The Americans told the Germans they were surrounded by 600 soldiers—it was more like forty—and that American cruisers would presently begin shelling the installation. The Germans surrendered. In Steinbeck's account of the episode— the details were disguised to get it past the censors—the Germans realized they'd been tricked, but only after they were locked up in a heavily mined makeshift jail. Try to escape, they were warned, and we'll blow the place up. The Germans looked doubtful—in truth there were no mines—but they did not attempt escape.

Steinbeck was back home in New York in October, though he continued filing a backlog of reports for the *Herald Tribune* through early December. He still couldn't get any news about Mary's husband, Bill Dekker, who remained missing in Italy. The army could not even tell him where Dekker had last been seen. When they finally got an answer, it was the worst possible news. Dekker had been killed by friendly fire on July 13, 1943, days before he was reported missing.

Steinbeck told Toby Street that he was at work on a new book, one that was both funny and fun to write. This was almost certainly *Cannery Row*, which was evidently derived from his abandoned play, *God in the Pipes*. But it's not clear whether he was fully engaged in the project. Gwyn said he wasn't in any condition to write yet and made little progress. In January 1944, Gwyn discovered that she was pregnant. They took a trip to Mexico City. When they got back, Steinbeck started working again. He and Gwyn moved into the lower part of a brownstone on East Fifty-First Street. Steinbeck said it didn't look like a New York apartment and had a small yard that he could see from the upstairs room where he worked.

It was a rocky period. Steinbeck was in bad shape—much worse than he let on. He told Dook Sheffield that although he had not been hit during the war, he'd taken a beating just the same. In Mexico he'd suffered some kind of breakdown and had spent a couple of months staring out the window. He told Annie Laurie Williams he'd needed the rest more than he knew. Earlier, he'd confided to Toby Street that he was experiencing frightening episodes when he suddenly didn't know who or where he was. It was as if his brain went blank. He said these lasted only seconds and were followed by a "blinding headache" that also came and went in an instant. Eventually he learned that both eardrums had been ruptured during his time near heavy shelling, and though they were beginning to heal, his doctor told him he'd also suffered a concussion and that it could take a year or two for all of his symptoms to clear up. Steinbeck said there was no way to know how long it would be before other problems—the nervousness, nightmares, and insomnia that plagued him—would go away. Refusing to feel sorry for himself, Steinbeck noted that there were tens of thousands of men coming home with the same complaints.

He and Gwyn led a quiet life, rarely going out. Sometimes he worked at home and other times, especially if the weather was hot, he wrote in the air-conditioned Viking office on East Forty-Sixth Street. He said he didn't think his current manuscript was any good—the usual refrain—but that it had the virtue of taking his mind off the war. "I'm trying to forget that for the time being, not very successfully." Nobody could describe what war was like, and so nobody tried. He thought if you got it right, it couldn't be printed. Steinbeck believed the war would pick up speed in the coming months—D-Day was only weeks away. He was sorry not to be part of it, though in a way he felt as if he'd seen enough to know what it would be like. Besides, "I don't like fighting," he said, "and I've found very few who do once they've been in it." A month later, he told his sister Esther that Gwyn's pregnancy was going well—better than his book, which he was thinking of throwing away.

Steinbeck didn't give up on *Cannery Row*—even though he told Dook Sheffield he really did throw it away. Instead, he kept at it as Gwyn's due date approached. The baby, whom they named Thom, arrived by C-section on August 2. Thom was a "pudge." Unfortunately, Steinbeck reported, Thom seemed to resemble him. By September Steinbeck had corrected the galleys and *Cannery Row* was at the printer, scheduled for publication in early January 1945. At

Viking, Pascal Covici could not contain his excitement—pre-orders had topped 250,000 copies by November. Steinbeck sent a galley copy to Sheffield, who wrote back saying the book was entertaining and that he enjoyed reading it. But he worried that the critics would find it slight and unworthy of the author of *The Grapes of Wrath*. Sheffield thought the story, a humorous portrait of the denizens of the Monterey waterfront, was too much like *Tortilla Flat*, only with a cast of white characters who seemed more like irredeemable bums than did the fun-loving *paisanos*.

Sheffield must have hit a nerve. He didn't get an answer from Steinbeck, who didn't talk to him or write for the next eight years.

Covici disputed Sheffield's opinion of *Cannery Row* and did his best to assure Steinbeck that the critics would appreciate that he was not repeating himself. After all, Covici said, even the greatest writers, Shakespeare included, reworked and explored the dimensions of familiar themes and characters all the time. This was fair enough, though Covici didn't mention what was new in *Cannery Row*. Unlike *Tortilla Flat*, which was inspired by Sue Gregory's tales of the *paisanos*, *Cannery Row* had sprung directly from Steinbeck's own life, and its protagonist was a literal version of his best friend, Ed Ricketts. Apart from *Sea of Cortez* and his various reporting assignments, Steinbeck had written little about the world he inhabited. His experience only modestly informed his work, in his description of Corral de Tierra in *The Pastures of Heaven* and the lab in "The Snake." But now he paused and looked around at where he'd been. For many readers, *Cannery Row* would be Steinbeck's stop-time book, the one in which he and Ricketts were forever preserved in the amber of a charming, quirky town on the California coast where once the living had been free and easy, the cheap booze flowed, and the days were never, ever boring.

As many reviewers pointed out, *Cannery Row* is less a story than a collection of small stories, some of them not actually stories at all but only incidents, conversations, vignettes, sepia moods. The book is like a box of old postcards. In a brief introduction, Steinbeck describes the Row as "a poem, a stink, a grating noise, a quality of light, a tone, a habit, a nostalgia, a dream." His affection for Monterey and his love of Ricketts run deep and constant all the way through. This was a place and a time that belonged to the ages. The action, such as it is, revolves around Doc, the owner of Western Biological and a charmer and sage beloved by everyone on the Row. Doc is small, wiry, and has a face that is "half Christ and half satyr." He can't stand it if his head gets wet.

Steinbeck did not conceal his conviction that life on the Row back in the day was better than the life most people aspired to—that the motley collection of writers and artists and whores and layabouts who accepted one another as they were was preferable to what passed for civil society. This subtle restatement of Steinbeck's loathing of privilege puts a different light on the story, which is a celebratory parable. How fine the dregs of society were. You could find these marginalized, invisible sidewalk saints everywhere. They possessed nothing—and, in their intuitive way, comprehended everything: " 'It has always seemed strange to me,' said Doc. 'The things we admire in men, kindness and generosity, openness, honesty, understanding and feeling are the concomitants of failure in our system. And those traits we detest, sharpness, greed, acquisitiveness, meanness, egotism and self-interest are the traits of success. And while men admire the quality of the first they love the produce of the second.' "

Anyone who needs anything—advice, a medical diagnosis, a dollar—turns to Doc, and on the Row he is known as a "fountain of philosophy and science and art." He plays Gregorian music for the young women who work at Dora's Bear Flag Restaurant, the whorehouse across the street from the lab, and he reads Li Po, the eighth-century Chinese poet, to Lee Chong, owner of the grocery and general store. Everybody on the Row is in some way indebted to Doc, and everyone wishes they could return the favor and do something nice for him. That includes the residents of the Palace Flophouse, a grungy old fish-meal warehouse that Lee Chong owns on a hillside above the Row. It's rented to a group of men with nowhere else to be, no work to do or ambition to find it, and who have no problem with any of that. There's Mack—a character much like Danny in *Tortilla*

Flat—and Hazel, Eddie, Hughie, and Jones. On the Row they're simply "Mack and the boys." Things happen, and then other things happen, one irony at a time. Mack and the boys collect frogs for Doc, who has a big order for them, and they throw him a surprise party that goes wrong when everyone gets drunk and the lab is smashed up before Doc gets home. The frogs escape into the night. So they throw him another party.

Doc is the book's hero, but it was Steinbeck's close study of the layabouts who inhabit the aromatic Monterey waterfront that entertained readers—who smiled every time Mack said "I and the boys." *Cannery Row* touched readers and made some of the critics happy. One called the book a "small miracle," while several dismissed it as unserious and questioned Steinbeck's preoccupation with the underclass. The hard-to-please Edmund Wilson offered a complex view. He loved the book's lack of pretension and said it was the Steinbeck book that made the most pleasant reading. But Wilson disliked Doc's flat-line emotional engagement with the people around him. Doc likes everybody and treats everyone with respect. But he also regards people with detachment, the same objective coolness he relies on in studying invertebrates in the intertidal zone. Doc is a lusty man, but only in the carnal sense. His passion for life seems artificial. Wilson suspected that there was some unspecific "coarseness" in Steinbeck's view of the world that prevented him from inventing characters who lived up to their supposedly lofty ideals.

It was Wilson's standing complaint that Steinbeck reduced his characters to their biological traits, drawing stick figures rather than fully formed humans. Wilson had read and admired *Sea of Cortez* and surely recognized the other Doc-like characters in Steinbeck's work. How could he not be real? But Wilson would not surrender himself to Steinbeck, would never let himself believe freely in Steinbeck's imagination or allow for the possibility that he simply did not understand Steinbeck's world, which was so often cloaked in fog and hidden away in a far-off valley.

And that's funny in this case, because *Cannery Row* was in almost every way utterly true, right down to the street-level geography so reliable that a stranger could have navigated through Monterey with only the book as a map. Even Mack was based on an actual person, a well-known fixture on the Row named Harold Otis "Gabe" Bicknell. True, what happened was made up, but does that even count? After the book came out and made Ricketts famous, people again made pilgrimages to Monterey to see what Steinbeck had described. Ask anybody on Cannery Row today about the small, wooden building with the stairs going up the front that still stands as it did, and they'll conflate the man and the character and tell you that's the lab, of course, where Doc Ricketts used to live and work.

While Viking was putting the finishing touches on *Cannery Row*, Steinbeck decided to let their lease lapse on the New York apartment and move back to California. He said he never wanted to spend another sweltering summer in New York. Even though their apartment stayed cooler than many, they had to run fans constantly, and sometimes the only escape was to pile into the car and drive into the country. Besides, he missed the fog. He said he just wanted to sit on the rocks by the ocean and fish. He'd found a pair of adjoining houses in the Carmel Highlands near Pacific Grove that would give him room to write and space for Gwyn and the baby, plus a nanny. Gwyn would fly ahead to Los Angeles, and he would bring their things cross-country in their Buick station wagon, a trip he figured would take six to eight days—longer if he had tire trouble. He also told his sister Mary to stop renting the Eleventh Street cottage to the Lovejoys. They were "hard on property and don't take care of things at all," he said.

Cannery Row, a book written for laughs and to alleviate Steinbeck's postwar anxieties, had done its job. By the end, Steinbeck seemed his old self, and the moment it was completed he began the next project—a film and an accompanying book based on a story he'd picked up down in La Paz on the gulf trip. As Steinbeck had heard it, a local boy who earned his way diving for pearls had found an immense one, a pearl so perfect and enormous that he knew he would live from then on as a rich man, surrounded by everything he could desire. But when he'd tried to sell the pearl, the brokers in the town conspired to cheat him, so rather than sell the pearl for a pittance, he hid it. After that, terrible things befell the boy. He was followed and attacked and searched. Eventually he fled inland, but was caught and tortured. Convinced the pearl had brought this misfortune upon him, the boy hurled it back into the sea. Steinbeck thought this story was hard to believe—and therefore probably true.

The plan was that Steinbeck would work on the story of the pearl that autumn, finish it before Christmas in California, then head down to Mexico in January to oversee the movie version and draft the shooting script on the spot. But the story went more slowly than Steinbeck planned—Covici teased him about being late—and Steinbeck didn't arrive in Monterey until October. Instead of renting the houses in Carmel, he impulsively bought a timeworn adobe in Monterey.

Built in the 1830s by a man named Jesus Soto, it was known by everyone as the Soto adobe, located on Pierce Street, in the heart of the city near Colton Hall, where the California constitution had been written. Steinbeck had seen the Soto adobe as a kid, and he told Covici he had always dreamed of someday living in it. It was a low-slung, one-story home that was not large but sat in the midst of a sprawling garden that covered eight city lots and was surrounded by an adobe wall. A cypress tree nearly as old as the house towered over the front lawn. Steinbeck sent a picture of the place to Pascal Covici, who said it looked like "an old Spanish mansion," though it appeared in need of a lot of fixing up. He said he wished he could work in the garden alongside Steinbeck. Meanwhile, Covici said orders for *Cannery Row* continued to climb a month ahead of publication. He predicted it would end up selling more than 250,000 copies.

Gwyn hated the house, which was solid but cramped and cold and tired. There was no central heat, only a small stove. The bathroom was an antique, with a claw-foot tub and a toilet with a tank above it on the wall. The kitchen, if it could be called one, was a lean-to outside in the back. The whole place needed rewiring, but with the war still on, they couldn't find anyone to do the work.

Steinbeck was thrilled to be back in California, but Gwyn was miserable. She didn't know anybody other than their nanny, Miss Diehl, a heavyset woman who wore a cape and had eyes like lumps of coal. She proved a dour companion, though Gwyn said that she took wonderful care of Thom. Steinbeck, noticing that Diehl wore shoes larger than his own, took to calling her "Platterfoot." Diehl, in turn, regularly let Steinbeck know she didn't approve of his language, which included a lot of swearing. Steinbeck must have found the company of his family and the nanny grating, because he abruptly decided to rent an office. When he gave the owner of the building his name, the man seemed unaware of who he was and asked what line of work he was in. Steinbeck said he was a writer. The man asked if he had a license for that. Steinbeck told him he didn't think one was required. Well then, the man said, I'm afraid I can't help you. He told Steinbeck he wanted only professional people, like doctors and insurance men, and certainly not writers or similar types. Steinbeck found this funny, and enjoyed not being recognized. He went home and cleaned out the woodshed at the adobe and set up his writing table there. It was like his days on San Francisquito Creek at Stanford.

Steinbeck finally finished *The Pearl* and went down to Cuernavaca, south of Mexico City, to begin work on the film. Gwyn came later. They stayed first at the Hotel Marik, but then found a house to rent. It was roomy, with a big garden and a swimming pool. The air in Cuernavaca was delicious in the rainy season. They had a dog named Willie with them who managed to "accidentally" fall in the pool several times a day. One day Willie disappeared, and Steinbeck got a ransom demand—which he paid. After that, they kept the dog chained up.

The baby Thom, Steinbeck said, was "growing like a weed and very black." Shortly after their arrival, word reached them that President Roosevelt had died. A few weeks later, Adolf Hitler put a bullet in his brain. Germany would soon be finished. The war's end, which everyone yearned for, was at hand, and he found that hard to believe.

That fall, the Nobel Prize for Literature went to the Chilean poet Gabriela Mistral—the first Latin American author to win the award. Pat Covici was willing to bet that Steinbeck would win the Nobel within three years. "It is inevitable," Covici declared.

A production company he'd never heard of called Pan-American Films approached Steinbeck about writing a film script for a movie about the Mexican revolutionary leader Emiliano Zapata. He told Annie Laurie Williams it was a story he loved and wanted to do, but that it would be some time before he could get to it. A few weeks later, though, he complained to Pascal Covici about the film business. He disliked turning *The Pearl* into a movie script. He had to make everything so literal for the camera that it drained all of the imagination from the story.

While he was in Mexico, Steinbeck reconsidered the idea of living in California. He'd felt more hostility in Monterey than he was prepared for. Old friends, though they didn't say it out loud, seemed to resent his success. Only Ed Ricketts treated him the same as before. And their difficulties in getting anyone to work on the adobe were suspicious. Steinbeck insisted there was a general distaste for writers there, one that he'd thought was funny when he tried to rent an office, but it now bothered him. Then, in July, Gwyn came down with dysentery. Her weight dropped to 102 pounds. As soon as she was back on her feet, Gwyn took Thom and returned to New York, where they moved into the Warwick Hotel on West Fifty-Fourth Street. Steinbeck visited them for a few days in September. The world was still absorbing the news about the atomic bomb, which had incinerated Hiroshima and Nagasaki in early August.

In October, Steinbeck was "back in the tropics," as he put it to his sister Mary. That was sad news, he said, because he didn't like warm weather, and a day spent in New York with a crushing hangover was preferable to a day stone sober in Mexico. The film production had moved to Acapulco, and he found the slow pace of moviemaking frustrating.

Late in the fall, Steinbeck bought what he called "twin houses" in New York that stood side by side on East Seventy-Eighth Street and shared a garden between them. The plan was to sell the extra house, but they ended up renting it to Nat Benchley—the son of *The New Yorker* humorist Robert—and his family. By March 1946, Steinbeck had moved into his writing room in the basement. It was windowless, which he figured would keep him from watching for the postman and daydreaming. There was a cement floor, gray concrete walls, and exposed pipes overhead. Steinbeck had started work on a new novel, *The Wayward Bus*. Gwyn was pregnant again, due in June. Thom was nearly two now. Steinbeck was deeply fond of him, though Thom's efforts at learning to talk mystified him. But then the idea that Thom was "his" was just as baffling. Perhaps he wasn't a normal parent, because Thom seemed to him in every way only one child among the myriad. The idea of any greater connection between them was an alien thought. Steinbeck thought he'd have the same feelings for any baby he was around.

John Steinbeck IV was born on June 12, 1946. Later they would nickname him "Catbird."

— 14 —

A ROCK FALLS
INTO THE WATER

I N THE WINTER of 1946, Steinbeck enlisted his sister Mary's help
in selling the Soto adobe in Monterey, in the end taking a loss.
He also worked on a musical intended for Broadway tentatively
called *The Wizard*, which was at one time a short novel titled *The
Wizard of Maine*. The lyricist and composer Frank Loesser was to do
the music. But it never came together and in March Steinbeck told
Mary that he'd suffered an "emotional bust-up" over it. The fact that
he'd had to throw it away wasn't so bad as the fact that he'd ever tried
it in the first place. "It was silly of me ever to think I could do it," he
confessed. "Presumptuous in fact."

By May of 1946, just before John IV was born, Steinbeck was deep
into *The Wayward Bus*. For a change, New York was cool that summer, the most pleasant he'd ever experienced there. The novel progressed quickly, in spurts of 2,000 words a day. A book seems to take
forever when you're writing it—and then to have happened in no time
at all after you've finished. In August, Ed Ricketts's mother died.
Steinbeck wrote him a letter of condolence, and included some money
for anything Ricketts might need.

In early October, Steinbeck was revising *The Wayward Bus*. He
considered it a "strange" book that would make enemies. As soon as
he was finished with it, he and Gwyn were going to Scandinavia for
five weeks, planning to return by Thanksgiving. The boys—John IV

was only four months old—would stay in New York with their nanny, Miss Diehl.

Steinbeck wrote to his sister Esther from aboard the SS *Drottning-holm*, bound for Copenhagen. It was a rough passage, the ship rolling heavily in "a gray, angry sea." But it was better than the last time he'd crossed the ocean, when they'd had to keep watch for submarines and would not have been surprised to hear an explosion onboard at any moment. They followed the edge of the Gulf Stream, and in spite of their unsteady progress over the pitching ocean, Steinbeck could not get enough of the food, which he thought was terrific. In Copenhagen, Steinbeck was met by a swarm of reporters. He was astonished that writers were received so enthusiastically there. The city looked in good shape after the war, having escaped heavy bombing. He noticed that air-raid shelters were everywhere but nearly invisible, having been covered over by neatly manicured lawns. That was so like the Danes. From there they went on to Stockholm, where Steinbeck got together with Bo Beskow, an author and painter he and Carol had met when they'd come over years before. The trip ended a week early—Steinbeck and Gwyn discovered they missed their children—and they flew home.

Christmastime that year was beautiful. A blizzard hit New York, leaving several feet of snow in the streets. Cars were buried, and there was a hush in the city. Steinbeck and Nat Benchley fixed Bloody Marys and went out exploring. They came back with sleds in the still-falling snow and played outside all day like little boys, building a snow fort and starting snowball fights with their wives.

Viking published *The Wayward Bus* in February of 1947, moving it ahead of *The Pearl*—which Steinbeck had already published in *The Woman's Home Companion*. Steinbeck sent a copy to Esther, warning her there was no chance she would like it. If she didn't, she had company among many—though by no means all—of the book's reviewers. As Steinbeck anticipated, *The Wayward Bus* hit a lot of people the wrong way. A few liked it; no one seemed indifferent. Steinbeck wrote to Max Wagner's brother Jack, who had worked with him on the film set of *The Pearl*, saying that it was a mistake to read reviews of his own work. The good ones canceled the bad ones, and vice versa—and all this did was confuse him. But Steinbeck did allow that the split decision made the book controversial, and in the end this would be good for it. Nothing like an argument over a book to help sales, he said.

Not that *The Wayward Bus* needed help. Steinbeck's latest was in demand well ahead of publication. The Book-of-the-Month Club ordered a jaw-dropping printing of 600,000 copies, and Viking reported another 150,000 in pre-orders. The people who were going to attack the book, Steinbeck noted, seemed eager to buy it. As he did every year now, Steinbeck protested that he would still need to borrow money to pay his income taxes.

Reviewers agreed that *The Wayward Bus* was a departure for Steinbeck—though as most of the critics recognized, Steinbeck was always trying something new. Set in central California, the book was lush with Steinbeck's unerring descriptions of the terrain, the muted colors of the landscape, the bruised skies that bring rain, the cascading torrents that rush down the near-desert hillsides when the clouds open. And it had the clean economy of *Of Mice and Men*—the same elemental dialogue and uncanny ear for the way real people speak—though much of this is internalized. *The Wayward Bus* is about what people think. Not surprisingly, it turns out that the things people think about include money, careers, their appearance, the unpleasantness or attractiveness of other people, dreams of a life that will never be actualized, and—coming in well ahead of everything else—sex.

Steinbeck explores an ensemble of these inner monologues as they play through the minds of a handful of bus passengers and their driver over the course of a single day that begins at dawn in a diner and ends just beyond a treacherous, rain-slicked mountain pass. The bus slides off the road and becomes mired long enough for its driver, a handsome and muscled man named Juan, to seduce one of the passengers, a worldly but sex-starved college girl named Mildred. Mildred is traveling with her stuffy parents, who are sufficiently lost in their own thoughts that they fail to notice when their daughter chases after Juan after he goes to summon help. Mildred is sure Juan will be waiting for her somewhere down the gloomy road, and she's right about that and about what will take place when she finds him.

Almost nothing else happens in *The Wayward Bus*. It's a group character study of several types. There are Mildred's parents—a businessman and a housewife; a traveling salesman who's come back from the war wielding a "get up and go" that hides his shattered nerves; a naive waitress who hopes to find a new life in Hollywood; Juan's awkward, acne-plagued mechanic; and an old-timer who warns everyone against even starting out in such terrible weather. The group's quiet conscience is a voluptuous blonde named Camille, who claims to be a dental hygienist but in reality is a stripper who works stag parties. Camille's bigger secret, though, is that she knows what everyone else on the bus is thinking. Nothing gets past her. In the film version of *The Wayward Bus*, released ten years later, the part went to Jayne Mansfield.

Carlos Baker, who would go on to write a seminal biography of Ernest Hemingway, reviewed the book for the *New York Times*. Baker admired its strong imagery and felt readers who had disliked the interwoven chapters in *The Grapes of Wrath* would be delighted by the book's straightforward construction, which he thought was Steinbeck at his best. *The Wayward Bus*, Baker said, was a "twentieth-century parable on the state of man." Parables, however, impart lessons, and it's hard to say what the lesson is in *The Wayward Bus*—unless it's that everybody wants what they don't have.

The critics who disagreed with Baker felt as strongly the other way. Orville Prescott, offering a contrary opinion in the *New York Times*, called it a tedious retelling of an old and worn-out story. Prescott found the characters better people than the "worthless riffraff" in *Cannery Row*, and yet Steinbeck seemed to prefer the latter—a curious observation that suggested Prescott had missed the points of both books. Ralph Habas, writing in the *Chicago Tribune*, kept it short. It was, he said, too bad that Steinbeck had bothered to write this book, which among its defects had didn't seem to involve an actual story.

Steinbeck, who reliably argued that his detractors failed to understand his books, took comfort in the extravagant sales for *The Wayward Bus*. Written in a rush and aimed to disturb, the book had hit its mark. And Steinbeck had amused himself in small ways, too, hiding obscure references to people he knew and places he'd gone by using their names in the book. When the salesman offers to meet up with Mildred's father to discuss business, he gives him an address in Hollywood—the Aloha Arms apartments, where Gwen Conger had introduced herself to Steinbeck and given him a hot bath.

It wasn't unusual for the Steinbecks to find themselves at a party in Manhattan where guests gathered around a piano. It seemed that everyone had at least a little show business in them. But Steinbeck didn't like it when Gwyn sang in public—or so she later claimed. She surmised that he wanted to be the center of attention—though this would have been the opposite of the way he felt about Carol, whom he enjoyed showing off in the more relaxed life they'd led in California. Early on, Gwyn had come to terms with the fact that it made Steinbeck unhappy when she performed. So she had to have been delighted in the spring of 1947 when Steinbeck bought her a piano and had it lifted into their second-floor living room. Gwyn wanted to compose lullabies—eventually she wrote a dozen or so, and recorded ten of them with a full orchestra.

One night in mid-May, around ten o'clock, they were in the living room when Steinbeck thought he heard someone in the courtyard below the open window and went to have a look. When he leaned over the railing, which had been removed and reinstalled for the piano delivery, it gave way and he fell to the ground, narrowly missing a spike-studded iron fence and sustaining a broken kneecap that required surgery. Toward the end of the month, he was allowed to sit up and write a couple of letters, though it made him dizzy. He expected to be getting around on crutches soon, but he would have to be careful of the knee for some time. He'd been lucky. He easily could have broken his back. By the first week of June, he was out of the hospital and walking with a cane.

Steinbeck was glad to be back on his feet. With *The Pearl* set to come out in the fall he wanted to take time for a longer trip to Europe and especially the Soviet Union, regions still reeling from the war. He approached the *New York Herald Tribune* about doing a series of articles that would help pay for it. Steinbeck hoped to travel with the famous war photographer Robert Capa, whom he'd met in London during the Blitz and had later seen in North Africa and Italy. One day earlier that spring, as Steinbeck was having a drink at the bar in the Bedford Hotel in New York, Capa walked in and they got to talking. Capa suggested that they could join forces and visit parts of Russia away from Moscow that weren't being reported on. The *Herald Tribune* agreed to send them.

Steinbeck and Gwyn first went to Paris for a few weeks. They stayed at the Hotel Lancaster on the Rue de Berri. Everything was expensive. But they had a grand time. Burgess Meredith was staying in the same hotel with his wife, the actress Paulette Goddard, who'd married him after leaving Charlie Chaplin. One night the four of them attended a costume party, and Steinbeck—who refused to get dressed up—doubled over with laughter when he saw Goddard dressed as Marie Antoinette, wearing a hoopskirt so wide she had trouble getting out of the hotel elevator. The weather was unusually lovely, "cool and delightful" enough to remind Steinbeck of Monterey. He and Gwyn were excited about being in the city for Bastille Day, and planned to stay up all night partying. Gwyn would go home on July 18, and Steinbeck would head up to Stockholm and then on to Moscow with Capa. He expected to be back in New York by the start of October 1947.

At Viking, Pascal Covici looked forward to Steinbeck's reporting from the Soviet Union, not without a vested interest. Steinbeck's career seemed to have reached an intermission, as if the lights had come up and he'd gone to the lobby for a smoke. Covici wanted the old Steinbeck back. He thought the Russian reporting would be turned into a book, but more importantly it might put Steinbeck on track for a novel to follow. He didn't say it directly, but Covici dreamed of another book like *The Grapes of Wrath*, a book written in anger. In a letter to Steinbeck in Paris, Covici subtly suggested that the trip might rekindle Steinbeck's temper and his willingness to take on injustice, natural-born traits that had driven him to greatness and were being neglected in his recent work. No other author, Covici believed, could get so mad at the world with such grace: "There is a giant dormant in your soul and I want to see it stir with the compassion and generous understanding that is yours, yours above any other writer in America."

In a follow-up letter a week later, Covici told Steinbeck that whatever came of the Russian trip, he was sure it would put him in top shape to begin writing his long-contemplated book about the Salinas valley. This was an idea Steinbeck had mentioned from time to time for a big novel, longer than *The Grapes of Wrath*. Its slow gestation—plus Steinbeck's plan to make the book autobiographical—hinted that he imagined it would be his major achievement.

Steinbeck had chosen a volatile time to visit the Soviet Union, given the Allied occupation of Europe and Stalin's dominance over eastern Europe. U.S. mistrust of the Soviet leader—our recent ally—had intensified. America would soon launch the Marshall Plan, a $12 billion reconstruction effort for western Europe that was additionally intended to halt Soviet expansion beyond its satellite nations to the east. Named for its architect, former general of the army and now secretary of state George C. Marshall, the plan was in furtherance of the still-evolving Truman Doctrine, which promised American support to countries that resisted a Communist takeover. The United States's position was that it would no longer tolerate the steady spread of Communism. The Marshall Plan and the Truman Doctrine, later seen by historians as "two halves of the same walnut," laid the foundation for the establishment of the North Atlantic Treaty Organization. They also sketched in the outlines of the Cold War standoff between America and the Soviet Union—a confrontation pitting democracy against totalitarianism.

Steinbeck's account of his visit to Russia, accompanied by Capa's photographs, provided America with a casual, apolitical travelogue that peered behind what Winston Churchill the year before had called the "Iron Curtain" separating the Soviet Union and its satellites from the West. Steinbeck and Capa traveled through Russia for forty days. One of Steinbeck's telling early observations about Soviet society was that nobody did anything on their own if it seemed that permission might be needed from someone in an official capacity. This was most obvious whenever Capa aimed his camera at people. The appearance of the camera invariably led to the prompt arrival of a policeman, usually in plain clothes, and an inspection of their papers, which included permission for Capa to take photos. The officer—sometimes after reinforcements had arrived on the scene—would then telephone headquarters for advice on how to proceed. After some time, everyone would smile and Capa would be allowed to shoot. That was the way it always went. The police, Steinbeck noted satisfactorily, were unfailingly courteous about inconveniencing them.

In early August, Steinbeck and Capa visited a village in Ukraine called Shevchenko. There were still tank tracks and shell craters left over from heavy fighting there. Steinbeck reported that Shevchenko was a farming community, though a poor one owing to its pale, powdery soil. But its residents managed to grow a little wheat, and some millet and corn. Many of the town's men had been killed or wounded in the war. Everywhere they went it was like that—villages occupied by the elderly, women, and children—a whole generation of men gone. But the people who were left behind were cheerful and friendly. When they visited a field where cucumbers were being harvested and Capa got out his camera, the women stopped what they were doing and adjusted their kerchiefs, smoothed their blouses, and smiled broadly at their visitors. One woman waggled a cucumber at them and said she had been widowed twice, and that men now stayed away from her. Well, said Capa, how about marrying me right now?

An amused Steinbeck described what followed: "She rolled her head back and howled with laughter. 'Not you, look!' she said. 'If God had consulted the cucumber before he made man, there would be less unhappy women in the world.' The whole field roared with laughter at Capa."

As the end of August approached, Steinbeck grew weary of living out of a suitcase. He wrote to Gwyn and told her he looked forward to being home, where he could sit in one place and work again. And as much as he liked the Russian people, especially in rural areas, the wounds of war were everywhere. From Stalingrad he described for Gwyn the devastation. The city had escaped bombing, but artillery and machine-gun fire had reduced many buildings to rubble, and left others pocked with bullet marks. The city was all but destroyed. Steinbeck said the scale of the fighting must have been beyond comprehension.

Back in New York in October, Steinbeck began organizing the Russian material. He huddled with Mavis McIntosh and Elizabeth Otis about turning his reports for the *Herald Tribune*, as well as some others that had been picked up by *Ladies' Home Journal*, into a book. Eventually it was published as *A Russian Journal*. Steinbeck said it was going to be hard work and that he was desperate to get out from under it by summer so he could start his California book. He had come back from the Soviet Union with some 200 pages of notes, and Capa would have to choose from 5,000 photographs. Steinbeck rented an office in the Bedford Hotel. He said he worked better when he got dressed and out of the house.

This was new. Until then, Steinbeck had always enforced strict household rules about the quiet and absence of interruptions he needed to work. Gwyn liked to sleep late, and for a time this blended with Steinbeck's morning work schedule. But with the arrival of the boys and the addition of Miss Diehl, things were less peaceful and no longer under his control. And there were growing frictions between him and Gwyn. Besides the everyday chaos of two toddlers underfoot, Steinbeck resented the demands they placed on Gwyn. Even with Miss Diehl helping, Gwyn was often busy with the children and less attentive to him than Steinbeck thought she should be. Gwyn saw his jealousy growing. Often, when she was putting the boys to bed, Steinbeck would come up and stand just outside the room watching. Sometimes he played a little with Thom, but usually he just lurked in the doorway. Eventually he would ask her when she was coming downstairs.

Other times, Steinbeck was more insistent. He'd come up and interrupt Gwyn when she was with the children and tell her they needed to discuss something and could she please come downstairs. When she went down, Steinbeck would fix two cocktails and then sit down and start reading the newspaper. After a while, Gwyn would ask what it was he wanted to talk to her about—whereupon he would get up and make them two more drinks. If she asked him about dinner, he usually stalled, letting her wonder if he wanted to go out or stay in. Steinbeck hated being held to a rigid schedule for dinner, so a decision—and it was always his decision—was often slow in coming. Apparently neither of them was much of a cook. If they stayed in they usually had the same thing: bacon and eggs.

Gwyn knew that Steinbeck had come to resent the boys. Much later, she claimed that he'd gone along with having Thom only to prove that he wasn't too old to father a child with his pretty young wife. Or so she believed. Gwyn said many things later on that are hard to evaluate. She said that Steinbeck forced her to have a number of abortions and had not wanted her to have John IV. "My only mistake," Gwyn said bitterly, "was in having children," suggesting that had she not things would have otherwise been swell.

As Steinbeck plunged into *A Russian Journal*, Gwyn saw less of him. During the day he was at his office over at the Bedford, and at night they had stopped sharing a bed. Steinbeck now slept on the apartment's third floor. Whose idea this was, or why it happened, isn't clear. Gwyn maintained that Steinbeck's heavy drinking made him unpleasant in bed, behavior she described in venomous terms. Gwyn's complaints about Steinbeck were often outrageous and improbable. What seems most likely is that alcohol was a toxic habit for both of them, and that telling the truth was never Gwyn's strong suit.

Toward the end of the year, Viking published *The Pearl* in a slim volume, just weeks ahead of the release of the film based on it. The critics wrestled for consensus over Steinbeck's simple story about a gift whose beauty conceals its inherent ill fortune, though on balance they decided it was a fine piece of work. One who was less happy with Steinbeck's retelling of the Mexican folktale was Maxwell Geismar, who reviewed it for the *Saturday Review*. Geismar thought the little book was beautifully written, but found it regrettable that Steinbeck had set aside social criticism to return to a more primitive motif of the sort he'd explored in books like *To a God Unknown* and *Tortilla Flat*. Geismar argued that Steinbeck lacked the talent needed to make such an elemental story relevant to the problems of a modern materialistic culture—apparently believing that this was an obvious goal. Instead, Geismar said Steinbeck had reverted to his earlier themes, and that he was more amused by the Mexican natives than he was empathetic.

Geismar failed to notice, or didn't care about, the graceful images and ideas that glide through the beginning of the book—Steinbeck's beguiling portrait of the Gulf of California and the deft study of his theory of human behavior, his concept of the phalanx, the operation of a group as if it were a single biological unit. In *The Grapes of Wrath* this idea seemed forced, but in *The Pearl*, set by the life-cradling sea, where the tropical breeze smooths and settles everything, it felt natural and right.

The story opens with the dawn, in a cluster of brush huts next to an estuary by the ocean just beside the gleaming city of La Paz. A native fisherman and pearl diver named Kino is at home with his wife, Juana, and their baby, Coyotito. This domestic scene is shattered when a scorpion stings Coyotito on the shoulder. They take him to the doctor in La Paz, but he will not treat the child because they cannot pay him—and also because they are Indians. They go back to their hut, where it is still early and the "hazy mirage" that hangs over the gulf is playing tricks in the morning light, just as it had when Steinbeck visited years before.

Kino and Juana paddle out to the oyster beds in their canoe, Coyotito swollen and feverish under a blanket. Kino dives and he sees an oyster, an old one that is larger than the others nearby. Within its partly open shell, something gleams. Kino pulls the oyster loose and swims to the surface. In the canoe he pries open the shell and finds a "great pearl, perfect as the moon" within it. In the same moment, Kino and Juana look at Coyotito and see that the swelling has abated. He is getting better. When they are back at their hut, word of the pearl spreads through the village—which Steinbeck likens to a coral reef, an intricate living structure composed of many smaller living entities: "A town is a thing like a colonial animal. A town has a nervous system and a head and shoulders and feet. A town is a thing separate from all other towns, so that there are no two towns alike. And a town has a whole emotion. How news travels through a town is a mystery not easily to be solved. News seems to move faster than small boys can scramble and dart to tell it, faster than women can call it over fences.

"Before Kino and Juana and the other fishers had come to Kino's brush house, the nerves of the town were pulsing and vibrating with the news—Kino had found the Pearl of the World."

But Kino's prize brings only trouble. The greedy doctor tries to convince him that Coyotito is worse, not better, and for a price he can help. The pearl brokers in La Paz conspire to swindle him, and after he brushes aside their offers, Kino is repeatedly attacked in the night by robbers searching for the pearl. Soon his canoe is broken apart and his house is burned. Kino and his family flee, finding their way to the road that will take them north, to another, finer city than La Paz, where no one will know their business and the pearl will make them wealthy. On they go, traveling at night and hiding by day, always hurrying and always fearful, for like Pepe in Steinbeck's earlier story "Flight," they are being pursued. Death comes in the end this time, too, but not for Kino. He returns to his village and throws the pearl back into the sea.

Carlos Baker, the critic who had loved *The Wayward Bus*, was keen on *The Pearl*. Writing in the *New York Times Book Review*, Baker marveled at Steinbeck's clear voice. And unlike Maxwell Geismar, he thought Steinbeck's taste for parable was a refined thing, a sensibility that fitted *The Pearl* into the list of Steinbeck books as if it were a link in an intricate necklace. Most of all, Baker admired Steinbeck's restraint—his ability to hold back his prose and make it behave. Steinbeck's writing, he said, was powerful and yet always under control.

In February, Steinbeck went out to California to visit friends in Monterey and to do research in Salinas, where he walked the streets of his youth and read old newspaper files. He got into the countryside, out along the Salinas River and up into the weathered hills, kicking the dirt, inspecting the trees, and plucking up the sturdy dry grasses holding tight against the winter sun. It was intoxicating. And restful—something he realized he had needed badly only when he got there. Steinbeck stayed in a motor lodge called the Casa Munras and slept twelve hours at a stretch. He told Pascal Covici that he didn't know yet what the book would be like, only that he would need to reinvent his vocabulary for it, and that it would be long. He stated his usual warning against being rushed. This time, he said, his work would move at its own natural pace. This sounded like the book Covici wanted, and now he was on notice that he'd have to damn well wait for as long as it took. The working title for this ambitious novel was *Salinas Valley*, which sounded inartful and not suggestive of the momentous themes Steinbeck had in mind. Steinbeck believed it might take half a million words to get the story right.

This must have seemed all but impossible given Steinbeck's delicate mental state. Though he let everyone believe he was enjoying a lazy interlude in his home country, not all was well. The truth, which he confided to a diary he kept that year, was that he'd slipped into a profound depression, the worst he'd ever experienced. The fracture with Gwyn was surely a big part of it, but the gray void that clouded his mind seemed to come from all directions. He told himself to write in the journal every day for fear he might be putting down his last words. "Something is very wrong," he wrote, "and I am not in a frame of mind to do anything about it." He hinted that this "illness" was somehow overdue, that it was balancing out the times when all was well. He suffered terrible nightmares that haunted his daytime thoughts long after he was out of bed. He had been thinking how nice it would be to live again in the little cottage on Eleventh Street, the place that had always been his refuge. Now that he was nearby he felt drawn to it. But the grim struggle to hold his balance made it hard for him to do much. He slept and slept. Ricketts gave him some "cough medicine" that made him sleep even more. "I am worried about my mind," he wrote. "Think maybe I am a little nuts."

Steinbeck's depression may have been due to more than just the dark moods that sometimes overtook him. As we have learned more recently, head trauma can result in changes in the brain years or even decades after it occurs. These changes can precipitate or worsen a decline in cognition or play a role in depression. The damage can be cumulative—as it often is in athletes who absorb many smaller blows to the head over time—or it can be caused by a single traumatic event. Steinbeck never fully disclosed what happened during the artillery barrage in the war that left him with burst eardrums and a concussion whose symptoms he felt for many months afterward. Was it a single blast or a continuous shelling that went on for hours? Did it happen more than once—adding one concussion to another? More important—though unknowable—is whether it permanently altered structures inside his brain. If it did, this might explain many things about his later life—from his depressions to his mercurial behavior with his sons, to the difficulties he had with his writing long before his vital working life should have been over.

And Steinbeck would have had company in this—his old nemesis, Ernest Hemingway. When Hemingway checked into the Mayo Clinic in the fall of 1960 for electroshock treatment for depression, he was almost certainly suffering from chronic traumatic encephalopathy, or CTE, the brain disorder now widely seen in football players. Hemingway had suffered many concussions and subconcussive head injuries throughout his life, sustained over years of boxing, several car wrecks, and two airplane crashes. Ironically, the only time he and Steinbeck met—at a bar in New York in the spring of 1944—Hemingway had interrupted the otherwise dull evening by breaking a walking stick over his own head to prove he could.

On February 27—his forty-sixth birthday—Steinbeck had the flu. He was distracted by a lawsuit that had been filed against a planned film version of *Cannery Row* that Burgess Meredith hoped to make. Depressed and now physically ill, he made plans to return to New York in a couple of weeks. He fretted about money, though he expected to make enough to get by from films of "The Red Pony" and *The Pearl*. He kept having bad dreams that were powerful and vague and cruel, and that left him feeling panicked when he opened his eyes. He had a bad cough that sometimes gripped him in prolonged, convulsive episodes. In early March he drove up to Palo Alto to see Miss Mirrielees—whom he found much as he remembered her, only better—though he felt so sick on the way back that he wondered if he'd make it to his motel. On March 10 he took an overnight flight home to New York, where it was snowing when he got in.

Pat Covici was alarmed at Steinbeck's condition. When they met up Covici just stared at him anxiously, as if he expected Steinbeck to explode. Steinbeck could tell that Covici thought he was cracking up. "Maybe I am," he said. The anxiety came in waves. Steinbeck's sense of impending doom was paralyzing. "Something is going to happen," he told himself. "I am sure of it. I'm sure of it. There is no way out. There's something wrong."

Steinbeck underwent batteries of medical tests to see if there was something physical behind his malaise. This included an electroencephalograph, which Steinbeck said meant he was having his brain tested. But he said neither his doctors nor his old friend Covici could do anything for him, much as they wanted to help. Getting well, he said, was on him.

At some point Steinbeck started taking Dexedrine, a potent amphetamine related to the Benzedrine "energy pills" widely used by the Allies during the war. He hoped it would restore his strength and lift his mood. And it did. Amped up on speed by day, he sometimes had to take a sleeping pill at night before climbing into bed and encountering again the terrors of his dreams. Bouncing between uppers and downers, his days were a smear of roller-coaster emotions. On the plus side, he quickly dropped eleven pounds.

He tried to stick with the Salinas book. He wrote to tell Ed Ricketts that he had figured out how to write the book, but that the unifying theme within it was only beginning to appear. This seems to have been a reference to Ricketts's concept of breaking through, a suggestion that Steinbeck was striving to see the book whole and integrated into the larger reality of the life he had lived. Steinbeck desperately wanted the book to be good. "It may be my last," he wrote in his journal. "It may destroy everything for me but it has to be done." Steinbeck thought the book might "save" him. The more he thought about how the book would be, the more at peace he felt. In mid-April Covici came to see him and Steinbeck read him some of what he'd been writing. Covici at least pretended to like it, but indicated that it was going to be a hard job to get right. Steinbeck briefly switched medications but didn't like the new one and went back on Dexedrine.

A couple of years earlier, Steinbeck had explained his writing technique to his sister Mary. It began with the faint idea for a story. This was followed by a long period of contemplation, during which he invented one character after another and began to study them. He said it was important to set aside time every day for this—it could be a couple of hours in the morning, though he admitted he usually spent more time than that. The main thing was to think about the characters until he could see them. Eventually he learned everything about them. Where they were from, how they dressed, what their voices sounded like, the shape and texture of their hands—the total picture. Once they were clearly visible to him, he started building their back stories, adding details and events to their lives from before he knew them. He wouldn't use all of this information, but it was important to have it in order to better gauge the characters, to the point where they stood free of his conscious involvement and began to think and act independently. Gradually, he said, they would begin to talk to him on their own, so that he not only heard them speaking but started to have an idea about why they said the things they did. As the characters came to life, they inhabited his thoughts day and night, especially just before he went to sleep. Then he could "let things happen to them" and study their reactions. Eventually, he reached a point where he started fitting them into the story he had begun. Once the characters were his full partners, that's when he started to write. He thought this method could work for anyone, and said the real secret was to stay under control and resist the temptation to push too hard. Some writers worked for a fixed period of time every day. Others counted their words—as he did. Sticking to one method or the other was important, he said, otherwise your eagerness to be done takes over. He said writing a long novel goes on for months or years. When it's done you feel "terrible." That was how it was for him.

For a time that winter, Steinbeck was involved in a new medium that offered less room for such a leisurely approach—television. He'd helped organize and promote a venture called World Video, which hoped to produce and distribute documentaries and dramatic programs. Steinbeck also invested in it. Robert Capa was involved, too, and the driving force was a man named Harry White, who believed television had the potential to overwhelm other media, including books. Steinbeck ended up writing more letters to White than scripts for television, and the whole enterprise was short-lived. But it did win a Peabody Award in 1948—the first ever given to a television project. It was for a program called *Actors Studio*, a drama series featuring one-act plays and short stories. Steinbeck worked on the series with the celebrated director Elia Kazan. World Video also produced a short-lived quiz show for CBS that went by several titles, including *Riddle Me This*.

In late April, Steinbeck checked into the hospital to have the varicose veins in his legs removed. He said they didn't hurt but could cause blood clots. And they didn't look nice. He admitted he should have had them taken care of a long time ago.

The operation lasted four hours, and Steinbeck emerged from the hospital at the end of the month weak and exhausted. He wasn't supposed to climb stairs, so he planned to sleep at his office in the Bedford, which also offered the comfort of air-conditioning. He told his sister Mary that he'd now lost nineteen pounds and planned to drop another ten. Like a boxer before a fight, he was getting into shape. The "sound" of the Salinas book was never out of his thoughts now. He told Mary he'd been practicing for this new book all of his life. "Never was ready for it before," he said, "but I think I am now. If I'm not then I never will be." It had been nearly a decade since he'd told Dook Sheffield he was done writing novels.

Gwyn had been sick with minor ailments on and off all spring. Steinbeck thought she was making herself ill intentionally, willing herself toward death. But he confessed that he probably imagined it. Maybe his destiny now was to stagger from one crisis to the next. That seemed to be the pattern, one that could only be his own fault. He hinted that his spirits tended to lift later in the day, and he considered whether he should write more in his journal in the evenings. He was still losing weight, but more slowly now.

Out in Monterey, on the evening of May 8, 1948, a crowd turned up at Ed Ricketts's lab. It was Saturday night, and it promised to be a long one, so Ricketts decided to go out for some steaks to feed his friends. His ancient sedan, which was hard to start and almost as hard to keep running, was parked out front. He climbed in and eased onto Cannery Row, then turned onto Drake Avenue to go up the hill. It was dusk, the time of day when outlines blur in the failing light. The road was steep just before it crossed the tracks of the Southern Pacific Railway, and it passed close by a corrugated iron warehouse that made it hard to see to the left. As Ricketts pulled across the tracks—or maybe he drove onto them and stalled—the massive black steam locomotive pulling the Del Monte Express from San Francisco slammed into the driver's side of the car and carried it a hundred yards down the tracks.

Ricketts was pulled alive from the wreck and laid out on the grass, where he appeared to be gravely injured and went into shock. His eyes were unfocused, and there was blood coming from his mouth, though he did manage to say that nobody should blame the engineer. At the hospital he was taken into surgery, where Dr. John Gratiot—who knew Ricketts and had spent hours listening to music with him at the lab—removed his ruptured spleen. But Ricketts's injuries were extensive, and included punctured and collapsed lungs and severe head trauma. He lapsed in and out of consciousness for three days. Gratiot sensed that Ricketts knew he was dying. Finally, his heart stopped. Ricketts was fifty years old.

Steinbeck got word of the accident from Ritchie Lovejoy, who cabled him at three in the morning on May 9. He wanted to go to Monterey at once to see if he could do anything, but he hesitated. There was an encouraging update from Lovejoy, but Steinbeck knew that serious injuries could result in complications days later. On May 10 he decided to fly out. But his plane was delayed and he did not arrive before Ricketts died. He struggled to grasp that his friend—the "greatest man I have known and the best teacher"—was gone. He knew his life would not be the same. After a brief funeral service that many of Ricketts's friends skipped, Steinbeck went over to the lab and found it full of people he didn't know. He was beside himself, demanding to know who had any business being there and at one point threatening to burn the place down. What had been the incandescent core of Monterey for so many of them was now only a hollow shack on a busy, smelly waterfront, the ocean groaning at its feet. It no longer seemed part of this world.

Ricketts had designated Steinbeck as the executor of his will, and he also left Steinbeck all of his papers—journals, correspondence, and manuscripts. Ricketts hoped that one day Steinbeck would edit and publish some of this writing, but he never did. Most of the material, along with Ricketts's library, would make its way to the Hopkins Marine Station—but not before Steinbeck went through everything, tearing out pages on which Ricketts had made notes about women he was involved with, and burning the letters, many of which were from him. Ricketts kept a large safe at the lab. Its outer door was never locked, but an inner one was. Steinbeck called in a locksmith, and when they got it open, he found only a bottle of Scotch and a note that read, "What the hell did you expect to find in here? Here's a drink for your trouble."

Ricketts's love life remained messy even in death. He'd ended his six-year relationship with a woman named Toni Jackson not long before he died, though after their breakup he'd written to her saying he loved her more than ever. A week later he married a twenty-five-year-old student at Berkeley named Alice Campbell. None of his friends even knew who she was. After Ricketts died, Alice learned that he'd never finalized his divorce from Anna years before. A man named George Robinson, who'd become a close friend of Ricketts after the war, later estimated that Ricketts had slept with "about half" of the women on the Monterey Peninsula. He didn't think that was an exaggeration.

Steinbeck got to know Robinson, and they enjoyed remembering Ricketts over drinks at the Eleventh Street cottage. One time, Steinbeck shocked Robinson by saying he thought Ricketts had died at the right time. Ricketts, he said, hated things that were past their prime and would never have wanted to become an old man. Steinbeck said the thing in life Ricketts feared most was the inevitable waning of his unbridled libido.

Back in New York after ten days in Monterey, Steinbeck wrote a bitter, fatalistic letter to Toby Street, who was tidying up Ricketts's estate. He told Street that he had recently loaned Ricketts a thousand dollars, and he needed it back to pay his income taxes. Steinbeck insisted that, contrary to what everyone believed, he didn't have any money and had to go into debt every year at tax time. Like so many who feel the cold shadow of their own death pass over them when someone close has died, Steinbeck was in a morbid frame of mind. And he hinted at some unspecified trouble on the horizon. He was starting in on a long book and his life was a mess. Plus, he was sure there wasn't much of it left. He said he didn't think he was a real writer yet, and that if that was ever going to happen it had better be now.

Two days later, he wrote to Ritchie and Tal Lovejoy in an even more somber mood. He urged them not to torment themselves over what had happened. It was possible to imagine almost anything. Reality was at best provisional. What if, Steinbeck wondered, they were all just fleeting products of Ricketts's imagination and would now cease to exist at all? Would they fly apart and be scattered across all eternity? The one thing he knew was that nothing about him was the same as it had been when Ricketts was alive. "The rock has dropped in the water," he said, "and the rings are going out and God knows where they will go or for how long or what patterns they will change obliquely."

A few days later, Steinbeck put aside his book and went to Mexico for a couple of weeks to begin research for the film script on Emiliano Zapata. He figured it would take him until Christmas to finish it. The movie, *Viva Zapata!*, which came out in 1952, reunited Steinbeck with Darryl Zanuck at 20th Century Fox and was directed by Elia Kazan. Almost comically, it starred Marlon Brando sporting a black mustache, slathered in brown makeup, and speaking in an accent that came and went. Steinbeck admitted to Bo Beskow that he needed the diversion. The implication was that he wasn't ready to work on the Salinas book so close to Ricketts's death. But he also mentioned that Gwyn was taking the boys to visit her mother in California for two months.

In July, Steinbeck was back down in Mexico working on Zapata. He went on a three-day drinking binge that ended in what he called, without elaboration, a collapse. Nothing like it had ever happened to him and he wished it to never happen again. He laid off booze and resumed taking Dexedrine. He hoped to hear from Gwyn. When he didn't, he assumed she'd decided they were done. He felt lonely and thought idly that he'd always wished Gwyn loved Mexico the way he did. "I wish she loved anything," he said. "Maybe she does and I don't know about it."

Back in New York, Steinbeck was uncertain as to where things stood with Gwyn. At some point she'd had an affair with their neighbor, Nat Benchley, and Steinbeck knew about it. But now he didn't think she was seeing anyone else, and he wasn't either, which only made it harder to fathom what had gone wrong between them. Gwyn's later accounts of how their marriage failed—bitter and unreliable like so much of what she pretended to remember—failed to mention Steinbeck's true feelings for her, though she could not have been unaware of them. In his journal he wrote that he was still in love with Gwyn despite her betrayals and the deepening chill between them. "If she would only let me help her—I would," he said. "I love her and always will no matter what happens."

It was hellish. Steinbeck told himself he was a "sucker" for hanging on. He was concerned about the boys. Maybe they'd be happier if he and Gwyn parted. One evening in August, they went out for dinner and then went dancing. It was nice. As they swayed to the music, Gwyn looked up at him and said she wanted a divorce. By the end of the month, they'd signed a separation agreement that Steinbeck said gave Gwyn everything, including the boys. She planned to go to Reno for the formal divorce. Steinbeck thought he'd probably move back to California. New York had never felt like home. He talked to Toby Street about the two of them getting up to Fallen Leaf Lodge at Lake Tahoe. They never went, but it was comforting to think about.

Steinbeck said he was finished with marriage. It didn't agree with him. He liked women, but they caused him misery when they became wives. Thinking about how Gwyn had been mad at him for so long, it occurred to him that Carol was always mad at him, too, which he figured was more than coincidental. He seemed to have trouble remembering how long he and Gwyn had been married. Was it four years or five? Or was it one good year followed by four bad ones? But he was feeling okay, all things considered. After trying to hold his marriage together, it was a relief when the strain was lifted and there was nothing to hang on to anymore.

The feeling didn't last. Steinbeck moved to Pacific Grove that fall, back into the little house on Eleventh Street. The place was empty, a string of non-rent-paying tenants having made off with the furniture—as well as the dishes, pots, pans, and flatware. Steinbeck bought a bed and set up a card table to work on. He said he could get whatever else he needed at Woolworth's. He dug in the garden and painted the house inside and out. Pascal Covici told Steinbeck that he envied his retreat into physical labor—but also warned him that he was in a more fragile state than he realized and could count on "waves of loneliness and depression." The main thing, Covici said, was to finish the movie script and get on with the Salinas book. Steinbeck, alone in his barren cottage, sat by the fire as the fog rolled in and the tolling of the bell buoy and the barking of sea lions sounded in the distance. He'd come home, but home was not what it had been. He admitted to moments of panic, but at least it was peaceful. It was hard to believe that two decades had gone by since he and Carol had landed there, young and penniless and in love, with a whole world to conquer.

Steinbeck had tried to add a provision to the divorce decree requiring Gwyn to lead a "chaste" life thereafter—a preposterous demand she rejected, telling him it was an insult. When the divorce was finalized in October, Steinbeck read about it in the Reno papers—which also brought news about what Gwyn had been up to while she was there. According to the report, Gwyn had stayed at the Silver Saddle Dude Ranch and had become involved with a twenty-eight-year-old man named Leonard Wolff, whose father was a Denver stockbroker. One night they went out gambling and Wolff lost $86,000 at blackjack. Wolff took Gwyn back to her room. He was later found dead in his car in the desert, a bullet through the head and a pistol still in his hand. Gwyn, who'd been the last person to see him alive, was summoned to an inquest. Steinbeck, who believed Gwyn had gone to Reno to spare the boys publicity, was shocked by the mess in which their life together had come to a close. He hoped she'd get out of there fast. "I'm sick to my stomach about this."

Steinbeck continued working on Zapata in Pacific Grove and down in Mexico. It was a struggle—the first time in his life that writing seemed close to impossible. In November a woman named Mildred Lyman, who worked at McIntosh & Otis, stopped in to see Steinbeck in Pacific Grove and found him in bad shape. She said he seemed unbalanced and fretful that he couldn't work. He would soon return to Mexico, she said, and if the script didn't go well, it was hard to say what might happen next. Steinbeck needed discipline—something he had never before been short of—but as the days slipped by when he accomplished nothing this had become a self-reinforcing pattern. Not being able to write was depressing, and being depressed made him unable to write. Lyman suspected the Mexican trip was more about a woman he was seeing there than about working. In general, Lyman said, Steinbeck was living a chaotic, disorganized, and utterly unproductive life. He slept and ate at odd hours, and exhibited what Lyman said was a troubling attitude about women, without specifying what it was. Steinbeck bought Thanksgiving presents for the boys, an odd occasion for it. He wondered, bizarrely, if he should suggest that Thom start taking Dexedrine with his milk to see if it made him "more confident." Late at night he sat up writing letter after letter, as the damp Pacific air curled around the little house.

Steinbeck boasted to Bo Beskow that since his split from Gwyn he'd slept with fifty women. This was a result of his not sleeping with Gwyn at the end, leaving him with pent-up desires that were hard to satisfy. He said the sex was wonderful, but that he could not bear to spend the night in bed with a woman after they'd made love, because when he stayed his skin crawled and he had bad dreams. And yet not every shred of normalcy was gone: He said he had to somehow get to work because he owed $30,000 in taxes and didn't have it.

Just before Thanksgiving, Steinbeck was informed that he'd been elected to the American Academy of Arts and Letters. He wrote back thanking them—saying it was an honor and a unique experience for him. He said he'd been "blackballed from everything from the Boy Scouts to the United States Army." He told friends privately that he wasn't much impressed by joining the Academy. It seemed, he said, like a premature embalming job.

Christmas came and Steinbeck seemed to feel better—as if some sort of dam were bursting inside him. In another week the worst year of his life would be over. He'd be glad to see it gone. It was a quiet time. He talked with Carol on the phone and they had a pleasant conversation. The cottage was nice. Steinbeck wished, though, that he'd hung onto the Soto Adobe on Pierce Street. It would have cost a fortune to make it livable, but it would have been a joy to do some of the work himself. "What a shame I sold it," he said.

By the spring of 1949 Steinbeck was beginning to work again. He told Pat Covici that he couldn't explain it. He also wrote to Gwyn to let her know he wanted the boys with him for two months that summer. He hoped to make them do a little growing up, he said. He was going to listen to them and take them seriously. He planned to make them help out around the house and in the yard, but he was also going to let them wander and do as they would. These manly goals may have struck his friends as unrealistic. Thom would turn five in August, and John IV was not quite three.

Steinbeck spent some time in Los Angeles before the boys came out. He had an affair with Paulette Goddard—who'd separated from Burgess Meredith—that made the gossip columns. So did a report about his guests up in Pacific Grove over Memorial Day weekend. Steinbeck was friends with the actress Ann Sothern, and he'd invited her up for a visit. Sothern arrived with a friend named Elaine Scott. Scott was the daughter of a Texas oil man. She'd worked in the theater in New York, as a casting director and a stage manager, before moving to Los Angeles. She was thirty-five, trim, pretty, and had a lively wit. Elegant and stylish, Scott was also—according to people who would know—eager and energetic in bed. Steinbeck fell for her right off. Technically, she was still married to the actor Zachary Scott, whom she'd met at the University of Texas. They had an adolescent daughter named Waverly, but their marriage was strained. Within a week Steinbeck wrote Elaine a funny letter that—like their relationship—started with a bang. He told her he was a cowboy from Arizona and he hoped she would visit him and contemplate his vast land holdings dotted with purple sage. He thought they could indulge in just enough sin to make it fun.

Elaine was not ready for her husband and daughter to know about Steinbeck, so for a while he wrote to her in care of Max Wagner.

Toward the end of June he told Elaine that he'd bought a small, two-room trailer and parked it across the street from the Eleventh Street house for the boys to live in that summer. He said it looked like a house, not a trailer, and was nicely furnished. As a bonus, he said, they could put it to alternative uses when the boys were not around.

Steinbeck flooded Elaine with letters, and they saw each other when they could. By November Elaine had told Zachary Scott she was leaving him. Steinbeck was elated. He told her he adored her and was glad he could say that at last without feeling guilty about it. He said he'd wanted her from the start, but that she had to come to him on her own terms. He sent Elaine his mother's engagement ring. He wanted Thom to have it someday, but for now it was hers. Having at different times sworn off novels and wives, Steinbeck again committed himself to both.

Steinbeck and Elaine had agreed to move to New York—close to the theater for Elaine and handy to the boys for Steinbeck. Steinbeck started out at the Plaza Hotel, but they soon found a pair of apartments on East Fifty-Second Street—one for Elaine and Waverly, the other one directly above it for Steinbeck. Cold weather arrived just before Christmas, a string of the kind of clear, bracing days that Steinbeck loved best in the city. He walked everywhere, taking in the holiday sights and looking forward to having the boys with him on Christmas Eve. He told Bo Beskow that his life had turned another corner. He had the right partner now, and was working well again, feeling that he'd managed to heal the wounds that had nearly broken him.

Elaine made Steinbeck happy in an important way that neither Carol nor Gwyn had done—as he put it, by not being in competition with him. Steinbeck, conveniently forgetting Carol's vital contribution to *The Grapes of Wrath*, said it was nice that he could work in the same room with Elaine and not worry that she would bother him. It helped, too, that when he read her a passage from something he was working on he didn't have to listen to a critique.

Elaine did not go back to work—Steinbeck asked her not to—but she introduced him to theater people she knew, including Richard

Rodgers and Oscar Hammerstein, who would end up producing a play that Steinbeck suddenly decided to write that winter. It's easy to imagine that Steinbeck was stimulated by being around show people—but it's even easier to think it was a convenient way of putting off work on the big book about the Salinas Valley. Steinbeck's explanation was that he did it for the money, which he needed desperately to pay Gwyn's alimony and child support, not to mention financing the two households he was running with Elaine. However it got started, he wrote it in twenty-two days that January. The working title, *In the Forests of the Night*, was from William Blake's poem "The Tyger." Later it became *Burning Bright*, from an adjacent line in the same poem.

Burning Bright adhered to a format that Steinbeck had invented: the play-novella. It appeared as both a book and on Broadway in October of 1950. But it fell far short of what he had accomplished in *Of Mice and Men* and *The Moon Is Down*. It's the story of a man haunted by his inability to have a child, and what happens when his attractive young wife decides to give him one by sleeping with another man. This three-way drama is observed by a fourth character—inspired again by Ed Ricketts—and the small cast appears in three acts, each of which shifts to a new setting. Placing the same characters in different contexts—at the circus, on a farm, aboard a ship—was clever, and, as Steinbeck learned to his dismay, hard to pull off. He was enthusiastic about trial runs of the play in New Haven and then Boston. Steinbeck thought the cast—which included Howard Da Silva and Barbara Bel Geddes—was fine, but that the play's fate would be impossible to predict until it got to New York.

When it did, both the book and the play failed. Steinbeck told Toby Street that no magazine would take the novella and that the Book-of-the-Month Club didn't want it either. He thought audiences liked the play—but the critics had other ideas, and it closed after thirteen performances.

Steinbeck and Elaine had spent the previous summer in the country, in a house they rented in Rockland County not far from Burgess Meredith's. The boys came out, and Steinbeck set them loose exploring and being gnawed at by mosquitoes. He told Gwyn they were great company and, thanks to constant exercise, had gotten "hard as nails." Steinbeck worked on a profile of Ed Ricketts—making it clear that Ricketts had been the model for Doc in *Cannery Row*. It was for a new edition of *Sea of Cortez* that dispensed with the phyletic catalogue, keeping only the narrative of the trip. Viking published it the following year as *The Log from the Sea of Cortez*.

On December 28, 1950, Steinbeck and Elaine were married at the home of Harold Guinzburg, the president of Viking Press. Steinbeck said everyone cried. The boys loved Elaine's daughter, Waverly, and wanted her to come live with them. Steinbeck and Elaine spent their wedding night at the St. Regis Hotel, leaving a trail of rice everywhere when they arrived. They honeymooned at the Cambridge Beaches Resort in Bermuda, in a cottage only steps from the water. It was beautiful—warm but not too hot, and only three and a half hours by air from New York. He told Pat Covici they moved lazily from bed to the dining room to the beach every day, and that in the nights he had unusual dreams that were like a newsreel of his life running in reverse. One day the wind came up and they built a fire against the chill as the waves rode onto the beach. All of it, the snug cottage, the gray ocean, the tattered clouds, felt wonderful and familiar at the same time.

— 15 —

EACH BOOK DIES
A REAL DEATH

THE DATE WAS January 29, 1951:

"Dear Pat: How did the time pass and how did it grow so late? Have we learned anything from the passage of time? Are we more mature, wiser, more perceptive, kinder? We have known each other now for centuries and still I remember the first time and the last time.

"We come now to the book. It has been planned a long time."

With these words to his editor, Pat Covici, Steinbeck promised that he had come unstuck. The book he still called *Salinas Valley* was about to get underway. He and Elaine were moving into their new house on East Seventy-Second Street, and two more weeks would pass before he tried to begin writing. He didn't know for sure what he had left, but he said he was eager to find out. The past few years had cost him dearly—he said he would have had to have been made of stone to come through them unscathed. For the longest time he had thought this book would be another experiment with a new form and a new vocabulary. Now, he said, he knew that was all wrong. This book would be straight and lean, and at its center would be a philosophy that was both "old and yet new born." It was going to be about the place he was from and it was going to be about him—the book, as he had said before and would say again in the days to come, that he was meant to write.

Steinbeck decided to start each working day with a letter to Covici

on the left-hand pages of the journal before moving to the manuscript, which he wrote on the right-hand pages. He called this a
"double entry" approach, as if he were keeping a balance sheet. He
wrote in pencil, his miniature handwriting moving across the page
in jagged waves. The letters were not actual correspondence in the
sense of being put in the mail—Covici later had them typed up—but
were instead a working journal like the one he'd kept for *The Grapes
of Wrath*. Talking to Covici at the beginning of a session about the
passage he was working on, and about everyday matters, got him
warmed up and supplied a momentum that made it easier to tackle
the book. He felt ready for the rigors of a big novel, but humble given
the scale of what he hoped to accomplish. The time had come at last
to see if years of practice had gotten him ready to write the book he
felt destined to write.

After getting settled in the new house, he spent a week staring at
the blank pages before it began to come. He seemed reluctant to start,
spending Valentine's Day visiting the boys at the house he had shared
with Gwyn. They were uncomfortable with him—Thom especially,
who had become reluctant to go to school and who looked sullen. His
unease troubled Steinbeck. But then, a couple of days later, Steinbeck
actually started writing. It came without warning—as it always did,
he said. Only this time he felt less urgency than before. With other
books he'd been "frantic" to proceed once he began. But not now. He
said he was happier than he had ever been. Steinbeck had been smoking pipes lately, and he said he wanted to get a small Meerschaum. If
he smoked it every day, it would be perfectly broken in just about the
time he finished the book. Pipe smoking while he worked also helped
him cut back on his longtime cigarette addiction. He still had a constant cough, but it was better. Steinbeck thought he owed his sunny
frame of mind to Elaine. Everything seemed to please him. The new
house, even with the distraction of carpenters still working in it, was
wonderful. His sex life was robust. He lost weight. Nothing bothered
him anymore, he claimed. He admitted that he was worried about
Thom and John IV—a real concern, of course—but that was all. Not
even the war in Korea seemed to matter.

But of course it did matter. At the end of World War II, the United States and the Soviet Union had taken control of the Korean peninsula, which had been in Japanese hands. They partitioned it into North and South along the 38th parallel. Over the next few years, as they relegated greater autonomy to dictators on both sides of the line, American officials prepared for an invasion from the North, which was more heavily armed. But they relied on military advisers in the South as a deterrence against aggression from the North. What both sides understood was that Korea could become a proxy fight over competing visions of the postwar world. Since a move by the North would have to be sanctioned by the Soviets—and could also involve China—any conflict on the peninsula would inevitably test the whole concept of American opposition to Communist expansionism.

And in June of 1950, that's what happened. Kim Il Sung, the ruler of North Korea, invaded South Korea. The larger, better-equipped, and more disciplined army of the North marched steadily southward until, on June 27, President Truman promised to intervene. This abrupt decision surprised both Moscow and Peking, where the Soviets and the Chinese realized they had underestimated American resolve. Truman hadn't bothered to ask Congress for a declaration of war, but Americans didn't seem to mind. Eager to confront Communism, Congress gave the president what he wanted, extending the draft and authorizing military "assistance" to South Korea. The first hot flame of the Cold War had been lit. When the undeclared Korean War ended in stalemate three years later, more than 36,000 American soldiers had been killed, and North and South Korea were back where they had begun, staring at each other across the 38th parallel.

Steinbeck cut down on his drinking and started writing earlier in the mornings. Within a week he was averaging about 1,500 words a day, a pace he would mostly maintain to the end. Sometimes he held it to 1,000 words for a few days, worried about his tendency to rush once he got going. He admitted that he felt silly spending part of each morning writing letters that Covici would not see for months. But

Covici would find it interesting to read them later on. Steinbeck had begun to think of the book and the time he spent working on it as the "inside." Everything else belonged to the "outside." When everyday matters got in the way of his work, he felt the outside pushing in on him and couldn't wait to get back inside the confines of the world he was making. These slumps were unavoidable but rare. At some point that spring, Covici began stopping over to pick up the manuscript as Steinbeck's work progressed.

As May came into view, Steinbeck had finished nearly 100 hand-written pages—about a quarter of the book. At that rate he said he might finish by November. It was the old calculus: days ahead, days lost—the steady accretion of words and pages. Steinbeck was still putting the final touches on the Zapata screenplay, too, and some-times Elia Kazan—"Gadge," as he was called by his friends—showed up to work with him on it. There wasn't anything to be done about this except to try to push ahead on both projects.

In May, one of Elaine's distant relatives—a Texas oil man—stopped by for dinner and talked with Steinbeck about the book. The man didn't know anything about literature, but he told Steinbeck he didn't like the title. Who would care about the Salinas Valley? The book should be called something more universal. Steinbeck—always on the lookout for a better title than the one he started with—thought the man had a point. Maybe, he said, it should be called *My Valley*. When Covici said he didn't like it, Steinbeck sulked. He said he'd "never been a title man" and didn't give a damn what it was called.

In truth, the book was stirring deep and sometimes anguished thoughts in Steinbeck. He believed that empathy—his feeling that the whole range of human thought and emotion was familiar to him—was his great strength as a writer. At least he hoped this was true, because he would be a "better writer for it" if it was. But at the same time, he knew he was capable of feelings that no one else could understand, as if his intimate connection to the rest of humanity were a one-way street. He told Covici that while he did not have a death wish, he was ambivalent about *being* alive. For as long as he could remember—going back to his childhood, Steinbeck said—he would have "preferred to have never existed." He wasn't like other writers, striving for success and immortality—writers who looked at their books lined up on a shelf and felt pride. He didn't care if his words outlived him. His books became meaningless to him the moment they were done. "The book dies a real death for me when I write the last word," he said. "I have a little sorrow and then go on to a new book which is alive."

Despite his claim that he didn't care what the book was called, Steinbeck searched for a title. He told Covici he needed one that would explain what the book was about, which he said was the "oldest story in the world," a story that illuminated all human desires and failings. After a long day of work in early June, Steinbeck went back to what he considered the original source of that ancient story, writing out by hand the sixteen verses from Chapter 4 of Genesis that tell of Cain and Abel. Steinbeck said the story changed and blared with "flashing lights" when he wrote it down—and that when he'd come to the end, he had his title:

And Cain went out from the presence of the Lord, and dwelt in the land of Nod, on the east of Eden.

Eager to have more time with his sons—and convinced that nothing could derail the book—Steinbeck decided he and Elaine would spend the summer with the boys in Siasconset, on Nantucket. They arrived in mid-June. Steinbeck had briefly entertained the idea that this was some kind of research trip, during which he'd study the history and culture of the island and then write a series of articles about it. He'd even asked Elizabeth Otis what she thought of the idea. But this plan evaporated when they got there. He told Otis the island was beautiful and that the boys loved it. He did, too, or would once he got back to work on the book. It was hard to be happy when he wasn't working.

To Steinbeck's surprise, he was able to write despite the warm temptations of the sand and sea. On a day they could repeat at will, Elaine would take the boys to the beach and have a picnic lunch. With luck he'd be done working when they came back in the afternoon. The book's title, *East of Eden*, now seemed set. Steinbeck said he could tell when the day was going to be good for working, as he could feel a tingle in his stomach and an itch to get at it. The book, he told Covici, "does go on and on." He wanted Covici to let him know if the story was holding up; it was hard for him to tell. He thought it was good, but he was so deeply immersed in it that he couldn't be sure. As June came to an end he felt the manuscript was nearly half done.

Covici, ever the cheerleader, wrote often to assure Steinbeck he was doing something wonderful. He described one chapter as "a whole orchestra with every instrument playing its part." He told Steinbeck to stop worrying about how long the book would be. He claimed the book held his attention "like a vise." At the end of July, Covici and his wife visited the island. Steinbeck's nerves, frayed by work, got the better of him and he was boorish at a dinner just before they departed. He wrote them immediately to apologize, talking about what had happened as if he and the book were a single entity that had briefly spun out of control. Chagrined, he said he couldn't explain it. By the end of August, Covici had a typescript in hand that ran to more than 170,000 words. And it was far from finished.

When they got home in mid-September, Steinbeck forced himself to take a week off. He was exhausted, but the downtime was restorative. Not that it would be easy to get started again—that part was always hard. But he looked forward to regaining his rhythm. "I can't work all the time," he realized, "but I should." He got started unusually early on October 4 so that he could go to the opening game of the World Series between the New York Yankees and the New York Giants. The day before, the Giants had won their three-game National League playoff series against the Dodgers on Bobby Thomson's electrifying ninth-inning home run. Steinbeck called it probably the best baseball game ever played. This World Series was to be the last one for the Yankees' Joe DiMaggio—and the first for their phenomenal young outfielder, Mickey Mantle. Mantle wrecked his knee in Game 2, but the Yankees beat the Giants in six games.

Steinbeck was counting down the days now. On October 10, he

told Covici he might spend the day just thinking, as he was "a day ahead." He thought he'd be done soon. A week later he wrote 3,000 words in one sitting. But the book stretched on. And then, in the first week of November, it was done. He told his sister Mary that he'd worked on it almost every day since February, and that it was the "longest, hardest and most complex piece of work that I have ever taken on." He said he hoped it was his best.

Steinbeck and Elaine took a car trip through New England to unwind. It snowed the whole time.

By the following spring, Pascal Covici was sure. *East of Eden*, set for publication in September, was going to be Viking's biggest book since *The Grapes of Wrath*. Steinbeck, who was on a six-month tour of Europe and North Africa, got regular updates—in Paris, Casablanca, Madrid, and Seville, where they'd gone to see the bullfights. In Rome, it was too hot and they escaped to the Amalfi coast below Naples. They also stopped off in Algiers, which Steinbeck described as "clean and beautiful" compared to the way it had been when he'd been there during the war. A local French official had invited them to an all-night party, where "oceans of Champagne" were served. He said the trip was the longest time he could remember when he hadn't written anything. In what sounded like a minor aside that was actually a preview of their life ahead, he held that "Elaine loves this life." In August they finished up their travels in Ireland, where Steinbeck went in search of the Hamilton family's ancestral home.

According to Covici, booksellers were apparently thrilled that there would be no book-club edition or magazine serialization of *East of Eden*, as this meant more revenue for them. Covici tried to reassure Steinbeck that the Book-of-the-Month Club's decision against taking the book was of little importance, though he had heard only "vague rumors" about what had happened. He said the problem seemed to be that a couple of the club's judges felt parts of the novel set in a whorehouse bordered on the obscene—or were at least likely to offend their subscribers. Otherwise, Covici went on, the advance word was good, though there were hints that the reviews were likely to be mixed. Covici tactfully pointed out that this was nothing new for Steinbeck. And it didn't dim Viking's enthusiasm. In spring, Covici had told Steinbeck to expect a first printing of 50,000 copies and an even bigger second printing. Covici predicted sales would top 100,000 copies. Shortly after Steinbeck and Elaine got home that month, Pat Covici's wife, Dorothy, gave birth to a son. They named him John.

East of Eden, the book John Steinbeck was meant to write, was published on September 19, 1952. The critical reception ranged from reverence to ambivalence to unvarnished hostility. People loved it or despised it—or both—though almost everyone agreed that it was riveting. One of the more memorable reviews—it captured almost perfectly the split opinion on the book—came from Orville Prescott, writing in the *New York Times*. Prescott started by calling the book Steinbeck's best since *The Grapes of Wrath*. But, he said, at a quarter of a million words long, it was "clumsy in structure and defaced by excessive melodramatics and much cheap sensationalism." One thing Prescott appreciated was that Steinbeck had moved away from the "weak and contemptible animals" that passed for human beings in his lesser recent works such as *Cannery Row* and *The Wayward Bus*, apparently unable to imagine that Steinbeck regarded them as neither weak nor contemptible. But Prescott didn't think Steinbeck had learned anything in the thirteen years since *The Grapes of Wrath*, pursuing one dead end after another, using his enormous gift to no purpose. He seemed to be mixed up about what he believed about the human condition.

Whether they liked his books or not, critics admired Steinbeck's ability to live inside other cultures, other races. He brought people to life who were otherwise invisible and voiceless—because he could, and because he liked them better than the characters who lived in other writers' work.

Like most other reviewers, Prescott was struck by *East of Eden*'s complex construction, which wove together the long progress of two Salinas Valley families in the early decades of the twentieth century. The Hamiltons, based on Steinbeck's own family on his mother's side, are sober, honest, and intelligent. The patriarch, Samuel, has little to show for a life of labor on his parched farm, but he is rich with understanding and sparkling with worldly knowledge and possessed of a rare nobility that impresses itself on everyone with whom he comes into contact. Then there are the Trasks, a fictional family that has come to the valley more recently, and in whom good and evil grapple for supremacy. Adam, the father, is a dour easterner who brings with him a pretty but damaged and dangerous wife, Cathy—perhaps the most memorably nasty and treacherous character in all of American literature. Cathy is a murderer, a prostitute, and eventually, after she abandons and nearly kills Adam, the owner of a brothel. What happens there stays there, but Cathy's patrons are mindful that she knows things about all the supposedly proper men in town that could ruin them. In what is as close as the book comes to a central plot, Adam and Cathy's two sons—Cal and Aron—play out their symbolic roles as a modern Cain and Abel. Aron, the favored son, can seemingly do no wrong. Cal, the misfit, can't understand what's wrong with him. And for the longest time, neither of them knows a thing about Mom.

Orville Prescott found Cathy unbelievable and repellent. Her presence, he said, was ruinous to the book. But not fatally, Prescott said, as the plain fact was that he liked *East of Eden* despite its flaws. It was a good read, full of life and well-told by a master storyteller.

The many people who think they know this book because they've seen the film version—remarkable for James Dean's taut performance as the mopey Cal Trask and for its nimble direction by Steinbeck's friend Elia Kazan—would be surprised to learn how little of the novel is in the movie. Nor does Steinbeck himself turn up in the film, as he does in the book. Steinbeck surely knew that inserting himself into the narrative would cause trouble—just as he had known readers would stumble over the interstitial chapters in *The Grapes of Wrath*. But this was the book he was meant to write, and so it was impossible for him not to have a say in it.

Steinbeck's thinking about the phalanx, the power of humans in groups, had evolved. He believed now that humanity faced a crisis that had arisen because of "collective" behavior, whether it occurred on the mass production line or within the apparatus of a totalitarian government. He thought the world had become an "unhappy and confused" place because people were relinquishing everything— economics, politics, thought, even religion and the concept of God— to a soulless and unforgiving collectivism. This, he was convinced, was a suicidal course—one he paused to examine in his own voice in *East of Eden,* heedless that it sounded like he was talking about the Cold War in the middle of a story set decades before it began:

"And I believe this: that the free, exploring mind of the individual human is the most valuable thing in the world. And this I would fight for: the freedom of the mind to take any direction it wishes, undirected. And this I must fight against: any idea, religion, or government which limits or destroys the individual. This is what I am and what I am about. I can understand why a system built on a pattern must try to destroy the free mind, for that is one thing which can by inspection destroy such a system. Surely I can understand this, and I hate it and I will fight against it to preserve the one thing that separates us from the uncreative beasts. If the glory can be killed, we are lost."

Steinbeck's intermittent presence as the book's narrator made little impression on the reviewers. Most ignored it, or dismissed it as superfluous. An exception was the acid-penned critic for *The New Yorker,* Anthony West—who called Steinbeck's voice in his own book "unfortunate." West, an accomplished novelist and essayist with a literary pedigree—his parents were H. G. Wells and Rebecca West— found Steinbeck's writing dripping with "verbal syrup." In a well-honed takedown, West argued that Steinbeck had gone so far over the top, particularly in making Cathy's depravity the epitome of evil, that he was blind to evil in its more sinister and familiar guises—the evil that "sits smiling in the family group or mingles with the guests at a wedding in a neat suit." The overall effect, West said, was that the book was a contest between blandness and melodrama that looked like a draw. The only thing missing, he thought, were black-hatted villains twirling their mustaches. When Steinbeck saw West's review, it intrigued him. Where could such poisonous outrage have come from? Steinbeck said he'd like to meet West sometime and ask him.

While waiting for the book to be published, Steinbeck had been in a contemplative mood. He hadn't heard from Dook Sheffield in years. But a postcard from Sheffield the winter before had caught up with him in Europe, and now he replied at length. He was mildly surprised to be fifty years old. He said his hair was receding and he could no longer lose the slight paunch around his middle. But the diminishments of age were gradual, and he let himself ignore them. Now that he could afford good liquor, his hangovers weren't so bad. Their European tour had been fine, but it was good to be home in their comfortable house. He looked forward to the coming winter— his favorite time in New York—when he could light the coal in the small fireplace in their library and read while the icy blast buffeted the windows. He and Elaine led a quiet life, going out now and then to dinner or the theater and occasionally having people over. It was counterintuitive, but life in Manhattan seemed to move more slowly than life in a small town.

Steinbeck admitted he had enjoyed and admired Hemingway's new book, *The Old Man and the Sea*. He thought the widespread praise was deserved, especially in light of how Hemingway's last book, *Across the River and Into the Trees*, had been savaged. Steinbeck said he was probably going to get his share of criticism for *East of Eden*, even though he was sure it was the best thing he'd done.

Steinbeck puzzled over the divergence in their lives. They had once been so alike. He had long thought that the cause of the break between him and Sheffield had been his offer to finance Dook's studies for a doctorate, which Steinbeck had failed to see was hurtful and insulting. Steinbeck was convinced that Sheffield could have been a great scholar, and couldn't comprehend why he seemed without ambition. It was if their roles had gotten reversed. Dook should have been the successful one. But now, divorced and alone, Dook lived quietly in an old barn in an orchard near Stanford. It had taken years for Steinbeck to see that Sheffield had a different idea about contentment, that he didn't measure himself the way Steinbeck did. Sheffield had lived a modest life that made him happy—something that Steinbeck respected and wished he could emulate. Steinbeck's own life was confusing and illusory. He was never entirely convinced that it had happened to him the way it had. Maybe it was all a dream. It often seemed so to him.

When Sheffield wrote back about *East of Eden*, he told Steinbeck he liked the book. Steinbeck was gratified, though speaking of it was like remembering the dead. Making the final revisions had been like putting a corpse into a nice suit for his burial. Thinking about the book now was like thinking about Ed Ricketts. What was the point?

The years began to fly away. Steinbeck and Elaine traveled often and far, vacationing on St. John and touring Europe. Paris and London and the annual *fiesta* in Seville became familiar haunts. Steinbeck felt a special affinity for Spain—especially measured against Mexico, its dull offspring. He enjoyed looking at the paintings at the Prado in Madrid, and was particularly fond of a small El Greco portrait of St. Paul holding a book. And he loved the bullring at Seville, where the sand, dredged from the Guadalquivir River, was the color of gold. One time at the *fiesta* he picked up a saying about drinking hard liquor that he never forgot: "The first with water, the second without water, the third like water." It sounded even more perfect in Spanish.

Right after the publication of *East of Eden* Steinbeck got involved in the presidential campaign. At first he favored Eisenhower, but then he switched his allegiance to Adlai Stevenson and ended up writing position papers and speeches for Stevenson's surrogates. He told his sister Esther that Stevenson "seems to be a truly great man and we need one right now." Three days after Eisenhower's landslide victory, Steinbeck wrote a note to Stevenson—whom he had yet to meet—telling him not to give in to despair. He said it had been an honor to work on his behalf. He hoped Stevenson would come by his place for a drink sometime. They could share sad stories about the fates of kings. And he reminded Stevenson that if things went badly, there were always the protections of impeachment. When Stevenson ran again four years later, Steinbeck once more signed on to the campaign. But Stevenson lost a second time.

In early 1953, Steinbeck worked on a musical adaptation of *Cannery Row* called *Bear Flag*. Frank Loesser signed on as the composer and lyricist, and later, after Loesser bowed out, Oscar Hammerstein and Richard Rodgers took over. Eventually, Steinbeck's project morphed into a forgettable sequel to *Cannery Row* called *Sweet Thursday*, which was published in 1954. The Rodgers and Hammerstein musical, *Pipe Dream*, based loosely on *Sweet Thursday*, opened on Broadway in the fall of 1955 to awful reviews and ran for a few months until the advance sales petered out. Steinbeck complained throughout rehearsals that his story about Doc's affair with an ex-hooker had been sanitized beyond recognition. The play was nominated for nine Tony awards, but lost out for best musical to *Damn Yankees*.

Sweet Thursday had been a wan attempt to reanimate Doc and his friends, and its contribution to Steinbeck's literary legacy was negligible—perhaps because it signaled a lack of interest in what was happening in the world. The book was published only a couple of months after the United States tested the first hydrogen bomb at Bikini Atoll in the Marshall Islands. The unexpectedly powerful explosion—there had been a miscalculation in how the fuels would interact—was the equivalent of one thousand "Little Boy"s, the bomb that had leveled Hiroshima. Five more tests were conducted that spring, until Japan pleaded with the United States for a halt when tuna in the Pacific Ocean were found to be radioactive. People began adjusting to a new reality, in which the threat to humanity from nuclear war was less about being blown to bits and more about the prospect of the entire planet being fatally contaminated with radioactive fallout from a fearsome new weapon.

The country was being transformed in other ways. Even before the end of World War II, the government had anticipated the coming problem of reintegrating some 16 million veterans when they came home. Everyone still remembered the Bonus Army's protest in Washington in 1932 and wanted to avoid a replay of it. In June of 1944, Congress passed the Servicemen's Readjustment Act—the G.I. Bill—and President Roosevelt signed it into law. The law provided tuition and living expenses for veterans attending college, and also backed home mortgages. Eventually, nearly 8 million veterans went to college on the G.I. Bill. A soaring middle class of newly minted professionals flooded the suburbs, millions of them with government-insured home loans. America was in a good mood again, the prospect of nuclear catastrophe notwithstanding. Late on the night of Monday, July 5, 1954, a nervous young truck driver recorded a song called "That's All Right (Mama)" at the Sun Records studio in Memphis. Three days later the record was playing nonstop on the radio and Elvis Presley made his debut.

The fast-changing times moved away from John Steinbeck, whose grasp of the culture hadn't progressed much since the days before and after the Great War. Toward the end of the year, in an apartment in the North Beach section of San Francisco, a young poet named Allen Ginsberg started work on a long poem that began:

I saw the best minds of my generation destroyed by madness . . .

"Howl" established Ginsberg as one of the defining voices of the so-called Beat Generation—Jack Kerouac's term for a small but potent antiestablishment movement among nonconformist writers that included Ginsberg; William Burroughs, the author of *Naked Lunch*; and, of course, himself, with *On the Road*. Beat writers indulged in explicit, sometimes salacious celebrations of sex and drug use and a generalized distaste for rules and conventions. Kerouac wrote the first draft of *On the Road* in a caffeine- and Benzedrine-fueled blur in 1951, though it took another six years for it to find a publisher. He later drank himself to death at forty-seven. Ginsberg and Burroughs survived court cases charging them with obscenity. Steinbeck liked the Beats, but surely felt a greater kinship with writers who adhered to more conventional themes—like James Jones in the earthy *From Here to Eternity*, and J. D. Salinger, with a string of elegant, urbane, intensely current stories that appeared throughout the decade following his 1951 masterpiece, *The Catcher in the Rye*. It was harder for Steinbeck to relate to sui generis postapocalyptic fiction, such as Ray Bradbury's *Fahrenheit 451* or Nevil Shute's *On the Beach*, sorting through the debris from the collapse of civilization altogether. Steinbeck, still exploring the pastoral frontier of the Salinas Valley or wandering along the byways of Cannery Row, seemed to be from a different age, out of place in the present one.

His boys remained a challenge. He missed them when they were with Gwyn, but grew impatient with their noise and untidiness, especially when he was trying to work. They seemed, as he often told them, completely selfish. And Steinbeck was determined to instruct them, from an early age, that they would make their way through life on their own and that it would not be easy for them. He had rigid ideas about discipline that could erupt into disproportionate anger and even physical abuse. Once, when John IV was around three, he let Steinbeck's poorly trained sheep dog into the apartment. The dog shat on the floor. When Steinbeck discovered the mess, he grabbed the boy and rubbed his face in it. Another "lesson" involved trust— and how it must be earned and never taken for granted. John IV was encouraged to leap from his high chair and land giggling in his father's outstretched arms. Again and again, the ecstatic jump into space and the laughing embrace—until one time Steinbeck pulled back his hands at the last moment and John IV fell to the floor, crumpled and wailing. This was a reminder that Steinbeck delivered many times and in different ways to both of his sons: I will not always be there to help you. John IV would later say that the great epiphany of his childhood was realizing that his father was an asshole.

John IV recalled that his parents often drank too much. Alcohol was a contagion in both households that fueled erratic behavior and made many mornings-after somber. On New Year's Eve of 1951, at the age of five, John IV was either offered champagne or managed to sneak some—he couldn't remember which—and experienced his first blackout, waking up "in a little ring of vomit" the next day. By then he already knew how to count and liked to entertain Steinbeck's friends by reciting the second law of thermodynamics, a trick his father had taught him. "Entropy always increases!" he'd shout in a small voice. He later said it was a fair description of growing up a Steinbeck.

Thinking they'd be better off away from Gwyn, Steinbeck insisted that both boys be sent off to boarding schools in New England—and not the same one. "For reasons that were never made clear, at least not to us, my father felt early on that it would be good if my brother and I were separated," John IV wrote in a memoir years later. Thom went first, starting in 1953 at the Malcolm Gordon School for boys, on the Hudson River near West Point, and later at the Forman School in Connecticut. John IV was eventually sent off to Eaglebrook School in Massachusetts, where one of his classmates was Michael Douglas. Thom hated school and had to be moved to one after another until Steinbeck said he would soon run out of places to which he could be banished. Steinbeck pleaded with him to do better. He told Thom that he had known many men who got through life without an education, doing manual labor. This was an honest but boring and exhausting way to live, and he recommended against it. Steinbeck believed he understood the life of the common man all too well and he didn't want it for his sons.

One advantage of their being away was that Steinbeck communicated with Thom and John IV—he was by now "Catbird"—mostly by letter, always his preferred means. Many of the letters hinted at a much happier relationship between the father and his sons. He wrote often to tell them he was proud of their accomplishments, to say how much he missed them. He always looked forward to their next visit, and never failed to mention how grand one had been when it was over.

But Steinbeck seemed impatient for his sons to grow up. For Thom's twelfth birthday he sent him a Winchester Model 94 .30-30, the rifle John Wayne carried in the movies and that Steinbeck described as "instrumental in settling the West." Steinbeck's father had given him the same gun and he still had it. He did warn Thom that it was a powerful weapon. "It will kill a deer or a bear or a man," though he didn't offer any opinion as to what the boy was supposed to use it for at prep school. In the same letter, Steinbeck scolded Thom for getting fat and told him to lose weight.

In the fall of 1958, as Catbird was about to head back to school, Steinbeck wrote him a letter of encouragement, extolling the virtues of hard work and telling him life was messy and harsh, and that getting by often meant coping with change. These were things he had to know *now*—Steinbeck felt he could not count on having time for this discussion later. "By the nature of things," Steinbeck wrote, "you will live a great part of your life without me. That is not sentimental. It is just a natural law. That is why I want to impress on you how much I love you because that is immortal and I am not."

Steinbeck did not obsess about his mortality, but he could not ignore the small reminders of it that come to everyone eventually. Just before he and Elaine went to Europe in the spring of 1954—they took the boys with them this time—Steinbeck applied for a life insurance policy. But he failed the physical. He didn't know much about the findings, but the exam indicated he had an "abnormally small heart." Steinbeck promised he'd find a doctor in Paris when they got there and get a second opinion. But regardless of anything he learned, he was not going to become "one of those heart cripples who spread their psychopathy around." He said his heart had always been good to him and he wasn't going to insult it now by being careful with it. As for the insurance—well, that would be tough luck for his heirs. He was sorry about it, but thought that the whole concept was like betting against yourself anyway. They'd raised the odds on him, but he didn't plan to change the way he lived.

Steinbeck did see a doctor in Paris and reported that he'd been told his heart was fine for someone his age. Actually, the doctor told him his heart beat too fast. But he'd heard that before and said he planned to forget about it. There was also a suggestion that he quit smoking, or at least cut down. Steinbeck said maybe he would try quitting, to see how hard it was.

A year earlier, in the summer of 1953, Steinbeck and Elaine rented a cottage in Sag Harbor, a former whaling port on Gardiners Bay near the eastern end of Long Island. Steinbeck found the sea air and the steady pulse of the ocean and tides bracing. It was fine to "smell the good wind" again. That was the problem with New York: In the city, you forgot what you longed for. Two years later, Steinbeck bought a small house in Sag Harbor, a place to escape to when the city grew tiresome. It was surrounded by oaks and had a protected frontage on the water. He'd gone from one edge of the continent to the other, putting a familiar ocean behind him and a new one at his doorstep. He'd come home.

Steinbeck ordered a boat, a twenty-foot skiff with a 100-horsepower engine—suitable for almost anything he wanted to do and steady in even a heavy sea. Steinbeck told Toby Street he could cross the Atlantic in it if he could carry enough gasoline, but that it had a shallow draft and could navigate close to shore, too. There was fine fishing for bluefish off Montauk that summer. Blues were delicious, when brought back alive and cooked at once. He said being close to the ocean eased his concerns about ever starving. The seafood on the East Coast was amazing—lobster, crabs, oysters, an endless variety of fish. He told Street he was going to winterize the house so they could visit in the cold months and fish through the ice when the cove froze over.

There was a blizzard on Long Island in March of 1956. Eighteen inches of snow piled up around the house at Sag Harbor. Steinbeck was thinking about politics, as he'd signed on with a dozen newspapers to cover the upcoming presidential nominating conventions. Whether this was the cause or merely a coincidence, Steinbeck found himself suddenly writing a political satire that became a slim novel called *The Short Reign of Pippin IV*, a fantasy in which the monarchy is restored in postwar France. When he finished it in November, he told Elizabeth Otis that nobody at Viking seemed to like it. He confessed to Pat Covici that he'd written it strictly for fun. He was shocked when the Book-of-the-Month Club made it a selection the following spring. For some time, Steinbeck had been worried about keeping up with the high cost of being John Steinbeck. Two houses. Alimony. Taxes. Child support. Private-school tuition. And near-constant travel, usually with stays at only the best hotels—a lifestyle that suited both him and Elaine, whom he said was ready for anything the minute she saw a suitcase. So the overhead was tremendous. But now the money was steady and increasing. *East of Eden* had earned back its advance, and he was collecting royalties that were boggling—$40,000 from sales in Europe alone on his most recent statement. He wondered about selling the house in the city, less because he didn't like it than because he'd paid $55,000 for it and thought it would probably now fetch $100,000. He told his sister Mary that at last it looked as if he and Elaine were "going to have to face solvency." In the same letter, he also mentioned that he looked forward to going to England soon.

That fall, Steinbeck had rekindled his boyhood fascination with *Le Morte d'Arthur*. In 1934, a partial manuscript composed shortly after the death of Thomas Malory, in 1471, had been discovered at

Steinbeck with his third wife, Elaine, at Sag Harbor shortly after learning he'd won the Nobel Prize. Carol had made him a writer. Gwen/Gwyn had made him crazy. Elaine made him happy. *(Bettmann via Getty Images)*

Winchester College in England. Steinbeck thought this version was the closest thing to Malory's original text, and it included important material that William Caxton had excluded from his printed edition. Steinbeck believed there would be a readership for *Le Morte d'Arthur* if it were translated into contemporary English and syntax. And he thought he was the man for the job. Whether that was true—whether, in fact, it was even a job that needed doing—was debatable. But even thinking about it elevated Steinbeck's spirits. In January of 1957, he wrote to Elizabeth Otis from Sag Harbor to tell her he had been furiously reading Malory. It was brutally cold outside, the bay partly frozen over, so that as the tide rose and receded, shards of loose ice scraped against one another and made a sound that was like a singing voice.

Steinbeck was struck by how the story became clearer and more sharply rendered as it went along. Malory—who was literate but in prison when he wrote the book—had to learn how to write as he went. Steinbeck vowed that whatever he saw fit to translate or change in his version, he would strive to preserve Malory's steady growth. Who knows, he said, maybe he'd learn something, too? Thinking about it was sometimes almost too much for him. One night, unable to sleep but too tired and jangled to read, Steinbeck took himself outside for a walk. The night was odd. Inside it had seemed to press in on him and fall away again. When he went out into the darkness it was only six degrees. Steinbeck said the cold seeped through his skin at first and then plunged deep within him, until he was thoroughly chilled, almost anesthetized. And then he felt calm. His nerves, which had been raging like the whitecaps far out on the bay, settled. He felt like a bear. It was a good thing, he said, that he'd come back inside before discovering a hollow log and crawling inside for the winter.

Steinbeck also wrote to his sister Mary, asking her if she knew where his *Boy's King Arthur* might be. He said their aunt Molly had given it to him when he was about ten, and that it was the first book he'd owned. He said that it had a red-brown cover, and if it could be found, he wanted very much to have it back. Mary ended up joining him and Elaine when they traveled in March to Italy, where Steinbeck plunged into the Vatican's archives. He was astonished at the vastness of the holdings, which included mountains of "Maloryana." Steinbeck was beguiled by the dusty solitude of scholarly research and contemplation.

The Arthurian legend, which might or might not have been inspired by an actual person, dates to the twelfth century, when an Oxford cleric named Geoffrey of Monmouth composed a *History of the Kings of Britain*, among them a bold ruler named Arthur, who was touched by the magic of a wizard named Merlin, and who lived in the time after the end of Roman rule in Britain. Forever indeterminate and shrouded in myth, Arthur presumably died around 540 AD, though the details of his passing are in doubt, as he was carried off to the mysterious island of Avalon after being wounded in battle, never to be seen again. Some elements of the story, such as King Arthur's Round Table, were supplied by later storytellers. How much of this is true, if any of it is, has been an open question for centuries. As one of Arthur's many creators said of him hundreds of years ago, "The tales of Arthur are not all lies nor all true. So much have the story-tellers told and so much have the makers of fables fabled to embellish their stories that they have made everything seem a fable."

Malory's Arthur, real or mythical or a combination thereof, ruled over a sprawling empire and a band of powerful knights. In the epic story of his life, Arthur rose to power in Camelot, fought wars, conquered distant lands, and ultimately searched for the Holy Grail—a chalice from the Last Supper that, like Arthur himself, was as much a legend as an actuality. What had always puzzled Steinbeck about *Le Morte d'Arthur* were the unequal failings of the characters. Why did Launcelot fall short in his quest for the Grail, while Galahad succeeded? Why did Queen Guenivere betray Arthur with Launcelot? And what justice was there in Launcelot saving Guenivere from the flames after Arthur condemned her to the stake?

In a long, self-involved letter to Elizabeth Otis from Rome, Steinbeck said it had all suddenly come clear to him: Launcelot was Malory's alter ego—the "self-character" that all novelists deploy in their books as stand-ins for themselves. And as such, Launcelot had to be imperfect because Malory was imperfect. Steinbeck said that, sooner or later, all men learn that whatever is the object of their quest in life, they will never win it. For a writer—like Malory or himself— that meant that their characters were always as flawed as they were.

Steinbeck thought this seemed to explain everything. And perhaps it did.

From Rome, the Steinbecks went to England, where they met a professor from the University of Manchester named Eugène Vinaver. Vinaver was an expert on the Middle Ages and an Arthurian scholar. Steinbeck discussed his project and began what would be a long correspondence and deepening friendship with Vinaver. He said he hoped Vinaver would not mind getting his letters, which were bound to be long and packed with questions.

The fall of 1957 was a difficult one. In September, Steinbeck attended a PEN writers' congress in Tokyo, where he was besieged by reporters and came down with the flu, which left him bedridden for several days. The illness followed the harrowing first day of the meeting, when Steinbeck learned at the last minute that he was to deliver the closing address of the opening session. Panicky and half-blinded by the glare of the stage lights, he gripped the lectern and stammered for a few minutes as he read from a scrap of paper. Later, he was told his brevity had impressed everyone. On the way home, he met up with his sisters, Esther, Beth, and Mary, in San Francisco. By the time he was back in New York, he was under doctor's orders to rest. On October 5, Steinbeck was—like everyone else in the country—startled at the news that a shiny, two-foot-wide metal ball called *Sputnik* was orbiting the earth. The Soviet Union had launched the first man-made satellite the day before, beating the United States into space and opening a new age. In December, Elaine's daughter, Waverly—who'd gotten married the year before—announced that she was getting divorced. Steinbeck judged Waverly's attitude the same as it was for all "weak and lazy people." She blamed it all on her mother.

Steinbeck was in England again the following year, touring places said to have been visited by Arthur. He told Vinaver that he felt a kinship with Malory. What difference did a few centuries make between fellow writers? Steinbeck believed that if he could see for himself the places Malory knew and described, he would be better able to interpret his work.

Back in Sag Harbor, he wrote Elizabeth Otis that he had at last started on his translation of Malory. He said it made him feel fine and free, as if he wanted to sing. He also mentioned that he was set up temporarily in the garage while his new workroom—a snug, six-sided office with windows all around that would sit near the water like a stubby lighthouse—was being built. It was going to be just big enough for a writing desk and a chair. Eventually he named it Joyous Gard, after Launcelot's castle in the North. Later that fall, back in New York, Steinbeck was happy to get a letter from Thom, now fourteen and in school in Connecticut, saying that he'd fallen in love with a girl named Susan. Steinbeck wrote back, counseling his son that being in love was good—even if the person you were in love with turned out not to be in love with you. The important thing, he said, was not to love selfishly to satisfy your own ego, but instead to see that the object of your love is someone "unique and valuable." He understood that Thom wasn't asking how he should feel, only what to do about it. Steinbeck said the only thing he could do was tell the girl and not worry about the consequences. "Nothing good gets away," he said reassuringly, though of course there was no way he could have believed that.

— 16 —

THE BEST I COULD DO

S TEINBECK'S PLAN TO translate Malory was causing trouble with his publisher. Pat Covici had initially expressed support for the idea and even started reading up on the Arthurian legend. Covici said he had ordered a copy of T. H. White's *The Once and Future King*, a retelling of Arthur's story that had just appeared in England and that incorporated several of White's earlier books on the subject. Covici didn't say it, but he had to be thinking that White's book—which became the smash Broadway musical *Camelot* a couple of years later—could make Steinbeck's more literal rendering of Malory irrelevant.

In the fall of 1958, Covici visited Steinbeck in Sag Harbor and found him agitated. He felt old and was having trouble working. He was down to 175 pounds, a weight he'd last seen in high school, and had recently told his sister Mary that he knew his years were not "unlimited." He and Elaine had committed to make the most of the time they had remaining. Covici wrote to remind Steinbeck that he was only fifty-six, but that with so many important books to his credit, he was entitled to take his time on the next one. What became clear in the coming months was that even though Covici maintained a pretense of enthusiasm for it, Viking had little interest in a modernized version of Malory's Arthur. Steinbeck was wounded. In December, he wrote an aggrieved letter to Elizabeth Otis, complaining that after all the years and all the money he'd made for Viking, their only interest in him was how his next book would do. Even though he'd stuck with Viking and always would—despite the many publishing houses that would rush to sign him if he so much as hinted at making a change—their loyalty to him trailed their focus on profits. He accused Covici of constantly pretending to be worried when he wasn't writing but in reality being worried only that he wasn't writing something that would sell.

Steinbeck wrote a more restrained letter to Covici. He spoke again about making the most of the time he had left, which was becoming a running theme, though there was no reason to think his time was short. Nonetheless he would not be rushed. He told Covici that he understood that publishing was a business. He said he knew all too well that his creative impulses ebbed and flowed, and that his books sometimes were a long time in getting started—an odd admission in that, with a couple of exceptions, the truth was just the opposite. Steinbeck had been an unusually prolific and fast writer. He said that the result of his efforts weren't necessarily the best, but that each book was always "the best I could do."

Ignoring the signals from his publisher, Steinbeck and Elaine traveled to southwest England once again, landing this time near the village of Bruton, in Somerset—the heart of Arthurian country. It was only four miles from a onetime Roman outpost known now as Cadbury Castle—not a castle in the usual sense, but a massive earthen fortification that rose plateau-like against the horizon. It had become an active archaeological site. Speculation circulated that it was the location of Camelot. The Steinbecks rented a sturdy Hillman station wagon and leased an ancient stone house with walls three feet thick and a thatched roof. It was called Discove Cottage, and was listed in the Domesday Book, the survey of England and Wales made for William the Conqueror in 1086. After a flurry of attention from reporters, they settled in. It was March of 1959.

Steinbeck believed the cottage must have once been the home of a religious hermit. There was a small but comfortable upstairs room for him to work in, and it had timeless views of the surrounding fields and forests. There was a garden to tend and other chores that required

Steinbeck's attention, but he said his only real job was the manuscript. He felt as though he belonged there. Elaine kept busy by making friends and often went into Bruton, where her Texas accent charmed everyone. She taught one of the locals to greet them as "y'all." After two weeks, Steinbeck told Elizabeth Otis that it seemed they'd lived there forever.

Steinbeck had decided to start over with his translation, though he didn't begin until toward the end of the month. As Steinbeck worked on the manuscript, he realized that he was remaking the story in the same way Malory had—guided by what had existed in legend but putting it down in his own way. For a long time he had thought that while he was going to bring Malory's language forward into a more contemporary idiom, he should not make any fundamental changes to the story. But why not put in some of his own ideas? Everyone else did. The legend evolved continually, as legends will. Steinbeck decided he would modify Malory but not remake him. He'd be walking a narrow line, but if it worked, he could make Arthur's life a story that was alive in our time. It was wonderful to be fully immersed at last, though he could not escape the complications of his life back in New York. Otis wrote to tell him that he owed $21,500 in income taxes—news that barely seemed like news anymore. Steinbeck wondered idly if they'd underpaid or the tax law had changed—and he kept on working. By the middle of April, he had a draft of the first chapter and sent it out to be typed.

On the last day of April, Steinbeck hiked to Cadbury Castle and climbed the ramparts of the ancient hill fort—his first visit to Camelot. It was a clear day. From the top, he could see the Bristol Channel. He began to weep. He told Eugène Vinaver he planned to go back again and again. At night. In foul weather and in every season. A few days later, he sent Elizabeth Otis the first installment of his manuscript. He was nervous about it. Maybe the reason nobody had done this before was that it could not be done. But he didn't believe that. Still, he wanted her opinion. Was he off on the wrong foot? He didn't think so, but he'd been wrong about that in the past.

Otis's answer was immediate. She did not like it at all.

Steinbeck was mortified. He wrote back saying he would not quit. He wasn't sure what she'd been expecting, but he said the worst thing was that she was *disappointed*. Honestly, he had hoped she would tell him the opposite. He wrote again the next day, after a sleepless night. His self-pitying words must have fallen on Otis like sledgehammer blows. She knew—and did not need reminding—how fragile even the greatest and most successful writers can be. Steinbeck said maybe what he'd written so far was no good—maybe he was wrong to even think it could be good. Perhaps this meant that he was wrong about a lot of things. Or everything. He mentioned the stage musical *Camelot*, which was being written by Alan Jay Lerner, with music by Frederick Loewe, and said it would no doubt earn millions. But that kind of popular entertainment wasn't what he wanted to do. He was sure there was something larger and more enduring in Malory, and that was what he was after. He couldn't stop using the word "wrong." If that's what he was, then he was wrong on an epic scale. This made him sad, as did the thought that he might never get it right. He said he would continue on with Malory through the summer and into the fall—and if it still wasn't working he'd surrender. But he couldn't quit easily. "I believe in this thing," he said. "There's an unmistakable loneliness in it. There must be."

An unmistakable loneliness. Was that it? Was that what he was after? Not being the first author of the tale, Steinbeck didn't necessarily have to find his own character in the story. But of course there was one—Arthur, the great and fallen king. So often lately, Steinbeck remarked on the vacancy of his long career, about how his books died for him when they were done, about not having much time left. He feared his quest was coming to an end before he could fully fail at it, as he knew he must. And the loneliness—that was the writer's lot, the nature of the trade. Writers want solitude, and often they get it. To be swallowed up by loneliness, to stand alone against the world— maybe this was the oldest story there was, one that took root in the legend of Arthur.

Steinbeck wrote to Vinaver, saying he was having trouble with his agent back in New York, where everyone had been expecting

something more like *The Once and Future King*. Steinbeck was probably mistaken about that—nobody would have wanted an imitation
from him—but it left open the question of what, exactly, would make
Viking happy. Covici—always averse to a discouraging word—stayed
diplomatically in the background. Steinbeck kept working, sending
confident-sounding updates to Elizabeth Otis—but no more copy.
On the evening of the summer solstice, he and Elaine visited Cadbury Castle, where legend had it that the ghost of Arthur rode across
the plain beneath the fortress on that night. Later in the summer,
Steinbeck's sister Mary visited. Mary had not been the same since
her husband was killed in Sicily. Steinbeck thought she looked like
a ghost—restless, apprehensive, and ungrounded. Maybe she should
see a therapist. If nothing else it might make her feel less lonely. Mary
snapped at him that she felt exactly the way she wanted to feel.

Toward the end of August, Steinbeck told Vinaver that the
deeper he went into the Arthurian legend, the more daunting his
task became. He'd begun to doubt he was good enough to do it right.
Everything he'd written so far was disappointing and small alongside
the pure poetry that was Malory. In instance after instance he could
in no way improve on the original telling, forgetting that this was not
his purpose. This *thing* he pursued had now become his special hell.
Disconsolate, he said he was in almost physical pain. He told Vinaver
that he believed writers were like knights, bound by duty and honor
to seek perfection. Whether anyone could ever achieve perfection was
immaterial. And that, he said, is why writers are not merely lonely
but *lost*. It was as if life had taught him nothing. "I come toward the
ending of my life with the same ache for perfection I had as a child."

In September of 1959, as their days in Somerset were winding
down, Steinbeck wrote to Pat Covici, making the same glum pro-
nouncement. Covici wrote back that he was more worried about
Steinbeck's emotional well-being than his writing. Putting the
Malory translation in the past tense, Covici suggested something
different. Why not write a novel about Launcelot? This wasn't help-
ful at all. Steinbeck and Elaine packed up, and in early October went
to London and checked into the Dorchester Hotel before heading

home. Steinbeck told Vinaver that his time in England's "most noble realme" had been wonderful. He was both sad and relieved to be leaving.

Back in New York, Steinbeck still longed for the Middle Ages, for a time when leaders had an imposing bearing and morality was not relative but enforced by the laws of God and by powerful knights. He was appalled by the abundance of daily life, as well as the pervasive corruption and violence. Just before his return, several popular television quiz shows had been canceled after it was discovered that they were rigged—a scandal that seemed to lay bare the country's craven dysfunction. Although most of the guilt lay with the producers, who were manipulating the shows for ratings, Steinbeck thought the contestants were shameful petty criminals who were symptoms of a wider corruption that had taken hold of American culture. He missed the simple, honest ways of Bruton, where there had been only one policeman, who kept the peace in five villages with no gun and only a bicycle for transportation. Steinbeck wondered how he could raise his sons to be virtuous in a country where success so often depended on treachery and cunning self-interest, a place where charity had become first and foremost a tax deduction.

Just after Thanksgiving, Steinbeck turned in early one evening, saying he didn't feel well. Elaine went to check on him and found him unconscious and the bed on fire from a cigarette he'd dropped. When Steinbeck arrived at the emergency room he was having difficulty speaking and couldn't move one of his hands. But these symptoms disappeared quickly. He spent ten days in the hospital, where no firm conclusion was reached about what had happened, though it seemed apparent that he had suffered a minor stroke. He was sent home to rest and then continued to recuperate at Sag Harbor after Christmas. Steinbeck and Elaine went back down to St. John in January for a few weeks of even more intense relaxation.

Steinbeck wrote Vinaver that he had no doubt his illness had been caused by his struggle with Malory. He believed he'd reached such a state of exhaustion and confusion that his body had simply forced him to stop. When he wrote to Elizabeth Otis, he said there was more to it—much more—than that. He felt he had been off track for close to fifteen years. Alluding to the distinction he liked to make between the inside world, in which he worked best, and the outside world, where other people intruded, Steinbeck believed his big mistake had been made long ago, when he took his writing outside. He'd done too much work too many times for the money, turned himself into a paid performer—like a cook flipping hotcakes in the front window of a breakfast joint. He also told Otis that he'd had a much closer call than many people realized, that in the hospital he'd been near death—and that death had appeared to him as a door. If he went through it, he would depart the world of the living, but he understood that this time, at least, it was his decision. At first he had run toward the door, longing to plunge through it. But he had stopped short, and the door had swung closed. He was convinced that if he didn't act like an invalid, he wouldn't be one.

Within weeks he was hard at work again, the words pouring out of him. It was 1960, a new decade. He'd started in on a novel, a story of domestic disharmony, moral decay, and financial turmoil in which Steinbeck explored some of the problems he felt were plaguing America. It was called *The Winter of Our Discontent.*

By spring, Steinbeck was well along with *The Winter of Our Discontent* and already thinking about the next book. In the fall, he planned to take a driving trip around the country and set down what he saw. Elaine would meet up with him from time to time, but he would mostly travel alone, avoiding big cities and zigzagging on country roads to avoid freeways when he could. New York was not America, and he wanted to reacquaint himself with his own country. He'd bought a pickup truck with a fully furnished and well-equipped camper top in the bed—he called it an "apartment"—and named the vehicle Rocinante, after Don Quixote's horse. He packed fishing and hunting gear and imagined that he would camp in the truck and talk to people as he met them in the heartland.

Both Pat Covici and Elizabeth Otis approved of the travel book,

A salty Steinbeck during the Whalers Festival at Sag Harbor
in the summer of 1966. *(Bettmann via Getty Images)*

though Otis tried to talk Steinbeck into going by bus and staying in motels—a suggestion he did not take well. He told her firmly that not only was he sticking to his plan, he was no longer taking anybody's suggestions about anything. He didn't bring up the Malory fiasco, but it was surely on his mind. He said allowing himself to be talked out of what he wanted to do was exhausting. Who wants to be told they're wrong all the time? He was sick of being wrong about things, which he thought was a function of being made to feel uncertain about what he was doing. He was going to do the travel book his way, lest the advice of others ruin the whole project.

Steinbeck did make one important change in his plans. He decided not to go alone. Elaine had a standard poodle that had been a gift from him. He asked her if he could take the dog along for the ride. Elaine was nervous about the trip, and this seemed like an excellent idea. Steinbeck didn't want the dog with him for protection, but as an advertisement to strangers that he wasn't dangerous or insane. He probably also realized that it would be nice to have someone to talk to—on the road and in the book. The dog's name was Charley.

In June 1960, Steinbeck told Pat Covici that he hadn't written him lately because he'd been writing—a way of putting it that he found funny. A few weeks later, he made a similar joke, telling Covici how ironic it was to be writing a book called *Winter* in July. By August it was done, and Steinbeck was revising. Covici was delighted with the book and thought maybe his old friend was back on track.

By September, Steinbeck was ready to leave in Rocinante. He had to wait for Hurricane Donna to pass—it had arrived on Long Island on September 12, trailing a path of destruction across Florida and up the Atlantic seaboard. Steinbeck was half-drowned saving his boat when the storm hit. He later admitted that for a time he had secretly hoped something might prevent him from going—the prospect of a three-month road trip was less appealing than the comforts of home. A sudden illness could save him from traveling, but his hospitalization the winter before was a big part of why he was going in the first place. After getting sick, he'd listened sourly to the usual advice: Slow down, lose weight, watch your cholesterol, and remember, you're not as young as you used to be. Steinbeck thought this was a kind of living death, one in which a formerly vigorous man steadily becomes childlike and delicate—all in exchange for a small and by no means certain increase in life expectancy. He just couldn't see himself living that way: "For I have always lived violently, drunk hugely, eaten too much or not at all, slept around the clock or missed two nights of sleeping, worked too hard and too long in glory, or slobbed for a time in utter laziness. I've lifted, pulled, chopped, climbed, made love with joy and taken my hangovers as a consequence, not as a punishment. I did not want to surrender fierceness for a small gain in yardage. My wife married a man; I saw no reason why she should inherit a baby."

Steinbeck drove less across the country than around it, circumnavigating the lower-48. He went first through New England and into Maine, then around the Great Lakes and into the Midwest, up through Wisconsin—which he found beautiful beyond description— across Minnesota and into North Dakota and Montana, a state he loved, then through Washington and Oregon and down into California, stopping off in Monterey for drinks on Alvarado Street like old times, south to Bakersfield, where he must have felt ghostly emanations from the nearby site of the Weedpatch migrant camp, and then back east through Arizona, New Mexico, Texas, and the Deep

South, a region riven by racial tensions and where he witnessed a vile anti-integration protest in New Orleans, before turning north again and making his way, finally, back into Manhattan, where he got lost. By then it was early December. He'd been gone two and a half months. Pulling Rocinante to the curb while he tried to remember how to get home, Steinbeck was approached by a friendly cop who, after making sure he wasn't drunk, gave him directions to East Seventy-Second Street.

In January of 1961, president-elect Kennedy invited the Steinbecks to attend his inauguration in Washington. Steinbeck and Elaine motored to the event in a limousine they shared with John Kenneth Galbraith and his wife. Later that winter they went to Barbados. Steinbeck thought it a wonderful place, an island designed for doing nothing—though he planned to work. Word came during this vacation that both the Literary Guild and the Book-of-the-Month Club wanted *The Winter of Our Discontent*. The people at Viking thought this might be the first time both clubs had offered the same book to their subscribers. Steinbeck wrote several letters to Elizabeth Otis with updates on the manuscript of the travel book, which he'd begun the day after their arrival. Every day, after starting with coffee at 7:30, he wrote until noon, tearing through a thousand or more words a day and sometimes twice that. The Steinbecks returned to New York in early March. While they were away, things had gone awry between the boys and Gwyn. This was not surprising, given her growing dependence on alcohol and pills. Catbird sometimes helped himself to the plentiful supplies of codeine and sedatives in the medicine cabinet and eventually made himself sick enough that he had to be treated for opiate withdrawal at the age of seven. The boys never knew when they'd come into the house and find their mother passed out from drinking, sometimes nude and lying on the floor, not always alone. In the nights, plastered and raging, Gwyn would scream at them that if they'd never been born the divorce would not have happened. Occasionally she hurled an empty liquor bottle in their direction to emphasize the point. By their mid-teens the boys had had enough. One day Catbird loaded his .22 rifle and held it to the head of one of Gwyn's boyfriends as they lay drunkenly asleep. He didn't pull the trigger, but he realized it was time to go for good. When Steinbeck and Elaine got home, they found Thom and Catbird waiting for them at the Seventy-Second Street house, demanding to move in, and they did.

A year later, during an ill-advised visit to his mother on his sixteenth birthday, Catbird and Gwyn got into a physical altercation. Gwyn was drunk and abusive, as usual. Catbird erupted. He threw a TV out the window and then began to bust up the furniture. He punched Gwyn in the face and then pummeled her until she fell to the floor.

In June, while Steinbeck continued working on what would become *Travels with Charley: In Search of America*—a journalistic title that would one day cause trouble—Viking published *The Winter of Our Discontent*. Covici had warned Steinbeck to expect mixed reviews. This turned out to be an understatement. The reviews were mostly terrible. Critic after critic dismissed the book as an unbelievable fable intended as an indictment of the crumbling morality of an affluent modern society that fell far short of the mark.

The novel—Steinbeck's last—centers on a man named Ethan Hawley, a good husband and loving father of two teenagers, whose life in the imaginary Long Island village of New Baytown is falling apart, although he's doing his best to ignore it. The Hawley name is an old one in New Baytown. Ethan and his family still live in the grand old whaling-era house that his great-grandfather built, but they're no longer people of means. Ethan clerks in a grocery store he used to own. When Ethan realizes that what's holding him down is his own decency, he sets aside his principles, which of course leads to disaster.

Reviewing the book for the *New York Times Book Review*, Steinbeck's old admirer Carlos Baker said it was good to have a serious novel from Steinbeck after a long fallow period, and this one was most readable. Baker also thought the book was a kind of coming-out for Steinbeck as an East Coast writer. But Baker couldn't conceal his disappointment. He thought many readers would be puzzled by a novel about social and economic malaise that didn't seem to be clear on either the nature of the problem or what might be done about it. Baker's fellow *Times* critic, Orville Prescott, put his finger more precisely on the problem many reviewers had with the book—a whimsical style that didn't quite suit the edgy satire Steinbeck intended. "Mr. Steinbeck's anger and bitterness are the underlying forces that drove him to write this book," Prescott wrote. "But once it was started a sort of verbal cheerfulness kept breaking in and blunted the edge of his wrath." Prescott's deployment of the word "wrath" could not have been lost on Steinbeck.

Steinbeck found the reviews of *The Winter of Our Discontent* depressing. Reviews always made him feel that way, even the good ones. But this time around was hard to take. He told Elizabeth Otis he'd known the book would be "vulnerable"; he just hadn't expected such a harsh response. He'd get over it, but—alluding again to his mortality—he added that the less time he could look forward to, the less optimistic he could be. Steinbeck's energies were quickly transferred to *Travels with Charley*, which he continued to work on, though with less enthusiasm. He told Pat Covici the book was coming, but that it had lost its shape and seemed to lack any reason for being written. At least that made it realistic, as everything he saw around him seemed aimless and pointless.

On July 2 that summer, Ernest Hemingway pressed his forehead against the muzzle of a shotgun in the vestibule of his house in Idaho and killed himself. It was a blow that Pat Covici said he felt deeply. Something about Hemingway's death told him to encourage Steinbeck to "keep on," though Steinbeck could no more stop writing than a fruit tree could stop bearing. Covici urged Steinbeck to listen to his "hidden voice" and let his instincts take him forward. When Covici visited Steinbeck in Sag Harbor that month, he caught him several times staring out the window, lost in thought and seemingly a million miles away.

Steinbeck delivered the finished manuscript of *Travels with Charley* in September and left with Elaine, Thom, and Catbird on a planned ten-month, around-the-world trip. They hired the future playwright Terrence McNally—who'd been recommended by Elia Kazan—to come along as a tutor. This didn't sit well with Thom, who was now seventeen and as resistant to study as ever. They went first to London and then down to Bruton. In Dublin they got word that longtime Viking president Harold Guinzburg had died. Then, in November, they were in Milan when Steinbeck suffered another stroke-like episode that left him weak and briefly unable to travel. Steinbeck ominously called it a "tap on the shoulder." McNally took the boys ahead. Steinbeck wrote to Elizabeth Otis to assure her he was okay, just very tired. It wasn't much of a letter, he admitted, mainly proof of life, "just mist on a glass." He regretted that he'd scared Elaine and now her. After the boys rejoined them, Steinbeck was determined that they would go on with the trip but he would heed his doctors' advice to take it more slowly. In Greece they could decide whether to continue on. As for the other instructions he'd been given—to stop drinking, smoking, and overeating, or doing anything that might be exciting—he said there was no way. It was too late for him to change.

In January of 1962, a proof of *Travels with Charley* caught up with Steinbeck in Capri. Covici told him orders for the book were strong. A few weeks later, Covici reported that the Viking sales team liked the book better than any other Steinbeck had written—and that it would be the lead title in their spring catalogue. Covici, who had been enthusiastic about the book all along, now said it was a "good book," which sounded slightly flat. He realized it had been a hard slog for Steinbeck, but he thought that in a way it was a distillation of his entire body of work. "Almost everything that you ever thought, felt, smelled and expressed about people and things in your other books is here," he said.

On February 27, Steinbeck turned sixty. They stayed on in Capri until April, and by May were in Greece, where Steinbeck learned that *Travels with Charley* had been chosen by the Book-of-the-Month Club. Viking planned to publish it in July.

The Steinbecks cut short their trip and were back in New York by June—in time to enjoy the appreciative reviews of *Travels with Charley* the following month. Near the close of the book, Steinbeck had said that his only purpose in taking to the road was to see what his countrymen were like. In the *New York Times*, the reliably perceptive Orville Prescott begged to differ. Observing, as Steinbeck had, that Americans were losing their regional distinctions and becoming more alike didn't tell us much—but Prescott agreed with the consensus that Steinbeck had produced a thoroughly likable and amusing book. Prescott thought Steinbeck had gotten the country about right in describing its "expanding cities, the roaring superhighways, the good breakfasts and wretched dinners available along the highways, racial strife in New Orleans and the beauty of nature everywhere."

Enthusiastic readers then—and ever since—loved the book's genial modesty and gentle humor. Steinbeck presented himself as a down-to-earth, open-minded traveler and a fellow citizen happy to lend an ear to what people wanted to tell him. From the outset, he seemed determined to reconnect with a commonsense brand of Americanism and self-reliance that had faded on the urbanized coasts and in the mass media. He also hinted early in the book that real journalism eluded him and that he was not a reliable correspondent: "I've always admired those reporters who can descend on an area, talk to key people, ask key questions, take samplings of opinions, and then set down an orderly report very like a road map. I envy this technique and at the same time do not trust it as a mirror of reality. I feel that there are too many realities. What I set down here is true until someone else passes that way and rearranges the world in his own style."

Too many realities? That sounded, not surprisingly, like something a novelist would say. In his review, Orville Prescott indicated that his enjoyment of the book didn't mean he bought everything Steinbeck was peddling. Prescott accused Steinbeck of some wild exaggeration and possibly some made-up stories, based, apparently, on the assumption that when it comes to realities there is only one. Prescott thought the many passages of pure commentary were fine not because they were deeply reported, but because Steinbeck was a good writer. As it turned out, Prescott was on to something. Much of *Travels with Charley* did not happen the way Steinbeck claimed. Steinbeck's search for America took place more inside his own head than through encounters with his salt-of-the-earth brethren on country back roads. In fact, quite a lot of *Travels with Charley* was invented—later revealed when someone else did pass the same way, asking questions as he went.

In 2010, a former newspaper reporter named Bill Steigerwald retraced Steinbeck's 10,000-mile odyssey ahead of the fiftieth anniversary of *Travels with Charley* and discovered that not only was the book mostly fiction, it was, in Steigerwald's view, "something of a fraud." Reconstructing Steinbeck's trip as carefully as he could, based on his own time behind the wheel and from the limited record, Steigerwald concluded that Steinbeck rarely camped in Rocinante, preferring comfortable motels, cozy country inns, and the occasional five-star hotel. Steigerwald also calculated that for forty-five of Steinbeck's seventy-five days on the road, Elaine was with him—an undisclosed fact that puts a dent in the whole just-me-and-Charley charm of the story. Most disturbing was Steigerwald's claim that many of the conversations with regular people that Steinbeck recorded in the book could not be trusted. One particularly improbable passage, almost certainly created out of thin air, was the book's well-known account of Steinbeck's supposed meeting with a Shakespearean actor near Alice, North Dakota, which rambles across eight pages. Steinbeck's search for the real America was, in a word, inauthentic.

Steigerwald wrote a magazine piece and eventually a book pointedly titled *Dogging Steinbeck*. In April of 2011, the *New York Times* reported on Steigerwald's research, though neither his reporting nor the coverage of it ignited the sort of controversy Steigerwald thought they might. Steinbeck scholars showed little interest on the grounds that Steinbeck's license in *Travels with Charley* had always been taken for granted. Steigerwald, they said, had only discovered something that was already known about *Travels with Charley*. That's probably true—though, in fairness to Mr. Steigerwald, it should be noted that researchers, including biographers, usually attach cosmic significance to even the most minor details about their subjects— from a humdrum scrap of irrelevant correspondence to obscure clues about their private lives. *Travels with Charley* is fair game. Steiger-wald's "scoop" went unappreciated, which must have rankled. But Steigerwald could be forgiven for applying the rules of journalism to a work that purported to be journalism. First among those rules is that facts matter.

For a new introduction to the book on its fiftieth anniversary, the Penguin Group (the parent company of Viking) added a few lines alerting readers that Steinbeck "took liberties with the facts" and that the book could be considered "true" only in the way that a well-crafted novel is true.

And therein lies the wisdom of revisionist history. *Travels with Charley* was regarded as an honest and intimate portrait of America for fifty years—until it became something else. In hindsight, it's not surprising. There's Steinbeck's own admission in the book that he was no shoe-leather reporter. But more telling was his reluctance to go at all, coupled with Elizabeth Otis's suggestion that he take a bus. Everybody seemed to know, including Steinbeck, that he wasn't up to the rigors of hard travel and daily reporting that were supposed to be his method in *Travels with Charley*. Plus, he'd already decided what was wrong with the country, and that made it easy for him to find the antidote without needing to literally find it.

Travels with Charley does contain at least one mistake nobody has bothered to correct. In recalling his acquaintance with Sinclair Lewis—Steinbeck was reminded of it when he drove through Lewis's Minnesota hometown of Sauk Centre—Steinbeck said he'd read *Main Street* in high school. That would have been hard, as the book was published the year after Steinbeck graduated.

Long before Bill Steigerwald raised his objections, Steinbeck's own family had been skeptical of the book. According to Catbird:

"Thom and I are convinced that he never talked to any of those people in *Travels with Charley*. He just sat in his camper and wrote all that shit. He was too shy. He was really frightened of people who saw through him. He couldn't have handled that amount of interaction. So the book is actually a great novel."

In October of 1962, U.S. intelligence discovered the reason for a recent increase in Soviet shipping traffic to the island of Cuba. The Russians were building offensive missile installations there, just ninety miles from the U.S. mainland. President Kennedy ordered a naval blockade of Cuba to halt further deliveries and demanded that the Soviets remove the equipment already in place. Tensions were high and war seemed possible. The blockade took effect on October 24. The next day Steinbeck and Elaine, who were out in Sag Harbor, switched on the evening news to find out the latest on the crisis and were startled by a different headline: John Steinbeck had won the Nobel Prize in Literature.

The day following the announcement, he appeared at a press conference at the Viking offices, dressed in a pinstripe suit and jauntily smoking a cigar. He fielded questions from reporters for an hour. Steinbeck said his initial reaction had been "disbelief." Then he was "stunned and happy." Someone asked him which of his books he liked best, and Steinbeck predictably replied, "I have no favorite. Only the one I'm working on." Inevitably, he was asked who his favorite writers were. He answered Faulkner and Hemingway. When he was asked why writers write, he said he couldn't answer that one because it had been a long time since he'd wondered why. Toward the end, a reporter asked him if he thought he deserved the Nobel Prize. "That's an interesting question," he said. "Frankly, no."

Of course it was not an interesting question—it was a challenge. The only right answer, which Steinbeck did not choose to give, would have been "I hope so." It's possible that in the moment, caught off guard and wounded by the question, Steinbeck was simply being his angry, contrarian self. But it's also possible that he meant it, that he believed *nobody* could deserve such a prize. After all, there had to be an unmistakable loneliness in being a Nobel laureate.

Steinbeck had been nominated for the prize eight times previously, beginning in 1943—much closer in time to the books that might have made him deserving of the Nobel. But that was not the position taken by the Swedish Academy. The prize committee specifically cited the critically dismissed *The Winter of Our Discontent* as the work that made Steinbeck worthy of the prize, saying that the book had returned him, after more than two decades, to the "towering standard" he had set with *The Grapes of Wrath* in 1939. The academy did seem to acknowledge the greater weight of Steinbeck's older body of work, praising *Of Mice and Men* and *The Long Valley*. Steinbeck's feeling for "the oppressed, the misfits and the distressed" was his unique strength, the academy remarked. In an odd aside, the academy added that Steinbeck "more than holds his own" with previous American winners of the prize, which besides Hemingway and Sinclair Lewis included William Faulkner, Eugene O'Neill, and Pearl Buck—plus T. S. Eliot, who'd been born in America before resettling in England.

On October 26, the day after the announcement and as part of its extensive coverage, the *New York Times* published an editorial complaining about the award. The *Times* questioned a Nobel Prize for an author who "produced his major work more than two decades ago." The paper thought giving the prize to Steinbeck demonstrated that the Nobel committee was out of touch with the "main currents of American writing." There were any number of more deserving writers, the *Times* sniffed, writers who were more significant and influential and profound—though the paper declined to name any of them. The editorial insisted it was in no way intended to detract from Steinbeck's accomplishments, though of course that was exactly what it did.

There was more to come. In a lacerating profile for the *New York Times* the day before the Nobel ceremony in December, Arthur Mizener seconded Steinbeck's assertion that he didn't deserve the prize. Mizener, a college professor and biographer of F. Scott Fitz-

Steinbeck at work in his Manhattan apartment, 1958.
(Erich Hartmann/Magnum)

gerald, autopsied many of Steinbeck's major works and decided that in most instances—and in some cases to an "intolerable" extent—Steinbeck insisted on finding a sentimental moral to every story. Mizener especially detested the phrase "mystic sorrow," which Steinbeck had used in reference to Danny's house in *Tortilla Flat*, and which seemed another expression of the freighted emotions he found in the Arthurian legend. Mizener thought this dopey sorrow "spread like a cancer" through many of Steinbeck's books. *The Red Pony*, the only Steinbeck work Mizener seemed to like even slightly, was pretty good, he allowed. It contained only a glimmer of the "third-rate" portentousness that infected Steinbeck's subsequent works, though the seeds were there, too. Mizener speculated that the Swedish Academy must have figured it was time to again give the prize to an American, and Steinbeck happened to be the only one they could think of who didn't already have it.

Steinbeck bore the criticism stoically—as he always had. Though he had often complained that readers, including critics, failed to understand his work, they were entitled to their opinions. If people thought he didn't deserve a Nobel Prize, who was he to tell them that he did? When the New York critics had assailed *Burning Bright* years earlier, Steinbeck accepted their decision—and displayed an uncharacteristic open-mindedness about the verdict they'd rendered on his work. "They," he wrote of the reviewers, "are the custodians of the public interest and if their judgments were not usually accurate they would have neither the following nor the power they possess."

But Steinbeck must have struggled with the complaint that his best work had come decades before. It didn't seem that way to him. He had trouble even comparing one book to another, as he tended to view each as something that lived with him while he was writing it and not afterward. When he finished a book he felt he had "outgrown" it, and to move on to another in the same vein would have been intolerable. This was the reason no two of his books were alike. By his way of thinking, if he listened to the critics who argued that his latest book wasn't as good as the previous one, he'd have to believe that he'd started writing when he was at zero—and had gone steadily down ever since.

A decade after the Nobel backlash, a scholar named James Gray offered a more judicious review of Steinbeck's career—in a slim but penetrating monograph published as part of a University of Minnesota series on American writers. Gray argued that Steinbeck's critics during his lifetime had been distracted by the shifting of gears and shuffling of themes in his books, by his experimentation with different forms, by the appearance that he was always starting over. The official position on Steinbeck hardened, Gray said, into this: He was a perennial apprentice. Was Steinbeck first-rate? The critics were left perpetually waiting to find out.

Gray didn't share these reservations. Steinbeck, he wrote, was a powerful storyteller and a "quintessential dramatist." What the critics saw from book to book—but failed to detect as a linkage among all of them—was Steinbeck's anger. He was America's most pissed-off writer. "All his work," Gray wrote, "steams with indignation at injustice, with contempt for false piety, with scorn for the cunning and self-righteousness of an economic system that encourages exploitation, greed, and brutality."

Despite the blowback over the Nobel, congratulations flooded in. Steinbeck told Dook Sheffield he would need to be "castrated of self-consciousness" and that he was afraid of the "corrosive" effects of the prize. He wrote to Tal Lovejoy that he was trying to put it all in the proper perspective. The prize was important, he said, though not as important as, say, the fact that Thom and Catbird were both doing better in school.

Steinbeck heard from Vinaver in England, and he wrote back thanking him for his cable. Steinbeck said the Nobel was nice, but that he'd be careful not to let it mark his ending as writer. For too many who won it, the Nobel was a kind of epitaph. And he talked about going back to work on Malory—not, this time, on a translation of *Le Morte d'Arthur* into modern English, but on a looser reinterpretation he referred to as "the Acts."

Steinbeck and Elaine made their travel plans right away, booking a flight to Stockholm on December 8, two days ahead of the ceremony. Steinbeck wanted to follow protocol. There was one thing he did not look forward to: the acceptance speech. He wrote a plaintive letter to Adlai Stevenson, who was now the ambassador to the United Nations, saying it was ironic that he, who had always been ready to criticize other people's speeches, now had to give one. He suggested, not seriously, that maybe Stevenson could do it in his stead. Steinbeck said this would make them even for everything he had done for him.

Steinbeck looked regal in white tie and tails at the presentation ceremony on December 10. He began his speech by thanking the Swedish Academy for finding his work worthy of the prize. "In my heart," he said, "there may be doubt that I deserved the Nobel award over other men of letters whom I hold in respect and reverence—but there is no question of my pleasure and pride in having it for myself." He went on to say that the "ancient commission" of the writer in society was unchanged. The writer "is charged with exposing our many grievous faults and failures, with dredging up to the light our dark and dangerous dreams, for the purpose of improvement." But the writer's task was not wholly somber. It also included the obligation to reflect "man's proven capacity for greatness."

Steinbeck specified what he meant by "dark and dangerous dreams" without using the actual words nuclear holocaust, though that was clearly what he meant. "Fearful and unprepared, we have assumed the lordship over the life and death of the whole world, of all living things. The danger and the glory and the choice rest finally with man." Humankind had become the greatest hazard to itself, but also "our only hope."

Steinbeck was not done. In the fall of 1964, he received the Medal of Freedom at the White House. Other recipients that year included T. S. Eliot, Helen Keller, and Walt Disney. In October, Pat Covici died. "Pat Covici was much more than my friend," Steinbeck said of him later. "He was my editor. Only a writer can understand how a great editor is father, mother, teacher, personal devil, and personal god. For thirty years Pat was my collaborator and my conscience. He demanded more of me than I had and thereby caused me to be more than I should have been without him." Steinbeck joined Saul Bellow and Arthur Miller in delivering eulogies at the memorial service.

For a time Steinbeck could not bear the idea of visiting the Viking office. Then, in 1966, he published a book of essays and photos, *Amer-*

ica and Americans—an illustrated *Travels with Charley*. The photographers involved in the project—nearly sixty of them—included prominent artists such as Ansel Adams and Henri Cartier-Bresson. Steinbeck's commentary, woven among images that explored the range of the American experience, spoke to his own unease with a changing world. But he was hopeful. Americans were, as ever, ready to reach beyond the next horizon. "We cut ourselves off from the self-abuse of war by raising it from a sin to an extinction," he wrote. "Far larger experiences are open to our restlessness—the fascinating unknown is everywhere." Considering the book a few years later, the Minnesota scholar James Gray doubted that Steinbeck's heart was still in his work. *America and Americans*, he said, was shrewd in places and moved along appealingly, but "a tone of autumnal melancholy broods over its pages."

Another problem was that we were not "cut off" from war. American intervention in Vietnam had reached what would turn out to be the halfway point in 1965, a year that saw heavy bombing of the North and the deployment of the first U.S. ground troops to the region. It was another proxy war pitting American democracy against Communist expansionism. By the end of the year, 200,000 American soldiers were fighting in Southeast Asia. By 1966, as the American commitment continued to escalate, both of Steinbeck's sons were in the army and headed to war. Catbird had been drafted and Thom enlisted. Catbird arrived in Vietnam at the end of 1966, and Thom followed shortly after.

Steinbeck went, too—spending six months in Vietnam as a correspondent for *Newsday* from December 1966 to May 1967. Unable to escape his fame—and dismissive of any restrictions on reporters—he hung out with generals and sometimes carried an M16 in the field. Steinbeck filed fifty-eight essays over that time. He was a strong anti-Communist and supporter of the war then, and friendly with President Lyndon Johnson. Lady Bird and Elaine had known each other at the University of Texas, and Steinbeck's loyalty to the Democratic Party remained firm. Later on, Steinbeck began to question his hawkishness. After coming back, he visited with Johnson in the White

House and offered suggestions for "winning the war" and ending the things he felt the United States was doing wrong in Vietnam—but he wasn't convinced that either was possible. In August of 1967, he told Elizabeth Otis Vietnam was a lost cause. He said America could not win the war. Nobody, he added, could ever win a war. Steinbeck thought the old principles no longer applied, that the United States would ultimately be defeated by an ideology it could not kill. Steinbeck had come to the conclusion that even if America prevailed on the ground, defeating the supposed enemy in the usual sense, we would be just an occupying army in an alien environment. Even that, he said, was out of reach. By any measure, old or new, America was losing to a force better suited to the circumstances and driven by a conviction stronger than ours.

During his time in Indochina, Steinbeck had again developed severe back pain. By October of 1967 he was hospitalized and in traction, scheduled for a spinal fusion operation. On the morning of the procedure Steinbeck turned on the TV and saw on the news that Catbird, who was back in the States and living in Washington, DC, had been arrested in connection with a bust in his apartment involving twenty pounds of marijuana. The weed was not his, and Catbird insisted that he'd been set up. He managed to get his trial postponed and was ultimately acquitted by a jury that deliberated all of forty-five minutes.

His father was less understanding. Catbird had testified before Congress about drug use in Vietnam and openly opposed the war. Despite his own doubts about the Vietnam War, Steinbeck didn't like antiwar protesters. Or the drug-fueled hippie scene, which now touched his family. Catbird had embarrassed him, ruffled his and Elaine's friendship with LBJ and Lady Bird, and generally besmirched the Steinbeck name. As he had been since childhood, Catbird was an inconvenience and an annoyance. "They should have jailed you," Steinbeck told his son. And then Steinbeck never spoke to him again, though whether he intended for things to end that way isn't known. Their estrangement became protracted and then awkward to resolve as Steinbeck's health issues mounted over the coming year. Still, Steinbeck evidently kept track of Catbird, who traveled back to Vietnam as a journalist.

In the months ahead, Steinbeck's heart problems worsened. Steinbeck was amused by the sanitized language used to describe them. Some were "incidents," others "episodes." He could never tell which he was having. There was a scare in August of 1968 when his pulse raced out of control and his blood pressure was "strange," as Elaine put it. By October he needed physical therapy for his left arm and hand, which had become twitchy and useless. At some point he was cleared to resume more normal activity, but according to Elaine he preferred napping and taking oxygen and was usually ready for bed by the afternoon.

That fall, Richard Nixon narrowly defeated Hubert Humphrey in the presidential election. Elaine and Steinbeck thought this was awful news. They'd been at Sag Harbor, but now Steinbeck's doctor recommended they move back into the city. Before doing so, Steinbeck suffered a string of additional "little incidents" with his heart and evidently had another minor stroke.

In December, Steinbeck knew his time was short. He'd spent

With Charley.
(Rolls Press/Popperfoto via Getty Images)

decades anguished by the thought that life was always slipping away, each day subtracting from the total. Now all he could manage was to wait for the end. He didn't want to be in the hospital, so he stayed home with Elaine. He spent some time looking over the galleys of Catbird's Vietnam book, *In Touch*. On December 20 the phone rang. It was Max Wagner, his boyhood friend. Steinbeck hadn't been up to taking calls, but said he wanted to talk with Wagner and got on the line. He thanked Wagner for asking after him and said he'd be all right. He handed the phone back to Elaine, who spoke briefly with Wagner. Sometime later, Elaine asked the doctor to administer morphine to make things easier. John Steinbeck died at 5:30 that afternoon. Outside, the temperatures were mild, in the forties. It was the kind of New York weather he'd never liked.

John Steinbeck was survived by his wife, Elaine, sons Thomas and John IV, two ex-wives, and a large group of people who never existed but will live forever: Kino the pearl diver; bindle stiffs George Milton and Lennie Small; Jody Tiflin, who owned a pony; Mack and the boys; Doc; the Joad family—Ma, Pa, Tom, Rose of Sharon, and the rest—Adam, Cathy, Aron, and Cal Trask; a carefree *paisano* named Danny; Elisa Allen, keeper of chrysanthemums. Steinbeck told many stories, and many were told about him, including this one: A long time ago, late at night in the town of Salinas, California, a boy named Glenn Graves stirred in his sleep. He got up and walked in his pajamas to the window, rubbing his eyes. He looked out and saw curtains of fog hanging above Central Avenue. It was quiet. Nothing moved. But he could see across the way, to a window in the upstairs bedroom of the big house on the other side, and there was a light on in it.

ACKNOWLEDGMENTS

I AM INDEBTED to Susan Shillinglaw, English professor at San Jose State University and, during the time of my research, director of the National Steinbeck Center in Salinas. I relied time and again on Dr. Shillinglaw's unrivaled and generously shared knowledge of Steinbeck. I also profited from her close reading of the original manuscript. Thanks, Susan, for your friendship and encouragement. Thanks, as well, to Susan's husband, Dr. William Gilly, biology professor at Stanford's Hopkins Marine Station, for telling me about the Gulf of California and for his congenial company on my many visits to Monterey and Pacific Grove.

Thanks, also, to Dr. Robert DeMott, Edwin and Ruth Kennedy Distinguished Professor Emeritus at Ohio University, and Steinbeck scholar extraordinaire.

I am especially grateful to Toni Heyler for allowing me to read Steinbeck's letters to his sister Mary Steinbeck Dekker.

This book was inspired by conversations I had over the course of many months with my longtime friend and mentor, Dr. Michael Lannoo, professor of anatomy and cell biology at the Indiana University School of Medicine. In a way, it feels like we've been having one continuous conversation that has now passed the twenty-year mark. A neuroanatomist by trade, Mike is a polymath who knows everything about the human brain—and a lot about many other subjects, from wildlife ecology and conservation biology to the life and work of Ed Ricketts. I thank him for getting me started on the subject of John Steinbeck.

Special thanks to Lisa Josephs, archivist at the National Steinbeck Center, for guiding me through their vast holdings, including the many hours of taped interviews recorded almost a half century ago with people who knew Steinbeck—an unusual and important resource.

Thank you to Donald G. Kohrs, librarian at the Hopkins Marine Station; to Dennis Copeland, historian and museum arts and archives manager for the City of Monterey; to Will Ray, editor of the online newsletter *Steinbeck Now*; to Eric Mora, Yessenia Guzman, and the late Carol Robles of the National Steinbeck Center; to Richard Astro, Distinguished Professor of English at Drexel University; and to Michael Hemp, keeper of the memory of Cannery Row.

Thanks to Tim Noakes of Stanford University's Special Collections and Archives, and to the entire staff; to Nick Taylor and Peter Van Coutren of the Martha Heasley Cox Center for Steinbeck Studies at San Jose State University; to Rick Watson and the staff of the Harry Ransom Center at the University of Texas; and to everyone who helped me at the Pierpont Morgan Library in New York, the Butler Library at Columbia University, the Monterey Public Library, the John Steinbeck Library in Salinas, and the Minneapolis Central Library.

Thanks to Gavin Jones, Frederick P. Rehmus Family Professor of the Humanities at Stanford; and to Bill Steigerwald.

Special thanks to Nancy Steinbeck, John IV's widow, who welcomed me into the sometimes-perplexing world of a father-in-law she never knew but knows all about—and for her patience in answering my endless questions. Thank you, too, to Nancy's husband, Galen Lambert, who shared thoughts about Steinbeck that led me to consider CTE as a possible factor in parts of his life. More thanks, as well, to John Lovejoy, who talked with me on many occasions about his parents, Ritchie and Tal, and their place in the solar system of friends that orbited John Steinbeck and Ed Ricketts. John also shared photos and letters with me.

Thanks to scholar and author Jackson Benson for his *The True Adventures of John Steinbeck, Writer*, the seminal biography and the one against which all others are measured.

I am fortunate to have had the wise and good-natured John Glusman as my editor at W. W. Norton & Company. John's passion for clear writing—and his low tolerance for the other kind—kept me on track, and his patience and enthusiasm kept me going. Thanks, also, to Helen Thomaides for shepherding the manuscript all the way through and for making many improvements to it.

Thanks, as usual, to my stalwart agent of many years, Chuck Verrill. I could have no better partner.

I am grateful to the members of my writing group for reading the manuscript as it progressed and for their always heartening company. Thank you, Frank Bures, Kim Todd, Jason Albert, Emily Sohn, Jason Good, and Mara Hvistendahl.

John Steinbeck's favorite Stanford professor, Edith Mirrielees, liked to say that writing can't be taught, only helped. For the better part of forty years, my friend and colleague, the brilliant Dan Kelly, has helped my writing. Dan read my manuscript in its embryonic form and showed me how to make it better. For that I thank him one more time.

I wrote the first chapter of this book in February 2016, at Marsha Dowler's guest house in Seaside, Florida, during my residence in the annual Escape to Create retreat for writers and artists. Thank you to Marsha, and to Karen Holland, Ed and Cathy Toole, Bert and Sue Trucksess, and to the enlightened citizens of that sun-splashed community who sponsor this superb program. And big all-around thanks to my fellow Escapees—Charis Cotter, Miki Caniato, Katrina Schwartz, and Jeff Black—for their excellent companionship.

Last but never least, thank you to my family.

NOTES

I HAVE DISPENSED with citations for searchable facts—dates, place names, major events, historical matters, and so on—as well as for general statements that are my own conclusions and inferences based on reading the record. Numerical entries at the end of citations from Stanford indicate their location within the collection thusly: Box Number/Folder Number.

John Steinbeck left a long paper trail. Over time, many of these documents have been copied and recopied, and have migrated among archives. Wherever I relied on such copies I have attempted to indicate their proper locations.

Abbreviations

CAJ	*Carol and John Steinbeck*
HRC	Harry Ransom Center/University of Texas
TCR	*John Steinbeck: The Contemporary Reviews*
JON	*Journal of a Novel*
SJSU	Martha Heasley Cox Center for Steinbeck Studies/ San Jose State University
NSC	National Steinbeck Center
PM	Pierpont Morgan Library
Dekker	Private correspondence with Mary Steinbeck Dekker
Stanford	Stanford University Libraries Dept. of Special Collections
ALL	*Steinbeck: A Life in Letters*
JSW	*The True Adventures of John Steinbeck, Writer*

Chapter One: The Boy No One Knew

3   *Once it was an arm of the sea*: Durham, "Geology of the Southern Salinas Valley Area, California," Geological Survey Professional Paper 819, U.S. Government Printing Office, 1974; Edward Hoit Nutter, "Sketch of the Geology of the Salinas Valley, California," *Journal of Geology* 9, no. 4 (May–June 1901).

3   *In the winter of 1902*: "Nearly Bank Full," *Salinas Daily Index*, February 27, 1902.

4   *That same day, in a large, Queen Anne–style house*: Personal observation. The Steinbeck house still stands, and is open to visitors and operates as a restaurant run by the Valley Guild and now called the Steinbeck House Restaurant.

4   *Thousands of years before*: Breschini et al., *10,000 Years on the Salinas Plain*, pp. 10–12.

4   *In 1602, a Spanish explorer*: Guinn, *History and Biographical Record of Monterey and San Benito Counties*, vol. 1, p. 42.

4   *In 1769, a Spanish expedition*: Breschini et al., *10,000 Years on the Salinas Plain*, p. 16.

5   *The Spanish established religious missions*: Guinn, *History and Biographical Record of Monterey and San Benito Counties*, vol. 1, pp. 56–73.

5   *They brought livestock*: Anderson, *The Salinas Valley*, pp. 7–10.

6   *Heavier-bodied beef cattle*: Ibid., pp. 23–32.

6   *Two rich aquifers were discovered*: California Groundwater Bulletin 118.

6   *By the late 1800s*: Anderson, *The Salinas Valley*, p. 70.

6   *At the turn of the century*: Ibid.

6   *Grains, hay, alfalfa, beans*: Breschini et al., *Early Salinas*, pp. 45–58.

6   *Beef, milk, and produce moved*: Anderson, *The Salinas Valley*, p. 45.

6   *Salinas sat in the midst of five large* ranchos: Breschini et al., *Early Salinas*, p. 11.

6   *But three years later*: Starr, *California*, p. 104.

6   *Then, in the 1860s*: Breschini et al., *10,000 Years on the Salinas Plain*, p. 34.

7   *The town occupied an eighty-acre tract*: Breschini et al., *Early Salinas*, p. 7.

7   *Salinas began as a stopping-off place*: Ibid.

7   *The line's most celebrated*: Ibid.

7   *As one childhood acquaintance put it*: Pauline Pearson interview with Sylvester Carriaga, March 17, 1981. NSC. This, along with many similar citations to follow, is from a series of interviews recorded by Pearson, George Robinson, and Paul Caswell for the Salinas Public Library in the 1970s and early 1980s. Pearson, who fittingly came originally from Oklahoma, was a fixture at the library. She had an encyclopedic familiarity with Steinbeck and his books, and her discretion and firm avoidance of salacious themes give the recordings their charm.

7   *People said he looked like*: Pauline Pearson interview with Herb Hinrichs, June 26, 1975. NSC.

7   *Until high school, John wore knee pants*: Pauline Pearson interview with Angelo Binsacca, October 3, 1975. (Herb Hinrichs also told Pearson about Steinbeck's short pants.) NSC.

8   *John's father, John Ernst, had been born*: JSW, p. 12. Note that here, and in all subsequent citations of Benson's biography, page numbers refer to the 1990 paperback edition by Penguin Books.

8   *Sam Hamilton had lived in Salinas*: Paul Caswell interview with Mildred Kellogg Hargis, January 1974. This was an informal conversation. Hargis did not know she was being recorded. NSC.

8   *But the Sperry mill closed in 1911*: Olive Steinbeck to Esther Steinbeck, February 1, 1911. Stanford M1063, 1/39.

9   *He complained of feeling "dippy"*: John Ernst Steinbeck to Esther Steinbeck, February 6, 1911. Stanford M1063, 1/41.

9   *He was, he confided*: John Ernst Steinbeck to Esther Steinbeck, February 6, 1911. Stanford M1063, 1/42.

9   *Olive reassured Esther that*: Olive Steinbeck to Esther Steinbeck, February 1, 1911. Stanford M1063, 1/39.

9   *They had been under the impression*: Ibid.

9   *John Ernst opened a feed store*: Pauline Pearson interview with Paul Pioda, March 17, 1975. NSC.

9   *Claus Spreckels was a German-born*: Breschini et al., *Early Salinas*, pp. 53–56.

9   *Main Street was wide*: Ibid., pp. 22–23, 33.

10 *There was an opera house in town*: Breschini et al., *10,000 Years on the Salinas Plain*, p. 55.

10 *There was a roller-skating rink*: Pauline Pearson interview with Paul Pioda, March 17, 1975. NSC.

10 *very evening at 8:00 p.m.*: Pauline Pearson interview with Henry J. Happ, September 29, 1981. NSC.

10 *Before Prohibition arrived in 1920*: Pauline Pearson interview with Herb Hinrichs, June 26, 1975. NSC.

10 *One, called the Stream, featured*: Breschini et al., *Early Salinas*, p. 28.

10 *There was a Chinatown*: Pauline Pearson interview with Sylvester Carriaga, March 17, 1981. NSC.

10 *John heard stories about*: Ibid.

10 *In early 1923*: Shillinglaw, *A Journey into Steinbeck's California*, p. 18.

10 *The job paid $250 a month*: Ibid.

10 *The Steinbeck children and their friends*: Salinas High School student interview with Dorothy Donahue, April 1968, and Pauline Pearson interview with Donahue, May 1975. NSC.

10 *John organized a boys' club*: Margaret Robinson and Pauline Pearson interviews with Glenn Graves, October and November 1974. NSC.

10 *He owned a terrier named Jiggs*: Ibid.

10 *One named Teddy figured in an incident*: Steinbeck to Kate Beswick, May 1, 1928. Stanford, M0263, 1/2.

11 *Ignatius Cooper, who belonged to*: Pauline Pearson interview with Ignatius Cooper, January 31, 1975. NSC.

11 *A joiner, she belonged to the*: Steinbeck, "Always Something to Do in Salinas," *Holiday*, June 1955.

11 *She was also a founder of*: Pauline Pearson interview with George Mors, April 4, 1980. NSC.

11 *When the town's first women's bridge club*: Paul Caswell interview with Mildred Kellogg Hargis, January 1974. NSC.

11 *John sometimes carried the cross*: Pauline Pearson interview with Herb Hinrichs, June 26, 1975. NSC.

11   *A piano stood in the Steinbecks' front parlor*: George Robinson, additional interview with Mildred Kellogg Hargis, December 8, 1976. NSC.

11   *One friend later recalled*: Pauline Pearson interview with William Black, July 6, 1975. (The story about the skull came from Max Wagner in his interview with Pearson, May 25, 1975.) NSC.

12   *She could make donuts*: Pauline Pearson interview with Max Wagner, May 25, 1975. NSC.

12   *One friend of John's thought*: George Robinson interview with Elvina Iverson Johnson, September 4, 1975. NSC.

12   *A girl who got invited to join*: Paul Caswell interview with Mildred Kellogg Hargis, January 1974. NSC.

12   *In the late 1800s, the area was*: McLane, *A Piney Paradise by Monterey Bay*, p. 3.

12   *In 1873, a Methodist minister from the East*: Ibid., p. 4.

12   *Eventually, the devout were outnumbered*: Ibid., p. 10.

13   *The Steinbeck cottage, small and square*: Personal observation. The cottage still stands at 147 Eleventh Street in Pacific Grove.

13   *The Gabilans, he thought, were friendly*: Steinbeck, *East of Eden*, p. 3.

13   *One time John's father helped drill a well*: Ibid., p. 4.

14   *Though he generally preferred his own*: Pauline Pearson interview with Max Wagner, May 25, 1975. NSC.

14   *The Graves property was big enough*: Margaret Robinson and Pauline Pearson interviews with Glenn Graves, October and November 1974. NSC.

14   *In the spring of 1906*: Ibid.

14   *Glenn once told his mother*: Pauline Pearson interview with George Mors, April 4, 1980. NSC.

14   *John told a classmate*: Pauline Pearson interview with Herb Hinrichs, June 26, 1975. NSC.

14   *When they were older*: Margaret Robinson and Pauline Pearson interviews with Glenn Graves, October and November 1974. NSC.

14   *Wagner had been born in Mexico*: Pauline Pearson interview with Max Wagner, May 25, 1975. NSC.

14   *John was delighted when he discovered*: Ibid.

15   *Wagner joined Glenn and John*: Ibid.

15   *Wagner later remembered*: Ibid.

15   *But the family demanded proper appearances*: Ibid.

15   *Once, when they were playing*: Ibid.

16   *Around 1906, John Ernst surprised John*: JSW, p. 14.

16   *Much later, Wagner would remember*: Pauline Pearson interview with Max Wagner, May 25, 1975. NSC.

16   *John was the ringleader*: Ibid.

16   *"He was a sharpie"*: Ibid.

16   *Wagner and Glenn Graves were privy*: Pauline Pearson interview with Max Wagner, May 25, 1975. NSC.

16   *John often visited his neighbors*: Margaret Robinson and Pauline Pearson interviews with Glenn Graves, October and November 1974. NSC.

16   *Another childhood friend said John liked talking*: Pauline Pearson interview with Sylvester Carriaga (the son), March 17, 1981. NSC.

17   *For a time, he struggled to read*: Steinbeck, *The Acts of King Arthur and His Noble Knights*, p. 1.

17   *Then, when he was nine*: Steinbeck to Mary Steinbeck Dekker, January 18, 1957. Apparently he was nine or ten.

18   *"I loved the old spelling"*: Steinbeck, *The Acts of King Arthur and His Noble Knights*, p. 1.

18   *John liked to ride Jill out into the fields*: JSW, p. 21.

18   *One summer John organized a trek*: George Robinson, additional interview with Mildred Kellogg Hargis, December 8, 1976. NSC.

19   *Like the other kids in Salinas*: Salinas High School student interview with Dorothy Donahue, April 1968, and Pauline Pearson, May 1975. NSC.

19   *After Baby School, John went*: Ibid.

19   *Sometimes he pretended*: Ibid.

19   *Unlike Mary, who would write*: John Ernst Steinbeck to Esther Steinbeck, January 20, 1911. Stanford, M1063, 1/38.

19   *John Ernst routinely asked*: John Ernst Steinbeck to Esther Steinbeck, October 27, 1910. Stanford, M1063, 1/31.

19   *His friends learned that if they*: Pauline Pearson interview with Sylvester Carriaga, March 17, 1981. NSC.

19   *Occasionally, he'd ask a few kids over*: Pauline Pearson interview with Max Wagner, May 25, 1975. NSC.

19   *One time Max Wagner showed up*: Ibid.

19   *The school was known as "the Old Brick Pile"*: Breschini et al., *Early Salinas*, p. 114. Beschini gives the nickname as the "Brick Yard," though "Brick Pile" seems to have been more common among Steinbeck's classmates.

19   *Elvina Iverson, a neighbor who came from*: George Robinson interview with Elvina Iverson Johnson, September 4, 1975. NSC.

20   *One year the English teacher required*: Pauline Pearson interview with Angelo Binsacca, October 3, 1975. NSC.

20   *Another girl who knew John*: Salinas High School student interview with Dorothy Donahue, April 1968, and Pauline Pearson, May 1975. NSC.

20   *Besides Malory, he read*: DeMott, *Steinbeck's Typewriter*, pp. 7–9.

20   *The Steinbeck house was full of books*: Ibid., p. 6.

20   *Some years later Steinbeck reckoned*: Steinbeck to Ben Abramson, February 1936. HRC.

21   *Almost everybody in the school attended*: Pauline Pearson interview with Elita Rose Hawley, December 9, 1974. NSC.

21   *He became interested in drama*: George Robinson interview with William Church, July 24, 1975. NSC.

21   *He was associate editor of*: El Gabilan, 1919. NSC.

21   *John was no athlete*: George Robinson interview with William Church, July 24, 1975. NSC.

21   *To everyone's astonishment*: El Gabilan, 1919. NSC.

21   *In 1895, the California National Guard*: Breschini et al., *10,000 Years on the Salinas Plain*, p. 63.

21   *One soldier in Pershing's army*: Berg, *Max Perkins*, photo insert after p. 246.

22   *The news reached Salinas a day later*: "Heir to Austrian Throne Slain by Young Student," *Salinas Daily Index*, June 29, 1914.

22   *In one battle that raged for months*: Strachan, *The First World War*, p. 195.

22   *Although many people in Salinas were*: Breschini et al., *Early Salinas*, pp. 100–101.

22   *Salinas High School maintained*: Pauline Pearson interview with Herb Hinrichs, June 26, 1975. NSC.

23   *Glenn Graves remembered a day*: Margaret Robinson and Pauline Pearson interviews with Glenn Tracy Graves, October and November 1974. NSC.

23   *Sometimes the boys went to*: Ibid.

23   *In the summers, the Cadets were often*: *El Gabilan*, 1919. NSC.

23   *One summer, John also did a stint*: Margaret Robinson and Pauline Pearson interviews with Glenn Tracy Graves, October and November 1974. NSC.

24   *John was good with his hands*: Pauline Pearson interview with Angelo Binsacca, October 3, 1975. NSC.

24   *The prediction for him*: Pauline Pearson interview with William Black, July 6, 1975. NSC.

24   *Max Wagner, who knew John*: Pauline Pearson interview with Max Wagner, May 25, 1975. NSC.

24   *Glenn Graves would sometimes wake up*: Margaret Robinson and Pauline Pearson interviews with Glenn Tracy Graves, October and November 1974. NSC.

24   *One day after school*: Pauline Pearson interview with William Black, July 6, 1975. NSC.

Chapter Two: Live, Not Hope to Live

25   *In October of 1919*: Sheffield, *John Steinbeck: The Good Companion*, p. 3. Steinbeck told his friend Ted Miller that his father acquired his first car "for Christmas" and that he was spending the first days of the new year teaching him how to drive it. Steinbeck to Ted Miller, January 7, 1931. Stanford, M0263, 2/2.

25   *The only other person*: Pauline Pearson interview with William Black, July 6, 1975. NSC.

25   *He'd sent some of them around*: JSW, p. 27.

26   *Opened in 1891*: Davis and Nilan, *The Stanford Album*, pp. 10–39.

26   *His father, a railroad tycoon*: Ibid., p. 10.

26   *Public sentiment had been against*: Tutorow, *The Governor*, vol. 2, p. 722.

26   *Unlike the elite eastern colleges*: Davis and Nilan, *The Stanford Album*, p. 41.

26   *Stanford occupied nearly 9,000 acres*: Ibid., p. 9.

27   *Inspired by a Swiss resort*: "The Bad Boys of Encina Hall," *Stanford* magazine, February 5, 2015.

27   *A favorite prank was*: Ibid.

27   *On registration day in October of 1919*: Pauline Pearson interview with George Mors, April 4, 1980. NSC.

27   *To Mors, Steinbeck seemed a friendly lug*: Ibid.

28   *In a sign of trouble to come*: Margaret Robinson and Pauline Pearson interviews with Glenn Graves, October and November 1974. NSC.

28   *Mors and Steinbeck roomed together*: Pauline Pearson interview with George Mors, April 4, 1980. NSC.

28   *Black had already tried to persuade*: Pauline Pearson interview with William Black, July 6, 1975. NSC.

28   *"We both liked John"*: Ibid.

28   *In the summer of 1920*: Pauline Pearson interview with George Mors, April 4, 1980. NSC.

28   *"You could only travel there on foot or horseback"*: Ibid.

28   *Steinbeck admitted he wasn't sure*: Pauline Pearson interview with Richard Albee, July 14, 1975. NSC.

28   *They worked only a short time*: Pauline Pearson interview with George Mors, April 4, 1980. NSC.

29   *She was pretty and had a figure*: Ibid.

29   *John Ernst asked Mors to*: Ibid.

29   *John Ernst came up to Stanford*: Ibid.

29   *Eventually they learned*: Ibid.

29   *Mrs. Mors spent several days*: Pauline Pearson interview with George Mors, April 4, 1980. NSC.

29   *They were in two classes together*: Pauline Pearson interview with Dook Sheffield, January 19, 1975. NSC.

29   *Sheffield remembered*: Ibid.

29   *Steinbeck told Sheffield story after story*: Sheffield, *John Steinbeck: The Good Companion*, p. 14.

30   *According to Sheffield, Steinbeck joined*: Pauline Pearson interview with Dook Sheffield, January 19, 1975. NSC.

30   *Sheffield said Steinbeck worked for a time*: Ibid.

30   *Steinbeck and Sheffield enjoyed boxing*: Ibid.

30   *In the spring of 1921*: Ibid. The conflict between Sheffield's and Mors's recollections are unresolvable but leave the same impression, that it was hard to keep track of Steinbeck during his Stanford days.

30   *Early one year—probably 1923*: Steinbeck to John Ernst Steinbeck, circa fall 1923. Stanford, M1063, 1/71.

31   *In the university's early days*: Davis and Nilan, *The Stanford Album*, pp. 109–11.

31   *Administrators' attempts to impede*: Ibid.

32   *At Stanford, alcohol was an essential*: Ibid.

32   *For the 1922 game, Steinbeck arrived*: Sheffield, *John Steinbeck: The Good Companion*, p. 8.

32   *Late one night, he came back to their room*: Ibid., pp. 24–25.

33   *On several occasions, Steinbeck came into*: Pauline Pearson interview with Dook Sheffield, January 19, 1975. NSC.

33   *One author he admired*: Ibid.

33   *Steinbeck also discovered*: Ibid.

33   *Sometimes, Sheffield said, Steinbeck would "try*: Ibid.

33   *Sheffield said Steinbeck shrugged this off*: Ibid.

33   *During his on-again, off-again career*: Sheffield, *John Steinbeck: The Good Companion*, p. 42.

34   *He completed fourteen English classes*: DeMott, *Steinbeck's Typewriter*, p. 9.

34   *In the spring of 1923*: Sheffield, *John Steinbeck: The Good Companion*, p. 28.

34   *I shall have really lived*: Untitled student poem, Sheffield, *John Steinbeck: The Good Companion*, p. 202.

34   *He got in after dark and had trouble*: Ibid., p. 33.

34   *He asked them to wait in the car*: Ibid., pp. 36–37.

34   *Before Sheffield left, the four of them*: Ibid., pp. 37–38.

35   *That summer, with Sheffield off to*: Ibid., p. 39.

35   *When they looked at them together years later*: Ibid., pp. 38–39.

35   *There was a group of Filipinos*: Ibid., p. 40.

35   *The following summer, Steinbeck and Sheffield*: Ibid., pp. 53–61.

35   *Street was a veteran who'd lost an eye*: George Robinson interview with Toby Street, April 27, 1975. NSC.

36   *Bailey had a house on campus*: Ibid.

36   *Bailey, for her part*: Sheffield, *John Steinbeck: The Good Companion*, p. 71.

36   *Beswick would eventually see*: "Marriage" and "To a Complacent Murderer," *Poetry*, June 1930.

36   *Toby Street said that*: George Robinson interview with Toby Street, April 27, 1975. NSC.

36   *But Steinbeck had made it comfortable*: Steinbeck to Carl Wilhelmson, n.d. 1924. Stanford, M0263, 7/6.

36   *The finishing touch was*: Ibid.

36   *Toby Street had the impression that*: George Robinson interview with Toby Street, April 27, 1975. NSC.

37   *He'd finished several stories*: Steinbeck to Carl Wilhelmson, n.d. 1924. Stanford, M0263, 7/6.

37   *Steinbeck did manage to publish*: *Stanford Spectator* 2, no. 5 (February 1924); *Stanford Spectator* 2, no. 9 (June 1924).

38   *Her name was Elizabeth Smith, but*: George Robinson interview with Toby Street, April 27, 1975. NSC.

38   *Steinbeck thought Breck had technical skill*: Steinbeck to Carl Wilhelmson, n.d. 1924. Stanford, M0263, 7/6.

38   *So Steinbeck didn't think much of it*: Sheffield, *John Steinbeck: The Good Companion*, pp. 78–79.

40   *As an academic discipline*: McGurl, *The Program Era*, p. 5.

40   *It wasn't until 1946*: Ibid., p. 184.

40   *Steinbeck enrolled in a class*: Sheffield, *John Steinbeck: The Good Companion*, p. 71.

40   *Two people died at Stanford in the quake*: Davis and Nilan, *The Stanford Album*, pp. 104–5.

41   *Mirrielees graduated a year later*: Ibid., p. 66.

41   *Slight and unassuming, Mirrielees in 1917*: Ibid., p. 161.

41   *Steinbeck hoped she could teach him*: Mirrielees, *Story Writing*, p. vi.

41   *At most, she said*: Ibid., pp. 3–5.

41   *[I]t is by no means necessary*: Ibid., p. 15.

42   *The story was titled*: Sheffield, *John Steinbeck: The Good Companion*, p. 71.

42   *In the fall of 1919*: Berg, *Max Perkins*, pp. 15–16.

42   *After Perkins prevailed*: Ibid., p. 16.

43 *In his review for the literary magazine*: Ibid., p. 19.

44 *In the fall of 1924*: Ibid., p. 63.

44 *Perkins wrote some months later*: Ibid., p. 87.

44 *Steinbeck was wary of Hemingway*: Sheffield, *John Steinbeck: The Good Companion*, p. 49.

44 *He told Dook Sheffield*: Ibid.

44 *Explain the point of a story*: Mirrielees, *Story Writing*, p. vii.

45 *In the spring of 1925*: Sheffield, *John Steinbeck: The Good Companion*, p. 42.

Chapter Three: The Long Winter

46 *John Steinbeck got his first glimpse*: "Autobiography: Making of a New Yorker," *New York Times*, February 1, 1953.

46 *Just before his final two quarters*: Steinbeck to Carl Wilhelmson, n.d. 1924. Stanford, M0263, 7/6.

46 *In November, he went down*: Sheffield, *John Steinbeck: The Good Companion*, pp. 79–80.

47 *Steinbeck watched gray whales*: Ibid., pp. 83–84.

48 *But Ainsworth paid for a night*: "Autobiography: Making of a New Yorker," *New York Times*, February 1, 1953.

49 *According to Dook Sheffield*: Sheffield, *John Steinbeck: The Good Companion*, p. 84.

49 *Steinbeck had rented a*: "Autobiography: Making of a New Yorker," *New York Times*, February 1, 1953.

49 *It was like a "fever dream"*: Ibid.

49 *Steinbeck didn't know what to do next*: Ibid.

49 *Joe Hamilton knew somebody*: Ibid.

49 *The pay was $25 a week*: Ibid.

49 *Steinbeck liked exploring New York*: Steinbeck to his family, n.d. Stanford, M1063, 1/79.

49 *Steinbeck worried that he was given*: Ibid.

50 *His hope was that*: Ibid.

50 *At Christmas he sent home some*: Steinbeck to his family, December 25, 1925. Stanford, M1063, 1/80.

50 *He told his parents he was doing fine*: Steinbeck to his family, n.d. Stanford, M1063, 1/79.

50 *Unhappily for Steinbeck*: "Autobiography: Making of a New Yorker," *New York Times*, February 1, 1953.

50 *They all worked in a single room*: Steinbeck to his family, n.d. Stanford, M1063, 1/79.

50 *Steinbeck later wondered if*: "Autobiography: Making of a New Yorker," *New York Times*, February 1, 1953.

50 *Steinbeck had moved to a sixth-floor room*: Ibid.

50 *On a gloomy afternoon*: Steinbeck to George Hamilton, n.d. 1926. Stanford, M1063, 1/81.

50 *As he continued, it became clear*: Ibid.

51   *Her name was Mary Ardath*: JSW, p. 93. Dook Sheffield, whose later recollections of his friendship with Steinbeck were sometimes inaccurate, remembered her as a concert pianist. He said that Steinbeck told him they lived in neighboring buildings and had "met" by seeing each other through their windows. Steinbeck, blurring the story further, claimed that he'd known her in California before coming to New York.

51   *She made enough money to take Steinbeck*: "Autobiography: Making of a New Yorker," *New York Times*, February 1, 1953.

51   *Steinbeck told his parents*: Steinbeck to his parents, March 5, 1926. Stanford, M1063, 1/83.

51   *He had shown half a dozen short stories*: Sheffield, *John Steinbeck: The Good Companion*, pp. 88–89.

51   *The city was beginning to close in*: "Autobiography: Making of a New Yorker," *New York Times*, February 1, 1953.

52   *Somehow he finished six more stories*: Sheffield, *John Steinbeck: The Good Companion*, pp. 89–90.

52   *He told Dook Sheffield that*: Ibid.

52   *But in May, he wrote a worryingly*: Steinbeck to his parents, May 25, 1926. Stanford, M1063, 1/86.

52   *Steinbeck also wrote to his sister Esther*: Steinbeck to Esther (Steinbeck) Rodgers, n.d. spring 1926. Stanford, M1063, 1/87.

53   *Steinbeck wrote to thank them*: Steinbeck to his parents, n.d. spring 1926. Stanford M1063, 1/88.

53   *Spring gave way to summer*: Sheffield, *John Steinbeck: The Good Companion*, pp. 90–91.

53   *"The city had beaten the pants"*: "Autobiography: Making of a New Yorker," *New York Times*, February 1, 1953.

53   *Halfway home, Steinbeck wrote*: Steinbeck to his parents, n.d. fall 1926. Stanford, M1063, 1/89.

53   *Steinbeck said he had gotten into*: Sheffield, *John Steinbeck: The Good Companion*, p. 91.

53   *Steinbeck wrote to congratulate*: Steinbeck to his parents, November 11, 1926. Stanford, M1063, 1/92.

54   *The courthouse was sometimes referred to*: George Robinson interview with Elvina Iverson Johnson, September 4, 1975. NSC.

54   *Olive never went there*: Ibid.

54   *In 1882, Dr. Charles Brooks Brigham*: Scott, *The Saga of Lake Tahoe*, pp. 139–41.

54   *The naturalist and wilderness advocate*: Ibid., p. 141.

55   *little cabin*: Steinbeck to his parents, n.d. fall 1926. M1063, 1/90. Steinbeck didn't always date his correspondence, so for some letters the date must be inferred. The curators at Stanford have done this in some cases by assigning such letters the same date as the postmarks on their envelopes when those exist. Obviously, Steinbeck often wrote letters that didn't get to the post office the same day, and dates assigned to undated letters should be regarded as approximations. This letter was dated merely "Sunday." Steinbeck's next letter was sent on Monday, November 1. So my guess is this letter was written on October 31.

55   *Ducks were beginning to appear*: Ibid.

55   *Steinbeck enjoyed eating snowshoe rabbit*: Ibid.

55 *He confessed that he had no idea*: Ibid.

55 *The first white man to see it*: Landauer, *The Mountain Sea*, p. 30.

56 *Through the first part of November*: Steinbeck to his parents, November 1, 1926. Stanford, M1063, 1/91.

56 *Steinbeck wrote to Street*: Steinbeck to Toby Street, n.d. 1926. ALL, pp. 3–4. I cite here, for the first time but not the last, *Steinbeck: A Life in Letters*, by Elaine Steinbeck and Robert Wallsten. Some letters published in this expansive collection—including this one—are edited versions of originals that reside in archives where I also worked. Others are reproduced verbatim. I have relied equally on both the published and the unpublished correspondence.

56 *He asked Street to send him*: Ibid.

56 *Steinbeck encouraged Street*: Ibid.

57 *One time Wilhelmson had defended*: Steinbeck to his parents, n.d. April 1927. Stanford, M1063, 2/34.

57 *Steinbeck told him that he hoped*: Steinbeck to Carl Wilhelmson, n.d. June 1928. Stanford, M0263, 7/6.

57 *Wilhelmson was in his element*: Steinbeck to his parents, n.d. December 1926. Stanford, M1063, 1/96.

58 *In December, the snow continued*: Ibid.

58 *The snow was so powdery*: Ibid.

58 *The dog had to "worm along"*: Ibid.

58 *Steinbeck wrote to his parents asking*: Ibid.

58 *In March, Steinbeck got a surprise*: Nakayama, *Uncollected Stories of John Steinbeck*, pp. 62–76.

58 *Steinbeck's friend, the well-connected*: JSW, 113.

58 *His sister Mary had become engaged*: Steinbeck to his parents, n.d. April 1927. Stanford, M1063, 2/6.

59 *He'd sent fifty pages of his manuscript*: Steinbeck to his parents, n.d. April 1927. Stanford, M1063, 2/6.

59 *He told his parents he'd caught a nine-pound*: Steinbeck to his parents, n.d. April 1927, Stanford, M1063, 2/7.

59 *Summer at Lake Tahoe was pleasant*: Steinbeck to his parents, July 1, 1927. Stanford, M1063, 2/14.

59 *He promised to make sure*: Steinbeck to Carl Wilhelmson, n.d. fall 1927. Stanford, M0263, 7/6. The date of this letter is uncertain. Stanford gives it as September 5, 1928, but it had to have been the previous year.

60 *While Steinbeck waited for Wilhelmson*: Steinbeck to his parents, n.d. fall 1927. Stanford, M1063, 2/25.

60 *The wind, meanwhile, moaned*: Steinbeck to his parents, n.d. fall 1927. Stanford, M1063 2/33.

60 *Blaine had a contract*: Steinbeck to his parents, n.d. fall 1927. Stanford, M1063, 2/34.

60 *Steinbeck called it a "biographical novel"*: Ibid.

61 *By December, Steinbeck had finished*: Steinbeck to his parents, n.d. December 1927. Stanford, M1063, 2/36.

61 *Just before Christmas, they paused*: Steinbeck to his parents, December 23, 1927. Stanford, M1063, 2/37.

61 *At the end of January*: Steinbeck to his parents, January 31, 1928. Stanford, M1063, 2/47.

61 *Before Wilhelmson left*: Steinbeck to his parents, February 4, 1928. Sanford, M1063, 2/49.

61 *It was tempting, but Steinbeck*: Ibid.

62 *It rained and rained*: Steinbeck to his parents, March 24, 1928. Stanford, M1063, 2/54.

62 *The level of the lake rose nearly*: Steinbeck to his parents, March 31, 1928. Stanford, M1063, 2/55.

62 *A stretch of highway and a stone bridge*: Steinbeck to his parents, n.d. spring 1928. Stanford, M0163, 2/56.

62 *Lloyd Shebley came and*: Steinbeck to his parents, March 24, 1928. Stanford, M1063, 2/54.

62 *"Lord how it snows"*: Steinbeck to his parents, March 31, 1928. Stanford, M1063, 2/55.

62 *He had been offered a job*: Steinbeck to his parents, March 24, 1928. Stanford, M1063, 2/54.

62 *Steinbeck sent his manuscript to Toby Street*: Steinbeck to Toby Street, n.d. 1928. Stanford, M0263, 5/25.

63 *When Miller read the manuscript*: Steinbeck to Kate Beswick, n.d. summer 1928. Stanford, M0263, 1/3.

63 *Steinbeck, who somehow deduced*: Ibid.

63 *At the end of February, he told Dook Sheffield*: Steinbeck to Dook Sheffield, February 25, 1928. Stanford, M2063, 5/8.

63 *Much as he wanted to begin*: Ibid.

63 *Steinbeck wondered if the "sharp agony"*: Ibid.

63 *He had been "drunken"*: Ibid.

63 *"It is sad," Steinbeck said in closing*: Ibid.

Chapter Four: Carol

65 *That spring, Steinbeck told a friend*: Steinbeck to Robert Cathcart, April 14, 1928. Stanford, M0263, 1/10.

65 *He wrote to Kate Beswick that*: Steinbeck to Kate Beswick, May 1, 1928. Stanford, M0263, 1/2.

65 *He wrote to Kate Beswick*: Steinbeck to Kate Beswick, n.d. May 1928. Stanford, M0263, 1/2.

66 *Luridly, Steinbeck told her*: Ibid.

66 *Celibacy, he said*: Steinbeck to Kate Beswick, n.d. June 1928. Stanford, M0263, 1/4.

66 *Steinbeck's insistence that he'd had*: Ibid.

66 *Work resumed at the fish hatchery*: Steinbeck to Kate Beswick, n.d. June 1928. Stanford, M0263, 1/4. There is more than one undated letter from June in this folder.

66 *He reassured himself that there would be*: Steinbeck to Kate Beswick, n.d. June 1928. Stanford, M0263, 1/4.

66   *Between shifts at the hatchery*: Steinbeck to Kate Beswick, June 26, 1928. Stanford, M0263, 1/4.

66   *"I thought I was too old to be stricken"*: Ibid.

66   *She and her sister, Idell, had come to Lake Tahoe*: CAJ, pp. 36–37.

66   *Carol worked at the Schilling spice company*: Ibid., p. 32.

66   *She owned her own car*: Ibid., p. 33.

66   *He didn't let the sisters leave*: Ibid., p. 37.

67   *He found Steinbeck and Carol*: Sheffield, *John Steinbeck: The Good Companion*, p. 99.

67   *Sheffield, who read the manuscript and the typescript*: Ibid., p. 100.

67   *When the sisters went back*: Ibid., p. 102.

67   *Toward the end of summer*: Steinbeck to Kate Beswick, n.d. August 1928. Stanford, M0263, 1/4.

67   *Steinbeck had heard nothing from Ted Miller*: Ibid.

67   *The book had been turned down twice*: Steinbeck to Kate Beswick, n.d. September 1928. Stanford, M0263, 1/4.

68   *That same month, Steinbeck decided*: Steinbeck to Kate Beswick, n.d. September 1928. Stanford, M0263.

68   *He told her that after his long celibacy*: Ibid.

68   *He found a job in a jute mill*: Steinbeck to Kate Beswick, September 30, 1928. Stanford, M0263, 1/4.

69   *Steinbeck admitted that the jute mill*: Steinbeck to Kate Beswick, n.d. November 1928. Stanford, M0263, 1/4.

69   *He asked Kate if he should rewrite it*: Steinbeck to Kate Beswick, n.d. late 1928. Stanford, M0263, 1/5.

69   *"I should like this opus to go to McBride's"*: Ibid.

69   *One weekend Steinbeck went down to Palo Alto*: Steinbeck to Kate Beswick, n.d. late 1928. Stanford, M0263, 1/5. Here again, there is more than one undated letter in this same folder. Where consecutive citations are identical, rather than "Ibid.," they refer to different letters.

69   *Street insisted that they call on*: Ibid.

69   *Street had written to tell him*: Steinbeck to his parents, September 15, 1927. Stanford, M1063, 2/18.

69   *Steinbeck confided to Beswick he had hoped*: Steinbeck to Kate Beswick, n.d. late 1928. Stanford, M0263, 1/5.

69   *Polly and a friend were vacationing*: JSW, pp. 136–37.

69   *After an abject apology*: Ibid., p. 137.

70   *Breck came to the door*: Steinbeck to Kate Beswick, n.d. late 1928. Stanford, M0263, 1/5.

70   *In a letter to Beswick, Steinbeck mentioned*: Steinbeck to Kate Beswick, n.d. late 1928. Stanford, M0263, 1/5.

70   *But Steinbeck insisted that she should not*: Steinbeck to Kate Beswick, n.d. December 1928. M0263, 1/4.

70   *He told Beswick that if she were rich*: Ibid.

70   *Steinbeck heard at last*: Steinbeck to Kate Beswick, December 17, 1928. Stanford, M0263, 1/4.

70   *He told Beswick he was headed*: Ibid.

71   *"I shall write and write"*: Ibid.

71   *On New Year's Eve*: Steinbeck to Kate Beswick, January 22, 1929. Stanford, Mo263, 1/6.

71   *Ted Miller wrote Steinbeck*: Steinbeck to Kate Beswick, n.d. late 1928. Stanford, Mo263, 1/5.

71   *Steinbeck told Beswick that some*: Steinbeck to Kate Beswick, n.d. December 1928. Stanford, Mo263, 1/4.

71   *Apparently that was going to be*: Steinbeck to Kate Beswick, January 2, 1929. Stanford, Mo263, 1/6.

71   *On January 21, 1929*: Ted Miller to Steinbeck, January 23, 1929. Stanford, Mo263, 7/13.

71   *Miller wired Steinbeck*: Ibid.

71   *Mahlon Blaine, who seemed to have*: Ibid.

71   *It was too late to add*: Ibid.

72   *Miller said they told him*: Ibid.

72   *Miller warned Steinbeck*: Ibid.

Chapter Five: Crash

73   *At Stanford, Edith Mirrielees had advised*: Mirrielees, *Story Writing*, p. viii.

73   *Carol had visited Steinbeck in Pacific Grove*: Steinbeck to Kate Beswick, January 28, 1929. Stanford, Mo263, 1/6.

73   *But when Carol left*: Ibid.

73   *Sometimes it felt as if a demon*: Steinbeck to Kate Beswick, n.d. February 1929. Stanford, Mo263, 1/6.

74   *He told Kate Beswick he wouldn't come east*: Steinbeck to Kate Beswick, n.d. February 1929. Stanford, Mo263, 1/6.

74   *She and Steinbeck were in bed one morning*: Steinbeck to Kate Beswick, February 19, 1929. Stanford, Mo263, 1/6.

74   *Steinbeck claimed he was having an affair*: Steinbeck to Kate Beswick, n.d. February 1929, Stanford, Mo263, 1/7.

75   *In March, Steinbeck got a look*: Steinbeck to Kate Beswick, n.d. March 1929. Stanford, Mo263, 1/7.

75   *Steinbeck was "a little shocked"*: Ibid.

75   *He also mentioned that he planned*: Steinbeck to Kate Beswick, n.d. March 1929. Stanford, Mo263, 1/7.

75   *By the end of April*: Steinbeck to Kate Beswick, n.d. late April 1929. Stanford, Mo263, 1/7.

75   *An early fragment of the novel's manuscript*: Stanford, Mo263, 8/14, 8/15, 8/16, 8/17, and 8/18.

76   *Sometime over the summer*: Steinbeck to Kate Beswick, August 15, 1929. Stanford, Mo263, 1/8.

76   *He was working feverishly*: Steinbeck to Kate Beswick, n.d. early September 1929. Stanford, Mo263, 1/8.

76   *He figured he'd owe*: Ibid.

76   *But when he showed part of it*: Ibid.

76   *Street would later insist*: George Robinson interview with Toby Street, April 27, 1975. NSC.

76   *Annoyed by Street's criticism*: Steinbeck to Kate Beswick, n.d. early September 1929. Stanford, Mo263, 1/8.

76   *Steinbeck said he had hoped*: Ibid.

76   *But in the end he got only*: Ibid.

76   *Steinbeck had heard that*: Ibid.

76   *Writing in the* New York Herald Tribune: TCR, p. 3.

77   *A review in the* St. Louis Star: Ibid.

77   *In December, a long review by Paul Teal*: Ibid., p. 5.

77   *This was an improvement over*: Ibid., p. 4.

78   *In April of 1924*: Berg, *Max Perkins*, pp. 60–67.

78   *The Great Gatsby sold slowly*: Ibid., pp. 82–83.

78   *The reviews were mixed*: Bruccoli, *Some Sort of Epic Grandeur*, p. 221.

78   *Scribner's first printing of 21,000 copies*: Ibid., p. 220.

78   *Gatsby was decisively outsold by*: Ibid., p. 221.

79   *American drivers of both kinds*: Cowley, *Exile's Return*, pp. 37–38.

79   *After the war, Cowley lived for a time*: Ibid., pp. 48–80.

79   *American writers were "launching or drifting"*: Ibid., p. 19.

79   *"Literature, our profession"*: Ibid.

80   *As Malcolm Cowley observed decades later*: Ibid., p. 42.

81   *An unsigned review in the* New York Times: "Marital Tragedy," *New York Times*, October 31, 1926.

81   *Hemingway said that he developed his*: Hemingway, *A Moveable Feast*, p. 13.

81   *He claimed that the lean syntax*: Ibid.

83   *The* New York Times *reported that the total losses*: "Losses Recovered in Part," *New York Times*, October 25, 1929.

83   *The humorist Will Rogers*: "The Jumpers of '29," *Washington Post*, October 25, 1987.

83   *In the middle of that terrible day*: "Financiers Ease Tension," *New York Times*, October 25, 1929.

83   *"As word went out in Wall Street"*: Ibid.

84   *Thomas W. Lamont, senior partner at J.P. Morgan*: Ibid.

84   *Things were back to normal on Friday*: "Wall Street Hums on the Day of Rest to Catch Up on Work," *New York Times*, October 28, 1929.

84   *But on Monday the markets plunged*: "Premier Issues Hard Hit," *New York Times*, October 29, 1929.

84   *Share prices of many*: Ibid.

84   *On October 29, stock prices collapsed*: "Closing Rally Vigorous," *New York Times*, October 30, 1929. The *Times*'s strangely optimistic headline did not capture the substance of the story, an otherwise glum summary of Black Tuesday.

85   *But in the end, the day that would come to be known*: Ibid.

85   *Fewer than one in ten Americans*: Watkins, *The Great Depression*, p. 54.

85   *In Florida, land speculators had created*: Galbraith, *The Great Crash 1929*, pp. 18–19.

85   *This was a feature*: Ibid., pp. 11, 169.

85   *Some people blamed the banks*: Ibid., p. 169.

85   *"Speculation on a large scale"*: Ibid.

85   *He insured it for $500*: Steinbeck to Kate Beswick, n.d. late September 1929. Stanford, Mo263, 1/8.

86   *Steinbeck's struggle with* The Green Lady: Ibid.

86   *When he heard from Ted Miller*: Steinbeck to Kate Beswick, n.d. October 1929. Stanford, Mo263, 1/8.

86   *McBride's efforts on behalf*: Steinbeck to Kate Beswick, October 8, 1929. Stanford, Mo263, 1/8.

86   *Steinbeck was most upset*: Steinbeck to Kate Beswick, October 21, 1929. Stanford, Mo263, 1/8.

86   *He and Carol had gone*: Ibid.

86   *He felt as though he'd already written*: Steinbeck to Kate Beswick, November 21, 1929. Stanford, Mo263, 1/8.

87   *He still wanted to go to New York*: Ibid.

87   *In the late fall of 1929*: Sheffield, *John Steinbeck: The Good Companion*, pp. 112–13.

87   *Steinbeck, Carol, and the Lovejoys*: Ibid., pp. 110–12.

87   *It all started with Ritchie*: Ibid.

87   *The Russians, Sheffield said*: Ibid., p. 114.

88   *And then, on January 14, 1930*: Marriage license, County of Los Angeles, January 14, 1930.

89   *On the marriage certificate*: Ibid.

89   *Celebrating back at the Sheffields'*: Ibid., p. 124.

89   *When he updated Kate Beswick*: Steinbeck to Kate Beswick, January 20, 1930. Stanford, Mo263, 1/8.

89   *Obtaining the house had been*: Sheffield, *John Steinbeck: The Good Companion*, p. 121.

89   *She saw potential in it*: Ibid.

89   *Steinbeck told Beswick he was ready*: Steinbeck to Kate Beswick, January 20, 1930. Stanford, Mo263, 1/8.

89   *The Sheffields liked sunbathing*: Sheffield, *John Steinbeck: The Good Companion*. pp. 132–33.

89   *One day, when it was just the Sheffields*: Ibid.

90   *When at last Steinbeck agreed*: Ibid.

90   *When Steinbeck finished* The Green Lady: Steinbeck to Kate Beswick, n.d. March 1930. Stanford, Mo263, 1/8.

90   *Sometime in early April 1930 he sent it*: Steinbeck to Kate Beswick, n.d. April 1930. Stanford, Mo263, 1/8.

90   *Beswick suggested submitting*: Ibid.

90   *The owners of the ancient house*: Sheffield, *John Steinbeck: The Good Companion*, pp. 133–34.

90   *Steinbeck and Carol moved*: Ibid., p. 134.

91   *Steinbeck and Carol split everything*: Steinbeck to Kate Beswick, n.d. April 1930. Stanford, Mo263, 1/8.

91   *"I'd be happier if I had a rejection"*: Steinbeck to Kate Beswick, n.d. May 1930. Stanford, Mo263, 1/8.

91   *McBride finally did reject*: Steinbeck to Kate Beswick, n.d. late July 1930. Stanford, Mo263, 1/9.

91   *Steinbeck acknowledged there was*: Steinbeck to Kate Beswick, August 6, 1930. Stanford, Mo263, 1/9.

91   *He finished a short manuscript*: Ibid.

91   *He told Kate Beswick he was going to*: Ibid.

91   *According to Dook Sheffield*: Sheffield, *John Steinbeck: The Good Companion*, pp. 129–30.

91   *The Sheffields liked to have people over*: Pauline Pearson interview with Richard Albee, February 23, 1975. NSC.

92   *When the latest house they were renting*: Steinbeck to Kate Beswick, August 6, 1930. Stanford, M0263, 1/9.

93   *Steinbeck said they'd be glad*: Ibid.

93   *In 1935, a woman in Kansas*: Jennie Babb to Sanora Babb, n.d. 1935. HRC.

Chapter Six: Such Good Friends as These

95   *When Steinbeck heard nothing*: Steinbeck to Kate Beswick, n.d. October 1930. Stanford, M0263, 1/9.

95   *Ted Miller had sent*: Ibid.

95   *Carol's mother had come*: Ibid.

95   *They had a new dog, an Airedale*: CAJ, p. 69.

95   *Steinbeck added a stone barbecue pit*: Steinbeck to Kate Beswick, n.d. October 1930. Stanford, M0263, 1/9.

95   *His most ambitious project*: Ibid.

96   *He even went into Palo Alto*: Ibid.

96   *Toby Street visited Pacific Grove*: Ibid.

96   *He and Steinbeck had had a passing acquaintance*: George Robinson interview with Carol Steinbeck Brown, May 1, 1977. NSC.

96   *There was a short-lived promise*: Steinbeck to Kate Beswick, n.d. early 1931. Stanford, M0263, 1/9.

96   *By then Steinbeck had resumed work*: Steinbeck to Carl Wilhelmson, October 1, 1930. Stanford, M0263, 7/6.

97   *He confided to Wilhelmson*: Ibid.

97   *"I don't know if he is shrinking"*: Ibid.

97   *When he wrote Wilhelmson again*: Steinbeck to Carl Wilhelmson, October 20, 1930. Stanford, M0263, 7/7.

97   *He told Wilhelmson he'd been at a party*: Ibid.

98   *They fished and caught crabs and eels*: Steinbeck to Kate Beswick, n.d. early 1931. Stanford, M0263, 1/9.

98   *On many days*: CAJ, p. 66.

98   *"We are very happy"*: Steinbeck to Kate Beswick, n.d. October 1930. Stanford, M0263, 1/9.

98   *Then McBride informed Steinbeck*: Steinbeck to Kate Beswick, November 14, 1930. Stanford, M0263, 1/9.

98   *Steinbeck said it was being met*: Ibid.

98   *He told Kate Beswick that all he needed*: Ibid.

98   *"Honestly," he said*: Ibid.

99   *In December 1930, he surprised Miller*: Steinbeck to Ted Miller, n.d. December 1930. ALL, pp. 32–33.

99   *Only a few days before*: Steinbeck to Ted (and "Mrs. Ted") Miller, December 3, 1930. Stanford, Mo263, 2/2.

99   *Now he reminded Miller that*: Steinbeck to Ted Miller, n.d. December 1930. ALL, pp. 32–33.

99   *He claimed he'd written* Murder at Full Moon: Ibid.

99   *In early January 1931*: Steinbeck to Ted Miller, January 7, 1931. Stanford, Mo263, 2/2.

100   *And then he got to*: Steinbeck to Ted Miller (enclosed with), January 7, 1931. Stanford, Mo263, 2/2.

100   *Steinbeck knew which agent*: Ibid.

100   *Miller, no doubt pleased*: ALL, p. 40. Citations from *Steinbeck: A Life in Letters* that do not reference a specific letter refer instead to one of the many comments included throughout from editors Elaine Steinbeck and Robert Wallsten.

100   *Carl Wilhelmson had finished another novel*: Steinbeck to Ted Miller (enclosed with), January 7, 1931. Stanford, Mo263, 2/2.

100   *Just a couple of months after*: Steinbeck, "About Ed Ricketts," appendix to *The Log from the Sea of Cortez*, p. 229.

101   *Ricketts's sister Frances backed up*: Rodger, *Renaissance Man of Cannery Row*, pp. xxii–xxiii.

101   *But other people who knew them*: George Robinson interview with Carol Steinbeck Brown, May 1, 1977. NSC.

101   *Carol's memory was that she*: Ibid.

101   *Ricketts was compact—under five feet six inches*: Ricketts's draft registration gave his height as five feet seven inches, though that could simply be the information he provided. A perhaps more honest estimate came from Toby Street, who said Ricketts was shorter than Burgess Meredith, a frequent guest at the lab. Meredith was five feet six inches. Pauline Pearson interview with Toby Street, December 3, 1978. NSC.

101   *"He had a neatly trimmed, red-brown-golden beard"*: George Robinson interview with Carol Steinbeck Brown, May 1, 1977. NSC.

101   *Edward Flanders Ricketts was born*: Rodger, *Renaissance Man of Cannery Row*, p. xv.

101   *At eighteen, he briefly attended*: Hedgpeth, *The Outer Shores*, Part 1, pp. 3–5.

102   *Ricketts left the University of Chicago*: Ibid., pp. 4–5.

102   *He roomed for a time*: Rodger, *Renaissance Man of Cannery Row*, pp. xx–xxi.

102   *He and Nan and the baby settled*: Hedgpeth, *The Outer Shores*, Part 1, p. 8.

102   *Ricketts and Galigher restarted their business*: Rodger, *Renaissance Man of Cannery Row*, p. xxi.

103   *Researchers over at the Hopkins station*: Hedgpeth, *The Outer Shores*, Part 1, pp. 6–8.

103   *Ricketts was a compulsive organizer*: Rows of Ricketts's meticulously detailed index cards today sit neatly in the stacks of the Hopkins station library.

103   *The company was headquartered in a warehouse*: Hedgpeth, *The Outer Shores*, Part 1, p. 6.

103   *Three stories high, Holman's covered*: McLane, *A Piney Paradise by Monterey Bay*, p. 169.

103   *Ricketts and Galigher parted ways*: Rodger, *Renaissance Man of Cannery Row*, pp. xxi–xxii.

103   *In 1928, Ricketts moved*: Hemp, *Cannery Row*, p. 99.

104   *This was the California sardine*: Ibid., p. 61.

104   *In the 1920s, as bigger, diesel-powered boats*: Ibid., pp. 54–56.

104   *At one time there were sixteen cross-overs*: Ibid., p. 86.

105   *In the early 1920s*: Ibid., p. 54.

105   *In the 1934–35 season*: Ibid., p. 83.

105   *The reckoning came in*: Ibid., p. 82.

105   *Ricketts's lab was in a little house dwarfed*: Ibid., pp. 94–100.

105   *The Wing Chong Market was*: Ibid., pp. 118–21.

105   *Somehow, Ricketts never seemed to notice*: Steinbeck, "About Ed Ricketts," appendix to *The Log from the Sea of Cortez*, p. 265.

105   *He left space for a handwritten chart*: George Robinson interview with Carol Steinbeck Brown, May 1, 1977. NSC.

106   *The Lloyds had saved enough money*: George Robinson interview with Marjory Lloyd, April 7, 1976. NSC.

106   *Xenia had lost her virginity*: Tamm, *Beyond the Outer Shores*, pp. 15–16. Steinbeck mentions this indiscretion—an outrage by today's standards—in his profile of Ricketts for *The Log from the Sea of Cortez*: "When I first met him he was engaged in a scholarly and persistent way in the process of deflowering a young girl." Steinbeck's jocular, boys-will-be-boys tone coarsens the unseemliness of the story.

107   *Marjory Lloyd, who was only twenty-two*: George Robinson interview with Marjory Lloyd, April 7, 1976. NSC.

107   *Carol, on the other hand*: Ibid.

107   *With everyone drinking wine, smoking*: Ibid.

108   *Marjory said that because nobody*: Ibid.

108   *Sometimes the Steinbecks would talk everyone into*: Pauline Pearson interview with Marjory Lloyd, April 28, 1987. NSC.

108   *Marjory found Ed Ricketts quiet and gentle*: Ibid.

108   *Carol considered Ricketts introspective*: George Robinson interview with Carol Steinbeck Brown, May 1, 1977. NSC.

108   *Ricketts had peculiar superstitions*: Steinbeck, "About Ed Ricketts," appendix to *The Log from the Sea of Cortez*, p. 239.

108   *He had fine, lustrous hair*: Ibid., p. 234.

108   *Carol agreed that the legend*: George Robinson interview with Carol Steinbeck Brown, May 1, 1977. NSC.

109   *For a time during Jean's on-and-off*: Tamm, *Beyond the Outer Shores*, p. 248.

109   *At one point, Jean got Bruce to agree*: Jean Ariss to Ed Ricketts, n.d. late 1930s. Courtesy John Lovejoy. The notes and letters from Ariss to Ricketts that I have been able to see were undated, though all appear to be from the same period. In one, she mentions that Ricketts is "forty-one now," which would indicate that it was written in the spring of 1938.

109   *Bruce, she said, was good to her*: Jean Ariss to Ed Ricketts, n.d. late 1930s. Courtesy John Lovejoy.

109 *In one anguished letter, she told him*: Jean Ariss to Ed Ricketts, n.d. late 1930s. Courtesy John Lovejoy.

109 *At one party Steinbeck got into*: JSW, pp. 208–9.

110 *Ingels had a sharp tongue*: George Robinson interview with Marjory Lloyd, April 7, 1976. NSC.

110 *For as long as people could remember*: Steinbeck to Ted Miller, n.d. mid-1931. Stanford, Mo263, 2/2.

110 *By the spring of 1931*: Steinbeck to Mavis McIntosh, May 8, 1931. ALL, pp. 42–43.

111 *He asked Ted Miller if he liked the plan*: Steinbeck to Ted Miller, n.d. mid-1931. Stanford, Mo263, 2/2.

111 *Mavis McIntosh wrote telling him*: Steinbeck to Ted Miller, n.d. mid-1931. Stanford, Mo263, 2/2. The letter cited immediately above was enclosed with this one. The estimate of a "mid-May" date seems slightly off. It was more likely early May.

111 *He thought that McIntosh had laid it on*: Ibid.

111 *Steinbeck wrote a long answer*: Steinbeck to Mavis McIntosh, May 8, 1931. ALL, pp. 42–43.

111 *In August, Dook and Maryon Sheffield visited*: Steinbeck to Carl Wilhelmson, September 1, 1931. Stanford, Mo263, 7/7.

111 *Sheffield—who later misremembered*: Sheffield, *John Steinbeck: The Good Companion*, pp. 108–9.

112 *He'd gotten into something he was allergic to*: Steinbeck to Carl Wilhelmson, September 1, 1931. Stanford, Mo263, 7/7.

112 *When he returned home*: Ibid.

112 *He told Carl Wilhelmson he almost wished*: Ibid.

112 *He wrote to Wilhelmson that he wished he could*: Steinbeck to Carl Wilhelmson, September 16, 1931. Stanford, Mo263, 7/7.

112 *The only thing that kept him from asking*: Ibid.

112 *What he really missed*: Ibid.

112 *He wanted to wait until he was done*: Ibid.

112 *When he finished* The Pastures of Heaven: Steinbeck to Ted Miller, n.d. mid-December 1931. Stanford, Mo263, 2/3.

112 *Mavis McIntosh didn't like it*: Steinbeck to Ted Miller, February 16, 1932. Stanford, Mo263, 2/3.

113 *"I'm getting pretty sick of my"*: Ibid.

113 *A publisher had accepted*: Steinbeck to Ted Miller, February 27, 1932. Stanford, Mo263, 2/3.

Chapter Seven: A Unit of the Greater Beast

117 *Ballou told Steinbeck how much*: Steinbeck to Ted Miller, March 14, 1932. Stanford, Mo263, 2/3.

117 *There was a brief scramble*: ALL, p. 60.

117 *Mavis McIntosh told him he now had*: Steinbeck to George Albee, n.d. March 1932. ALL, pp. 61–62.

117   *Steinbeck got a congratulatory letter*: Steinbeck to George Albee, n.d. March 1932. ALL, pp. 59–60.

117   *Steinbeck affected a nonchalance*: Ibid.

118   *In late January of 1932*: Egan, *The Worst Hard Time*, p. 113.

118   *Ed Ricketts was paying his sister Frances*: George Robinson interview with Carol Steinbeck Brown, May 1, 1977. NSC.

118   *Ricketts's father was always there*: Ibid.

119   *Carol's office was in*: Ibid.

119   *Carol said they were small and docile*: Ibid.

119   *She came to the lab in a*: Ibid.

119   *One of the main diversions*: Ibid.

120   *They measured these outings by*: Pauline Pearson interview with Richard Albee, July 14, 1975. NSC.

120   *One stormy day he and Carol*: Ibid.

120   *One afternoon, Carol's sister, Idell*: Pauline Pearson interview with Joseph Campbell, November 28, 1983. NSC.

120   *Although they'd exchanged letters*: Larsen and Larsen, *Joseph Campbell: A Fire in the Mind*, p. 165.

120   *Campbell remembered meeting Carol*: Ibid.

120   *Campbell later recalled*: Ibid., p. 167.

121   *At Columbia, where he earned*: Ibid., p. 75.

121   *The Steinbecks insisted that*: Ibid., p. 165.

121   *Steinbeck and Campbell stayed up*: Ibid., p. 166.

121   *He asked Campbell what he thought*: Ibid.

121   *Campbell was impressed*: Ibid.

122   *He found a place in Carmel*: Pauline Pearson interview with Joseph Campbell, November 28, 1983. NSC.

122   *Campbell said his rent*: Ibid.

122   *Campbell felt he'd found something*: Larsen and Larsen, *Joseph Campbell: A Fire in the Mind*, p. 173.

122   *On Steinbeck's birthday*: Pauline Pearson interview with Joseph Campbell, November 28, 1983. NSC.

122   *One evening when the Steinbecks*: Ibid.

123   *"I was impressed by"*: Ibid.

124   *Campbell thought Steinbeck and Ricketts*: Ibid.

124   *Campbell had been in Pacific Grove*: Larsen and Larsen, *Joseph Campbell: A Fire in the Mind*, pp. 182–86.

124   *Campbell wandered back*: Ibid.

125   *In the journal Campbell kept*: Ibid.

125   *The next morning, Campbell staggered home*: Ibid.

125   *In the car, Campbell and Carol*: Ibid.

125   *In his journal, Campbell wrote that*: Ibid.

125   *"Life?" he mused*: Ibid.

125   *A few days later*: Ibid., pp. 187–89.

126   *About a month later*: Ibid., p. 200.

126   *There's another version of the story*: CAJ, p. 113.

127 *Months earlier there'd been yet another shake-up*: Steinbeck, *The Pastures of Heaven*, James Nagel introduction, p. xi.

127 *Steinbeck liked Ballou and agreed*: Steinbeck to Elizabeth Otis, May 13, 1932. Stanford, Mo263, 9/1. Stanford has Steinbeck's many years of correspondence with Otis in two forms: the original holographs and typed transcriptions. After satisfying myself that the transcripts are accurate, I relied on those versions.

127 *In June, Ballou had asked Steinbeck*: Steinbeck to Robert Ballou, June 10, 1932. ALL, pp. 62–63.

127 *A camera, he said*: Ibid.

127 *About the same time that the book came out*: Steinbeck to Carl Wilhelmson, December 8, 1932. Stanford, Mo263, 7/8.

127 *Steinbeck busied himself with his latest*: Ibid.

127 *He told Mavis McIntosh the reviews*: Steinbeck to Mavis McIntosh, November 2, 1932. Stanford, Mo263, 9/1.

127 *In* The New Yorker, *Robert Coates*: TCR, p. 13.

127 *Robert Coates in* The New Yorker *called*: Ibid.

130 *Anita Moffett, the well-regarded*: TCR, p. 15.

130 *There's some evidence that Beth Ingels*: Pauline McCleary interview with George Robinson, November 22, 1977. NSC.

131 *She said Steinbeck "hijacked"*: Ibid.

131 *In January of 1933, Steinbeck got a check*: Steinbeck to Robert Ballou, January 3, 1933. ALL, pp. 66–67.

131 *The change was small but good*: Ibid.

131 *Ballou had told him*: Steinbeck to Carl Wilhelmson, December 8, 1932. Stanford, Mo263, 7/8.

131 *Steinbeck felt he could not stop experimenting*: Ibid.

131 *Steinbeck sent the manuscript*: Steinbeck to Mavis McIntosh, February 1, 1933. Stanford, Mo263, 9/1.

131 *Steinbeck was sympathetic*: Steinbeck to Robert Ballou, February 11, 1933. ALL, pp. 68–69.

131 *He admitted that he and Carol*: Ibid.

131 *In March, Olive Steinbeck fell ill*: CAJ, pp. 128–29.

132 *For Steinbeck, each passing hour*: Steinbeck to Carl Wilhelmson, August 9, 1933. Stanford, Mo263, 7/8.

132 *Nobody told John Ernst*: Steinbeck to George Albee, n.d. March 1933. ALL, pp. 70–71.

132 *At the end of May, Olive suffered*: Steinbeck to Robert Ballou, June 1, 1933. ALL, pp. 71–72.

132 *He was working on a long story*: Steinbeck to George Albee, n.d. March 1933. ALL, pp. 70–71.

132 *He told George Albee he was writing it*: Steinbeck to George Albee, n.d. 1933. ALL pp. 73–74. This letter is probably from April.

132 *He also said he had started to think*: Ibid.

132 *He told Dook Sheffield he was at the start*: Steinbeck to Dook Sheffield, June 30, 1933. ALL, p. 78.

133 *He had no idea what to do*: Ibid.

133　*He was studying philosophy*: Pauline Pearson interview with Richard Albee, February 23, 1975. NSC.

133　*Ricketts, who liked to think about*: Ibid.

133　*Albee believed that he was a "catalyst"*: Ibid.

133　*"I came out of school with my head full*: Ibid.

134　*That summer, with his mother's labored breathing*: Steinbeck to Dook Sheffield, June 21, 1933. Stanford, M0263, 5/8.

135　*Steinbeck told Sheffield that although*: Ibid.

136　*It was a term Richard Albee added*: Pauline Pearson interview with Richard Albee, February 23, 1975. NSC.

137　*He said he found four instances*: Steinbeck to George Albee, n.d. summer 1933. ALL, pp. 79–82.

Chapter Eight: Get Me Out of This Sort of Thing

138　*On March 4, 1933*: McElvaine, *The Great Depression*, p. 130.

138　*Congress was split on this question*: Ibid., p. 142.

139　*When he listened to a relief plan*: Ibid., p. 152.

139　*He bathed Olive and claimed*: Steinbeck to George Albee, n.d. June 1933. ALL, pp. 82–83.

139　*Steinbeck turned down offers*: Steinbeck to Carl Wilhelmson, August 9, 1933. Stanford, M0263, 7/8.

140　*But Steinbeck said he trusted Ballou*: Ibid.

140　*In August, Steinbeck corrected and returned*: Ibid.

140　*As if taking care of his mother*: Ibid.

140　*Gregory taught Spanish*: George Robinson interview with James Costello, June 22, 1975. NSC.

141　*That fall, John Ernst finally collapsed*: Steinbeck to Edith Wagner, November 23, 1933. ALL, pp. 89–90.

141　*Steinbeck sent him over to*: Ibid.

141　*But Steinbeck thought that if his mother*: Steinbeck to Robert Ballou, November 20, 1933. ALL, pp. 88–89.

141　To a God Unknown *was published*: Steinbeck, *To a God Unknown*, Robert DeMott introduction, p. xxxvi.

141　*In the earliest fragment of the novel*: Steinbeck and Street, *The Green Lady* (fragment), Stanford, M0263, 8/14–8/18.

142　*Back in the fall of 1930*: Steinbeck to Carl Wilhelmson, October 20, 1930. Stanford, M0263, 7/7.

142　*He thought about why he felt*: Ibid.

143　*After Robert Ballou sent him some*: Steinbeck to Robert Ballou, n.d. 1933. HRC.

144　*He remembered how awful*: Ibid.

144　*The critics, he said, were "lice"*: Ibid.

144　*In a smart review*: TCR, pp. 23–24.

145　*"C.S." in the* Saturday Review: Ibid., pp. 25–26.

145　*Steinbeck grudgingly agreed*: Steinbeck to George Albee, February 25, 1934. ALL, pp. 90–92.

145 *He could not shake the image*: Steinbeck to George Albee, n.d. 1934. ALL, pp. 92–94.

145 *And his father was in some ways*: Ibid.

146 *Against all evidence, Steinbeck insisted*: Ibid.

146 *His agents managed to sell*: Steinbeck, *The Long Valley*, John H. Timmerman introduction, p. xiv.

146 *After* To a God Unknown, *Steinbeck told*: Steinbeck to Carl Wilhelmson, August 9, 1933. Stanford, M0263, 7/8.

150 *When he showed the story to Carol*: Steinbeck to George Albee, February 25, 1934. ALL, pp. 90–92.

150 *When he sent* Tortilla Flat *to Mavis McIntosh*: Steinbeck to Mavis McIntosh, n.d. 1934. Stanford, M0263, 9/1.

154 *The son of a junk peddler*: Covington, *The Argus Book Shop*, p. 3.

154 *Abramson put out a chatty, informative catalogue*: Ibid., pp. 14–15.

154 *Toward the end of 1934*: JSW, p. 313.

154 *He asked Mavis McIntosh*: Friede, *The Mechanical Angel*, p. 123.

154 *Covici wrote Steinbeck saying that*: Steinbeck to George Albee, n.d. 1935. ALL, pp. 101–2.

154 *Steinbeck told George Albee admiringly*: Ibid.

155 *Covici was a burly, opinionated Romanian*: Fried, *The Mechanical Angel*, p. 80.

155 *Covici was already a minor legend*: Ibid., p 81.

155 *Steinbeck was also paid*: Steinbeck to Mavis McIntosh, March 2, 1935. Stanford, M0263, 9/1.

155 *He called it "a short life of a Communist"*: Steinbeck to Mavis McIntosh, February 4, 1935. Stanford, M0263, 9/1.

155 *Steinbeck told Mavis McIntosh it was*: Ibid.

155 *Covici-Friede sent Steinbeck a contract*: Steinbeck to Wilbur Needham, n.d. early 1935. ALL, pp. 106–7.

155 *They also promised to*: Ibid.

155 *George Albee's novel*: Steinbeck to George Albee, n.d. 1935. ALL, pp. 101–2.

155 *It's possible that Albee had recommended*: Steinbeck to Mavis McIntosh, n.d. February 1935. Stanford, M0263, 9/1.

155 *He told Mavis McIntosh he'd also heard*: Ibid.

155 *He told Mavis McIntosh if that was the case*: Ibid.

156 *Steinbeck was already on edge*: Steinbeck to Mavis McIntosh, February 23, 1935. Stanford, M0263, 9/1.

156 *He sent the questionnaire*: Ibid.

156 *About a week later*: Steinbeck to Mavis McIntosh, March 2, 1935. Stanford, M0263, 9/1.

156 *He reminded McIntosh that*: Ibid.

156 *An assistant editor named Harry Bloch*: Chamberlain, *A Life with the Printed Word*, p. 53.

156 *He fired off a three-page rejection*: JSW, p. 315.

156 *He complained to Mavis McIntosh*: Steinbeck to Mavis McIntosh, n.d. April 1935. Stanford, M0263, 9/1.

156 *He added that he was discouraged*: Ibid.

156 *Steinbeck had hoped he and Carol*: Ibid.

157   *This time Steinbeck got some help*: Steinbeck to Elizabeth Otis, May 13, 1935. Stanford, Mo263, 9/1.

157   *In early May he told her*: Steinbeck to Elizabeth Otis, May 7, 1935. Stanford, Mo263, 9/1.

157   *He'd also had a visit*: Steinbeck to Elizabeth Otis, May 9, 1935. Stanford, Mo263, 9/1.

157   *About the same time, Elizabeth Otis wired Steinbeck*: Ibid.

157   *Feeling he had the upper hand*: Ibid.

157   *Within a few days*: Steinbeck to Elizabeth Otis, May 13, 1935. Stanford, Mo263, 9/1.

Chapter Nine: Take Off Your Hat, Lennie

158   *Lewis Gannett, writing in the* New York Herald Tribune: TCR, p. 34.

158   *A reviewer for the* San Francisco Chronicle: Ibid., pp. 32–33.

158   *He told Elizabeth Otis he was surprised*: Steinbeck to Elizabeth Otis, June 13, 1935. Stanford, Mo263, 9/1.

159   *Steinbeck instructed his agents to avoid*: Ibid.

159   *By midsummer, Steinbeck said he was*: Steinbeck to Mavis McIntosh, July 30, 1935. Stanford, Mo263, 9/1.

159   *The magazine, run by*: Ibid.

159   *He told Mavis McIntosh that if she wanted*: Ibid.

161   *Although it has over time*: It was a critic named Harry Hansen, writing in the *New York World Telegram*, September 19, 1938, who called "The Snake" synthetic. TCR, p. 137.

161   *When it appeared in the story collection*: TCR, p. 143.

161   *Steinbeck had no idea how*: Steinbeck to Mavis McIntosh, July 30, 1935. Stanford, Mo263, 9/1.

161   *But in August, the* New York Times: "Book Notes," *New York Times*, August 25, 1935.

161   *George Albee relayed a rumor that*: Steinbeck to Mavis McIntosh, August 29, 1935. Stanford, Mo263, 9/1.

161   *In the fall, with* The Pastures of Heaven: Steinbeck to Elizabeth Otis, November 3, 1935. Stanford, Mo263, 9/1.

161   *Soon after their arrival*: Steinbeck to Mavis McIntosh, September 12, 1935. Stanford, Mo263, 9/1.

162   *He doubted that Hollywood could*: Steinbeck to Elizabeth Otis, November 3, 1935. Stanford, Mo263, 9/1.

162   *He was more candid with George Albee*: Steinbeck to George Albee, n.d. 1935. ALL, pp. 117–18.

162   *He said the air was thick*: Ibid.

162   *She had been collecting pottery figures*: Ibid.

162   *They had planned to stay in Mexico until*: Steinbeck to Elizabeth Otis, November 3, 1935. Stanford, Mo263, 9/1.

162   *When he got home*: Steinbeck to Joseph Henry Jackson, n.d. late 1935. ALL, pp. 118–19.

162   *He wrote to Joseph Henry Jackson*: Ibid.

163   *In California, the Cannery and Agricultural Workers*: McWilliams, *Factories in the Fields*, pp. 213–18.

163   *By 1933, it was the second-most*: Starr, *Endangered Dreams*, pp. 74–75.

164   *Cotton pickers went on strike*: McWilliams, *Factories in the Fields*, p. 220.

164   *The* New York Times *reported*: "4 Killed, 2 Dying in Coast Strikes," *New York Times*, October 11, 1933.

164   *Lettuce pickers striking in Watsonville*: Ibid.

164   *To prevent future strikes*: McWilliams, *Factories in the Fields*, pp. 231–33.

164   *The Associated Farmers were supported*: Ibid.

164   *Most importantly, they organized*: Ibid, pp. 238–39.

164   *In the summer of 1934*: Ibid.

164   *Many carried both*: Ibid.

165   *They initially opposed Roosevelt*: Ottanelli, *The Communist Party of the United States*, p. 72.

165   *When Steinbeck learned that two Communist organizers*: JSW, pp. 296–97.

166   *In the spring of 1935 Covici slipped*: Chamberlain, *A Life with the Printed Word*, p. 53.

166   *Chamberlain also knew Harry Bloch*: Ibid.

166   *Chamberlain told Covici*: TCR, pp. 53–55. Chamberlain recounted Covici's invitation to second guess Harry Bloch in his review of *In Dubious Battle* for the *New York Times* in January of 1936.

168   *It all comes to a tragic conclusion*: Steinbeck to Mavis McIntosh, February 4, 1935. Stanford, Mo263, 9/1.

168   *At the* New York Times, *John Chamberlain's breathless*: TCR, pp. 53–55.

168   *In the* San Francisco Chronicle: TCR, pp. 51–53.

169   *In an annoyed review for* The Nation: TCR, pp. 64–65.

169   *Steinbeck was still working out*: "Argument of Phalanx," fragment. I am indebted to Bob DeMott for sharing a photocopy of this essay with me. The original is at the Bancroft Library at Berkeley.

169   *By failing to observe and understand groups*: Ibid.

170   *As for Harry Bloch*: Chamberlain, *A Life with the Printed Word*, p. 53.

170   *Steinbeck considered Bloch the kind of half-hearted*: Steinbeck, "A Primer on the 30's," *Esquire*, June 1960.

170   *He told Elizabeth Otis to let*: Steinbeck to Elizabeth Otis, April 4, 1936. Stanford, Mo263, 9/1.

171   *It was "hardly a book for a child"*: Steinbeck to Ben Abramson, n.d. early 1936. HRC.

171   *Steinbeck claimed that once, in Salinas*: Ibid.

171   *That was the reason, he said*: Ibid.

171   *He told Elizabeth Otis it would be done by*: Steinbeck to Elizabeth Otis, May 27, 1936. Stanford, Mo263, 9/1.

171   *The house was simple but ample*: Sheffield, *John Steinbeck: The Good Companion*, p. 159.

171   *For a while, Steinbeck called his short novel-in-progress*: JSW, p. 327.

172   *An editor for the* San Francisco News: Steinbeck, *The Harvest Gypsies*, Charles Wollenberg introduction, pp. v–vi.

172   *He bought a used bakery delivery truck*: Ibid., p. vii.

173   *"But if you take off the cover"*: Lord, *To Hold This Soil*, p. 5.

173   *Even though the total population*: Stein, *California and the Dust Bowl Migration*, p. 6.

174   *Steinbeck went first to*: ALL, p. 129.

174   *Housing at Weedpatch*: Steinbeck, *The Harvest Gypsies*, p. 38.

174   *More than 400 people were living*: Report for the weeks ending August 22 and August 29, 1936, Arvin Migratory Labor Camp. SJSU. These regular reports, filed meticulously by Tom Collins, illuminated the scale of the problem the government was doing what it could to address.

174   *Of the eighty-four groups in the camp*: Ibid.

174   *But rumors circulated that the Associated Farmers*: Ibid.

175   *If anyone doubted the growers' resolve*: Ibid.

175   *One typical respondent*: Ibid.

175   *In one case that month*: Ibid.

175   *"How fine are these people!"*: Ibid.

175   *Collins and Steinbeck called his truck*: Steinbeck, *The Harvest Gypsies*, Charles Wollenberg introduction, p. ix.

176   *He reported that at least 150,000*: Steinbeck, *The Harvest Gypsies*, p. 19.

176   *"Thus in California we find a curious attitude"*: Ibid., p. 20.

176   *"The squatters' camps are located all over"*: Ibid., p. 26.

177   *When the Associated Growers in one county*: Ibid., p. 37.

177   *"The new migrants to California"*: Ibid., p. 62.

177   *Steinbeck wrote to thank him*: Steinbeck to Ted Miller, n.d. 1936. ALL, pp. 131–32.

178   *Steinbeck told George Albee they were holding the stories*: Steinbeck to George Albee, n.d. fall 1936. ALL, pp. 132–33.

178   *Before that, Steinbeck had managed*: Ibid.

178   *Steinbeck told Ben Abramson*: Steinbeck to Ben Abramson, n.d. fall 1936. HRC.

178   *On November 25, 1936*: Hemp, *Cannery Row*, p. 95.

179   *Although he had insurance*: Rodger, *Renaissance Man of Cannery Row*, p. xxxi.

179   *Steinbeck loaned Ricketts*: Pauline Pearson interview with Toby Street, December 3, 1978. NSC.

179   *That same month, Steinbeck sent a radio*: Report for the week ending November 28, 1936, Arvin Migratory Labor Camp. SJSU.

179   *Collins said they hoped to find*: Ibid.

179   *George Albee wrote Steinbeck after*: Steinbeck to Mr. and Mrs. George Albee, January 11, 1937. ALL, pp. 133–34.

179   *Elizabeth Otis informed Steinbeck*: Steinbeck to Elizabeth Otis, January 15, 1937. Stanford, M0263, 9/1. Apparently Pascal Covici had already sent a wire about the selection, but it was garbled and he asked Otis to elaborate.

179   *He told Otis that any amount of money greater*: Steinbeck to Elizabeth Otis, January 27, 1937. Stanford, M0263, 9/1.

179   *He also said his new book*: Ibid.

180   *When Steinbeck wrote to Pat Covici*: Steinbeck to Pascal Covici, February 28, 1937. ALL, pp. 135–36.

180   *A month later, sales were averaging*: CAJ, p. 190.

180 *Steinbeck told Covici that their travel plans*: Steinbeck to Pascal Covici, February 28, 1937. ALL, pp. 135–36.

180 *Kaufman agreed*: ALL, p. 136.

180 *Steinbeck wrote to Williams before*: Steinbeck to Elizabeth Otis and Annie Laurie Williams, March 19, 1937. Stanford, M0263, 9/1.

180 *He'd already instructed Covici to stop*: Ibid.

180 *If people demanded to know something*: Ibid.

181 *Richard Albee said that Steinbeck was*: Pauline Pearson interview with Richard Albee, July 14, 1975. NSC.

183 *Heywood Broun, in a review*: TCR, pp. 87–88.

183 *Wilbur Needham, in the* Los Angeles Times: Ibid., pp. 81–82.

183 *Mrs. Roosevelt chose to find*: Ibid., p. 90.

Chapter Ten: The Hundred-Day Siege

184 *In 1937, CBS sent a twenty-nine-year-old*: Persico, *Edward R. Murrow*, p. 113.

184 *Murrow, who was from*: Ibid., p. 15.

184 *Americans turned up their radios*: Ibid., p. 144.

185 *They sailed to Europe on*: Steinbeck to "Everybody," n.d. May 1937. Stanford, M0263, 9/1. "Everybody" meant his representatives at McIntosh & Otis.

185 *They arrived back in New York*: Steinbeck to Lawrence Clark Powell, August 23, 1937. ALL, pp. 139–40.

185 *Steinbeck was shy around Kaufman*: JSW, p. 358.

185 *"I wouldn't pay ten dollars"*: Steinbeck to Lawrence Clark Powell, August 23, 1937. ALL, pp. 139–40.

185 *After the curtain came down*: Steinbeck to Elizabeth Otis, Annie Laurie Williams, and Mavis McIntosh, November 24, 1937. Stanford, M0263, 9/1.

185 *Pascal Covici had wired after*: Ibid.

185 *George Kaufman was more measured*: Ibid.

186 *In his next-day review*: TCR, pp. 112–13.

186 *After the play was a hit*: TCR, pp. 116–18.

186 *Steinbeck wrote George Kaufman*: Steinbeck to George S. Kaufman, n.d. November 1937. ALL, pp. 144–45.

186 *Arnold Gingrich published "The Snake"*: Steinbeck to Elizabeth Otis, Annie Laurie Williams, and Mavis McIntosh, November 24, 1937. Stanford, M0263, 9/1.

186 *Steinbeck told his agents*: Ibid.

186 *Gingrich sent him a watch*: Steinbeck to Arnold Gingrich, January 5, 1938. ALL, pp. 151–52.

186 *Zeppo Marx called*: Steinbeck to Elizabeth Otis and Annie Laurie Williams, n.d. December 1937. ALL, pp, 148–49.

186 *Myron Selznick's office offered*: Ibid.

187 *He and Carol finally got*: Ibid.

187 *The new one could type accents*: Steinbeck to "All," n.d. November 1937. Stanford, M0263, 9/1. "All" meant his representatives at McIntosh & Otis.

187 *Exasperated, he wired Annie Laurie Williams*: Steinbeck to Annie Laurie Williams (telegram), December 8, 1973. ALL, p. 149.

187   *The next day he wrote Williams a letter*: Steinbeck to Annie Laurie Williams, December 9, 1937. ALL, pp. 149–50.

187   *If one small scene*: Ibid.

187   *When the play opened in January*: Steinbeck to Mr. and Mrs. Joseph Henry Jackson, n.d. January 1938. ALL, pp. 152–53.

187   *A pregnant woman named Alice*: Steinbeck to Elizabeth Otis, n.d. February 1938. Stanford, Mo263, 9/2.

187   *According to Richard Albee*: Pauline Pearson interview with Richard Albee, n.d. October 1976. NSC.

188   *When he couldn't stand any more*: Steinbeck to George Albee, n.d. early 1938. ALL, pp. 156–57.

188   *But Steinbeck had it all wrong*: Pauline Pearson interview with Richard Albee, n.d. October 1976. NSC.

190   *an inflamed letter*: Steinbeck to Elizabeth Otis, n.d. 1938. Stanford, Mo263, 9/2.

190   *But within days*: Steinbeck to Elizabeth Otis, February 14, 1938. Stanford, Mo263, 9/2.

190   Life *magazine asked him*: Steinbeck to Elizabeth Otis, March 7, 1938. Stanford, Mo263, 9/2.

191   *Steinbeck returned after a week*: Ibid.

191   *He said any notion that*: Ibid.

191   *She'd tried to photograph*: Gordon, *Dorothea Lange*, pp. 133–34.

191   *Lange had had better luck*: Ibid., pp. 236–39.

192   *Sanora Babb had been born*: Babb, *Whose Names Are Unknown*, Lawrence R. Rodgers introduction, pp. ix–x.

193   *"Malnutrition is a subtle disease"*: Babb, "San Joaquin Valley" (fragment), n.d. HRC.

193   *Babb sometimes walked with Tom Collins*: Babb, *On the Dirty Plate Trail*, p. 123.

194   *After her first day in the field*: Ibid., p. 130.

194   *Tom Collins told her it had been*: Ibid.

194   *He came to see Steinbeck at Los Gatos*: Steinbeck to Elizabeth Otis, February 14, 1938. Stanford, Mo263, 9/2.

194   *Steinbeck was introduced to James Cagney*: Ibid.

194   *He told Steinbeck that*: Steinbeck to Elizabeth Otis, n.d. March 1938. Stanford, Mo263, 9/2.

194   *He reminded Elizabeth Otis*: Ibid.

195   *Steinbeck's talk with LeRoy prompted*: Ibid.

195   *In March he told Elizabeth Otis*: Steinbeck to Elizabeth Otis, March 23, 1938. Stanford, Mo263, 9/2.

195   *That same month Tom Collins wrote*: Tom Collins to Sanora Babb, March 19, 1938. HRC.

195   *Floundering, Steinbeck promised*: Steinbeck to Elizabeth Otis, March 23, 1938. Stanford, Mo263, 9/2.

195   *Yet in May he wrote back*: Steinbeck to Elizabeth Otis, May 2, 1938. Stanford, Mo263, 9/2.

195   *If Otis didn't like it*: Ibid.

196   *Usually it was money, but*: Steinbeck to Elizabeth Otis, n.d. May 1938. Stanford, Mo263, 9/2.

196   *Meanwhile, George Kaufman was insulted*: ALL, p. 165.

196 *He said he wouldn't travel across the country*: Steinbeck to Elizabeth Otis, n.d. May 1938. Stanford, Mo263, 9/2.

196 *And the New York Drama Critics' Circle*: Ibid.

196 *In the cable*: Steinbeck to the Critics' Circle (telegram), April 23, 1938. ALL, p. 164.

196 *By the beginning of June*: Steinbeck to Elizabeth Otis, June 1, 1938. Stanford, Mo263, 9/2.

196 *Steinbeck envisioned a manuscript of*: Steinbeck, *Working Days*, entry for June 11, pp. 25–26. *Working Days*, edited by Robert DeMott, is the published version of the diary Steinbeck kept while he worked on *The Grapes of Wrath*.

197 *Steinbeck told Elizabeth Otis that, at last*: Steinbeck to Elizabeth Otis, June 1, 1938. Stanford, Mo263, 9/2.

197 *Steinbeck asked Otis to not tell*: Steinbeck to Elizabeth Otis, June 17, 1938. Stanford, Mo263, 9/2.

197 *He wanted to finish by*: Steinbeck, *Working Days*, entry for May 31, pp. 19–20.

197 *Steinbeck told Covici he considered*: Steinbeck to Pascal Covici, n.d. 1938. HRC. Steinbeck said much the same thing to Annie Laurie Williams.

197 *In late June Covici informed*: Steinbeck to Elizabeth Otis, July 22, 1938. Stanford, Mo263, 9/2. McIntosh & Otis were monitoring the situation closely. They'd wired Steinbeck the month before to let him know that Covici was under "severe" financial pressure. But they assured him his interests would be protected.

198 *The company was $170,000 in debt*: "Valuable Property," *Time*, August 29, 1938. *Time* reported that Covici-Friede had cleared some $35,000 on *Of Mice and Men* alone—but could not pay Steinbeck's overdue royalties.

198 *Steinbeck was owed some $6,000*: Ibid.

198 *Steinbeck asked McIntosh and Otis to start*: Steinbeck to Elizabeth Otis, July 22, 1938. Stanford, Mo263, 9/2.

199 *Ed Ricketts came over*: Ibid., entry for June 27, pp. 34–35.

199 *On the last day of the month*: Ibid., entry for June 30, pp. 36–37.

199 *Ritchie and Tal and Ed came over*: Ibid., entry for July 5, pp. 37–38.

199 *The asking price, $16,000*: Ibid., editor's note, p. 153.

199 *There were so many distractions*: Ibid., entry for July 13, pp. 42–43.

199 *The manuscript had reached nearly*: Ibid., entry for July 15, pp. 44–45.

200 *On July 18, Steinbeck got a letter*: Ibid., entry for July 18, p. 45.

200 *It was followed a day later*: Ibid., entry for July 20, pp. 46–47.

200 *He and Carol could get by*: Ibid.

200 *The short-story collection already had*: Ibid., entry for July 22, pp. 47–48.

200 *At the end of the month*: Ibid., entry for August 1, pp. 49–50.

200 *Then Broderick Crawford showed up*: Ibid.

200 *He realized he'd been foolish*: Ibid.

200 *In early August Steinbeck decided*: Ibid., entry for August 8, p. 53.

200 *When he got back, he found that*: Ibid., entry for August 9, pp. 53–54.

200 *Viking Press had purchased his contract*: "Valuable Property," *Time*, August 29, 1938.

200 *Covici sent a telegram*: Pascal Covici to Steinbeck (telegram), August 12, 1938. HRC.

200 *Toward the end of the month*: Steinbeck to Pascal Covici, August 29, 1938. HRC.

201 *And then, in early September*: Steinbeck, *Working Days*, entry for September 3, p. 65.

201 *As she typed the manuscript*: Steinbeck to Elizabeth Otis, September 10, 1938. Stanford, M0263, 9/2.

201 *He asked Otis to keep all this*: Ibid.

201 *He couldn't bring himself*: Ibid.

201 *Steinbeck noted that this happened*: Ibid.

202 *With all of this going on at once*: Steinbeck to Elizabeth Otis, September 10, 1938. Stanford, M0263, 9/2.

202 *On another front*: Steinbeck, *Working Days*, entry for August 16, p. 56.

202 *One time, Steinbeck was at home*: JSW, pp. 383–84.

202 *In August, Steinbeck and Pare Lorentz*: Steinbeck, *Working Days*, entry for August 23, pp. 59–60.

202 *The ever-attentive Wilbur Needham*: TCR, p. 133.

202 *William Soskin at the* New York Herald Tribune: TCR, pp. 134–35.

203 *One critic called the book*: TCR, p. 135. The reviewer was Lewis Gannett, writing for the *New York Herald Tribune* a day after Soskin.

204 *The first people who looked at*: Steinbeck, *Working Days*, entry for September 5, p. 66.

204 *During the first week of September*: Ibid., entry for September 6, pp. 66–67.

204 *A month later they were "camped"*: Steinbeck to Pascal Covici, n.d. October 1938. HRC. The date of this letter is disputed. HRC assigns a date of November 23, 1938, but the October date given in ALL, p. 172, seems more likely.

204 *The Farm Security Administration asked him*: Steinbeck, *Working Days*, entry for September 9, pp. 69–70.

205 *It was, he thought, far too much*: Ibid., entry for September 26, pp. 76–77.

205 *Now he had a cough*: Ibid., entry for September 22, p. 75.

205 *The Hollywood gossip columnist*: Ibid., entry for September 30, p. 80.

205 *But Steinbeck said he was frightened*: Ibid., entry for September 26, pp. 76–77.

205 *Carol's typescript reached*: Ibid., entry for October 24, pp. 91–92.

205 *Steinbeck's sister Mary*: Ibid., entry for October 10, p. 85.

205 *Pat Covici was planning a trip*: Ibid., entry for October 14, pp. 87–88.

205 *He confided in his journal*: Ibid., entry for October 25, p. 92.

205 *He concluded the final entry*: Ibid., entry for October 26, p. 93.

Chapter Eleven: *I'll Be There*

212 *Carol registered as a member*: U.S. Military Intelligence Service report, 1943. SJSU. The War Department investigated Steinbeck in connection with his request for an officer's commission. This file was later shared with the FBI, though the Bureau never conducted its own independent investigation of Steinbeck.

212 *Eleven months later*: Ibid.

212 *Pat Covici proposed a large print run*: Steinbeck to Elizabeth Otis, n.d. November 1938. Stanford, M0263, 9/2.

212 *Steinbeck was against*: Ibid.

213   *Paramount wanted to make*: Ibid.

213   *He told Elizabeth Otis to not*: Ibid.

213   *They met in Los Angeles*: Steinbeck to Pascal Covici, January 1, 1939. ALL, pp. 174–75.

213   *Otis felt that the book's language had to be*: CAJ, p. 203.

213   *Steinbeck grudgingly consented*: Ibid.

213   *When Otis and Carol phoned Western Union*: ALL, p. 176.

213   *Steinbeck explained to Pat Covici*: Steinbeck to Pascal Covici, January 3, 1939. HRC. The date of this letter is from ALL, p. 175. HRC incorrectly gave it as January 13.

214   *Collins wrote that for a time*: Report for the week ending May 23, 1936, Arvin Migratory Labor Camp. SJSU.

214   *Thatcher had lived mostly*: Mel Thatcher diary. NSC.

216   *Back in 1935, long before*: John Gross interview with Mel Thatcher, March 21, 1978. NSC.

216   *In early January 1939, Pat Covici told Steinbeck*: Pascal Covici to Steinbeck, January 9, 1939. HRC.

216   The Grapes of Wrath, *a book that*: Ibid.

216   *Covici continued, in the same letter*: Ibid.

217   *Covici once told Steinbeck that*: Pascal Covici to Steinbeck, July 2, 1941. HRC.

217   *It took a week for Covici's letter*: Steinbeck to Pascal Covici, January 16, 1939. ALL, pp. 178–79.

218   *"It's her book and"*: Steinbeck to Pascal Covici, January 31, 1939. HRC.

218   *In late March, Covici told Steinbeck*: Steinbeck to Elizabeth Otis, March 27, 1939. Stanford, M0263, 9/2.

219   *Sales would soon approach*: Steinbeck, *Working Days*, editor's note, p. 97.

219   *In a thoughtful and balanced review*: TCR, pp. 159–61.

219   *Malcolm Cowley, writing in*: TCR, pp. 166–67.

219   *An unsigned review in* Colliers: TCR, pp. 174–75.

219   *In* The Nation, *Louis Kronenberger wrote*: TCR, pp. 155–57.

219   *Clifton Fadiman, in* The New Yorker: TCR, pp. 154–55.

220   *Steinbeck said he and Carol*: Steinbeck to Elizabeth Otis, February 12, 1939. Stanford, M0263, 9/2.

220   *Meanwhile,* Of Mice and Men *had been sold*: Steinbeck to Elizabeth Otis, February 9, 1939. Stanford, M0263, 9/2.

220   *He told Elizabeth Otis that Wallace Ford*: Ibid.

221   *Broderick Crawford was out, too*: Ibid.

221   *More than a month before*: Steinbeck to Elizabeth Otis, March 4, 1939. Stanford, M0263, 9/2.

221   *Toby Street warned him to be careful*: Ibid.

221   *He'd learned of an episode*: Ibid.

221   The Grapes of Wrath *was banned*: Wartzman, *Obscene in the Extreme*, p. 10.

221   *Three copies were burned*: Ibid.

221   *. . . and one in Bakersfield*: Ibid., pp. 149–51.

221   *The formal resolution denounced*: Ibid., p. 8.

221   *Steinbeck invited him to*: Steinbeck to Carl Wilhelmson, June 7, 1939. Stanford, M0263, 7/8.

221 *He also wrote to Dook Sheffield*: Steinbeck to Dook Sheffield, March 19, 1939. Stanford, Mo263, 5/8.

222 *. . . and Steinbeck offered to pay*: Sheffield, *John Steinbeck: The Good Companion*, pp. 162–63.

222 *Steinbeck told him that when he drank*: Steinbeck to Dook Sheffield, March 19, 1939. Stanford, Mo263, 5/8.

222 *Some months later, Sheffield visited*: Sheffield, *John Steinbeck: The Good Companion*, pp. 166–67.

222 *When Steinbeck's dog, Toby*: Steinbeck to Carl Wilhelmson, June 7, 1939. Stanford, Mo263, 7/8.

223 *Steinbeck loved it at the ranch*: Steinbeck to Elizabeth Otis, April 13, 1939. Stanford, Mo263, 9/2.

223 *When he got home a couple of months later*: Steinbeck to Dook Sheffield, June 23, 1939. Stanford, Mo263, 5/9.

223 *Hollywood scared him*: Ibid.

224 *Steinbeck told Dook Sheffield that*: Ibid.

224 *Some years later Steinbeck related*: ALL, p. 187.

224 *Steinbeck also gave materials*: Steinbeck to Dook Sheffield, June 23, 1939. Stanford, Mo263, 5/9.

225 *As W. W. Alexander, head of the*: "Violations of Free Speech and Rights of Labor, etc." Alexander testified in a hearing pursuant to Senate Resolution 266 by the Committee on Education and Labor. U.S. Government Printing Office, 1941.

225 *In a probing examination*: Wilson, "The Boys in the Back Room," from *Literary Essays and Reviews of the 1930s & 40s*, pp. 504–12.

228 *Early in 1939, before Steinbeck's book came out*: Babb, *Whose Names Are Unknown*, Lawrence R. Rodgers introduction, p. xi.

228 *Cerf concurred with*: Cerf to Sanora Babb, August 16, 1939. HRC.

228 *Cerf ruefully wrote to Babb*: Ibid.

228 *Cert urged Babb to sign on*: Ibid.

230 *Roosevelt wrote to Joseph Kennedy*: Hastings, *Inferno: The World at War, 1939–1945*, p. 180.

230 *In the fall of 1939, as the bombs fell*: Ibid., p. 182.

230 *In June he'd pleaded with*: Steinbeck to Elizabeth Otis, June 22, 1939. Stanford, Mo263, 9/2.

230 *One woman named Irma wrote to him*: Steinbeck to Elizabeth Otis, September 18, 1939. Stanford, Mo263, 9/3.

230 *Not long after this, Steinbeck started*: Steinbeck to Elizabeth Otis, n.d. July 1939. Stanford, Mo263, 9/3.

230 *One day, one person and then another*: Ibid.

230 *He told Elizabeth Otis he was thinking*: Ibid.

231 *Jack Benny mentioned*: Steinbeck to Elizabeth Otis, n.d. October 1939, Stanford, Mo263, 9/3.

231 *Lately they'd spread a rumor*: Steinbeck to Elizabeth Otis, July 20, 1939. Stanford, Mo263, 9/3.

231 *Steinbeck believed the campaign against him*: Steinbeck to Elizabeth Otis, July 24, 1939. Stanford, Mo263, 9/3.

232 *Steinbeck figured it was going to be*: Ibid.

Chapter Twelve: At Sea

233   *Steinbeck was introduced to Conger by*: Pauline Pearson interview with Max Wagner, May 25, 1975. NSC.

234   *Wagner had moved to Hollywood*: Ibid.

234   *The three of them shared an apartment*: Halladay, *The Closest Witness*, p. 33.

234   *Gwen said Max fell in love*: Ibid, pp. 33–34.

234   *She said that when he had a few drinks*: Ibid., p. 34.

234   *Max had last seen Steinbeck*: Pauline Pearson interview with Max Wagner, May 25, 1975. NSC.

234   *According to Wagner, he took Steinbeck*: Ibid.

234   *She had reddish-blonde hair*: CAJ, p. 211.

234   *As Gwen herself told it*: Halladay, *The Closest Witness*, p. 39.

234   *A couple of days later*: Pauline Pearson interview with Max Wagner, May 25, 1975. NSC.

235   *Gwen's version of the story was*: Halladay, *The Closest Witness*, pp. 34–39.

237   *Steinbeck headed back to Los Gatos*: Ibid., p. 41.

237   *"I have known girls more beautiful"*: Ibid., p. 305.

238   *He told his old friend Toby Street*: CAJ, p. 210.

238   *During the time he worked on it*: Arvin, *Herman Melville*, p. 196.

238   *Dorothea Lange had promised*: Steinbeck to Elizabeth Otis, July 30, 1939. Stanford, M0263, 9/3.

239   *He was going to get away from*: Ibid.

239   *They stayed at the Garden of Allah*: Ibid.

239   *Offering few specifics, Steinbeck told*: Steinbeck to Elizabeth Otis, August 20, 1939. Stanford, M0263, 9/3.

239   *Now he told Otis that Carol*: Ibid.

239   *But a few days later, he said*: Steinbeck to Elizabeth Otis, August 24, 1939. Stanford, M0263, 9/3.

239   *Only days after this update*: Steinbeck to Elizabeth Otis, August 28, 1939. Stanford, M0263, 9/3.

239   *He said they continued to savage him*: Ibid.

239   *Rumors were spread that he was*: Ibid.

240   *In September Steinbeck and Carol*: Steinbeck to "All" [Elizabeth Otis, Mavis McIntosh, and Annie Laurie Williams], September 15, 1939. Stanford, M0263, 9/3.

240   *He'd become a "public domain"*: Steinbeck, *Working Days*, entry for October 16, 1939, pp. 105–7.

240   *A few days later*: Ibid., date uncertain. DeMott gives October 20 and 27, or November 3 as possibilities.

240   *Another big check—this one for $13,000*: Steinbeck to Elizabeth Otis, December 15, 1939. Stanford, M0263, 9/3.

240   *"But I know it will be found"*: Steinbeck, *Working Days*, entry for October 16, 1939. pp. 105–7.

240   *Steinbeck wrote to Dook Sheffield*: Steinbeck to Dook Sheffield, November 13, 1939. Stanford, M0263, 5/9.

242 *Steinbeck and Ricketts made a collecting trip*: Hedgpeth, *The Outer Shores, Part 1*, p. 32.

242 *He experienced a "crash within myself"*: Steinbeck, *Working Days*, entry for January 4, 1940, pp. 109–10.

242 *After about ten days she came over*: Ibid., entry for January 12, 1940, pp. 111–13.

242 *Steinbeck bought a fancy microscope*: Steinbeck to Elizabeth Otis, December 15, 1939. Stanford, M0263, 9/3.

242 *He said it looked almost like a documentary*: Steinbeck to Elizabeth Otis, December 15, 1939. Stanford, M0263, 9/3.

243 *John Ford was friends with the Irish writer*: Thomas Flanagan, "John Ford's West," *New York Review of Books*, December 20, 2001.

244 *In February, Steinbeck and Carol were*: Steinbeck to Elizabeth Otis, February 24, 1940. Stanford, M0263, 9/3.

244 *Steinbeck had an idea now*: Ibid.

244 *The cost of the six-week charter was*: Enea, *With Steinbeck in the Sea of Cortez*. p. 3.

244 *Steinbeck was paying, so he asked*: Steinbeck to Elizabeth Otis, February 24, 1940. Stanford, M0263, 9/3.

244 *It turned out that many of the boat owners*: Enea, *With Steinbeck in the Sea of Cortez*, pp. 1–3.

244 *After being turned down by several*: Bailey, *The Western Flyer*, p. 8.

244 *Steinbeck inspected the engine room*: This and all further descriptions of the ship, the crew, the voyage, and what happened along the way are from *Sea of Cortez*, *The Western Flyer*, and *With Steinbeck in the Sea of Cortez* unless otherwise stated.

247 *America hung on the words of Ed Murrow*: Persico, *Edward R. Murrow*, p. 145.

249 *Much of the Gulf of California is flanked*: Ives, Ronald L., "Recurrent mirages at Puerto Penasco, Sonora," *Journal of the Franklin Institute* 352, no. 4 (October 1951).

253 *Ricketts had a fresh draft*: Hedgpeth, *The Outer Shores, Part 2*, pp. 161–70. Ricketts titled it "Essay on Non-teleological Thinking."

253 *Years later, the literary critic Alfred Kazin*: "The Unhappy Man from Happy Valley," *New York Times Book Review*, May 4, 1958.

257 *They arrived back in Monterey*: CAJ, p. 232.

258 *Edward R. Murrow—in a broadcast*: Persico, *Edward R. Murrow*, p. 170.

258 *A reporter following her asked*: ALL, p. 202.

258 *Steinbeck wrote to Mrs. Roosevelt*: Steinbeck to Mrs. Franklin D. Roosevelt, April 24, 1940. ALL, p. 202.

259 *Their houseboy at the ranch said*: Steinbeck to Elizabeth Otis, May 8, 1940. Stanford, M0263, 9/4.

259 *He figured that Saroyan would be*: Steinbeck to Elizabeth Otis, May 7, 1940. Stanford, M0263, 9/4.

259 *Steinbeck admitted to having*: Ibid.

259 *He signed it over to his friend*: Lovejoy, John, "The Man Who Became a Steinbeck Footnote," *Steinbeck Review* 5, no. 2 (November 25, 2008).

259 *He wrote to Elizabeth Otis from Mexico*: Steinbeck to Elizabeth Otis, May 8, 1940. Stanford, M0263, 9/4.

260 *Gwen—whose recollections of this time*: Halladay, *The Closest Witness*, p. 46.

260 *He bought himself a new pen*: Steinbeck to Elizabeth Otis, December 29, 1940. Stanford, M0263, 9/4.

260   *In January 1941, he was in*: Steinbeck, *Working Days*, entry for January 20, 1941, pp. 124–25.

260   *He told Pat Covici that humankind*: Steinbeck to Pascal Covici, January 1, 1941. ALL, pp. 220–22.

261   *Toward the end of the month*: Steinbeck, *Working Days*, entry for January 28, 1941, pp. 125–26.

261   *"And if we seem a small factor"*: Steinbeck and Ricketts, *Sea of Cortez*, pp. 3–4.

Chapter Thirteen: Conceived in Adventure and Dedicated to Progress

265   *Alone in Pacific Grove*: Steinbeck, *Working Days*, entry for January 29, 1941, pp. 126–27.

265   *Steinbeck claimed he was "ill in the mind"*: Ibid., entry for January 30, 1941, pp. 127–28.

265   *After working a couple of weeks*: Steinbeck to Elizabeth Otis, February 1, 1941. Stanford, Mo263, 9/4.

265   *He counseled Elizabeth Otis*: Steinbeck to Elizabeth Otis, February 17, 1941. Stanford, Mo263, 9/4.

266   *Gwen came up to Pacific Grove*: ALL, p. 228.

266   *In what seems the more truthful version*: Hallady, *The Closest Witness*, pp. 46–48.

266   *Steinbeck confided to Mavis McIntosh*: Steinbeck to Mavis McIntosh, April 16, 1941. ALL, pp. 227–28.

266   *When Gwen arrived*: Hallady, *The Closest Witness*, pp. 46–48.

267   *He told Steinbeck to skip a third draft*: Pascal Covici to Steinbeck, July 2, 1941. HRC.

268   *He told Gwen's mother that*: Halladay, *The Closest Witness*, p. 57.

268   *Covici, who by this time knew*: Pascal Covici to Steinbeck, July 2, 1941. HRC.

268   *A poll the day before the election*: Hastings, *Inferno: The World at War, 1939–1945*, p. 184.

269   *At the start of 1941*: "The American Century," *Life*, February 17, 1941.

270   *But he admitted to feeling free at last*: Steinbeck to Mavis McIntosh, n.d. 1941. SJSU.

270   *The house was "easy"*: Ibid.

271   *Mavis McIntosh had suggested*: ALL, p. 233.

271   *There was no point, he said*: Ibid.

271   *Steinbeck had remained friendly*: Steinbeck to Toby Street, October 18, 1941. ALL, p. 234.

271   *Meanwhile,* The Forgotten Village *had run afoul*: Steinbeck to Toby Street, November 17, 1941. ALL, pp. 235–36.

271   . . . *though Charles Poore of the* New York Times: TCR, pp. 203–4.

272   *Writing in the* Monterey Peninsula Herald: TCR, pp. 205–6.

272   *"It is amazing," he wrote*: Steinbeck, *Sea of Cortez*, p. 10.

273   *A month later he was making revisions*: Steinbeck to Toby Street, January 12, 1942. ALL, pp. 239–40.

273   *In a faint echo of the dream*: Steinbeck to Toby Street, January 12, 1942. ALL, pp. 239–40.

273   *Steinbeck would pay her $100,000*: Steinbeck to Mavis McIntosh, n.d. 1941. SJSU.

274   *Gwyn, he said, worked*: ALL, p. 242.

275   *Some 85,000 copies were sold*: ALL, p. 242.

275   *Annie Laurie Williams sold the film rights*: Steinbeck to Toby Street, May 8, 1942. Stanford, Mo263, 5/27. Steinbeck reminded Street that he had to share this money with the play's producer and also pay his agents their commission. This meant he would net $162,000.

276   *The OWI rejected it for being defeatist*: Steinbeck, *The Moon Is Down*, introduction, pp. vii–ix.

276   *That spring, while still waiting*: Steinbeck to Francis Biddle, n.d. spring 1942. SJSU.

277   *The FBI maintained at the time*: Memorandum from J. Edgar Hoover for the attorney general, May 21, 1942. SJSU.

277   *But the Bureau did eventually*: FBI file 100–106224. SJSU.

278   *He told Toby Street he hoped to sign on*: JSW, p. 512.

278   *In January of 1943*: Steinbeck to Annie Laurie Williams, January 8, 1943. ALL, p. 249.

278   *Steinbeck was sufficiently annoyed*: Steinbeck to Annie Laurie Williams (telegram), February 19, 1944. ALL, p. 267.

278   *In mid-March, Toby Street informed*: ALL, p. 250.

278   *His friend Richard Albee*: Pauline Pearson interview with Richard Albee, April 25, 1975. NSC.

279   *But Steinbeck was drunk in New Orleans*: Halladay, *The Closest Witness*, pp. 111–17.

280   *It was hot and cloudy in London*: Steinbeck to Gwyn Steinbeck, July 4, 1943. ALL, p. 256.

280   *In August, after not writing for a few days*: Steinbeck to Gwyn Steinbeck, August 13, 1943. ALL, pp. 258–59.

280   *In a story he filed*: Steinbeck, *Once There Was a War*, pp. 105–8.

280   *He said he'd probably be back in London*: Steinbeck to Gwyn Steinbeck, August 13, 1943. ALL, pp. 258–59.

280   *Toward the end of the month*: Steinbeck to Gwyn Steinbeck, August 28, 1943. ALL, pp. 261–62.

280   *Steinbeck hurt his knee*: Steinbeck, *Once There Was a War*, pp. 131–33.

281   *The troops he went in with*: Ibid., pp. 126–28.

281   *Everyone noticed Steinbeck's courage*: Fairbanks Jr., *A Hell of a War*, pp. 190–96.

281   *Steinbeck became an object of fascination*: JSW, p. 536.

281   *One dark night when*: Fairbanks Jr., *A Hell of a War*, pp. 190–96.

282   *In Steinbeck's account*: Steinbeck, *Once There Was a War*, pp. 175–87.

282   *He still couldn't get any news*: Steinbeck to Toby Street, n.d. November 1943. Stanford, Mo263, 6/4.

282   *When they finally got an answer*: Personal communication, Susan Shillinglaw.

282   *Steinbeck told Toby Street*: Steinbeck to Toby Street, December 13, 1943. ALL, pp. 265–66.

282   *Gwyn said he wasn't*: Halladay, *The Closest Witness*, p. 147.

282   *In January 1944*: Ibid.

282   *They took a trip to Mexico City*: Ibid., pp. 147–54.

282   *He and Gwyn moved into the lower part*: Steinbeck to Dook Sheffield, April 12, 1944. Stanford, Mo263, 5/10.

282   *He told Dook Sheffield that although*: Ibid.

282   *In Mexico he'd suffered a*: Ibid.

282   *He told Annie Laurie Williams*: ALL, p. 267.

282   *Earlier, he'd confided to Toby Street*: Steinbeck to Toby Street, December 13, 1943. Stanford, M0263, 6/5.

283   *Eventually he learned that*: Steinbeck to Dook Sheffield, April 12, 1944. Stanford, M0263, 5/10.

283   *Sometimes he worked at home*: Steinbeck to Toby Street, July 4, 1944. Stanford, M0263, 6/5.

283   *"I'm trying to forget that"*: Steinbeck to Esther Steinbeck Rodgers, April 3, 1944. Stanford, M1063, 2/99.

283   *Besides, "I don't like fighting"*: Ibid.

283   *A month later, he told Esther*: Steinbeck to Esther Steinbeck Rodgers, May 2, 1944. Stanford, M1063, 2/100.

283   *. . . even though he told Dook Sheffield*: Steinbeck to Dook Sheffield, May 10, 1944. Stanford, M0263, 5/10.

283   *Thom was a "pudge"*: Steinbeck to Mary Steinbeck Dekker, August 4, 1944. Dekker.

283   *Unfortunately . . . Thom seemed to resemble*: Steinbeck to Mary Steinbeck Dekker, n.d. August 1944. Dekker. By middle age he would look like his father's twin.

283   *At Viking, Pascal Covici could not contain*: Pascal Covici to Steinbeck, November 15, 1944. HRC.

284   *Steinbeck sent a galley copy*: Sheffield, *John Steinbeck: The Good Companion*, pp. 174–75. Steinbeck managed to convince himself that the falling out was Sheffield's doing. In the spring of 1946 he complained to Carl Wilhelmson that he never heard from Sheffield anymore.

284   *Covici disputed Sheffield's opinion*: Pascal Covici to Steinbeck, November 15, 1944. HRC.

286   *One called the book a "small miracle"*: TRC, pp. 271–72. The reviewer was Nathan L. Rothman, writing in the *Saturday Review.*

286   *The hard-to-please Edmund Wilson*: TCR, p. 278. Wilson's review as in *The New Yorker.*

287   *Even Mack was based on*: Tamm, *Beyond the Outer Shores*, pp. 131–32.

287   *He said he never wanted to spend another*: Steinbeck to Esther Steinbeck Rodgers, August 12, 1944. Stanford, M1063, 2/104.

287   *He'd found a pair of adjoining houses*: Steinbeck to Mary Steinbeck Dekker, September 2, 1944. Dekker.

287   *Gwyn would fly ahead*: Steinbeck to Mary Steinbeck Dekker, September 27, 1944. Dekker.

288   *Steinbeck thought this story was*: Steinbeck, *Sea of Cortez*, pp. 102–3.

288   *But the story went more slowly*: Pascal Covici to Steinbeck, December 1, 1944. HRC.

288   *Built in the 1830s*: "Monterey's Lara-Soto Adobe," Monterey County Historical Society.

288   *Steinbeck sent a picture of the place*: Pascal Covici to Steinbeck, December 12, 1944. HRC.

288 *Meanwhile, Covici said orders*: Pascal Covici to Steinbeck, December 19, 1944. HRC.

289 *. . . a heavyset woman who*: Halladay, *The Closest Witness,* pp. 186-87.

289 *Steinbeck must have found*: Steinbeck to Pascal Covici, n.d. November 1944. ALL, p. 275.

289 *They stayed first*: Steinbeck to Mary Steinbeck Dekker, April 20, 1945. Dekker.

289 *They had a dog named Willie*: Steinbeck to Mary Steinbeck Dekker, May 14, 1945. Dekker.

289 *One day Willie disappeared*: Steinbeck to Mary Steinbeck Dekker, July 9, 1945. Dekker.

289 *The baby Thom, Steinbeck said*: Steinbeck to Mary Steinbeck Dekker, May 14, 1945. Dekker.

290 *Pascal Covici was willing to bet*: Pascal Covici to Steinbeck, November 20, 1945. HRC.

290 *A production company he'd never*: Steinbeck to Annie Laurie Williams, June 26, 1945. ALL, pp. 282–83.

290 *A few weeks later, though*: ALL, p. 283.

290 *Old friends, though they didn't say it*: Steinbeck to Pascal Covici, n.d. spring 1945. ALL, pp. 280–81.

290 *Steinbeck insisted there was a general distaste*: ALL, pp. 279–80.

290 *Then, in July, Gwyn came down with*: Steinbeck to Mary Steinbeck Dekker, July 31, 1945. Dekker.

290 *As soon as she was back*: Ibid.

290 *In October, Steinbeck was "back in the tropics"*: Steinbeck to Mary Steinbeck Dekker, October 25, 1945. Dekker.

290 *The film production had moved*: Ibid.

291 *Late in the fall, Steinbeck bought*: Steinbeck to Mary Steinbeck Dekker, November 10, 1945. Dekker.

291 *By March 1946*: Steinbeck to Toby Street, March 17, 1946. Stanford, M0263, 6/7.

291 *It was windowless*: Ibid.

291 *But then the idea that*: Steinbeck to Carl Wilhelmson, n.d. early 1946. Stanford, M0263, 7/9.

Chapter Fourteen: A Rock Falls into the Water

292 *In the winter of 1946*: Steinbeck to Mary Steinbeck Dekker, February 12, 1946. Dekker.

292 *But it never came together*: Steinbeck to Mary Steinbeck Dekker, March 16, 1946. Dekker.

292 *Steinbeck wrote him a letter of condolence*: Steinbeck to Ed Ricketts, n.d. August 1946. ALL, p. 292.

292 *He considered it a "strange" book*: Steinbeck to Esther Steinbeck Rodgers, October 3, 1946. Stanford, M1063, 3/5.

292 *As soon as he was finished*: Ibid.

293 *Steinbeck wrote to his sister*: Steinbeck to Esther Steinbeck Rodgers, October 19, 1946. Stanford, M1063, 3/9.

293   *Steinbeck could not get enough*: Steinbeck to Mary Steinbeck Dekker, October 26, 1946. Dekker.

293   *In Copenhagen, Steinbeck was met*: Steinbeck to Elizabeth Otis, October 30, 1946. Stanford, M0263, 9/6.

293   *He noticed that air-raid shelters*: Ibid.

293   *From there they went on to Stockholm*: ALL, p. 294.

293   *The trip ended a week early*: Steinbeck to Esther Steinbeck Rodgers, November 19, 1946. Stanford, M1063, 3/11.

293   *Steinbeck and Nat Benchley fixed*: Halladay, *The Closest Witness*, pp. 199–200.

293   *Steinbeck sent a copy to Esther*: Steinbeck to Esther Steinbeck Rodgers, n.d. February 1947. Stanford, M1063, 3/15.

294   *Steinbeck wrote to Max Wagner's brother*: Steinbeck to Jack Wagner, February 16, 1947. Stanford, M0263, 7/4.

294   *The Book-of-the-Month Club ordered*: Steinbeck to Jack Wagner, January 12, 1946. Stanford, M0263, 7/3.

294   *The people who were going to attack*: Steinbeck to Bo Beskow, n.d. ALL, p. 296.

295   *Carlos Baker, who would go on*: TCR, pp. 295–96.

295   *Orville Prescott, offering a contrary opinion*: TCR, p. 298.

296   *Ralph Habas, writing in*: TCR, p. 297.

296   *One night in mid-May*: Steinbeck to Mary Steinbeck Dekker, May 27, 1947. Dekker.

296   *When he leaned over the railing*: Halladay, *The Closest Witness*, pp. 205–6.

297   *He approached the* New York Herald Tribune: ALL, p. 297.

297   *One day earlier that spring*: Steinbeck, *A Russian Journal*, pp. 3–4.

297   *Steinbeck and Gwyn first went*: Steinbeck to Esther Steinbeck Rodgers, July 12, 1947. Stanford, M1063, 3/21.

297   *One night the four of them attended*: Halladay, *The Closest Witness*, p. 212.

297   *The weather was unusually lovely*: Steinbeck to Esther Steinbeck Rodgers, July 12, 1947. Stanford, M1063, 3/21.

297   *He and Gwyn were excited*: Ibid.

297   *At Viking, Pascal Covici looked forward*: Pascal Covici to Steinbeck, July 10, 1947. HRC.

298   *In a letter to Steinbeck in Paris*: Ibid.

298   *In a follow-up letter a week later*: Pascal Covici to Steinbeck, July 17, 1947. HRC.

299   *Steinbeck's account of his visit*: Descriptions of this trip are from *A Russian Journal*.

300   *As the end of August approached*: Steinbeck to Gwyn Steinbeck, August 20, 1947. ALL, pp. 299–300.

300   *From Stalingrad he described*: Ibid.

300   *He huddled with Mavis McIntosh and*: Halladay, *The Closest Witness*, p. 218.

300   *Steinbeck said it was going to be*: Steinbeck to Toby Street, November 17, 1947. Stanford, M0263, 6/8.

300   *Steinbeck rented an office*: Steinbeck to Mary Steinbeck Dekker, October 10, 1947. Dekker.

301   *Often, when she was putting the boys*: Halladay, *The Closest Witness*, pp. 201–2.

301   *He'd come up and interrupt Gwyn*: Ibid.

301   *If they stayed in they usually had*: Ibid.

301   *Steinbeck now slept on*: Ibid., p. 227.

301 *She said that Steinbeck forced her*: Halladay, *The Closest Witness*, p. 195.

301 *"My only mistake was"*: Ibid.

301 *Gwyn maintained that*: Ibid., p. 227.

302 *One who was less happy*: TCR, pp. 315–16.

303 *Carlos Baker, the critic who*: TCR, pp. 318–19.

304 *He got into the countryside*: Steinbeck to Pascal Covici, n.d. February 1948. ALL, p. 304.

304 *. . . and slept twelve hours at a stretch*: Steinbeck to Bo Beskow, February 12, 1948. ALL, pp. 305–7.

304 *Steinbeck believed it might take*: Steinbeck to Ed Ricketts, n.d. April 1948. ALL, pp. 309–10.

304 *He told himself to write in the journal*: Steinbeck, 1948 journal, entry for February 3, 1948. PM. The handwritten journal is held at the Pierpont Morgan Library in New York. Susan Shillinglaw provided me with a copy of a transcript she made from the original.

304 *"Something is very wrong"*: Ibid.

305 *When Hemingway checked into*: Farah, *Hemingway's Brain*, p. 101.

306 *On February 27—his forty-sixth birthday*: Steinbeck, 1948 journal, entry for February 27, 1948. PM.

306 *In early March he drove up*: Ibid., entry for March 2, 1948. PM.

306 *When they met up Covici just stared*: Ibid., entry for March 24, 1948. PM.

306 *The anxiety came in waves*: Ibid., entry for March 22, 1948. PM.

306 *Steinbeck underwent batteries*: Ibid., entries for March 23–24, 1948. PM.

307 *He wrote to tell Ed Ricketts that he*: Steinbeck to Ed Ricketts, n.d. April 1948. ALL, pp. 309–10.

307 *A couple of years earlier*: Steinbeck to Mary Steinbeck Dekker, July 20, 1946. Dekker.

308 *In late April, Steinbeck checked into*: Steinbeck to Ed Ricketts, n.d. April 1948. ALL, pp. 309–10.

309 *He told his sister Mary that*: Steinbeck to Mary Steinbeck Dekker, May 1, 1948. Dekker.

309 *Steinbeck thought she was making herself ill*: Steinbeck, 1948 journal, entry for May 2, 1948. PM.

310 *At the hospital he was taken*: George Robinson interview with Dr. John Gratiot, April 14, 1975. NSC.

310 *Steinbeck got word of the accident*: Steinbeck, 1948 journal, entry for May 9, 1948. PM.

310 *There was an encouraging update*: Ibid.

310 *On May 10 he decided to fly*: Ibid., entry for May 10, 1948. PM.

310 *He struggled to grasp*: Steinbeck to Bo Beskow, May 22, 1948. ALL, pp. 312–14.

310 *Steinbeck called in a locksmith*: Pauline Pearson and William Cole interview with George Robinson, November 8, 1972. NSC.

311 *Steinbeck got to know Robinson*: Ibid.

311 *Back in New York after ten days*: Steinbeck to Toby Street, May 25, 1948. Stanford, M0263, 6/8.

311 *Two days later he wrote to Ritchie*: Steinbeck to Ritchie and Natalya Lovejoy, May 27, 1948. ALL, pp. 316–17.

312 *A few days later, Steinbeck put aside his book*: Steinbeck, 1948 journal, entry for June 7, 1948. PM.

312 *Steinbeck admitted to Bo Beskow*: Steinbeck to Bo Beskow, June 19, 1948. ALL, pp. 317–18.

312 *He went on a three-day drinking binge*: Steinbeck, 1948 journal, entry for July 26, 1948. PM.

312 *When he didn't, he assumed*: Ibid.

312 *But now he didn't think she was seeing*: Steinbeck to Mary Steinbeck Dekker, August 19, 1948. Dekker.

313 *In his journal he wrote that*: Steinbeck, 1948 journal, entry for May 26, 1948. PM.

313 *Steinbeck told himself he was a "sucker"*: Ibid., entry for August 15, 1948. PM.

313 *One evening in August, they went out*: Halladay, *The Closest Witness*, pp. 229–30.

313 *By the end of the month*: Steinbeck to Toby Street, August 27, 1948. Stanford, M0263, 6/8.

313 *He talked to Toby Street about the two of them*: Ibid.

313 *Steinbeck said he was finished*: Steinbeck to Bo Beskow, n.d. August 1948. ALL, pp. 321–22.

313 *The place was empty*: Steinbeck to Pascal Covici, September 12, 1948. ALL, pp. 330–31.

314 *Pascal Covici told Steinbeck that*: Pascal Covici to Steinbeck, September 15, 1948. HRC.

314 *He admitted to moments of panic*: Steinbeck to Pascal Covici, n.d. September 1948. ALL, pp. 329–30.

314 *Steinbeck had tried to add a provision*: Steinbeck, 1948 journal, entries for August 25–26. PM.

314 *According to the report*: Steinbeck included these newspaper reports in his journal on October 30, 1948.

314 *In November, a woman named Mildred Lyman*: ALL, p. 339.

315 *He wondered, bizarrely, if he should*: Steinbeck, 1948 journal, entry for November 17, 1948. PM.

315 *Steinbeck boasted to Bo Beskow*: Steinbeck to Bo Beskow, November 19, 1948. ALL, pp. 341–44.

315 *He wrote back thanking them*: Steinbeck to the American Academy of Arts and Letters, December 3, 1948. ALL, p. 344.

315 *It seemed, he said, like a premature*: Steinbeck, 1948 journal, entry for November 21, 1948. PM.

315 *He talked with Carol on the phone*: Ibid., entry for December 13, 1948. PM.

315 *Steinbeck wished, though*: Ibid., entry for December 28, 1948. PM.

316 *He told Pat Covici that*: Steinbeck to Pascal Covici, February 22, 1949. ALL, p. 349.

316 *He also wrote to Gwyn*: Steinbeck to Gwyndolyn Steinbeck, May 3, 1949. ALL, p. 351.

316 *He hoped to make them do*: Steinbeck to Bo Beskow, May 23, 1949. ALL, pp. 354–55.

316 *He had an affair with*: JSW, p. 631.

316 *So did a report about his guests*: ALL, p. 355. The *Monterey Peninsula Herald* ran a photo of Steinbeck, in a suit and bow tie, seated between Sothern and Scott while lunching at the Pine Inn.

316 *Within a week Steinbeck wrote Elaine*: Steinbeck to Elaine Scott, June 6, 1949, Stanford, M0263.

317 *Toward the end of June*: Steinbeck to Elaine Scott, June 20, 1949. Stanford, M0263.

317 *By November Elaine had told Zachary*: Steinbeck to Elaine Scott, November 7, 1949. Stanford, M0263.

317 *He told her he adored her*: Ibid.

317 *He sent Elaine his mother's*: ALL, p. 388.

317 *Steinbeck started out at the Plaza*: Steinbeck to Esther Steinbeck Rodgers, n.d. December 1949. Stanford, M1063, 6/12.

317 *Cold weather arrived just before*: Steinbeck to Bo Beskow, n.d. late December 1949. ALL, pp. 397–98.

317 *He walked everywhere*: Ibid.

317 *He told Bo Beskow that his life*: Ibid.

317 *Elaine made Steinbeck happy*: Steinbeck to Bo Beskow, January 24, 1950. ALL, p. 400.

317 *Steinbeck, conveniently forgetting*: Steinbeck to Bo Beskow, n.d. late July 1950. ALL, pp. 402–4.

318 *Steinbeck's explanation was that*: Steinbeck to Mary Steinbeck Dekker, February 2, 1950. Dekker.

318 *Steinbeck thought the cast*: Steinbeck to Toby Street, August 20, 1950. ALL, pp. 408–9.

318 *Steinbeck told Toby Street that*: Ibid.

319 *He told Gwyn they were great company*: Steinbeck to Gwyndolyn Steinbeck, August 22, 1950. ALL, pp. 406–7.

319 *On December 28, 1950*: Steinbeck to Mary Steinbeck Dekker, January 1, 1951. Dekker.

319 *The boys loved Elaine's daughter*: Steinbeck to Pascal Covici, January 5, 1951. ALL, p. 417.

319 *Steinbeck and Elaine spent their wedding night*: Ibid.

319 *They honeymooned at*: Steinbeck to Mary Steinbeck Dekker, January 1, 1951. Dekker.

319 *He told Pat Covici they moved lazily*: Steinbeck to Pascal Covici, January 5, 1951. ALL, p. 417.

319 *One day the wind came up*: Steinbeck to Mary Steinbeck Dekker, January 1, 1951. Dekker.

Chapter Fifteen: Each Book Dies a Real Death

320 *The date was January 29, 1951*: From the daily diary that Steinbeck kept for Covici on the left-hand side of the notebook in which he wrote *East of Eden* on the right-hand pages. This journal portion was later published by Viking as *Journal of a Novel*.

321 *He called this a "double entry" approach*: JON, p. 5.

321 *He seemed reluctant to start*: JON, pp. 11–14.

322 *He said he was happier than*: JON, p. 13.

322 *Steinbeck cut down on his drinking*: Ibid.

323 *He admitted that he felt silly*: JON, p. 16.

323 *At that rate he said he might finish*: JON, p. 68.

323 *Steinbeck was still putting*: JON, p. 69.

323 *In May, one of Elaine's distant relatives*: JON, pp. 81–82.

323 *Maybe, he said, it should be called*: Ibid.

323 *He said he'd "never been a title man"*: JON, p. 86.

323 *At least he hoped this was true*: JON, p. 89.

323 *He told Covici that while he did not have a death wish*: Ibid.

323 *"The book dies a real death for me"*: JON, p. 90.

323 *He told Covici he needed one*: JON, p. 104.

324 *Steinbeck said the story changed and blared*: Ibid.

324 *He'd even asked Elizabeth Otis*: Steinbeck to Elizabeth Otis, May 21, 1951. Stanford, M0263, 9/7.

325 *Steinbeck said he could tell*: JON, p. 109.

325 *The book, he told Covici*: Ibid.

325 *He described one chapter*: Pascal Covici to Steinbeck, July 3, 1951. HRC.

325 *He claimed the book held his attention "like a vise"*: Pascal Covici to Steinbeck, July 10, 1951. HRC. Covici's letters were typed by an assistant, so it's hard to know which of them to blame for spelling it "vice," but I thought it would be polite to fix it.

325 *He wrote them immediately*: Steinbeck to Mr. and Mrs. Pascal Covici, n.d. August 1951. ALL, pp. 426–27.

325 *By the end of August*: Pascal Covici to Steinbeck, August 21, 1951. HRC.

325 *He was exhausted, but the downtime*: JON, p. 160.

325 *He got started unusually early*: JON, p. 164.

325 *On October 10, he told Covici*: JON, p. 167.

326 *A week later he wrote 3,000*: JON, p. 169.

326 *He told his sister Mary that*: Steinbeck to Mary Steinbeck Dekker, October 21, 1951. Dekker.

326 *Steinbeck and Elaine took a car trip*: Steinbeck to Mary Steinbeck Dekker, November 9, 1951. Dekker.

326 East of Eden, *set for publication*: Pascal Covici to Steinbeck, June 6, 1952. HRC.

326 *They also stopped off in Algiers*: Steinbeck to Elizabeth Otis, March 27, 1952. Stanford, M0263, 9/7.

326 *According to Covici, booksellers were*: Pascal Covici to Steinbeck, May 14, 1952. HRC.

326 *Covici tried to reassure Steinbeck*: Pascal Covici to Steinbeck, April 23, 1952. HRC.

327 *And it didn't dim Viking's*: Pascal Covici to Steinbeck, May 2, 1952. HRC.

327 *Shortly after Steinbeck and Elaine got home*: Steinbeck to Pascal Covici, September 9, 1952. ALL, p. 455.

327 *One of the more memorable reviews*: TCR, pp. 383–85.

329 *He thought the world had become*: East of Eden, pp. 130–31.

329 *An exception was the acid-penned*: TCR, pp. 387–89.

330 *He was mildly surprised to be*: Steinbeck to Dook Sheffield, September 10, 1952. Stanford, M0263, 5/10.

331 *Making the final revisions had been*: Ibid.

331 *"The first with water"*: Steinbeck to Elizabeth Otis, April 21, 1954. Stanford, M0263, 9/8.

331 *He told his sister Esther*: Steinbeck to Esther Steinbeck Rodgers, October 16, 1952. Stanford, M1063, 3/35.

331 *Three days after Eisenhower's landslide*: Steinbeck to Adlai Stevenson, November 7, 1952. ALL, p. 461.

333 *Late on the night of Monday, July 5*: Guralnick, *Last Train to Memphis*, pp. 94–97.

334 *Once, when John IV was*: Steinbeck (John IV) and Steinbeck, Nancy, *The Other Side of Eden*, p 22. Nancy Steinbeck confirmed to me that Catbird had emphatically assured her more than once that this story was true.

334 *John IV would later say*: Ibid., p. 149.

334 *On New Year's Eve of 1951*: Ibid., p. 5.

334 *By then he already knew how*: Ibid., p. 2.

335 *"For reasons that were never made clear"*: Ibid., p. 67.

335 *He told Thom that he had known many*: Steinbeck to Thom Steinbeck, May 24, 1960. Benson.

335 *For Thom's twelfth birthday he sent him*: Steinbeck to Thom Steinbeck, August 2, 1956. Benson.

336 *In the fall of 1958, as Catbird*: Steinbeck to Catbird Steinbeck, September 11, 1958. Benson.

336 *Just before he and Elaine went to Europe*: ALL, p. 477.

336 *Steinbeck did see a doctor*: Steinbeck to Elizabeth Otis, June 13, 1954. Stanford, M0263, 10/1.

336 *A year earlier, in the summer of 1953*: JSW, p. 741.

337 *It was fine to "smell the good wind"*: Steinbeck to Elizabeth Otis, September 14, 1953. Stanford, M0263, 9/8.

337 *Steinbeck ordered a boat*: Steinbeck to Toby Street, July 5, 1955. Stanford, M0263, 6/10.

337 *Eighteen inches of snow piled up*: Steinbeck to Toby Street, March 20, 1956. Stanford, M0263, 6/10.

337 *When he finished it in November*: Steinbeck to Elizabeth Otis, November 19, 1956. Stanford, M0263, 10/3.

338 *But now the money was steady*: Steinbeck to Mary Steinbeck Dekker, January 18, 1957. Dekker.

338 *He wondered about selling the house*: Ibid.

338 *He told his sister Mary that*: Ibid.

339 *In January of 1957, he wrote*: Steinbeck to Elizabeth Otis, January 3, 1957. Stanford, M0263, 10/3.

339 *One night, unable to sleep*: Ibid.

339 *Steinbeck also wrote to his sister*: Steinbeck to Mary Steinbeck Dekker, January 18, 1957. Dekker.

340 *He was astonished at the vastness*: ALL, p. 552.

340 *As one of Arthur's many creators said*: Ashe, *The Discovery of King Arthur*, p. 13.

340 *In a long, self-involved letter*: Steinbeck to Elizabeth Otis, April 26, 1957. Stanford, M0263, 10/4.

341 *He said he hoped Vinaver*: Steinbeck to Professor and Mrs. Eugene Vinaver, July 20, 1957. ALL, p. 557.

341 *The illness followed the harrowing first day*: Steinbeck to Elaine Steinbeck, September 3, 1957. ALL, pp. 567–68.

341   *Steinbeck judged Waverly's attitude*: Steinbeck to Esther Steinbeck Rodgers, December 16, 1957. Stanford, M1063, 3/52.

341   *He told Vinaver that he felt*: Steinbeck to Professor and Mrs. Vinaver, June 27, 1958. ALL, pp. 591–92.

341   *Back in Sag Harbor, he wrote*: Steinbeck to Elizabeth Otis, July 9, 1958. Stanford, M0263, 10/5.

341   *Later that fall, back in New York*: Steinbeck to Esther Steinbeck Rodgers (and Beth and Mary), November 29, 1958, 3/60.

341   *Steinbeck wrote back, counseling his son*: Steinbeck to Thom Steinbeck, November 10, 1958. ALL, pp. 600–601.

Chapter Sixteen: The Best I Could Do

343   *Covici said he had ordered a copy of*: Pascal Covici to Steinbeck, July 16, 1958. HRC.

343   *In the fall of 1958, Covici visited Steinbeck*: Pascal Covici to Steinbeck, October 2, 1958. HRC.

343   *In December, he wrote*: Steinbeck to Elizabeth Otis, December 7, 1958. Stanford, M0263, 10/5.

344   *Steinbeck wrote a more restrained letter*: Steinbeck to Pascal Covici, December 26, 1958. ALL, pp. 609–10.

344   *The Steinbecks rented a sturdy Hillman*: Steinbeck to Esther Steinbeck Rodgers, February 20, 1959. Stanford, M1063, 3/61.

344   *It was called Discove Cottage*: ALL, p. 615.

344   *Steinbeck believed the cottage must have once been*: ALL, p. 617.

345   *Elaine kept busy by making friends*: Steinbeck to Mr. and Mrs. Graham Watson, Mar. 14, 1959. ALL, pp. 615–16.

345   *She taught one of the locals to greet them*: Ibid.

345   *After two weeks, Steinbeck told Elizabeth*: Steinbeck to Elizabeth Otis, March 23, 1959. Stanford, M0263, 10/5.

345   *Otis wrote to tell him he owed $21,500*: Ibid.

345   *By the middle of April, he had a draft*: Steinbeck to Esther Steinbeck Rodgers, April 13, 1959. Stanford, M1063, 3/63.

345   *On the last day of April, Steinbeck hiked*: ALL, p. 629.

345   *He told Eugene Vinaver*: Ibid.

346   *He wrote back saying he would not*: Steinbeck to Elizabeth Otis, May 13, 1959. ALL, pp. 633–34. This is one of a number of letters to Otis, including some I am unsure about, that appear in *A Life in Letters* but that I did not find in the Stanford collection. Researchers in doubt should check both locations.

346   *He wrote again the next day*: Steinbeck to Elizabeth Otis, May 14, 1959. ALL, pp. 634–35.

346   *"I believe in this thing"*: Ibid.

347   *Toward the end of August*: Steinbeck to Eugene Vinaver, August 27, 1959. ALL, pp. 648–49.

347   *"Mary snapped at him*: Steinbeck to Elizabeth Otis, June 7, 1959. ALL, pp. 640–41.

347   *In September of 1959, as their days*: Pascal Covici to Steinbeck, September 17, 1959. HRC. Steinbeck's letter to Covici is long lost but can be inferred from Covici's letter cited here. This kind of thing happens a lot.

347   *Covici wrote back to say*: Ibid.

348   *Steinbeck told Vinaver*: Steinbeck to Professor and Mrs. Eugene Vinaver, n.d. October 1959. ALL, p. 651.

348   *. . . Steinbeck thought the contestants were*: ALL, p. 653.

348   *Elaine went to check on him*: ALL, p. 655.

348   *Steinbeck wrote Vinaver*: ALL, p. 656.

348   *When he wrote to Elizabeth Otis, he said*: Steinbeck to Elizabeth Otis, December 30, 1959. Stanford, Mo263, 10/6.

350   *. . . though Otis tried to talk Steinbeck into*: Steinbeck to Elizabeth Otis, n.d. June 1960. Stanford, Mo263, 10/6.

350   *In June 1960, Steinbeck told*: Steinbeck to Pascal Covici, June 20, 1960. ALL, pp. 671–72.

351   *Steinbeck was half-drowned*: Steinbeck, *Travels with Charley*, pp. 12–16.

351   *"For I have always lived violently"*: Ibid., p. 20.

352   *Steinbeck and Elaine motored*: JSW, p. 891.

352   *Word came during this vacation*: Ibid.

352   *The people at Viking thought*: Ibid.

352   *Catbird sometimes helped himself*: Steinbeck, John IV, and Steinbeck, Nancy, *The Other Side of Eden*, pp. 63–64.

352   *One day Catbird loaded his .22 rifle*: Ibid., p. 71.

353   *A year later, during an ill-advised visit*: Ibid., p. 93.

353   *Reviewing the book for the* New York Times: TCR, pp. 460–61.

354   *Baker's fellow* Times *critic*: Ibid., pp. 457–58.

354   *He told Elizabeth Otis he'd known*: Steinbeck to Elizabeth Otis, June 26, 1961. Stanford, Mo263, 10/7.

354   *He told Pat Covici the book*: Steinbeck to Pascal Covici, n.d. July 1961. ALL, pp. 702–3.

354   *It was a blow that Pat Covici said he felt*: Pascal Covici to Steinbeck, July 7, 1961. HRC.

354   *Covici urged Steinbeck to*: Ibid.

354   *When Covici visited Steinbeck*: Ibid.

355   *Then, in November, they were in Milan*: ALL, p. 726.

355   *Steinbeck ominously called it*: Pauline Pearson interview with Dook Sheffield, January 19, 1975. NSC.

355   *Steinbeck wrote to Elizabeth Otis*: ALL, p. 726.

355   *Covici told him orders for tzhe book*: Pascal Covici to Steinbeck, February 8, 1962. HRC.

355   *Covici, who had been enthusiastic*: Ibid.

355   *"Almost everything that you ever thought"*: Ibid.

356   *In the* New York Times: TCR, pp. 481–82.

356   *"I've always admired those reporters who"*: Steinbeck, *Travels with Charley*, p. 76.

357   *In April of 2011, the* New York Times: "A Reality Check for Steinbeck and Charley," *New York Times*, April 3, 2011.

358 *According to Catbird*: Steinbeck, John IV, and Steinbeck, Nancy, *The Other Side of Eden*, p. 151.

359 *The next day Steinbeck and Elaine*: ALL, p. 742.

360 *The prize committee specifically cited*: "Steinbeck Wins Nobel Prize for His 'Realistic' Writing," *New York Times*, October 26, 1962.

360 *In an odd aside*: Ibid.

360 *On October 26, the day after the announcement*: "Literature Award," *New York Times*, October 26, 1962.

360 *In a lacerating profile*: "Does a Moral Vision of the Thirties Deserve a Nobel Prize?" *New York Times*, December 9, 1962.

362 *"They," he wrote*: "Critics, Critics, Burning Bright," *Saturday Review*, November 11, 1950.

362 *Gray argued that Steinbeck's critics*: Gray, "John Steinbeck," University of Minnesota Pamphlets on American Writers, no. 94, 1971.

363 *"All his work," Gray wrote*: Ibid.

363 *Steinbeck told Dook Sheffield he would need to be*: Steinbeck to Dook Sheffield, November 1, 1962. Stanford, Mo263, 5/11.

363 *He wrote to Tal Lovejoy*: Steinbeck to Natalya Lovejoy, n.d. November 1962. ALL, pp. 744–45.

363 *Steinbeck heard from Vinaver*: Steinbeck to Professor and Mrs. Eugene Vinaver, November 6, 1962. ALL, pp. 748–49.

363 *Steinbeck and Elaine made their*: Steinbeck to Bo Beskow, November 1, 1962. ALL, pp. 747–48.

363 *Steinbeck wanted to follow protocol*: Ibid.

363 *He wrote a plaintive letter to Adlai Stevenson*: Steinbeck to Adlai Stevenson, November 20, 1962. ALL, pp. 755–56.

364 *"In my heart," he said*: www.nobelprize.org/prizes/literature/1962/steinbeck/speech/.

364 *"Pat Covici was much more than"*: "Covici: Steinbeck's Editor, Collaborator, and Conscience," *Saturday Review*, June 25, 1966.

364 *Steinbeck joined Saul Bellow and Arthur Miller*: Parini, *John Steinbeck*, p. 460.

365 *"We cut ourselves off from the self-abuse of war"*: Steinbeck, *America and Americans*, p. 143.

365 *Considering the book a few years later*: Gray, "John Steinbeck," University of Minnesota Pamphlets on American Writers, no. 94, 1971.

365 *After coming back, he visited*: JSW, p. 1014.

366 *In August of 1967:* Steinbeck to Elizabeth Otis, August 31, 1967. Stanford, Mo263, 11/3.

366 *On the morning of the procedure*: Steinbeck, John IV, *In Touch*, p. 112.

366 *"They should have jailed you"*: Steinbeck, John IV, and Steinbeck, Nancy, *The Other Side of Eden*, p. 150. Years before John IV began working on this book, his brother Thom—a sometimes unreliable source—attempted to convince Terry Halladay that Catbird and Steinbeck had reconciled during Steinbeck's final illness. Nancy Steinbeck, John IV's widow, assured me no such reconciliation ever occurred.

367   *Some were "incidents"*: Steinbeck to Dook Sheffield, August 17, 1968. ALL, p. 855.

367   *There was a scare in August*: Elaine Steinbeck to Esther Steinbeck Rodgers, August 29, 1968. Stanford, M1063, 4/87.

368   *It was Max Wagner*: Pauline Pearson interview with Max Wagner, May 25, 1975. NSC.

368   *John Steinbeck died at 5:30*: ALL, p. 861.

BIBLIOGRAPHY

Adam, Peter. *Art of the Third Reich*. New York: Henry N. Abrams, 1992.

Albee, George Sumner. *By the Sea, By the Sea*. New York: Simon & Schuster, 1960.

Allee, W. C. *Animal Aggregations, a Study in General Sociology*. Chicago: University of Chicago Press, 1931.

———. *Cooperation Among Animals*. New York: Henry Schuman, 1938.

———. *The Social Life of Animals*. New York: Abelard-Schuman, 1938.

Allee, W. C., et al. *Principles of Animal Ecology*. Philadelphia: W.B. Saunders, 1949.

Anderson, Burton. *The Salinas Valley: A History of America's Salad Bowl*. Salinas: Monterey County Historical Society, 2000.

Ariss, Bruce. *Inside Cannery Row: Sketches from the Steinbeck Era*. San Francisco: Lexikos, 1988.

Arvin, Newton. *Herman Melville*. New York: William Sloane, 1950.

Ashe, Geoffrey. *The Discovery of King Arthur*. London: Guild Publishing, 1985.

Astro, Richard. *John Steinbeck and Edward F. Ricketts: The Shaping of a Novelist*. Minneapolis: University of Minnesota Press, 1973.

Astro, Richard, and Hayashi, Tetsumaro, eds. *Steinbeck: The Man and His Work*. Corvallis: Oregon State University, 1971.

Avina, Rose Hollenbaugh. *Spanish and Mexican Land Grants in California*. New York: Arno Press, 1976.

Babb, Sanora. *On the Dirty Plate Trail: Remembering the Dust Bowl Refugee Camps*, ed. Douglas Wixson. Austin: University of Texas Press, 2007.

———. *An Owl on Every Post*. New York: McCall, 1970.

———. *Whose Names Are Unknown*. Norman: University of Oklahoma Press, 2004.

Bailey, Kevin M. *The Western Flyer*. Chicago: University of Chicago Press, 2015.

Barden, Thomas E. *Steinbeck in Vietnam: Dispatches from the War*. Charlottesville: University of Virginia Press, 2012.

Beegel, Susan F., et al. *Steinbeck and the Environment*. Tuscaloosa: University of Alabama Press, 1997.

Beevor, Antony. *The Second World War*. Boston: Little, Brown, 2012.

Benson, Jackson J. *Looking for Steinbeck's Ghost*. Reno: University of Nevada Press, 2002.

———. *The True Adventures of John Steinbeck, Writer*. New York: Viking, 1984.

Berg, A. Scott. *Max Perkins: Editor of Genius*. New York: Dutton, 1978.

Bloom, Harold, ed. *John Steinbeck: Modern Critical Views*. New York: Bloom's Literary Criticism, 2008.

———. *John Steinbeck's* The Grapes of Wrath. New York: Chelsea House, 1988.

Boodin, John Elof. *Cosmic Evolution: Outlines of Cosmic Idealism*. New York: Macmillan, 1925 (reprint edition).

———. *The Social Mind*. New York: Macmillan, 1939.

Bradley, Sculley, et al. *The American Tradition in Literature*, 3rd ed. New York: W. W. Norton, 1967.

Breschini, Gary S., et al. *10,000 Years on the Salinas Plain: An Illustrated History of Salinas City, California*. Carlsbad: Heritage Media, 2000.

———. *Early Salinas*. Charleston: Arcadia, 2005.

Bruccoli, Matthew J. *Some Sort of Epic Grandeur: The Life of F. Scott Fitzgerald*. New York: Harcourt Brace Jovanovich, 1981.

Byrne, Donn. *Destiny Bay*. Boston: Little, Brown, 1928.

———. *Messer Marco Polo*. New York: The Century, 1922.

———. *The Strangers' Banquet*. New York: Harper & Brothers, 1919.

Cabell, James Branch. *Jurgen*. New York: Robert M. McBride, 1919.

Campbell, Joseph. *The Hero's Journey: Joseph Campbell on His Life and Work*. New York: Harper & Row, 1990.

Chamberlain, John. *A Life with the Printed Word*. Chicago: Regnery Gateway, 1982.

Congdon, Don, ed. *The '30s: A Time to Remember*. New York: Simon & Schuster, 1962.

Conway, J. D. *Monterey*. Charleston: Arcadia, 2003.

Copeland, Dennis, and McCombs, Jeanne. *A Monterey Album: Life by the Bay*. Charleston: Arcadia, 2003.

Covington, D. B. *The Argus Book Shop: A Memoir*. West Cornwall, CT: Tarrydiddle Press, 1977.

Cowley, Malcolm. *Exile's Return: A Literary Odyssey of the 1920s*. New York: W. W. Norton, 1934.

———. *A Second Flowering: Works and Days of the Lost Generation*. New York: Viking, 1973.

Dakin, Susanna Bryant. *The Lives of William Hartnell*. Stanford: Stanford University Press, 1949.

Davis, Margo, and Nilan, Roxanne. *The Stanford Album: A Photographic History, 1885–1945*. Stanford: Stanford University Press, 1989.

DeMott, Robert. *Steinbeck's Typewriter: Essays on His Art*. Troy, NY: Whitston Publishing, 1997.

Dickstein, Morris. *Dancing in the Dark: A Cultural History of the Great Depression*. New York: W. W. Norton, 2009.

Egan, Timothy. *The Worst Hard Time*. New York: Houghton Mifflin, 2006.

Enea, Sparky. *With Steinbeck in the Sea of Cortez*. Los Osos: Sand River Press, 1991.

Evans, Harold. *The American Century*. New York: Knopf, 1999.

Evans, Richard J. *The Third Reich in Power*. New York: Penguin Books, 2005.

Exquemelin, Alexander O. *The Buccaneers of America*. trans. Alexis Brown. Mineola, NY: Dover, 1969.

Fairbanks, Douglas Jr. *A Hell of a War*. London: Robson Books, 1995.

Farah, Andrew. *Hemingway's Brain*. Columbia: University of South Carolina Press, 2017.

Fensch, Thomas. *Steinbeck & Covici: The Story of a Friendship*. The Woodlands, TX: New Century Books, 1979.

Fitzgerald, F. Scott. *This Side of Paradise*. New York: Scribner, 1920.

Fontenrose, Joseph. *John Steinbeck: An Introduction and Interpretation*. New York: Holt, Rinehart and Winston, 1963.

Freeman, Joseph. *An American Testament*. New York: Farrar & Rinehart, 1936.

French, Warren. *John Steinbeck's Fiction Revisited*. New York: Twayne, 1994.

Friede, Donald. *The Mechanical Angel*. New York: Knopf, 1948.

Galbraith, John Kenneth. *The Great Crash 1929*. New York: Houghton Mifflin Harcourt, 2009 edition.

Gordon, Linda. *Dorothea Lange: A Life Beyond Limits*. New York: W. W. Norton, 2009.

Gray, James. *John Steinbeck*. University of Minnesota Pamphlets on American Writers, no. 94. Minneapolis: University of Minnesota Press, 1971.

Guinn, J. M. *History and Biographical Record of Monterey and San Benito Counties*, vol. 1. Los Angeles: Historic Record, 1919.

Guralnick, Peter. *Last Train to Memphis: The Rise of Elvis Presley*. New York: Back Bay Books, 1994.

Halladay, Terry Grant, ed. *The Closest Witness: The Autobiographical Reminiscences of Gwyndolyn Conger Steinbeck*. Master of Arts thesis. Nacogdoches: Stephen F. Austin University, 1979.

Hamilton, Ian. *Writers in Hollywood, 1915–1951*. New York: Harper & Row, 1990.

Hannigan, Robert E. *The New World Power: American Foreign Policy, 1898–1917*. Philadelphia: University of Pennsylvania Press, 2002.

Hastings, Max. *Inferno: The World at War, 1939–1945*. New York: Vintage, 2011.

———. *The Korean War*. New York: Simon & Schuster, 1987.

Hayashi, Tetsumaro, ed. *John Steinbeck: The Years of Greatness, 1936–1939*. Tuscaloosa: University of Alabama Press, 1993.

———. *Steinbeck's Literary Dimension: A Guide to Comparative Studies, Series II*. Metuchen, NJ: Scarecrow Press, 1991.

Heavilin, Barbara, ed. *The Critical Response to John Steinbeck's* The Grapes of Wrath. Westport, CT: Greenwood Press, 2000.

Hedgpeth, Joel W. *The Outer Shores, Part 1: Ed Ricketts and John Steinbeck Explore the Pacific Coast*. Eureka: Mad River Press, 1978.

———. *The Outer Shores, Part 2: Breaking Through*. Eureka: Mad River Press, 1978.

Hemingway, Ernest. *A Farewell to Arms*. New York: Scribner's, 1929.

———. *in our time*. Paris: Three Mountains Press, 1924.

———. *In Our Time*. New York: Scribner's, 1925.

———. *A Moveable Feast: Sketches of the Author's Life in Paris in the Twenties*. New York: Scribner's, 1964.

———. *The Sun Also Rises*. New York: Scribner's, 1926.

Hemp, Michael Kenneth. *Cannery Row: The History of John Steinbeck's Old Ocean View Avenue*. Carmel: The History Company, 2015.

Holmes, Kenneth, and Holmes, Karen. *John Steinbeck: A Descriptive Bibliographical Catalogue of the Holmes Collection*. Privately published, 2013.

Jeffers, Robinson. *Selected Poems*. New York: Random House, 1963.

Karman, James. *Robinson Jeffers: Poet and Prophet*. Stanford: Stanford University Press, 2015.

Kazin, Alfred. *An American Procession: The Major American Writers from 1830 to 1930—The Crucial Century.* New York: Knopf, 1984.

———. *On Native Grounds: An Interpretation of Modern American Prose Literature.* Fiftieth Anniversary Edition. New York: Harcourt Brace, 1942.

Kerouac, Jack. *Road Novels 1957–1960,* ed. Douglas Brinkley. New York: Library of America, 2007.

Kiernan, Thomas. *The Intricate Music: A Biography of John Steinbeck.* Boston: Little, Brown, 1979.

Kohrs, Donald G., ed. *The Life and Letters of Edward F. Ricketts Including Personal and Professional Correspondence with Friends and Acquaintances.* Unpublished manuscript.

LaFeber, Walter, et al. *The American Century: A History of the United States since the 1890s,* 7th ed. Armonk, NY: M.E. Sharpe, 2013.

Landauer, Lyndall Baker. *The Mountain Sea: A History of Lake Tahoe,* 3rd ed. Honolulu: Flying Cloud Press, 1996.

Lannoo, Michael J. *Leopold's Shack and Ricketts's Lab.* Berkeley: University of California Press, 2010.

Larsen, Stephen, and Larsen, Robin. *Joseph Campbell: A Fire in the Mind.* Rochester, VT: Inner Traditions, 1991.

Larsh, Ed B. *Doc's Lab: Myth & Legends from Cannery Row.* Monterey: PBL Press, 1995.

Larson, Erik. *Dead Wake: The Last Crossing of the* Lusitania. New York: Crown, 2015.

Lebrun, Bernard, and Lefebvre, Michel. *Robert Capa: The Paris Years 1933–1954,* trans. Nicholas Elliot. New York: Abrams, 2012.

Lee, Charles. *The Hidden Public: The Story of the Book-of-the-Month Club.* Garden City, NY: Doubleday, 1958.

Levant, Howard. *The Novels of John Steinbeck.* Columbia: University of Missouri Press, 1974.

Lisca, Peter. *John Steinbeck: Nature & Myth.* New York: Thomas Y. Crowell, 1978.

———. *The Wide World of John Steinbeck.* New Brunswick: Rutgers University Press, 1958.

Lord, Russell. *To Hold This Soil.* Washington, DC: U.S. Department of Agriculture, Miscellaneous Publication no. 321, 1938.

Mak, Geert. *In America: Travels with John Steinbeck.* London: Harvill Secker, 2014.

Malory, Sir Thomas. *Le Morte Darthur,* ed. R. M. Lumiansky. New York: Collier Books, 1982.

McElrath, Joseph R. Jr., et al. *John Steinbeck: The Contemporary Reviews.* Cambridge: Cambridge University Press, 1996.

McElvane, Robert S. *The Great Depression: America, 1929–1941.* New York: Times Books, 1984.

McGurl, Mark. *The Program Era: Postwar Fiction and the Rise of Creative Writing.* Cambridge, MA: Harvard University Press, 2009.

McLane, Lucy Neely. *A Piney Paradise by Monterey Bay: Pacific Grove, the Documentary History of Her First Twenty-Five Years and a Glimpse of Her Adulthood.* San Francisco: Lawton Kennedy, 1952.

McWilliams, Carey. *Factories in the Field: The Story of Migratory Farm Labor in California.* Santa Barbara: Peregrine Publishers, 1971.

Meredith, Burgess. *So Far, So Good: A Memoir.* Boston: Little, Brown, 1994.

Mirrielees, Edith R. *Stanford: The Story of a University.* New York: Putnam, 1959.
———. *Story Writing.* Boston: The Writer Inc., 1947.
Moore, Harry Thornton. *The Novels of John Steinbeck: A First Critical Study.* Chicago: Normandie House, 1939.
Morella, Joe, and Epstein, Edward Z. *Paulette: The Adventurous Life of Paulette Goddard.* New York: St. Martin's, 1985.
Nakayama, Kiyoshi. *Uncollected Stories of John Steinbeck:* Tokyo: Nan'Un-Do, 1986.
Neiberg, Michael S. *The Path to War: How the First World War Created Modern America.* New York: Oxford University Press, 2016.
Olmstead, Kathryn S. *Right Out of California: The 1930s and the Big Business Roots of Modern Conservatism.* New York: The New Press, 2015.
Osio, Antonio Maria. *The History of Alta California: A Memoir of Mexican California,* trans. Rose Marie Beebe and Robert M. Senkewicz. Madison: University of Wisconsin Press, 1996.
Ottanelli, Fraser M. *The Communist Party of the United States: From the Depression to World War II.* New Brunswick: Rutgers University Press, 1991.
Owens, Louis. *John Steinbeck's Re-Vision of America.* Athens: University of Georgia Press, 1985.
Palumbi, Stephen R., and Sotka, Carolyn. *The Death & Life of Monterey Bay: A Story of Revival.* Washington, DC: Island Press, 2011.
Parini, Jay. *John Steinbeck.* New York: Henry Holt, 1995.
Persico, Joseph E. *Edward R. Murrow: An American Original.* New York: McGraw-Hill, 1988.
Peschel, Bill. *Writers Gone Wild: The Feuds, Frolics, and Follies of Literature's Great Adventurers, Drunkards, Lovers, Iconoclasts, and Misanthropes.* New York: Perigee, 2010.
Pitt, Leonard. *The Decline of the Californios: A Social History of the Spanish-Speaking Californians, 1846–1890.* Berkeley: University of California Press, 1966.
Pyle, Howard. *Howard Pyle's Book of Pirates,* ed. Merle Johnson. New York: Harper & Brothers, 1921.
Railsback, Brian, and Meyer, Michael J., eds. *A John Steinbeck Encyclopedia.* Westport, CT: Greenwood Press, 2006.
Ricketts, Edward F., and Calvin, Jack. *Between Pacific Tides.* Stanford: Stanford University Press, 1939.
Riggs, Susan F. *A Catalogue of the John Steinbeck Collection at Stanford University.* Stanford: Stanford University Libraries, 1980.
Ritter, William Emerson. *An Organismal Theory of Consciousness.* Boston: The Gorham Press, 1919.
———. *The Probable Infinity of Nature and Life.* Boston: The Gorham Press, 1918.
Rodger, Katharine A., ed. *Renaissance Man of Cannery Row: The Life and Letters of Edward F. Ricketts.* Tuscaloosa: University of Alabama Press, 2002.
Royce, Josiah. *Race Questions, Provincialism, and Other American Problems.* New York: Macmillan, 1908 (Leopold Classic Library On-Demand edition).
Schmitz, Anne-Marie. *In Search of Steinbeck.* Los Altos, CA: Hermes, 1978.
Schultz, Jeffrey, and Li, Luchen. *Critical Companion to John Steinbeck: A Literary Reference to His Life and Work.* New York: Checkmark Books, 2005.

Scott, Edward B. *The Saga of Lake Tahoe.* Lake Tahoe: Sierra-Tahoe Publishing, 1957.

Sheffield, Carlton A. *John Steinbeck: The Good Companion: His Friend Dook's Memoir.* Berkeley: Creative Arts Book Company, 1983.

Shillinglaw, Susan. *Carol and John Steinbeck: Portrait of a Marriage.* Reno: University of Nevada Press, 2013.

———. *John Steinbeck: Centennial Reflections by American Writers.* San Jose: Center for Steinbeck Studies, San Jose State University, 2002.

———. *A Journey into Steinbeck's California*, 2nd ed. Berkeley: Roaring Forties Press, 2006.

———. *On Reading* The Grapes of Wrath. New York: Penguin, 2014.

Shlaes, Amity. *The Forgotten Man: A New History of the Great Depression.* New York: HarperCollins, 2007.

Sobel, Robert. *The Great Bull Market: Wall Street in the 1920s.* New York: W. W. Norton, 1968.

Spisak, James W., ed. *Caxton's Mallory: Le Morte Darthur.* Berkeley: University of California Press, 1983.

Starr, Kevin. *California.* New York: Modern Library, 2005.

———. *Endangered Dreams: The Great Depression in California.* New York: Oxford University Press, 1996.

Steigerwald, Bill. *Dogging Steinbeck: Discovering America and Exposing the Truth about Travels with Charley.* Pittsburgh: Fourth River Press, 2012.

Stein, Walter J. *California and the Dust Bowl Migration.* Westport, CT: Greenwood Press, 1973.

Steinbeck, Elaine, and Wallsten, Robert. *Steinbeck: A Life in Letters.* New York: Viking, 1975.

Steinbeck, John. *The Acts of King Arthur and His Noble Knights.* New York: Farrar, Straus and Giroux, 1976.

———. *America and Americans.* New York: Viking, 1966.

———. *Bombs Away.* New York: Viking, 1942.

———. *Burning Bright.* New York: Viking, 1950.

———. *Cannery Row.* New York: Viking, 1945.

———. *Cup of Gold.* New York: Robert M. McBride, 1929.

———. *East of Eden.* New York: Viking, 1952.

———. *The Grapes of Wrath.* New York: Viking, 1939.

———. *The Harvest Gypsies.* Berkeley: Heyday, 1988. Originally published in the *San Francisco News*, 1936.

———. *In Dubious Battle.* New York: Covici-Friede, 1936.

———. *Journal of a Novel: The* East of Eden *Letters.* New York: Viking, 1969.

———. *The Log from the Sea of Cortez.* New York: Viking, 1951.

———. *The Long Valley.* New York: Viking, 1938.

———. *The Moon Is Down.* New York: Viking, 1942.

———. *Of Mice and Men.* New York: Covici-Friede, 1937.

———. *Once There Was a War.* New York: Viking, 1958.

———. *The Pastures of Heaven.* New York: Robert O. Ballou, 1932.

———. *The Pearl.* New York: Viking, 1947.

———. *A Russian Journal.* New York: Viking, 1948.

———. *The Short Reign of Pippin IV.* New York: Viking, 1957.

———. *Sweet Thursday.* New York: Viking, 1954.

———. *To a God Unknown.* New York: Robert O. Ballou, 1933.

———. *Tortilla Flat.* New York: Covici-Friede, 1935.

———. *Travels with Charley: In Search of America.* New York: Viking, 1962.

———. *The Wayward Bus.* New York: Viking, 1947.

———. *The Winter of Our Discontent.* New York: Viking, 1961.

———. *Working Days: The Journals of* The Grapes of Wrath, ed. Robert DeMott. New York: Viking, 1989.

Steinbeck, John, and Ricketts, Edward F. *Sea of Cortez.* New York: Viking, 1941.

Steinbeck, John IV. *In Touch.* New York: Knopf, 1969.

Steinbeck, John IV, and Steinbeck, Nancy. *The Other Side of Eden: Life with John Steinbeck.* Amherst, NY: Prometheus Books, 2001.

Strachan, Hew. *The First World War.* New York: Viking, 2004.

Tamm, Eric Enno. *Beyond the Outer Shores: The Untold Story of Ed Ricketts, the Pioneering Ecologist Who Inspired John Steinbeck and Joseph Campbell.* Vancouver: Raincoast Books, 2004.

Taylor, J. Golden, ed. *A Literary History of the American West.* Fort Worth: Texas Christian University Press, 1987.

Tedlock, E. W. Jr., and Wicker, C. V., eds. *Steinbeck and His Critics: A Record of Twenty-Five Years.* Albuquerque: University of New Mexico Press, 1957.

Tolkien, J. R. R. *The Fall of Arthur,* ed. Christopher Tolkien. Boston/New York: Houghton Mifflin Harcourt, 2013.

Tutorow, Norman E. *The Governor: The Life and Legacy of Leland Stanford,* vols. 1–2. Spokane: Arthur H. Clark, 2004.

Valjean, Nelson. *John Steinbeck, The Errant Knight: An Intimate Biography of His California Years.* San Francisco: Chronicle Books, 1975.

Wagner-Martin, Linda. *John Steinbeck: A Literary Life.* London: Palgrave Macmillan, 2017.

Watkins, T. H. *The Great Depression: America in the 1930s.* Boston: Little, Brown, 1993.

Wartzman, Rick. *Obscene in the Extreme: The Burning and Banning of John Steinbeck's* The Grapes of Wrath. New York: Public Affairs, 2008.

Weintraub, Stanley. *Silent Night: The Story of the World War I Christmas Truce.* New York: Plume, 2002.

Wilhelmson, Carl. *Midsummernight.* New York: Farrar & Rinehart, 1930.

Wilson, Edmund. *The American Earthquake.* Garden City, NY: Doubleday, 1958.

———. *Literary Essays and Reviews of the 1920s & 30s.* New York: Library of America, 2007.

———. *Literary Essays and Reviews of the 1930s & 40s.* New York: Library of America, 2007.

Wilson, Edmund, and Wilson, Elena, eds. *Letters on Literature and Politics: 1912–1972.* New York: Farrar, Straus and Giroux, 1977.

Wyatt, David, ed. *New Essays on* The Grapes of Wrath. Cambridge: Cambridge University Press, 1990.

INDEX

Abramson, Ben, 154, 171
Across the River and Into the Trees (Hemingway), 330
Actors Studio, 308
Adams, Ansel, 365
Ainsworth, Beth Steinbeck (JS's sister), 7, 20, 47, 48, 341
Albee, Anne, 188–90
Albee, George, 91, 117, 155, 161, 179, 187–88, 189
Albee, Richard
  on Anne Albee, 189–90
  influence on JS, 92, 133–34
  on JS's paranoia about fame, 187, 196
  on JS's personal characteristics, 278–79
  at lab gatherings, 106
  meets JS, 91–92
  on *Of Mice and Men,* 181
  phalanx theory and, 133, 134, 136
Alexander, W. W., 225, 405n
Allee, Warder Clyde, 102, 134
Alta California, 5–6
America and Americans (Steinbeck), 364–65
American Academy of Arts and Letters, 315
"American Century, The" (Luce), 269
Anderson, Sherwood, 110, 127–28
Animal Aggregations (Allee), 102
Ardath, Mary, 51, 382n

"Argument of Phalanx" (Steinbeck), 169
Ariss, Bruce, 106, 109, 159
Ariss, Jean, 106, 109, 391n
Arrowsmith (Lewis), 78
Arthurian legend. *See* Malory, Thomas
Associated Farmers of California
  anti-union organizing by, 164, 177, 191
  attacks on JS, 221, 224, 231–32, 239
  Dust Bowl migrants and, 174–75
Atkinson, Brooks, 185–86

Babb, Sanora, 192–94, 195, 228–29
Babbitt (Lewis), 78, 80
Bailey, Margery, 35–36
Baker, Carlos, 295, 303–4, 353–54
Ballou, Robert O., 117, 127, 131, 139, 140, 143, 153
"Battle Hymn of the Republic, The" (Howe), 201
Bear Flag, 332
Beat Generation, 333
Bellow, Saul, 217, 364
Benchley, Nat, 291, 293, 312
Benny, Jack, 231
Berry, Tony, 244, 245, 247–48, 250
Beskow, Bo, 293, 312, 315
Best, Marshall, 216
Beswick, Katherine, *37*
  assists JS with manuscripts, 63, 67, 74
  Cup of Gold and, 69